perspectives

Social Problems

Academic Editor
Robert P. McNamara
Furman University

St. Paul • Bellevue • Boulder • Dubuque • Madison

Our mission at **coursewise** is to help students make connections—linking theory to practice and the classroom to the outside world. Learners are motivated to synthesize ideas when course materials are placed in a context they recognize. By providing gateways to contemporary and enduring issues, **coursewise** publications will expand students' awareness of and context for the course subject.

For more information on **coursewise,** visit us at our web site: http://www.coursewise.com

To order an examination copy:
Houghton Mifflin Sixth Floor Media 800-565-6247 (voice) / 800-565-6236 (fax)

coursewise publishing editorial staff

Thomas Doran, ceo/publisher: Journalism/Marketing/Speech
Edgar Laube, publisher: Political Science/Psychology/Sociology
Linda Meehan Avenarius, publisher: **courselinks**™
Sue Pulvermacher-Alt, publisher: Education/Health/Gender Studies
Victoria Putman, publisher: Anthropology/Geography/Environmental Science
Tom Romaniak, publisher: Business/Criminal Justice/Economics
Kathleen Schmitt, publishing assistant

coursewise publishing production staff

Lori A. Blosch, permissions coordinator
Mary Monner, production coordinator
Victoria Putman, production manager

Interior design and cover design by Jeff Storm

Library of Congress Catalog Card Number: 98-073420

ISBN 0-395-90251-7

Printed in the United States of America by **coursewise publishing**, Inc.
1559 Randolph Avenue, St. Paul, MN 55105

10 9 8 7 6 5 4 3 2 1

from the
Publisher

Tom Romaniak
coursewise publishing

How many of your fellow students have developed a social conscience? Have you? How did that happen? Is it possible to act in the best interests of society while successfully competing in today's tough business environment? I think it is, but for me, the development of my social awareness happened over time.

I hold a degree in both accounting and finance from a small liberal arts college. My first job out of college was that of a financial analyst with a college publishing company focused on the social sciences. As my career progressed, I took a greater interest in the operational aspects of publishing. Through a fortuitous turn of events, I joined the editorial ranks and managed a list of books in the areas of anthropology, criminal justice and sociology.

Through this experience I became more aware of how society is made up of many interconnected groups. I also learned that my actions and behavior as an individual impact not only those close to me, but also many people who I will probably never meet. Likewise, the actions of others have an impact on me. This is a powerful concept, once you let it sink in.

I provide you with this background to give you some perspective on the importance I place on trying to understand and resolve the problems of society. We cannot truly realize our potential as a society until we recognize, take responsibility for, and make every effort to reduce and eliminate our society's problems. Which brings us to this reader.

This reader will personalize and intensify your learning experience. Robert McNamara, the Academic Editor of this volume, has selected key readings (most of which have not been previously published) on crime, poverty, education, and racial and gender inequalities. These readings will help you to connect the theory presented in class with events in the world around you.

This approach reflects how Robert McNamara teaches his students and is one of the reasons I asked him to craft this volume. One of Robert's goals is to get his students outside of the classroom and into the world around them. He wants them to experience firsthand some of society's problems and to show them that they play an important part in resolving those problems. Theory is great, but it becomes useless if it can't be applied.

To quote Albert Einstein: "Problems cannot be solved at the same level of awareness that created them." My hope for you and for our society is that through your studies, you can raise our collective awareness of social problems. Perhaps then we can begin to solve these problems and to reach our full potential as a society.

I wish you much success in your studies and in your life's work.

Tom Romaniak

P.S. Both Robert and I want to make this a better publication. We can't do that unless we hear from you. I urge you to send me your comments. My email address is tomr@coursewise.com. You can also complete one of the feedback forms available at our web site (www.coursewise.com).

Robert P. McNamara is assistant professor of sociology at Furman University. He is the author of several books, including *Crossing the Line: Interracial Couples in the South* with Maria Tempenis and Beth Walton; *Crime Displacement: The Other Side of Prevention; The Times Square Hustler: Male Prostitution in New York City; Sex, Scams and Street Life: The Sociology of New York City's Times Square; Beating the Odds: Crime, Poverty, and Life in the Inner City; Police and Policing* with Dr. Dennis Kenney; *The Urban Landscape: Selected Readings* with Dr. Kristy McNamara; *Social Gerontology* with Dr. David Redburn; and *Managing a Deviant Status: Field Research and the Labeling Perspective* with Deanna Ramey and Linda Henry. Dr. McNamara has also written numerous articles on a variety of topics and has been a consultant for state, federal, and private agencies on such topics as AIDS, drug abuse, urban redevelopment, homelessness, policing, gangs, and healthcare.

from the Academic Editor

Robert P. McNamara

Furman University

The study of social problems is a fundamental part of the sociological mission. This was true in the early days of the discipline, when scholars such as Emile Durkheim, Karl Marx, and Max Weber all attempted to come to grips with the changes to society brought about by the Industrial Revolution. Today, sociologists still struggle to understand the problems that plague our communities. In fact, the rapid changes that technology—particularly the Internet—have brought about may be changing society on a scale similar to that found during the Industrial Revolution.

Because this is an introductory level course, which draws people from all disciplines, some of you who have not been exposed to the social sciences may have difficulty with the issues discussed in this book. For example, students who major in biology, chemistry, and math sometimes struggle with the idea that no single answer exists for social problems. Their training compels them to find a single correct solution. This is not to say that students who major in these areas cannot grasp the concepts or succeed in the course. Nor does it mean that students familiar with the social sciences have an unfair advantage. Rather, I think that the problems that some students experience call attention to the need to step out of one's comfort zone—to work outside the usual paradigm and really think about the issues presented in this text. In some ways, this is relatively easy to do. After all, what makes the study of social problems so interesting is that these issues have a direct impact on how we live our lives.

I hope you enjoy reading *Perspectives: Social Problems.* I have tried to compile readings that are interesting, informative, and on the cutting edge of the research on each topic. Perhaps one day you will find yourself studying one or more of these problems and will use this text as a reference.

Editorial Board

We wish to thank the following instructors for their assistance. Their many suggestions not only contributed to the construction of this volume, but also to the ongoing development of our Social Problems web site.

WiseGuide Introduction

Critical Thinking and Bumper Stickers

Question Authority

The bumper sticker said: Question Authority. This is a simple directive that goes straight to the heart of critical thinking. The issue is not whether the authority is right or wrong; it's the questioning process that's important. Questioning helps you develop awareness and a clearer sense of what you think. That's critical thinking.

Critical thinking is a new label for an old approach to learning—that of challenging all ideas, hypotheses, and assumptions. In the physical and life sciences, systematic questioning and testing methods (known as the scientific method) help verify information, and objectivity is the benchmark on which all knowledge is pursued. In the social sciences, however, where the goal is to study people and their behavior, things get fuzzy. It's one thing for the chemistry experiment to work out as predicted, or for the petri dish to yield a certain result. It's quite another matter, however, in the social sciences, where the subject is ourselves. Objectivity is harder to achieve.

Although you'll hear critical thinking defined in many different ways, it really boils down to analyzing the ideas and messages that you receive. What are you being asked to think or believe? Does it make sense, objectively? Using the same facts and considerations, could you reasonably come up with a different conclusion? And, why does this matter in the first place? As the bumper sticker urged, question authority. Authority can be a textbook, a politician, a boss, a big sister, or an ad on television. Whatever the message, learning to question it appropriately is a habit that will serve you well for a lifetime. And in the meantime, thinking critically will certainly help you be course wise.

Getting Connected

This reader is a tool for connected learning. This means that the readings and other learning aids explained here will help you to link classroom theory to real-world issues. They will help you to think critically and to make long-lasting learning connections. Feedback from both instructors and students has helped us to develop some suggestions on how you can wisely use this connected learning tool.

WiseGuide Pedagogy

A wise reader is better able to be a critical reader. Therefore, we want to help you get wise about the articles in this reader. Each section of *Perspectives* has three tools to help you: the WiseGuide Intro, the WiseGuide Wrap-Up, and the Putting It in *Perspectives* review form.

WiseGuide Intro

WiseGuide Intro

In the WiseGuide Intro, the Academic Editor introduces the section, gives you an overview of the topics covered, and explains why particular articles were selected and what's important about them.

Also in the WiseGuide Intro, you'll find several key points or learning objectives that highlight the most important things to remember from this section. These will help you to focus your study of section topics.

At the end of the WiseGuide Intro, you'll find questions designed to stimulate critical thinking. Wise students will keep these questions in mind as they read an article (we repeat the questions at the start of the articles as a reminder). When you finish each article, check your understanding. Can you answer the questions? If not, go back and reread the article. The Academic Editor has written sample responses for many of the questions, and you'll find these online at the **courselinks**™ site for this course. More about **courselinks** in a minute. . . .

WiseGuide Wrap-Up

Be course wise and develop a thorough understanding of the topics covered in this course. The WiseGuide Wrap-Up at the end of each section will help you do just that with concluding comments or summary points that repeat what's most important to understand from the section you just read.

In addition, we try to get you wired up by providing a list of select Internet resources—what we call R.E.A.L. web sites because they're **R**elevant, **E**xciting, **A**pproved, and **L**inked. The information at these web sites will enhance your understanding of a topic. (Remember to use your Passport and start at http://www.courselinks.com so that if any of these sites have changed, you'll have the latest link.)

Putting It in *Perspectives* Review Form

At the end of the book is the Putting It in *Perspectives* review form. Your instructor may ask you to complete this form as an assignment or for extra credit. If nothing else, consider doing it on your own to help you critically think about the reading.

Prompts at the end of each article encourage you to complete this review form. Feel free to copy the form and use it as needed.

The courselinks™ Site

The **courselinks**™ Passport is your ticket to a wonderful world of integrated web resources designed to help you with your course work. These resources are found at the **courselinks** site for your course area. This is where the readings in this book and the key topics of your course are linked to an exciting array of online learning tools. Here you will find carefully selected readings, web links, quizzes, worksheets, and more, tailored to your course and approved as connected learning tools. The ever-changing, always interesting **courselinks** site features a number of carefully integrated resources designed to help you be course wise. These include:

- **R.E.A.L. Sites** At the core of a **courselinks** site is the list of R.E.A.L. sites. This is a select group of web sites for studying, not surfing. Like the readings in this book, these sites have been selected, reviewed, and approved by the Academic Editor and the Editorial Board. The R.E.A.L. sites are arranged by topic and are annotated with short descriptions and key words to make them easier for you to use for reference or research. With R.E.A.L. sites, you're studying approved resources within seconds—and not wasting precious time surfing unproven sites.
- **Editor's Choice** Here you'll find updates on news related to your course, with links to the actual online sources. This is also where we'll tell you about changes to the site and about online events.

- **Course Overview** This is a general description of the typical course in this area of study. While your instructor will provide specific course objectives, this overview helps you place the course in a generic context and offers you an additional reference point.
- **www.orksheet** Focus your trip to a R.E.A.L. site with the www.orksheet. Each of the 10 to 15 questions will prompt you to take in the best that site has to offer. Use this tool for self-study, or if required, email it to your instructor.
- **Course Quiz** The questions on this self-scoring quiz are related to articles in the reader, information at R.E.A.L. sites, and other course topics, and will help you pinpoint areas you need to study. Only you will know your score—it's an easy, risk-free way to keep pace!
- **Topic Key** The Topic Key is a listing of the main topics in your course, and it correlates with the Topic Key that appears in this reader. This handy reference tool also links directly to those R.E.A.L. sites that are especially appropriate to each topic, bringing you integrated online resources within seconds!
- **Web Savvy Student Site** If you're new to the Internet or want to brush up, stop by the Web Savvy Student site. This unique supplement is a complete **courselinks** site unto itself. Here, you'll find basic information on using the Internet, creating a web page, communicating on the web, and more. Quizzes and Web Savvy Worksheets test your web knowledge, and the R.E.A.L. sites listed here will further enhance your understanding of the web.
- **Student Lounge** Drop by the Student Lounge to chat with other students taking the same course or to learn more about careers in your major. You'll find links to resources for scholarships, financial aid, internships, professional associations, and jobs. Take a look around the Student Lounge and give us your feedback. We're open to remodeling the Lounge per your suggestions.

Building Better Perspectives!

Please tell us what you think of this *Perspectives* volume so we can improve the next one. Here's how you can help:

1. Visit our **coursewise** site at: http://www.coursewise.com
2. Click on *Perspectives.* Then select the Building Better *Perspectives* Form for your book.
3. Forms and instructions for submission are available online.

Tell us what you think—did the readings and online materials help you make some learning connections? Were some materials more helpful than others? Thanks in advance for helping us build better *Perspectives.*

Student Internships

If you enjoy evaluating these articles or would like to help us evaluate the **courselinks** site for this course, check out the **coursewise** Student Internship Program. For more information, visit:

http://www.coursewise.com/intern.html

Brief Contents

Contents

section 1

Crime

section 2

Poverty and Inequalities

section 3

Racial Inequalities

section 4

Education

section 5

Gender Inequalities

Topic Key

This Topic Key is an important tool for learning. It will help you integrate this reader into your course studies. Listed below, in alphabetical order, are important topics covered in this volume. Below each topic, you'll find the reading numbers and titles relating to that topic. Note that the Topic Key might not include every topic your instructor chooses to emphasize. If you don't find the topic you're looking for in the Topic Key, check the index or the online topic key at the **courselinks**™ site.

Introduction

The study of sociology and social problems: A first look

Robert P. McNamara
Furman University

If you were to look at the various introductory textbooks for sociology, most of them would include a definition of sociology that says something like: *Sociology is generally defined as the scientific study of society, including the relationships between people and patterns of social life.* However, this brief definition says little about the subject matter of sociology and nothing about how sociologists approach their work.

The basic insight of sociology is that the groups to which we belong and the social interaction that takes place within those groups shape human behavior. In a variety of ways, sociology affects much of our daily lives and what we do in them. Moreover, our understanding of other societies is based largely on what sociologists discover.

The knowledge we derive from sociological inquiry is both subjective and objective. This implies that what we understand in the world around us goes beyond the objective recording of events. The social, political, and economic positions we hold in society color what we see or understand. We must be aware of this subjective coloring if we are to understand anything about society, the people in it, and the interactions among members of different groups.

The Sociologist

In *Invitation to Sociology*, Peter Berger (1963) states:

> One conception of a sociologist is this. The sociologist is a person intensively, endlessly, shamelessly interested in the doings of man. His natural habitat or environment is all the human gathering places of the world and while he/she may be interested in other things, his/her consuming interest remains the world of people, their history, their passions, their organization. And since he is interested in man, he will naturally be interested in the events that engage men's beliefs, their moments of tragedy and grandeur and ecstasy. But he will also be fascinated by the everyday, mundane aspects of man as well. He may be shocked and repulsed in pursuit of his answers to questions about man, but he will continue his pursuit. Another way of saying this is to say that the sociologist is similar to the man who must listen to gossip despite himself, who is tempted to look through keyholes, to open closed cabinets. In other words, what interests us is the curiosity that grips any sociologist in front of a closed door behind which there are human voices. (p. 18)

Because of what sociologists study and the techniques they employ, some people think sociology is little more than a common-sense approach to society. We may read sociological accounts and be puzzled because we have heard the findings somewhere before or think that we already sufficiently understand the issue—at least until we suddenly read an insight that radically questions everything we had previously assumed about this issue. At this point, we begin to sense the purpose of sociology.

The Sociological Perspective

Everyone understands something about life in society. Much of what we know is based on personal experience and on observation of the events that crowd into our and other people's lives. Personal experience can be a valuable teacher that enables us to understand the society in which we live and how we function in it. But personal experience does have its shortcomings.

First, personal experience does not provide us with any understanding of social worlds other than our own, even within our own culture. Most people, for example, have no firsthand experience with the world of heroin addicts. Second, using personal experience to understand society may lead to the acceptance of errors. For instance, many people consider America's "homeless" to be lazy, shiftless drunks. However, identifying a "typical" homeless person is probably impossible. Some lack motivation, but most of the homeless population has been driven to the streets by unemployment, lack of affordable housing, or domestic abuse. Many are children, while others are the mentally ill, who have nowhere else to live. Thus, the "common knowledge" view of the homeless—that they are lazy, shiftless drunks—is flawed.

In sum, personal experience usually provides firsthand knowledge of only a limited segment of one society, often leaving many unanswered questions and troublesome errors. But once we learn something in society, whatever the source of our information, breaking loose from that understanding is often difficult. We all have what Leon Festinger (1954) called a fundamental "need to know" or understand the physical and social world around us. As such, we seek answers to questions around us. We tend to take cues from people and things, and when enough cues emerge, we tend to categorize. If a person acts in a particular way, he or she must be *that* type of a person. If people look or dress unconventionally, then we often make sweeping generalizations about who those people are and what they believe.

This simplistic understanding of the world around us and the people in it leads to what phenomenologists call *typifications* or *categorizations*. We put people and things into categories so that we are able to understand where they fit into our world and, conversely, where we fit in the world as well. Fritz Heider (1958) called this categorizing a *naive psychology* in that we all do it, and for the most part, it is harmless. But is it? Does it reflect a myopic view of the world, in that everyone and everything must fit into some category?

An explanation for categorization lies, in part, in our perceptions. We tend to take our social world for granted, accepting our society and customs as unquestioningly as we do the physical world around us. Thus, while we want to understand our world, we often do not want to understand too much of it. As such, we fall victim to our own attitudes and perceptions (which are often based on our personal experiences or the experiences of people we know).

When we see the world this way, it narrows our personal worlds since we do not transcend our own experiences. This is why many people have firm but erroneous beliefs about "how things ought to be." They have not taken that next step in understanding, and for the most part, they do not want to. An added problem is that these simplistic typifications or categorizations can change over time, so that what constitutes a certain phenomenon in one instance may change dramatically at a later point in time. This is part of the idea that society and the world around us are socially constructed and do not exist in a natural state for us to exist within (see, for instance, Berger and Luckman 1968).

Sociologists avoid this problem by using a sociological perspective. C. Wright Mills (1959) discusses what he calls the *sociological imagination*. He states that the value of sociology is not found by focusing on the personal troubles of individuals, but rather on the broader social context in which those personal issues emerge. He says, "Our sociological imagination which helps us develop our perspective allows us a vivid awareness of the relationship between the individual and the wider society." The sociological perspective allows us to expand our vision and objectively see the society of which we are a part as though looking at it for the first time. It is a unique way of looking at the world—a lens of sorts that offers us a snapshot of the world that few others have a chance to see. Thus, the sociological perspective:

1. Removes us from familiar experiences
2. Forces us to examine critically and objectively
3. Requires us to make a conscious effort to question the obvious

The sociological perspective is one reason why sociologists continue to discover new and interesting things about social life that we thought we already understood. What we know or think we know has probably been discovered by a sociologist at one point in time. Thus, the first mission of sociology is to discover that much of what may initially appear to be one way may not be that way at all in practice. Sociology offers a unique way of looking at the world and posing crucial questions. Sociology and the sociological perspective encourage us to look beyond individual cases and immediate events, and to seek to understand them in the broader context of the society in which they occur. Sociologists place a specific crime, family breakup, or unemployment problem in the context of larger social events.

Social Problems

So what exactly is a social problem? A host of issues in society are problematic. Are all of them social problems? No. Practically everyone agrees that some issues, such as crime or racial discrimination, are social problems. About other issues, however, there is more disagreement.

One aspect of defining social problems is to distinguish between problems that affect individuals from those that involve the entire society. As mentioned earlier, C. Wright Mills (1959) distinguished between personal troubles and public issues, and perhaps that is the best place to start. Personal troubles affect individuals and those immediately around them. When parents discover that their daughter has a serious drug problem, it is a personal trouble that threatens the values and goals of only that family. In short, the trouble is primarily that family's difficulty.

Public issues, on the other hand, have an impact on large numbers of people, and are matters of public debate and collective solutions, rather than individual or familial ones. So when we examine statistics that indicate that our society loses millions of dollars each year because of accidents, suicide, and worker absenteeism due to drug abuse, we are dealing with a public issue because the values of the group are threatened. Of course, public issues may translate into personal troubles in the lives of some people, but not every personal trouble is a public issue. Mills' distinction reminds us that problems need to be viewed in the broad context of their impact on society.

According to Malcom Spector and John Kitsuse (1987) in their classic text on the subject, a social problem has the following elements:

1. **An influential group defines a social condition as threatening its values.** An influential group is one that can have a significant impact on public debate and social policy. Personal troubles do not become public issues then unless an influential group so defines them. The mere existence of a social condition does not make it problematic, no matter how harmful it may be. Smoking tobacco has been a contributing factor in lung cancer for as long as people have used it, but it was not defined as a social problem until people became aware of the link between smoking and cancer and an influential group decided to label it a problem.
2. **When the social condition affects a large number of people.** Social conditions do not typically become social problems unless they affect a large number of people. When they affect relatively few people, they are private issues and there is little public debate over them or a search for collective solutions. The more people they affect, the more likely they are to be publicly debated and defined as a problem that society should address.
3. **When the social condition can be remedied by collective action.** Finally, a social condition may satisfy the previous criteria but not be regarded as a social problem because the condition does not have social causes and cannot be remedied by collective human action. Earthquakes, tornadoes, and other natural disasters are harmful to society, but they are not considered social problems because social conditions do not produce them and changes in social policy cannot prevent them.

As objective conditions and subjective concerns change, social problems do as well. In other words, social problems are dynamic. In fact, a social problem for some may be a solution for others. For example, the billions of dollars spent on warfare is not a social problem for McDonnell Douglas or other weapons corporations that make huge profits from arming the world.

Social problems do not simply spring up. For decades, sociologists have claimed that social problems have a natural history or *life cycle*. Beginning in the 1940s, sociologists attempted to specify the general stages of a social problem. Robert Ross and Graham Staines (1971) offer the following contemporary version of the life cycle of social problems, which Richard Fuller and Richard Myers (1941) developed:

1. Defining a Social Problem

According to Ross and Staines (1971), social problems are defined largely in terms of an individual or group's perceived self-interest. This makes the initial definition a highly political event, especially when opposing interests get involved.

2. Transformation into a Public Issue

The next stage in the life cycle of a social problem involves the transformation of a problem into a public issue. Ross and Staines argue that this stage will only take place when the privately recognized problem is seen as publicly important and legitimate for public consideration. In this stage, the media are critical in making a problem visible and in determining its importance and legitimacy. Ross and Staines see the reaction or even nonreaction of public officials as another element in the equation. Sometimes, the media and officials conflict over whether a given problem deserves the status of public issue. Again, this may be a matter of perceived self-interest as officials try to downplay the importance of the problem and provide their own interpretation of the event.

3. Debating Causes and Solutions

Once a privately recognized social problem becomes a public issue, then debate about its causes begins. Ross and Staines distinguish between two different causal interpretations commonly brought to bear on social problems. On one hand, a problem may be caused by *systemic attribution;* that is, the system itself may be problematic and/or generate difficulties for individuals. On the other hand, a problem may simply be blamed on the people involved; their faults "cause" the social problem. This is referred to as *personal attribution*. Different groups assign either systemic or personal attribution to a social problem according to their perceived self-interests. Ross and Staines observe that public officials often prefer to blame the people facing problems for their troubles, rather than to encourage a belief that the prevailing order is itself somehow problematic. And to be fair, it seems likely that all dominant groups tend to favor personal attribution.

After opposing groups publicize their interpretations of the causes of a social problem, serious debate begins. The result is a complex bargaining process between authorities and the advocates of the social problem that eventually results in a compromise. The political outcome is often in the form of legislation or a change in social policy.

4. The Role of Power

The message implicit in Ross and Staines' discussion is that power determines how problems are ultimately defined and what solutions are likely to be considered. Those people or groups in power are in the best position to:

1. Determine whether a private problem becomes a public issue
2. Influence the causes of the problem
3. Control the ways the problem comes to be defined
4. Determine what, if anything, will be done to solve the problem

Where does sociology fit into this picture? How can sociologists help us to understand the impact of power and the overall study of social problems in society? Sociologists can offer a better understanding of social problems by:

1. Determining the extent of a problem by measuring its objective conditions
2. Using the tools of science to measure the subjective concern about social problems
3. Applying the sociological perspective to place the problem in a broader context
4. Identifying different ways to intervene in a social problem and evaluating likely consequences

This *Perspectives: Contemporary Social Problems* is designed to supplement traditional social problems textbooks but can also stand alone as the main text. In addition to providing up-to-date research on various topics, this book also offers a number of theoretical implications of particular social problems in American society. The **courselinks**™ site for this reader provides additional readings, exercises, displays, and web sites for you to expand your knowledge on any single subject and to greatly enhance discussions. Thus, while the answers to many social problems remain elusive, this book and the links to the Internet will provide some insights into their solutions.

References

Berger, P. 1963. *Invitation to Sociology*. New York: Doubleday.

Berger, P., and Luckman, T. 1968. *The Social Construction of Reality*. New York: Anchor.

Festinger, L. 1954. "A Theory of Social Comparison," *Human Relations* 7: 117–40.

Fuller, R., and Myers, R. 1941. "The Natural History of a Social Problem," *American Sociological Review* 6: 320–28.

Heider, F. 1958. *The Psychology of Human Relations*. New York: John Wiley and Sons.

Mills, C. Wright. 1959. *The Sociological Imagination*. New York: Oxford University Press.

Ross, R., and G. L. Staines. 1971. "The Politics of Analyzing Social Problems," *Social Problems* 20: 18–40.

Spector, M., and Kitsuse, J. 1987. *Constructing Social Problems*. Hawthorne, N.Y.: Aldine de Gruyter.

Article Review Form at end of book.

section

Crime

Crime may be the most serious social problem in society today. One reason for this is the fear that it generates. While a rare phenomenon, in that it occurs relatively infrequently, crime nevertheless evokes a sense of concern about the possibility of being victimized. In addition, the criminal justice system, which is the main mechanism our society has to fight crime, encounters difficulty in the administration of justice. The problems range from dealing with clogged courts to managing inmates in a volatile environment to handling unintended consequences of crime prevention programs.

The readings in this section examine crime as a social problem and also describe some of the practical problems of the criminal justice system. John Fuller's reading discusses the problematic nature of the "war on crime" and offers an interesting peacemaking perspective for understanding crime in American society. Robert McNamara then discusses one of the most noted events of our time, police brutality. In his discussion, he offers a way of understanding how and why officers engage in inappropriate conduct. Shelia Weaver LaFountain then examines the problems and difficulties of white-collar crime. Since white-collar crime is inextricably linked to conventional business practices, our understanding of it is somewhat limited, as are our options for dealing with the problem. John Feinblatt and Michele Sviridoff then describe an innovative proposal for solving quality-of-life or low-level crimes. The Midtown Community Court is being heralded as one of the most effective crime-fighting solutions in American society. Finally, Maria Tempenis offers us an interesting twist on the realities of imprisonment. Tempenis describes how our correctional institutions must struggle with the demands of varying religious faiths and the impact this has on the security of the institution.

Learning Objectives

After reading these articles, you should be able to

- Contrast peacemaking with traditional views of crime control.
- Understand the distinction between white-collar and street crime.
- Discuss police brutality from a sociological point of view.
- Describe the role of religion in prisons.

Questions

Reading 2. Why does Fuller think that waging a "war on crime" is an inappropriate metaphor? Why does he find this destructive to current social institutions? How would advocates of the labeling theory support opposition of the war perspective?

Reading 3. How do the subcultural influences found in policing result in behaviors such as corruption and the excessive use of force? Is it individual behavior or is there a sociological explanation? Why do you think the comraderie is so important in policing? Many candidates say this is one of the main attractions to a law enforcement career. What does this say about the type of people who become police officers? How does this need to be a part of the law enforcement community affect their attitudes, values, and beliefs as police officers?

Reading 4. When people talk about the crime problem, they usually refer to street crime and not white-collar crime. This is true even though the costs of white-collar crime, as well as the harm it inflicts on society, are far greater than all of street crime combined. Why is there such a moral ambiguity about white-collar crime? Why is it that white-collar crime is so difficult to detect? Perhaps more importantly, why would people engage in it? Many white-collar offenders have achieved success by societal standards. Why, then, do you think they engage in it? Some people might say it is simple greed, but is this a compelling explanation?

Reading 5. Do you think that the Midtown Community Court will be effective? Why or why not? Do you think that the assessment interview composed by the Midtown Community Court will be helpful in reducing crime? Why or why not? How can this have an impact on the overall court system? Do you agree with combining punishment and rehabilitation when addressing crime?

Reading 6. How much religious freedom do you think should be allowed in prison? Where do you draw the line and why? Do you agree with the assessment of prison subculture and with prisoners' adoption of religious practices as a way of coping? What positive implications does religion in prisons have for the prison system? How can religion be controlled to improve the prison system?

Why does Fuller think that waging a "war on crime" is an inappropriate metaphor? Why does he find this destructive to current social institutions? How would advocates of the labeling theory support opposition of the war perspective?

The War on Crime as a Social Problem

John Fuller

State University of West Georgia

Crime is clearly a social problem. It represents a type of unfortunate behavior that seriously damages not only individual victims, but also the entire fabric of healthy society. The level of crime in this country is high compared to other societies and has led the public to demand that politicians enact policies to do something, anything, to address this social problem.

Sometimes the cure is worse than the disease. To be sure, crime is a significant social problem in the United States, but the thesis of this essay is that the way we are addressing crime, by waging a war on it, is not only doomed to failure but also destroys the cherished rights of our citizens (Alexander 1990). The unanticipated consequences of the war on crime, particularly the war on drugs, has eroded the trust people have in the government, increased crime and the level of violence, and has made human life expendable because of the sensational nature of criminal penalties. These are serious charges to level at contemporary criminal justice policy, and to accept them causes one to envision alternative responses to the problems of crime and violence in society. The purpose of this essay is to do no less than propose the war on crime be ended and replaced by a peacemaking perspective that values the rights of victims, offenders, and society (Bartollas and Braswell 1993).

This essay is divided into three sections. The first section briefly discusses why war is an inappropriate metaphor to apply to social problems. The second section deals more extensively with the tactics of the war on crime and details how destructive to the social fabric of society this misguided policy has become. Finally, the third section proposes an emerging peacemaking perspective and suggests it will not only be more effective in addressing the problems of crime, but it will also allow a more comprehensive examination of social problems and provide a framework for a theoretically integrated and functionally-connected strategy to ameliorate their seriousness.

Of Metaphors and Wars

Metaphors are linguistic devices. They link two concepts and suggest a relationship whereby one takes on the characteristics and behavior of the other. They are also seductive devices because they suggest a simple way to comprehend complex ideas by comparing them to more readily-accessible concepts. The war on crime perspective is just such a seductive metaphor. By suggesting that the social problem of crime can be envisioned as an external enemy, we can employ the paramilitary methods and tactics of war to achieve the goal of victory. By couching the language of crime control in terms of a war, we obscure the true nature of criminal activity and give rise to inappropriate and socially-destructive tactics to engage the problem (Czajkoski 1990).

The most fundamental distinction between war and crime is the location of the problem. In a war, even a civil war, there is an identifiable enemy, an outside aggressor who can be subdued, defeated, or killed. Crime, on the other hand, presents no readily-identifiable target for social policy. Criminals are drawn from within society and cannot be targeted for action until after they have committed the unlawful behavior. Unlike a wartime enemy who conveniently wears a uniform and occupies a territory, the criminal is part and parcel of society. In a sense, we are all potential criminals and the tactics of war are unsuitable in a free and democratic society. To use the war on crime perspective is to essentially impose a police state, and this is something that most Americans are unwilling to consider.

The war metaphor is misleading in a fundamental way. While it is a concept that politicians can use to sound tough on crime, they do not literally mean that we should use the same tactics to address crime that we use to wage war against an external enemy. In a war we have to make significant sacrifices. During World War II, there was a massive mobilization of muscle into the armed forces and a change in the labor force, where significant numbers of women left the home and went to work in vital industries. This shift in the structure of the labor market was short-lived, however. When the men came back from overseas, they replaced the women in the labor force. The impact of the war on the way America worked was temporary. The sacrifices we were willing to make were bearable and desirable because they did not entail a permanent change in society. They were necessary because of the external threat posed by the Axis powers.

When posed with the metaphor of a war on crime, the politicians are not talking about temporary sacrifices but about dismantling the protection of the Constitution that has been developed for over two hundred years (Sutton 1991). There is no external enemy to conquer, as drug use is a social problem from within our society. Sure, we may hassle some Colombian drug lord or complain to Mexican politicians about drugs crossing our borders, but the demand for drugs in American society will be met by different entities even if we are successful in dealing with these two countries. The nature of the drug trade mutates as our policies change. At one time we believed the heroin distribution channel through France was the problem, but when it was successfully addressed, the heroin found other means to get to this country. The problem is not in *them*, but in *us*. This is the underlying reason why the war metaphor is so misleading and ultimately destructive. To wage a war on crime, especially on drugs, is to ask Americans to make permanent sacrifices in their protection from government. These sacrifices are not something the politicians emphasize when they espouse their campaign rhetoric (Gardiner and McKinney 1991).

Strategies, Tactics, and Sacrifices in the War on Crime

The war on crime has many fronts. While we may think the criminal justice system is where the war is being waged, the truth is that many of the institutions of our society have been enlisted to fight this war (Gottfredson and Hirschi 1989). School, family, health services, and other institutions have been drafted into this war, and the relationship with students, clients, and loved ones has been altered. This has done a great peril to the fabric of society. In the name of waging war, we have destroyed many of the delicate social bounds that hold us together in meaningful communities. By employing the simplistic war metaphor we have transformed the relationship between the individual and the government in ways that are producing unanticipated and unattractive consequences. Let's look at some of the methods and tactics employed by the war on crime and discuss their ramifications. This list is primarily taken from the book *Power, Ideology, and the War on Drugs: Nothing Succeeds Like Failure*, by Christina Jacqueline Johns (1992), and is presented here to highlight how intrusive this policy has become and to demonstrate how the war on crime has, itself, become a social problem of far-reaching dimensions.

1. ***The right to privacy and searches.*** Americans treasure their rights of privacy and the proscription in the Constitution against unreasonable searches. In fighting the war on crime, the government has requested that restrictions on searches be eased so that they can find illegal drugs and weapons. This presents a conflict in values as most people would agree that lawbreakers should be caught, but at the same time, do not want to be subjected to unnecessary and intrusive searches themselves. Some of the search tactics that citizens complain about include aerial surveillance where law enforcement agencies overfly private property looking for illegal drugs. Without probable cause, that is, without a good reason to suspect that someone is growing illegal drugs, it seems like a fishing expedition to fly over everyone's property in search of drug activities.

Another type of unfair search tactic is the targeting of individuals in airports because they fit a drug courier profile. These profiles are perceived to be racially and ethnically based and to select subjects for search based on stereotypes rather than on behavior. Law enforcement officers have gone through people's trash in an effort to find incriminating information and have used a variety of hidden electronic devices to listen to and record conversations. While these types of information-gathering activities have always been a part of law enforcement, the war on drugs has expanded their use into the lives of many citizens who do not consider themselves criminals and who resent this type of surveillance.

2. *The right of financial privacy*. The drug trade involves large sums of money. In an effort to prosecute drug traffickers the records of banks are routinely examined for evidence of money laundering. While most people might agree that the government should be allowed to freeze the accounts of criminals, they are also wary of the government secretly snooping into their private financial matters.

3. ***Illegally gathered evidence: The exclusionary rule***. One of the most vexing problems of law enforcement is when they find evidence of criminal activity and have the case thrown out of court because the evidence was not obtained legally. The Anti-Drug Abuse Bill of 1988 allows illegally gathered evidence to be used if, in the opinion of the court, it was gathered in good faith. To take a hypothetical example, let's say law enforcement officers entered a burning building with the goal of making sure there were no potential victims and in the search found illegal drugs. Usually, these drugs would not be admissible as evidence because the officer did not have a search warrant or probable cause to believe there were drugs in the building. However, because he went into the building in good faith to rescue people, the drugs found can be used as evidence under the law. The issue becomes one of deciding what is good faith and how it might be abused by law enforcement officers.

4. ***Drug testing.*** One of the ways the war on crime is being fought in not only the criminal justice system, but also in other institutions is through drug testing. In an effort to make for a safer society, the intrusive practice of drug testing is used in a vast number of contexts, some of which have little prospect for achieving the goal of less crime and some of which are blatant violations of citizens' rights, common decency, and fairness. Take for instance the driving laws in Georgia, where the presence of marijuana in the blood or urine is sufficient evidence to convict a driver of driving under the influence. Marijuana can be detected in the body weeks after it was smoked; therefore it is possible that someone could be convicted long after the marijuana had any type of debilitating effect on the brain or body that could contribute to an accident. By testing for marijuana in the body of an accident victim, it is not possible to determine if any marijuana found actually was responsible for a miscalculation. The law does not promote traffic safety but merely regulates life-style. For DUI drivers who use alcohol, the blood-alcohol level measured by a breathalyzer or blood test can give a reasonable indication of how much the driver was impaired by drinking. This is not the case with marijuana. Only the presence of marijuana can be detected, not the effect. We should not be fooled into thinking that drug testing can make the roads safer.

   Drug testing is used by the private sector also. Many employers test their workers to ensure a drug-free workplace. On one level this seems reasonable. Certainly none of us would want to fly on an airplane where the pilot was not in complete control of his or her faculties, and we would not want our children on a school bus where the driver was under the influence of drugs. Unfortunately, drug testing cannot ensure that we are safe. Again, the question of impairment is not measured. Additionally, there are many occupations that are subjected to drug testing where safety is not an issue. Employers are merely testing for life-style and imposing their own moral code on the employees. This is a controversial matter. If someone is doing a good job should they be fired because they use illegal drugs away from the workplace? Does the employer have the right to invade the privacy of the worker when there is no evidence that the worker is in any way affected by the drug use?

   There is one other use of drug testing that is of concern to many people. That is the home drug-testing kits that are being marketed to parents. One wonders about the family dynamics when parents randomly test their children for drug use. If the parents were involved with their children it would seem they would know from the child's behavior if there was cause for concern. By relying on drug testing, parents are attempting to get technology to do what they have been neglecting, that is, being intimately involved in the lives of their children. What is the effect of parents testing their children for drugs on the development of trust and responsibility? If these attributes are not taught early they may never be developed or refined in the youth. Drug testing is not a panacea for the problems of crime. In addition to being ineffective and intrusive, there are unanticipated consequences that make it a policy that should be considered only under restricted and special circumstances, such as when public safety is in question.

5. ***Due process and rights of defendants***. There is a widespread perception in the country that criminal suspects are protected by laws that allow them to escape justice by slipping through loopholes. People believe that guilty persons are routinely being set free because the hands of police and prosecutors are tied by the principle of due process. There are two types of law that govern the criminal justice system. Substantive laws proscribe acts such as murder and theft. Procedural law specifies how criminal justice practitioners may go about implementing the substantive law. Procedural law protects from the arbitrary and capricious actions of the government (Sutton 1991). Many of the principles of the Constitution are embedded in our procedural law, such as the right to a jury of our peers and the right to confront hostile witnesses. The interpretation of the Constitution is an ongoing matter for the Supreme Court, and as the balance of liberal to conservative judges shift, we find that many of the principles of procedural law are being contested. Bills are routinely introduced in Congress that would diminish the rights of criminal defendants and make it easier for the criminal justice system to convict. In addition to the exclusionary rule, the contested principles of due process include the number of appeals available to those under the sentence of death and the Miranda warnings, which advise suspects of their right to an attorney before they are questioned. There is tension in the criminal justice system as the rights of defendants and the rights of the victim and the public are being reconsidered in light of the war on crime (Levy 1996). It is hard to be sympathetic toward those who violate the law and do harm, but their rights against an overzealous criminal justice system protect all citizens and help ensure that innocent individuals are not railroaded through the system.

6. ***Public housing and public life***. The war on crime is not limited to the criminal justice system as witnessed by the laws concerning public housing. If drugs are sold in a public housing apartment, the occupants can be evicted. Even if the drugs are sold without the knowledge of the parents, the entire family can be prohibited from living in public housing. This is a situation that has wide support given the conditions of crime and abuse in some public housing projects. The solution to economic crimes such as drug sales does not lie in punishing the whole family for the transgression of one of its members, however. By making public housing the instrument of law enforcement, the war on crime limits the role that other institutions can play in the prevention and treatment of social problems. If our institutions do the bidding of the criminal justice system, then the supportive nature of these institutions is lost and the only approach to social problems is the punitive nature of the criminal justice system. That is not to say that other institutions do not play an important role in the development of social control. It is important, however, to recognize that there is a fundamental difference in not only the tactics, but in the missions of institutions. The separation of powers and purposes prevents the country from becoming a police state where we are under surveillance in all aspects of our lives.

7. ***Women, the unborn, and drugs***. In an effort to protect unborn babies from the addiction of their mothers to drugs and alcohol, there has been a great effort aimed at criminalizing the drug use of pregnant women. While using drugs when pregnant is clearly dangerous, the best way to deal with this public health problem is not through the criminal justice system. There are two issues here that speak to the problems associated with the war on crime. The first problem is how to best help the mother to provide a healthy prenatal environment for the unborn baby. By holding the sword of the criminal justice system over her head, the war on crime pits the doctor and hospital against

the mother. If she faces criminal charges for drug or alcohol use while pregnant, the woman will be less likely to seek prenatal care because her behavior could be discovered. The first time health professionals will become aware of the pregnancy is when there is a significant problem or when the baby is born. Much damage may already have been done by the time the woman's drug use and pregnancy are discovered. The alternative is to encourage women into prenatal programs and treat the drug use in a supportive way rather than in a punitive manner. Having a healthy baby can be a significant motivation for a woman to address her addiction to drugs.

A second problem with the war on crime as it relates to pregnant women revolves around the issue of the "crack baby." There has been a massive campaign warning about the dangers of crack use on the unborn and the resulting behavioral difficulties these children face as they reach school age. Horror stories about the diminished brain capacity of crack babies are repeated to warn pregnant women about drug use. Laudable as these efforts may be it is coming to light that the crack baby scare is exaggerated at best, and may be even nonexistent (Welch 1996, 426–27).

While no one is claiming crack is safe, no studies have scientifically established that there is such a thing as a crack baby. Women who took crack while pregnant also tended to drink alcohol. The indicators of fetal alcohol syndrome are the same indicators as those for what we call crack babies. The war on crime rhetoric has elevated crack use to crisis status when it may be a legal drug, alcohol, that is responsible for this situation. Furthermore, there is some evidence that these babies are not doomed to a dismal life and that after two years they essentially catch up with their peers in physical and intellectual development (Gavzer 1997).

8. *Expansion of the death penalty*. The death penalty is used sparingly in the United States. It is a rare occurrence that happens only after a long and protracted series of trials and appeals. Those who espouse the war on crime would like to change that. In addition to streamlining the process by limiting the number of appeals available to the defendant, those who advocate capital punishment would like to expand the range of crimes and circumstances for which the death penalty can be applied (Tobolowsky 1992). This is particularly true in the war on drugs where homicides revolving around drug sales would be held to a lesser criteria for application of the death penalty than are other murders. The thinking behind this policy is that it would deter individuals from engaging in the drug trade because if something went wrong and someone were killed, then the death penalty could be more readily used. This reasoning naively assumes that people who make a great deal of money will be deterred from the drug trade by expansion of the death penalty. The unintended consequence of such a policy may be that it will make drug trafficking more lucrative because of the increased risks, thereby drawing more people into the drug trade rather than frightening them away. Additionally, drug traffickers who do kill may be more willing to use deadly force on undercover agents or innocent bystanders because of the increased risks if caught.

9. *Schools and the war on crime*. Like the family, schools have been enlisted to fight the war on crime, and this can fundamentally alter the relationship between this institution and students. Of particular concern are the zero-tolerance policies adopted by some schools where minor and technical infractions of the rules can result in detention, suspension, or even dismissal. Discretion has been taken away from teachers and administrators by these zero-tolerance policies, and the schools have been changed from institutions that exert informal social control to those that engage in a pervasive, formal social control. While school safety is certainly an important issue, the way students are stripped of their rights and dignity has altered the affinity between the student and school. Schools routinely search students, their lockers, and their cars. Drug-sniffing dogs are used to detect deviant behavior even when there is no reason to suspect drugs. Small pocket knives or legally-prescribed drugs can be violations of rigid zero-tolerance policies and cause students to be disciplined. Student-athletes are tested for drug use and kicked off the team if they fail. Students can be denied financial aid if they have a history of drug use. While protecting children and youth from drugs and violence is a laudable goal, in many instances the schools have strayed too far from their

primary mission of education and have become arms of the criminal justice system in the war against crime. Precisely those youth who need to stay in school the most are the ones being driven to the streets by the war on crime. As kids are kicked out of school for infractions of rules or alienated by an atmosphere of social control rather than learning, the schools forfeit their potential to make meaningful changes in the lives of students for the more limited goal of enforcing rigid rules and regulations aimed at uniformity and an atmosphere of discipline.

10. ***Workplace surveillance***. In addition to drug testing many workers are finding their actions subject to greater scrutiny at the workplace. Cameras are used to monitor not only job performance but also social interaction. Off-the-job behavior can also be used to discipline or fire employees. Drug use that does not affect job performance is not tolerated by many organizations. In short, the workplace is another institution that is assisting the criminal justice system in the war on crime.

This list of issues and concerns surrounding how the war on crime impacts the rights of citizens and the civility of everyday life is offered as a suggestion that fighting crime at all costs is too expensive. The costs in terms of the quality of life in a democratic society are being eroded by simplistic and political rhetoric aimed not at strengthening our institutions so they can do a better job in meeting the needs of people, but rather in enlisting them into fighting a war on crime that is destructive to the social fabric of the nation.

As mentioned previously, war is an inappropriate and misleading metaphor for the work of the criminal justice system. The consequences for employing such a destructive way of envisioning our crime problem is evidenced by this long and disturbing list of unintended consequences. It is required to suggest an alternative way of addressing the real problems of crime. It is not fair to criticize present policy if one has nothing to offer as a better way to solve the problem. What is offered is not more of the same. What is advocated requires a fundamental change in thinking from the war on crime perspective. What is suggested is more in keeping with the values and principles of democratic institutions, and it is hoped, it will be more effective in dealing with crime and criminals than the status quo (Buckley 1996; Duke 1996).

A Plea for a Peacemaking Perspective

If the war on crime is failing, then what would be a sensible alternative? A peace perspective presents a framework for addressing criminal justice issues that not only holds more promise for dealing with those who have already broken the law, but also for the development of meaningful communities where citizens and government work together to meet the needs of everyone. A full explication of the peace perspective is beyond the scope of this chapter but can be found in *Criminal Justice: A Peacemaking Perspective* (Fuller 1998).

Where the war on crime perspective is based on deterrence and punishment, the peacemaking perspective is based on prevention and rehabilitation. Where the war on crime perspective finds the cause for crime in the motivation and personality of the individual offender, the peacemaking perspective looks at the culture and institutions of society to ask why certain environments so consistently produce high crime rates. Where the war on crime perspective is willing to sacrifice freedoms for the elusive goals of a drug-free and crime-free community, the peacemaking perspective realizes that a certain amount of deviant behavior is normal in society and that the ultimate answer to crime lies not in the criminal justice system but in other of society's institutions.

The peacemaking perspective is not new. The underlying fundamentals have been practiced not only in the criminal justice system but in many cultures for thousands of years. The peacemaking perspective requires us to step back from the ethnocentric way we view our country and to use our sociological imaginations (Mills 1959) to look historically and cross-culturally to see alternative methods of dealing with crime.

Pepinsky and Quinney (1991) locate the basis for the peacemaking perspective in three types of intellectual traditions. The religious and humanist traditions emphasize love, compassion, and forgiveness (Parrinder 1971). To reintegrate offenders into society we have to stop punishing them and help them find meaningful relationships and fulfilling work. These traditions draw on the world's great religions for guidance on how to inspire and serve people so they become connected to the dominant culture. The feminist traditions look at how our society has developed patriarchal and sexist norms that limit the potential for women and men to develop their true human potentials. Focusing on equal rights, equal opportunities, and cooperation, the feminist tradition requires that we rethink traditional sex-role behavior and look at how the relationships between and among women and men contribute to our crime problem (McDermott 1994). The critical intellectual traditions look at other variables, particularly social class, and emphasize social justice, enlightenment, and emancipation (Reiman 1995).

These traditions contribute to a peacemaking perspective that can be applied to more than the problem of crime. From the intrapersonal to the interpersonal to the institutional and societal to the global and international level, the peacemaking perspective provides an integrated and consistent guide for human behavior. It requires not only that the criminal justice system be reformed but also that we reconsider everything from our parenting skills to global economic systems. Crime, according to the peacemaking perspective, is intertwined in the patterns and relationships of society and can only be effectively addressed by getting beyond blaming the individual offender and looking at the entire way societies operate. This is not to say that individual offenders are blameless, but it does suggest that crime is a product of the organizational and institutional arrangement of countries and that it requires a more comprehensive look than only viewing the social deficiencies of individual offenders.

One of the most important principles of the peacemaking perspective is that it requires the criminal justice system to model the behavior it expects of its citizens. It is not surprising then that the peacemaking perspective opposes capital punishment, the war on drugs, and excessive use of police force (Skolnick and Fyfe 1993). Those who adopt the peacemaking perspective would support gun control and advocate a shift in criminal justice resources from punishment to prevention and rehabilitation. Maintaining law and order are only part of what our society should be striving for. We should, according to the peacemaking perspective, ensure that our institutions of social control accomplish their mandates in a nonviolent way that promotes social justice (National Criminal Justice Commission 1996).

The key to making society work is to make it fair. Everyone must feel that they have a stake in obeying the law and acting in a civil manner. The war on crime fails to provide the underlying theoretical justification for this and thus has become a serious social problem. It's sometimes hard to distinguish which is more destructive to society: crime or the way we address it with a war mentality.

References

Alexander, B. K. (1990) "Alternatives to the War On Drugs." *The Journal of Drug Issues* 20(1): 1–27.

Bartollas, C., and M. Braswell. (1993) "Correctional Treatment, Peacemaking, and the New Age Movement." *Journal of Crime and Justice* 16(2): 43–58.

Buckley, W. F. Jr. (1996) "The War on Drugs Is Lost." *National Review* 48(2): 36–38.

Czajkoski, E. H. (1990) "Drugs and the Warlike Administration of Justice." *The Journal of Drug Issues* 20(1): 125–129.

Duke, S. B. (1996) "The War on Drugs Is Lost." *National Review* 48(2): 47–48.

Fuller, J. F. (1998) *Criminal Justice: A Peacemaking Perspective.* Boston: Allyn and Bacon.

Gardiner, G. S., and R. N. McKinney. (1991) "The Great American War on Drugs: Another Failure of Tough-Guy Management." *The Journal of Drug Issues* 21(3): 605–616.

Gavzer, B. (1997) "Can They Beat the Odds? *Parade Magazine*, July 27, 4–5.

Gottfredson, M., and T. Hirschi. (1989) "War on Drugs Attacks Problem from Wrong Angle." *The Atlanta Journal/The Atlanta Constitution*, September 24, p. D3.

Johns, C. J. (1992) *Power, Ideology, and the War on Drugs: Nothing Succeeds Like Failure.* New York: Praeger.

Levy, L. W. (1996) *A License to Steal: The Forfeiture of Property.* Chapel Hill, NC: University of North Carolina Press.

McDermott, M. J. (1994) "Criminology as Peacemaking: Feminist Ethics and the Victimization of Women." *Women and Criminal Justice* 5(2): 21–44.

Mills, C. W. (1959) *The Sociological Imagination.* New York: Oxford University Press.

National Criminal Justice Commission. (1996) "Ten Recommendations to Shift the Fundamental Direction of U.S. Crime Policy." HYPERLINK http://www.ncianet.org/ncia/FIND.HTML.

Parrinder, G. (1971) *World Religions: From Ancient History to the Present.* New York: Facts on File Publications.

Pepinsky, H. E., and R. Quinney (eds.). (1991) *Criminology as Peacemaking.* Bloomington, IN: Indiana University Press.

Reiman, J. (1995) *The Rich Get Richer and the Poor Get Prison: Ideology, Class and Criminal Justice.* Boston: Allyn and Bacon.

Skolnick, J. H., and J. J. Fyfe. (1993) *Above the Law: Police and the Excessive Use of Force.* New York: The Free Press.

Sutton, L. P. (1991) "Getting around the Fourth Amendment," in C. B. Klockars and S. D. Mastrofski (eds.), *Thinking about Police: Contemporary Readings.* New York: McGraw-Hill, pp. 433–444.

Tobolowsky, P. M. (1992) "Drugs and Death: Congress Authorizes the Death Penalty for Certain Drug-Related Murders." *Journal of Contemporary Law* 18(1): 47–73.

Welch, M. (1996) *Corrections: A Critical Approach.* New York: McGraw-Hill.

Article Review Form at end of book.

How do the subcultural influences found in policing result in behaviors such as corruption and the excessive use of force? Is it individual behavior or is there a sociological explanation? Why do you think the comraderie is so important in policing? Many candidates say this is one of the main attractions to a law enforcement career. What does this say about the type of people who become police officers? How does the need to be a part of the law enforcement community affect their attitudes, values, and beliefs as police officers?

Police Brutality and the Socialization of the Police

Robert P. McNamara
Furman University

In 1991, Los Angeles police officers shocked the American public with the beating of Rodney King. In 1996, a South Carolina state trooper assaulted a motorist while she attempted to exit her vehicle after a traffic stop. Also in 1996, Los Angeles area officers were again accused of assaulting Hispanic motorists after a prolonged pursuit. Incidents like these raise many questions concerning the attitudes, values, and behavior of police officers around the country. Social scientists have offered differing and sometimes conflicting explanations for police use of authority and misconduct. One way is to suggest that officers are part of a larger group that socializes individuals to embody a set of behavioral expectations. I will have more to say on this in another section, but for now, a definition of what I mean by socialization is necessary.

The concept of socialization has been subjected to extensive analysis with the definitions of the concept varying widely. We can say the term socialization is used to describe the ways in which people learn to conform to their society's norms, values, and roles. Many sociologists contend that people develop their own unique personalities as a result of the learning they gain from parents, siblings, relatives, teachers, and other people who influence them throughout their lives (Elkin and Handel 1989). What is important about socialization, then, is that people learn to behave according to the expectations of their culture and transmit that way of life from one generation to the next. In this way, the culture of a society is reproduced (see Parsons and Bales 1955; Danziger 1971).

Socialization occurs throughout an individual's life as he or she learns the norms of new groups in new situations. There are three categories of socialization: *primary,* which involves the ways in which the child becomes a part of society; *secondary,* where the influence of others outside the family become important, and *adult socialization,* when the person learns the expectations of adult roles and statuses in society. This latter socialization includes learning the standards set by one's occupation.

The Socialization Process in Occupations

Of the many roles that a person is called upon to perform, few surpass the importance of possessing the skills and attitudes necessary for one's occupation. This is especially true in modern society where occupation has a central place in the life of the vast majority of adults. Occupation is challenged only by the family and the peer group as the major determinant of behavior and attitudes (Moore 1969). To the degree that adequate socialization occurs to permit one to perform in an occupation, an individual's world view, attitudes toward others, and well-being are influenced.

Interestingly, occupational socialization has not elicited the kind of scholarly interest that one might expect. While there are many studies on this topic, academic interest in socialization traditionally focused on infancy and childhood. It has only been within the last thirty years or so that researchers have become keenly interested in occupational socialization, or what is sometimes referred to as the sociology of work (see Erikson and Vallas 1995). The topics seem to focus on the normative dimensions of occupations; that is, the rules relating to the proper conduct and attitudes of an individual in a particular job or career.

For instance, in a classic study of socialization into an occupation, Becker et al. (1961) examined the process by which medical students are socialized into their profession. At the University of Kansas Medical School, Becker found that lower-class medical students, by virtue of their undergraduate education and commitment to becoming successful physicians, had clearly assimilated middle-class norms and values. Becker also found that first-year medical students had idealistic reasons for becoming a physician: helping people was more important than making money. In the beginning of their profession, then, there was a strong sense of idealism and many students felt that medical school would give them the opportunity to develop the skills needed to further that goal.

However, the process of medical training caused the students to alter their views. Early on, they adapted to the expectations of medical school and developed a strong appreciation of clinical experience (working with patients rather than reading about disease and studying it in the laboratory). They also learned to view disease and death as medical problems rather than as emotional issues. Additionally, despite their idealism, students in medical school quickly learned that they could not learn everything they need to know to practice medicine, and soon directed their efforts toward finding the most economical way of teaming. This meant guessing what their faculty wanted them to know so that the material could be studied for the examinations. Thus, during the course of their medical training, idealism was replaced with a concern for getting through the program. Becker observed that medical students may become cynical while in school, but he pointed out that these attitudes were often situational. As graduation approached, idealism seemed to return once the students were no longer under the intense pressure to "perform." That is, the immediate problem of completing their studies had passed. The lesson then is that when isolated in an institutional setting, the students adjusted to immediate demands. Once "released" from that setting, their attitudes changed to again conform to their new surroundings.

The broader implications of Becker's work are that individuals will be socialized to meet the expectations that important institutions or organizations place on them. Their attitudes, values, and beliefs will then become centered around fulfilling those expectations. In the case of the physician, where there is a great deal of autonomy, the original ideological concerns reemerge at the end of their training, largely because they have the ability to determine what type of medicine they will practice and under what circumstances. In those professions where there is an intense training period, less autonomy, and greater internal control by the organization, the individual is greatly influenced by the members of that organization. In other words, where there is greater freedom to practice one's profession, there is less of an impact in terms of the socialization process. However, in those professions where the individual is constrained by organizational rules and regulations, the more influential other members are on the thoughts and actions of the individual. This is exacerbated in professions that actively promote a sense of comraderie and solidarity among their members.

Resocialization

Perhaps the most significant aspect of the socialization process is that members within an organization (or, more broadly, within a society) internalize a set of norms that dictate appropriate behavior. When this fails to occur, the organization is forced to employ corrective methods to ensure conformity. Examples include deviants or criminals. Other people are resocialized because of a decision to join a new group. A good example of this occurs when an individual selects a particular career, such as soldier or police officer. It is here that the work of Erving Goffman plays a significant part in our understanding. In his classic *Asylums,* Goffman (1961) contends that the resocialization of individuals often occurs in *total institutions.* These are places where the individual's physical and social freedom are constrained and channeled in a certain direction. Goffman describes resocialization as a two-step process. First, there is what he calls the *mortification of the self*, where the attitudes, world views, and behavior patterns of the individual are stripped away. Goffman states:

> The recruit comes into the establishment with a conception of himself made possible by certain stable social arrangements in his home world. Upon entrance, he is immediately stripped of the support provided by these arrangements. In the accurate language of some of our oldest total institutions, he begins a series of abasements, degradations, humiliations, and profanations of self. His self is systematically, if often unintentionally, mortified. He begins radical shifts in his moral career, a career composed of the progressive changes that occur in the beliefs that he has concerning himself and significant others. The process by which a person's self is mortified are fairly standard in total institutions; analysis of these processes can help us to see the arrangements that ordinary establishments must guarantee if members are to preserve their civilian selves. (pp. 14–20)

This paves the way for the second step in resocialization, where a new set of attitudes,values, and beliefs are provided:

> . . . Once the inmate is stripped of his possessions, at least some replacements must be made by the establishment, but these take the form of standard issue, uniform in character and uniformly distributed. These substitute possessions are clearly marked as really belonging to the institution and in some cases are recalled at regular intervals to be, as it were, disinfected of identifications. . . . While the process of mortification goes on, the inmate begins to receive formal and informal instruction in what will here be called the privilege system. In so far as the inmate's attachment to his civilian self has been shaken by the stripping process of the institution, it is largely the privilege system that provides a framework for personal reorganization. (pp. 20–29)

For instance, in the case of the military, the new recruit or civilian is brought to a "boot" camp and stripped of any individual characteristics: clothes are taken away, haircuts are given, and rules on every aspect of life in the institution are explained. It is during this process that the sense of self gives way and the individual becomes a cog in a much larger machine. Only after this process is complete can the organization implement the second part of the resocialization process. Upon completion of boot camp, the recruit has a different sense of self, along with a new set of attitudes and behavior patterns.

A similar process occurs in law enforcement. After selection, the police academy (also considered to be a type of total institution) represents the first overt process of socialization. In addition to the skills and techniques needed to become an effective police officer, recruits are indoctrinated and exposed to the vernacular used by its members, the cultural norms dictating acceptable and unacceptable behavior, as well as the world view from the law enforcement perspective. In addition, these values, attitudes, and beliefs are reinforced informally as new officers interact with more experienced ones outside of the classroom. The "war stories" told by more seasoned officers reinforce the point made by the formal classroom lessons. Over time, recruits develop attitudes and behaviors that provide a consistent framework in which to understand the role of the police and the individual officer (see Radelet 1986).

This process continues after the academy, when the officer is usually assigned some sort of field training. The time spent in this phase of training varies by department, but can be up to six months. The field training officer (FTO) is responsible for teaching the new officer how to apply lessons from the academy to the tasks on the street. There is also an evaluative component to the process in that the FTO is charting the progress (or lack thereof) of the recruit. The style of the FTO, as well as the way in which the FTO interacts with citizens, will tend to be reflected in the recruit's behavior. In this way, FTO training is a part of the socialization process although it may not be a conscious process (Radelet 1986).

After FTO training, the officer remains on probation for a time, usually one year. During this time, a supervisor evaluates the officer's progress and overall performance in the job. As described by Becker et al. (1961) most recruits will admit that part of the learning process involves knowing the unique expectations their supervisor/teacher has for them. When this is learned, the officer will modify his or her behavior to conform with that of the supervisor (see also Radelet 1986). If, for instance, the officer learns that the sergeant places a great deal of emphasis on police-community relations, the officer will, in turn, have more community contacts. These learned behaviors are part of what Goffman (1961) refers to as *working* the system. More importantly, these behaviors are the essence of occupational socialization.

This is a normal part of the learning process. To be an effective police officer, the rookie officer must first learn the tricks of the trade and the most knowledgeable officers should impart their wisdom on their less learned colleagues. However, there is also the potential for various forms of misconduct to be taught as well as the proper procedures and attitudes.

Nature Versus Nurture in Policing

As mentioned, some contend that police officers have different personalities than people in other occupations. Others maintain that there is a cultural distinction that separates law enforcement from other occupations. Still others contend that officers have neither personality nor cultural differences from other occupations. In sum, what we know about the police culture and personality is dependent on how one views police behavior. While no single perspective provides a complete understanding of the varieties of police behavior, there is a long history of debate as to whether they have unique personalities or whether socialization and subcultures play a significant part in the behavior of police officers. What can be said with some confidence is that the roles and functions of the police set officers apart from other members of society (Radelet 1986).

The Socialization Argument

A number of researchers argue that personality is not fixed and rigid and is subject to change based on different personal experiences and socialization. This school of thought focuses on the role of the police in society and how professionalization, training, and socialization influence an individual's personality and behavior. Researchers operating from this paradigm study how the work environment, peers, and academy training shape and affect a police officer's personality and behavior. Many of these researchers, such as Adlam (1982), still focus attention on an individual's unique experiences and the development of individual personalities.

A somewhat different approach contends that socialization occurs, but it is more of a group experience than an individual one (Stoddard 1968; Van Maanen 1978). For example, Van Maanen disagrees with the idea that police officers have certain personality characteristics, such as authoritarianism. He argues instead for a perspective based on group socialization and professionalism. The latter is the process by which norms and values are internalized as an individual begins his or her new occupation. In this way, just as attorneys and physicians learn the values endemic to their profession, so too do police officers.

This perspective assumes that police officers learn their "social" personality from training and through exposure to the demands of police work. It follows then that if police officers become cynical or rigid, it is not because of their existing personality or individual experience, but because of the demands of the job and the shared experiences of others. Some research supports this idea. For example, Bennett (1984) found that while probationary officers' values are affected by the training process, little evidence was available that personalities were shaped by their peers in the department. Part of this explanation involves the legitimacy of newly hired officers, who do not become "real" police officers until they are accepted as a member in standing of the police subculture.

Other studies, such as Putti, Aryee, and Kang (1988) find that there may be a temporal factor at work in the socialization of police officers. That is, socialization into the subculture of police may occur at different points in the officers' careers. There is little evidence concerning the extent of how reference groups affect the personality of older officers, but it seems that in the beginning of his or her career, the officer's occupational values are shaped during the training and probationary process.

Still another model is offered by Kappler (1993), who contends that there is an acculturation process whereby the beliefs and values of police work are transmitted from one generation of officers to the next. In effect, the group socializes the individual officer into ways of acceptable and unacceptable behavior. This perspective draws heavily from an anthropological point of view and introduces the concept of the police subculture more concretely.

The Authoritarian Personality

Many researchers adopting this perspective feel that personality is fixed and does not really change by choice of occupation or experience. In other words, each person has a fixed personality that does not vary during the course of his or her life (Adlam 1982). This does not imply that personality is inviolate or does not have some degree of malleability, but generally it stays the same. As it applies to the police, most of the research in this area focuses on the personalities of people who choose to become police officers. This perspective assumes that people with certain personalities enter law enforcement as an occupation and behave in certain ways.

One of the most influential experts in this area is Milton Rokeach (Rokeach, Miller, and Snyder 1971). In comparing the values of police officers in Michigan with those of a national sample of private citizens, Rokeach found that police officers seemed more oriented toward self-control and obedience than the average citizen and officers were more interested in personal goals, such as "an exciting life." Officers were also less interested in larger social goals, such as "a world at peace." Rokeach also found evidence that the experiences as police officers did not significantly influence their personalities. He concludes that most officers probably have a unique value orientation and personality when they embark on their careers in policing.

In a similar study, Teevan and Dolnick (1973) compared values of officers in the Cook County, Illinois Sheriff Department with those Rokeach encountered in Lansing, Michigan. The findings suggest that the values of police officers in a large urban department are also far removed from those of the public. Some of the reasons, according to Teevan and Dolnick, are that officers are isolated within society, they are required to enforce unpopular laws, and there is a sense of self-imposed segregation as officers think of themselves as a last bastion of middle-class morality.

In describing the authoritarian personality, Adorno (1950) characterizes it in part by aggressive, cynical, and rigid behavior. People with these characteristics are said to have a myopic view of the world and that issues, people, and behavior are seen as clearly defined: good or bad, right or wrong, friends or enemies. They also tend to be conservative in their political orientation (see also Niederhoffer 1967; Bayley and Mendelsohn 1969). Levy (1967) proposes that certain personality traits established early in life were clues to whether a person would be more likely to find policing attractive as a profession. She states:

> We find that the appointees most likely to remain in law enforcement are probably those who are more unresponsive to the environmental stresses introduced when they become officers of the law than are their fellow-appointees. These stresses include becoming a member of a "minority" (occupationally speaking) group, need to adhere to semi-military regimen, community expectation of incongruous roles and the assumption of a position of authority complete with the trappings of uniform, badge, holster, and gun, and all these imply. The officers who remain in law enforcement may well be the sons of fathers who imposed a rigid code of behavior to which their children learned to adhere, and who do not feel a strong need to defy or rebel against authority. (p. 275)

On the other hand, some researchers have pointed to a few positive aspects of this type of personality in police officers. For instance, Carpenter and Raza (1987) have found that police applicants as a group are less depressed and more assertive in making and maintaining social contacts. Additionally they find that police officers are a more homogeneous group, which may be based on their similar interests in becoming police officers as well as sharing similar personality traits and world views.

Ultimately, many develop an occupational or *working personality,* characterized by authoritarianism, suspicion, and cynicism (Rubenstein 1973; Van Maanen 1978; Alpert and Dunham 1992; Neiderhoffer 1967). Skolnick (1966) provides perhaps the best description of the police personality:

> The policeman's role contains two principal variables, danger and authority, which should be interpreted in the light of a "constant" pressure to appear efficient. The element of danger seems to make the policeman especially attentive to signs indicating a potential for violence and lawbreaking. As a result, the policeman is generally a "suspicious" person. Furthermore, the character of the policeman's work makes him less desirable as a friend, since norms of friendship implicate others in his work. Accordingly, the element of danger isolates the policeman socially from that segment of the citizenry which he regards as symbolically dangerous and also from the conventional citizenry with whom he identifies. (p. 43)

An integral part of the police personality is cynicism: the notion that all people are motivated by evil and selfishness. Police cynicism develops among many officers through the nature of police work. Most police officers feel they are set apart from the rest of society because they have the power to regulate the lives of others. Moreover, by constantly dealing with crime and the more unsavory aspects of social life, their faith in humanity seems to diminish.

Probably the most well-known study of police personality was conducted by Arthur Neiderhoffer (1967). In *Behind the Shield,* Neiderhoffer builds off the work of William Westley (1970) that most officers develop into cynics as a function of their daily routines. Westley had maintained that being constantly faced with keeping people in line and believing that most people intend to break the law or cause harm to the officer lead officers to mistrust the people they are charged to protect. Neiderhoffer tested

Westley's assumption by distributing a survey measuring attitudes and values to 220 New York City police officers. Among his most important findings were that police cynicism did increase with length of service; that patrol officers with college educations became quite cynical if they were denied promotion; and that military-like academy training caused recruits to become cynical about themselves, the department, and the community. As an illustration, Niederhoffer found that nearly 80 precent of first day recruits believed the department was an "efficient, smoothly operating organization." Two months later, less than a third professed that belief. Similarly, half of the recruits believed that a supervisor was "very interested in the welfare of his subordinates," while two months later, those still believing so dropped to 13 precent. Niederhoffer states:

> Cynicism is an ideological plank deeply entrenched in the ethos of the police world, and it serves equally well for attack or defense. For many reasons police are particularly vulnerable to cynicism. When they succumb, they lose faith in people, society, and eventually in themselves. In their Hobbesian view, the world becomes a jungle in which crime, corruption, and brutality are normal features of the terrain. (p. 9)

In sum, the police personality emerges as a result of the nature of police work and of the socialization process that most police officers experience. To deal with the social isolation that is derived from their use of authority, some of it self-imposed, officers use other members of the profession to cope with social rejection. As a result, many, perhaps most, police officers become part of a closely knit subculture that is protective and supportive of its members, while sharing similar attitudes, values, and understandings, and views of the world.

The Subculture of Policing

Occupational socialization creates occupational subcultures (Radelet and Carter 1994). The idea of the police being a subculture is not new and has been well documented (see Westley 1970; Rokeach, Miller, and Synder 1971; Kirkham 1976; Bittner 1970). For our purposes, subculture may be defined as the meanings, values, and behavior patterns unique to a particular group in a given society. Entry into this subculture begins with a process of socialization whereby recruits learn the values and behavior patterns characteristic of experienced officers.

The development and maintenance of negative attitudes and values by police officers has many implications. Regoli and Poole (1979) found evidence that an officer's feelings of cynicism intensifies the need to maintain respect and increase the desire to exert authority over others. This can easily lead to the increased fear and mistrust of the police by the public. This, in turn, can create feelings of hostility and resentment on the part of the officer, creating what is sometimes known as *police paranoia* (Regoli and Poole 1979: 43). Regoli and Poole also found that these negative attitudes result in conservative attitudes and a resistance to change among the officers.

As mentioned, the creation of the police subculture also stems from this unique police personality. However, despite the evidence, many researchers disagree with the notion of a police subculture. Balch (1972) in his study of the police personality states:

> It looks like policemen may be rather ordinary people, not greatly unlike other middle Americans. We cannot be sure there is such a thing as a police personality, however we loosely define it. (p. 117)

Similarly, Tifft (1974) argues that while the attitudes of officers may be influenced by their work environment, the idea that officers maintain uniform personality traits developed through socialization or innate drives is fallacious. Therefore, he argues that the activities and responsibilities most officers engage in have a role to play in how they see the world, but in many ways this is symptomatic of many other occupations. He states:

> Task related values, attitudes and behavior are occupationally derived or created out of specialized roles rather than being primarily due to the selection factors of background or personality. (p. 268)

Therefore, the debate over whether officers possess a distinct working personality, as well as whether the subculture of policing is pervasive, continues. The nature of police work remains complex and the issues surrounding law enforcement have not been completely understood. Incidents like the Rodney King beating will, unfortunately, continue. Part of the reason for this is because we do not know the reasons why officers engage in police brutality. For some, it may be due to a psychological impairment, for others it may be that they are following the rules set out by the larger group in certain situations. Our task as researchers is to sufficiently understand the context in which those incidents occur and attempt to offer some insight as to why these behaviors develop and continue. The answers to these questions remain elusive.

References

Adlam, K. R. 1982. "The Police Personality: Psychological Consequences of Becoming a Police Officer." *Journal of Police Science and Administration* 10(3): 347–48.

Adorno, T. W. 1950. *The Authoritarian Personity.* New York: Harper and Brothers.

Alpert, G., and R. Dunham. 1992. *Policing Urban America.* 2nd ed. Prospect Heights, IL: Waveland Press.

Balch, Robert. 1972. "The Police Personality: Fact or Fiction?" *Journal of Criminal Law, Criminology and Police Science* 63: 117.

Bayley, D. H., and H. Mendelsohn. 1969. *Minorities and the Police: Confrontation in America.* New York: The Free Press.

Becker, H., B. Greer, E. Hughes, and A. Strauss. 1961. *Boys in White: Student Culture in Medical School.* Chicago: University of Chicago Press.

Bennett, R. R. 1984. "Becoming Blue: A Longitudinal Study of Police Recruit Occupational Socialization." *Journal of Police Science and Administration* 12(1): 47–57.

Bittner, E. 1970. *The Functions of Police in Modern Society.* Chevy Chase, MD: National Clearinghouse for Mental Health.

Carpenter, B. N., and S. M. Raza. 1987. "Personality Characteristics of Police Applicants: Comparisons across Subgroups and with Other Populations." *Journal of Police Science and Administration* 15(l): 10–17.

Danziger, K. 1971. *Socialization.* Harmondsworth, England: Penguin.

Elkin, F., and G. Handel. 1989. *The Child and Society: The Process of Socialization.* 5th ed. New York: Random House.

Erikson, K., and P. Vallas. (eds.) 1995. *The Nature of Work. Sociological Perspectives.* Washington, DC: American Sociological Association.

Goffman, E. 1961. *Asylums.* New York: Anchor.

Kappler, V. E., M. Blumberg, and G. W. Potter. 1993. *The Mythology of Crime and Criminal Justice.* Prospect Heights, IL: Waveland Press.

Kirkham, G. 1976. *Signal Zero.* New York: Ballentine.

Levy, R. 1967. "Predicting Police Failures." *Journal of Criminal Law, Criminology and Police Science* 58(2): 275.

Moore, W. 1969. "Occupational Socialization," in D. Goslin (ed.), *Handbook of Socialization Theory and Research.* New York: Rand McNally, pp. 861–84.

Neiderhoffer, A. 1967. *Behind the Shield: The Police in Urban Society.* Garden City, NY: Doubleday.

Parsons, T., and R. F. Bales. 1955. *Family, Socialization, and Interaction Process.* New York: The Free Press.

Putti, J., S. Aryee, and T. S. Kang. 1988. "Personal Values of Recruits and Officers in a Law Enforcement Agency: An Exploratory Study." *Journal of Police Science and Administration* 16(4): 245–49.

Radelet, L. 1986. *The Police and the Community.* 4th ed. New York: Macmillan.

Regoli, R., and E. Poole. 1979. "Measurement of Police Cynicism: A Facto Scaling Approach." *Journal of Criminal Justice* 7: 37–52.

Rokeach, M., M. Miller, and H. Snyder. 1971. "The Value Gap between Police and Policed." *Journal of Social Issues* 27: 155–71.

Rubenstein, J. 1973. *City Police.* New York: Farrar, Strauss, and Giroux.

Skolnick, J. 1966. *Justice Without Trial: Law Enforcement in a Democratic Society.* New York: John Wiley and Sons.

Stoddard, E. R. 1968. "The Informal Code of Police Deviancy: A Group Approach to Blue-Collar Crime." *Journal of Criminal Law, Criminology, and Police Science* 59(2): 201–203.

Teevan, J., and B. Dolnick. 1973. "The Values of the Police: A Reconsideration and Interpretation." *Journal of Police Science and Administration* 1: 366–69.

Tifft, L. 1974. "The Cop Personality Reconsidered." *Journal of Police Science and Administration* 2: 268.

Westley, W. 1970. *Violence and the Police: A Sociological Study of Law, Custom, and Morality.* Cambridge, MA: MIT Press.

Van Maanen, J. 1978. "On Becoming a Policeman," in P. Manning and J. Van Maanen (eds.), *Policing: A View from the Street.* Santa Monica, CA: Goodyear.

Article Review Form at end of book.

When people talk about the crime problem, they usually refer to street crime and not white-collar crime. This is true even though the costs of white-collar crime, as well as the harm it inflicts on society, are far greater than all of street crime combined. Why is there such a moral ambiguity about white-collar crime? Why is it that white-collar crime is so difficult to detect? Perhaps more importantly, why would people engage in it? Many white-collar offenders have achieved success by societal standards. Why, then, do you think they engage in it? Some people might say it is simple greed, but is this a compelling explanation?

White-Collar Crime

Or "I didn't really mean for *that* to happen!"

Sheila Weaver LaFountain

State University of West Georgia

Our social system is inextricably wrapped up in our economic system in American life as it is elsewhere. Here, our capitalistic pursuits formulate certain goals realized in business, governmental, and educational institutions, which many times create social problems because of actions we take in pursuit of those goals. White-collar crime is one manifestation of those social problems. What is it? Who is held responsible for it? Is it treated like any other crime? Are white-collar crimes really just *"unanticipated consequences"*? What is the boundary between a social problem left to the culture, the civil law, and social agencies to handle and an act for which the state pursues prosecution and punishment? White-collar crime treads the boundaries of crime and defies the classical understanding of unanticipated consequences. Many acts that we tolerate because they are committed in the course of business dealings are treated as errors in judgment that, if committed by an individual in the community at large, that individual would quickly be charged with theft, or assault and battery, or murder. If we can identify the problem as a systemic one, should the agent be held responsible? Should the corporation? Should we instead find that our American culture is at fault? This essay will answer these questions while perhaps raising others. Among those implicit questions is how economic analysis can be more fully integrated into the classical sociological analyses, providing a transformative insight by which we might not only make observations, but that will also allow us to identify changes that will correct those ills of our socioeconomic-legal system. Here the economic considerations go beyond the traditional class-based analysis usually proffered by traditional functionalist (e.g., Merton) or conflict (e.g., Quinney) sociologists. The individual is effectively acting independently in an organization but within a given set of parameters set by the American culture where the characteristics of a class are not the primary focal point. The pairing of economic, legal, and social analysis in white-collar crime yields insight into the consequences of actions motivated by factors more complex than traditional sociological analyses can illustrate.

Why Is This New Category So Challenging to the Traditional Theories of Crime?

Consider the phrase *"white-collar crime."* "White collar" seems to in-

Inspired by a grasshopper. All examples contained herein are mere hypotheticals and any resemblance to actual people, corporations or events is purely accidental and unintended.

dicate that this crime is different from other crimes. It clues us into some sort of exclusive nature of this type of crime. Who is the "white collar" committing the crime? While the definition has not been precisely agreed on by the experts, Edwin Sutherland provided us not only with the term "white-collar crime" but also with the hallmarks that carved out a new field of study for sociology, criminology, and law. "White collar crime may be defined approximately as a crime committed by a person of respectability and high social status in the course of his occupation" (Sutherland, 1983).

Some theories rely on class or poverty to explain the occurrence of crime. Even a quick glance at the examples that fall into the category of white-collar crime will illustrate how those theories are inadequate to explain all types of crime. If the theories that rely on class or poverty fail to explain these types of crimes, then do they adequately explain other types of crime? As Sutherland (1983) challenged the criminologists, if we examined only those crimes committed by those people with red hair would we be correct in surmising that the redness of their hair is the cause of their crimes?

Sutherland focused particularly on corporations that violated federal laws and profiled three case histories in detail. The violations he found involved looting of a corporation for personal profits by its officers, price fixing, infringing on patent rights, discriminating against union members, unfair trade practices, conspiracy to violate antitrust laws, making false advertising claims, and consolidation of reports for the purpose of avoiding taxes.

How Can a Corporation Commit a Crime?

A corporation is an entity, which the law treats as a person in many respects. Think of the many corporations whose services and products we purchase or consider purchasing every day. Legally, corporations exist independently of those who work for it and make the daily decisions. The actions of those people on behalf of the corporation are treated as actions of the corporation itself and they are called its *agents.*

False Advertising

Consider the fictional corporation we will refer to as SpiderWebs Unlimited. The Advertising director named Sneaky is planning a series of ads for television to promote the webs produced by the corporation. These ads claim that SpiderWebs has the biggest, most luxurious webs found anywhere. The video seems to support this claim and when you see the ad, the viewer is climbing onto what seems to be a web that stretches on forever. Each line of the web is perfectly spaced so that climbing through it is easy and fun. What the consumer cannot see, however, is that Sneaky has put a special lens on the camera that makes a six-inch long web appear to be two feet long. Using special effects generated by his computer, Sneaky makes the number of lines in the web double its actual number, reinforcing the impression of a much larger web.

Can we say that SpiderWebs Unlimited has violated the laws against false advertising? If we determine that SpiderWebs has influenced our desire to purchase the product, then they may be said to be guilty of false advertising. Surprisingly, false advertising does not mean that something that appears in the ad is false. If a cartoon fairy drops down from the sky in the ad and magically makes the web appear, then that too may be an example of an implicit false claim. Fairies don't exist, and fairies don't make webs appear. Merely being false is not enough to substantiate a false advertising claim. If it does not affect our decision to buy then legally it is not "misleading in a *material* respect" (Federal Trade Commission Acts 15). In the ad made by Sneaky, the number of lines in the web are double what we would find in a normal web purchase. The web itself appears to be about four times the size of what we would find in a normal web package. Our decision to buy a box with this web in it might reasonably be affected by this type of exaggerated advertising. In this example we might say that the deceptive ad shown by the corporation has *materially* or actually affected our decision to purchase the web made by SpiderWebs Unlimited.

Who Is at Fault—Sneaky or SpiderWebs Unlimited?

Since Sneaky is the director of advertising at SpiderWebs Unlimited, he is acting as an *agent* of the corporation. Sneaky's action as an agent will be attributed to the corporation. Sometimes it is possible that the corporation will be liable for those actions, and Sneaky may be liable for those actions too.

Historically, the law has sought an individual actor whose intentions were responsible for the crime committed. More recently, however, sociologists and criminologists (e.g., James Coleman) have shifted the focus of analysis by incorporating an economic perspective into the picture of crime, illustrating how we can conceive of *organizational crime* as opposed to white-collar crime, which suggests it is the individual who is solely at fault.

We are increasingly a nation of employees, working in one or another of vast bureaucracies and fearfully dependent upon the boss or the boss's boss. The "invisible hand" of the open marketplace is often attached to an awesome amalgamation of corporate and governmental power.

In many ways the organizations, and not individual employees, are the real perpetrators of organizational crimes. In many cases, criminal activities carried on to further organizational goals are rooted in a subculture and a set of attitudes that have developed over many years and cannot be traced to any single individual or group of individuals. Individual actors must still carry out the criminal deeds, but there is ample evidence to show that the attitudes and characteristics of the individual offenders are often of little importance (Coleman, 1985).

As director of advertising at SpiderWebs Unlimited, Sneaky is charged with creating ads that will attract more people to buy their webs than any other web, especially the number one web seller Megawebs, Inc. Megawebs sells the usual size six-inch web, but they have the patent that allows them to link the webs so that you can travel easily from one web to another. To compete, Sneaky realizes he must make SpiderWebs look wonderful just as they are since they haven't developed an alternative device to link them. Therefore, to be successful, the goal of Sneaky's work creates an incentive for him to project a false image of the product and one that is supposed to *materially* affect the customer's decision to purchase their web. We might say that Sneaky's primary intention is to keep his job and be successful in it and that it is the organizational goals that breed the intention for the employees to go beyond the limits that the law allows.

Is It Possible for SpiderWebs to Become Too Successful?

While competition is one of the hallmarks of the capitalist system, the most successful corporations will be those that can control their competition. When attempts to control competition go too far they are known as *antitrust* violations. Federal and state legislation prohibit corporations from attempting to fix the price of goods or services, from price discrimination, and from creating monopolies. The primary antitrust legislative acts include the Sherman Act (1890), the Clayton Act (1914), Federal Trade Commission Act (1914), and the Robinson-Patman Act (1936). The majority of the states have also passed antitrust laws based on these federal laws. State laws cover those companies doing business within the boundaries of the state while federal laws cover interstate commerce. Most of the time antitrust violations will be covered by state and federal laws even when the company only intends to keep its business within the boundaries of the state. How? The use of the telephone even for a local call brings the act within the purview of the federal interstate commerce laws.

If the director of distribution and sales for SpiderWebs attempted to work out an agreement with the web distributors that would prevent them from distributing webs made by MegaWebs, that would fall into the category of *exclusive dealing*. If the American Web Association, to which all web makers belong, tried to make the selling price of all webs the same then they might be guilty of *price fixing*. If MegaWebs bought all of the businesses that make the sticky stuff of webs and sold the sticky stuff at much higher prices to other web makers than it sold it to itself for webmaking, then MegaWebs might be guilty of *price discrimination* regarding its sales of sticky stuff. Finally, if MegaWebs bought all the companies that make webs, then they might be accused of trying to build a *monopoly*, another form of price discrimination. These practices are examples of unfair competition and were typical of the unfair business practices that characterized the late nineteenth century and early twentieth century. The laws established since that time, state and federal, make these kinds of practices illegal (Coleman, 1985).

As always with criminal law, we must identify a criminal *intent* before a conviction for an antitrust violation will be obtained. In other words we must ask questions such as: "Did MegaWebs *intend to monopolize* the web market?" "Has there been any exploitation of the market due to the advantage of their position as a monopoly?" "Was the monopolistic advantage obtained through illegal means?" If the answer to these questions is no, then there probably would not be a finding that MegaWebs has created an illegal monopoly. No one can be found guilty of a crime without a showing of an evil intent.

Doesn't a Crime Historically Involve Violence?

Usually when we think of crime our immediate thoughts are associated with some sort of violent act. The media floods us with those images each day. Theft, assault and battery, and murder take many forms and the corporate form can be as violent as those we see on television.

Name a Crime. Outside of the context of this book, many would respond "burglary" or "robbery" or "murder." Few would respond "monopoly" or "knowingly marketing unsafe pharmaceuticals" or "dumping of toxic wastes." (Mokhiber, 1988, 3)

Corporations have historically been able to charge excessive prices (theft?), ask workers to come into contact with chemicals that are harmful to their bodies and their minds (assault and battery?), and ask workers to work under conditions that ultimately lead to their death (murder?). Unmasking the façade of disinformation and misinformation that is disseminated by master manipulators of public impression is not easy. One need only look at the cases documented by Mokhiber (1988) and the length of time that was required to change the criminal behavior of the corporations involved. Jeffrey Reiman, a conflict sociologist, undertook a similar study. Reiman found that occupational diseases and deaths associated with health care delivery in the United States far exceed certain FBI crime statistics for murder and assault (Reiman, 1995).

Oil companies, automobile manufacturers, and pharmaceutical companies are examples of industries with the highest crime rates (Coleman, 1985). The most serious illegal corporate practices lead to violent results. Suppose that Slimy, the director of engineering for MegaWebs, has tested the links they are using to make large webs. During repeated testing the link has broken when the speeds used to run between the two webs are faster than the normal crawl. Slimy's contract with MegaWebs promised to deliver a link that could be developed, marketed, and sold this year. Everything worked out just fine during research and development except that Slimy's engineering crew couldn't develop a link that would withstand higher speeds. Slimy files the test results on the links in his desk drawer and tells the president that they are ready to run with the new links for MegaWebs. In the first three months of web sales an unprecedented number of fatal injuries occur. The deadly results from these types of design flaws are as lethal as the murderer who points the gun directly at her victim and pulls the trigger. Coleman has documented the irresponsible acts of corporations who produce and dispose of toxic chemicals such as vinyl chloride, asbestos, mercury, and others (Coleman, 1985). Many times the agents for these corporations deny the effects are related to the use or exposure to their product, even in the face of extensive statistical data that seems to refute their claims.

Many times the toxic effect of the chemicals involved does not provoke an immediate reaction. Sometimes it takes many years for symptoms to appear and years longer for any serious consequences. The use of Agent Orange during the Vietnam War; deadly gases released over Bhopal in 1984; black lung disease found in coal miners in West Virginia; brown lung disease found in the cotton mill workers; DBCP pesticide, which affected living creatures near the pesticide production facility; the Dalkon Shield; DES; overseas dumping of hazardous waste; asbestos; and the list goes on of chemicals and products that have had traumatic consequences for humans and other life forms (Mokhiber, 1988). In each of these toxic chemical cases, it took years to develop the correct associations between the symptoms and their causes. It took even longer to enact laws and change corporate practices to prevent people from being exposed to those toxic chemicals. Corporations do not easily give up profitable ventures after all, unless they are a *nonprofit* corporation, that is their mission.

Violence occurs not only secondarily, as a result of something that the company mines, makes, sells, or distributes, but also directly at the hand of the agents. Such *institutionalized violence* takes many forms. For instance, prisoners or inmates suffer violent acts committed by the employees of those institutions whose "authority" remains unchecked (Faith, 1996).

Abuse of power in the prison setting occurs in many different ways, from the outright beating of prisoners by guards and other officials to much more subtle forms that require thought and investigation to perceive how the abuse is legitimated. Officials might place female inmates imprisoned for child abuse in isolation for their own "protection." Some housing units may not be properly cleaned, prisoners may be strip-searched for inadequate reasons, the exam may be conducted in abusive ways, or visitation rights with family members may be denied (Faith, 1996). These types of excesses within the prison system seem closer to the kind of crime with which we are familiar. The element of violence and violation is tangibly present. We do not have to sort through financial documents and sources of authority to the same extent as in some corporate settings to find the wrong. Society, however, has historically found it easier to turn a blind eye to these problems because they were inflicted upon those who were viewed as criminals, and as such they might seem somehow deserving of their mistreatment within the system. During the late 1960s and 1970s the leading cases were won and primary legislation was enacted that provides the legal enforcement mechanisms that safeguard the human and civil rights of inmates.

Environmental Justice

Some of the most severe physical traumas are suffered by people who come into contact with toxic substances released into the environment. Many times these substances are either unregulated, minimally regulated, or they are legally entering the environment in some contexts. Robert Bullard (1994) has documented many such cases. At the forefront of these cases is the fact that it is primarily people of color and the poor who suffer a disproportionate amount of these injustices. Lacking the resources to address these problems through legislation and the court system, these victims suffer from pesticide pollution, toxic waste dumps, and the dangers of living near inadequately monitored landfills, incinerators, and coal-fired power plants.

While these communities have been relatively powerless in the past, a grassroots movement within these communities of color has taken shape enabling them to successfully attack such issues as "neighborhood disinvestment, housing discrimination and residential segregation, urban mass transportation, pollution, and other environmental problems that threaten public safety" (Bullard, 1994). They achieved formal organization in 1991 when the First National People of Color Environmental Leadership Summit was held in Washington, D.C. (Bullard, 1994). Through such a massive organization effort, which encompasses many different minority cultures and all fifty states, they have been able to document their successes and formulate plans of action, which can be duplicated by other communities. The "Principles of Environmental Justice" they adopted at this meeting:

- Affirms the sacredness of Mother Earth, ecological unity and the interdependence of all species, and the right to be free from ecological destruction.
- Demands that public policy be based on mutual respect and justice for all people, free from any form of discrimination or bias.
- Affirms the fundamental right to political, economic, cultural, and environmental self-determination of all peoples.
- Affirms the right of all workers to a safe and healthy work environment, without being forced to choose between an unsafe livelihood and unemployment.
- Affirms the need for urban and rural ecological policies to clean up and rebuild our cities and rural areas in balance with nature, honoring the cultural integrity of our communities, and providing fair access for all to the full range of resources.
- Calls for the education of present and future generations, which emphasizes social and environmental issues, based on our experience and an appreciation of our diverse cultural perspectives. (Bullard)

These statements are only a diverse sampling of the declarations adopted by the group. It is easy to see that their goals include not only the immediate concern of cleaning up and protecting the environment in which their communities exist, but they have the longer term goals of altering the commercial and legislative process that creates such a pattern of discrimination. *Environmental racism* was a term first used by Reverend Chavis in a report issued by his commission in 1987. Though the commission was first formed in response to the assassination of Medgar Evers in 1963, they have turned their focus to many different issues that affect people of color, from education to violence (Bullard, 1994). In 1982 their attention turned to the proposed dumping of PCBs in a predominantly African American county in North Carolina. When Chavis looked at other hazardous dumping grounds he found that the common link between them was that they were located in or near communities of color. Race was the single most significant variable at each of the sites examined in the study, economic conditions were not. Emelle, Alabama, location of the "largest [hazardous waste] landfill in the nation " was 80 percent African American and many were *middle class* (Bullard).

According to Chavis, *environmental racism is:*

> racial discrimination in environmental policymaking, the enforcement of regulations and laws, the deliberate targeting of communities of color for toxic waste facilities, the official sanctioning of the life threatening presence of poisons and pollutants in our communities, and the history of excluding people of color from leadership of the environmental movement. (Bullard 1994, 278)

The last point in Chavis' definition might seem surprising. In 1987, the ten largest groups whose focus was the environment had largely white males in the staff and leadership positions. The Sierra Club and the National Resources Defense Council immediately responded to this address by Chavis at the National Press Club by acknowledging the diversity deficiencies in their organization in the member populations as well as the focus of their issues. They also opened their arms and embraced the readiness of people of color to join their ranks in the fight against all forms of environmental degradation (Bullard, 1994).

Those who claimed it was the invisible hand of the market that directed such dealings countered the claims of environmental racism. Vicki Been (1995) contends that if market forces are the reasons for such things, then those forces must be taken into account as we seek solutions to the problem or, as she claims, "any solutions that do not take these forces into account will be only temporarily effective, at best." On the face of it there is plausibility in the assertion that something other than the race variable may be at issue. Most research into environmental racism looks at the *current* socioeconomic characteristics of those communities. As such they may not consider the actual conditions of the site at the time of its choosing. Been speculates that the existence of locally undesirable land uses (LULU) may further drive down prices and land values in the area, making it attractive for "poor and racial minorities to 'come to the nuisance'—to move the neighborhoods that host LULU—because those neighborhoods offered the cheapest available housing." The empirical research she offers to back such speculation makes it seem more than plausible. Her findings indicate that there was an increase in the minority race population after the siting of a LULU.

Why would those involved in the environmental racism movement be reluctant to recognize the economic variable in this equation? Much of the legislation and many of the cases brought forward in the name of environmental racism ignore this aspect of socioeconomic analysis under the protective umbrella of claims of unconstitutionality based on *suspect classification.* We all discriminate in many ways in our everyday life. We may prefer chocolate over vanilla ice cream. We might love eggplant and despise onions. Some preferences yield the type of discrimination that the Supreme Court has determined is unconstitutional when undertaken in some contexts. While the Supreme Court would not be concerned about discriminating against onions, and therefore would not declare root vegetables a suspect classification, there are some classifications that can serve as a basis for discrimination that rise to the level of unconstitutionality. These classifications become suspicious when they are used. These suspect classifications include race, sex, and national origin. The Supreme Court has historically refused to recognize economic classifications as a protected category. Those neighborhoods discriminated against because they are poor cannot receive any relief under the Equal Protection Clause. Whereas if they claim that they are discriminated against on the basis of race or national origins, they might receive relief under that same clause. When a claim is asserted under the Equal Protection Clause of the Fourteenth Amendment, one question that must be answered is, "Is a suspect classification involved?" because it is the suspect classifications the Supreme Court has recognized as being in need of protection. The way the Supreme Court enforces the Equal Protection Clause may point to the reason why Vicki Been's analysis may provide insight into the problem, yet be ineffective in offering an analysis that can legally be enforced at this time. If the interjection of market analysis is correct, however, Been is correct in asserting that any fixes that do not take the economic aspect of the problem into account will be a temporary fix at best and will be a source of frustration to everyone involved.

The special situation of Native Americans is even more problematic where some environmental issues are concerned. As the language implies, Native American reservations involve tracts of land removed from the public domain. These were supposed to be territories reserved for their own governance. In reality, the federal government remains as a *fiduciary* to the tribes. A fiduciary is one who has the duty to care for another. For the reservations, this means that the federal laws apply to these reservations while state laws do not.

This paternalistic attitude toward the Native Americans has not encompassed care and concern for the environment in which they live (Small, 1995).

In the 1970s approximately half of the 500,000 acre reservation of the Cheyenne in southeastern Montana was leased to coal companies by the Bureau of Indian Affairs (BIA) for seventeen cents per ton without anything in the lease that would even minimally protect the environment (Small, 1995). The tribe, already poor, spent many of its much needed resources and took fifteen years trying to undo the actions of the BIA claiming. The problem of the coal mines has not ended as each year the coal of the Cheyenne becomes even more valuable and each year the coal miners return. "Every year, the tribe debates again whether we can afford to continue refusing the offers of the coal companies" (Small). These efforts cannot, however, reach the problem that rests along their perimeter lined with the largest coal strip-mines in this country (Small).

Native Americans have valued natural resources as having intrinsic value as a part of their tradition and cultural heritage; therefore they have preserved what many groups sold off years ago. As a result, those reservations able to maintain the integrity of their environment at great financial and personal expense now sit on a wealth of coal, oil, uranium, timber, and other mineral resources (Bryant, 1995). On other reservations, the treaties protecting their fishing and mineral rights have proved worthless. Over four hundred treaties have been signed and broken by the U.S. government with the Native Americans (Bryant). Both groups are relatively poor and lack the resources to deal with these problems and resolve unemployment issues and other social problems (Bryant).

Computer Crime

Crimes committed using highly sophisticated computing skills encompass a broad range. Some of these criminals are kids who seek the thrill that comes with hacking. They want to "see if they can do it," as though their activities are a game. Those are indeed serious crimes worth exploration but in this section I will focus on those types of computer crimes committed by the white-collar criminal.

Whether for government or corporate *espionage,* "masquerading" has proven to be one of the most successful means of gaining criminal access to a computer system (Icove, 1995). The masquerader is using a known login; therefore all of the system logins will give the appearance of an authorized access to the system. When this happens it is as though someone who looks just like you is breaking into your room at college in broad daylight. Not only are confidential corporate and governmental records altered, copied, or destroyed (theft and destruction of property), the reputation of the true login owner is badly damaged in the process.

Computers are also tools used in the commission of corporate fraud. In 1973, a corporation using computer generated reports presented itself on paper as one of the fastest growing institutions worldwide. Corporate managers inflated the actual numbers of insurance policies held by around 300 percent and the subsequent losses to investors were an estimated $2 billion (Clinard, 1980). "Double billing" generates a similar problem. When sending bills to corporations and government agencies who process large volumes daily, double billing, sending a duplicate bill for the same services or products, results in double payment. Losses of greater than $500,000 have been documented in such fraud cases suffered by the Medicaid agency (Clinard, 1980). These crimes make significant use of the abilities of the computer, but all are the type of crime committed through manual bookkeeping systems; therefore they do not bear the same hallmark as the acts of the hackers.

Consider the computer fraud and abuse crimes committed by a graduate student at Cornell in 1988. He created a program called a *worm.* A worm is different from a computer virus, which affects, alters, and sometimes destroys, computer programs. Unlike a worm, a computer virus cannot exist as an independent program in its own right. A worm can exist independently of other programs and is usually malevolent in that it replicates itself to such a degree to use up system resources, sometimes completely. As with the 1988 worm incident, the replication of the program occurs not only on the original computer system in which the worm is placed but also across the network to any other computer systems connected to it (Icove, 1995). Imagine trying to get into your dorm room or office only to find that your books and papers have been doubling their size and number all day, and you can't get into the room because all available space has been consumed. In 1988, the worm was actually released from MIT in hopes of masking that it originated at Cornell. The graduate student knew the program was going to replicate itself even beyond the system at MIT as that is precisely what he had designed it to do. That alone would have caused some damage so far as it would have used up system resources. The more severe aspects of his deed appeared when the program replicated itself and infected other machines far more quickly than he had anticipated. As a result many machines crashed and or became catatonic. Even though the student enlisted the aid of a friend at Harvard and they attempted to devise a fix that would halt the progress of the worm, the message sent across the Internet was unable to be delivered because many machines had already shut down and the network was too clogged to reach those still viable. Eventually researchers at Berkeley and Purdue found and published ways to slow the action of the worm and to recover the system. The graduate student was convicted under Title 18, the Computer Fraud and Abuse Act, sentenced to three years of probation, 400 hours of community service, and fined $10,050 plus supervision costs. While this conviction may be satisfying at some level for those who were harmed, there was no restitution available for their damages suffered. The costs of dealing with the worm ranged from $200 to over $53,000 per site affected.

While the 1988 worm incident was the result of an unauthorized and illegal experiment gone awry, the other end of this extreme in computer crimes involves the computer hacker who seeks to reach out to another system and view, retrieve, or alter data. One of the more famous unauthorized access cases was pursued by an astronomer whose attention was captured by a mere $.75 discrepancy in a lab report. After much diligent investigation, which led the astronomer through a maze including the FBI and the CIA, the hacker was finally located in Germany. Though never brought to justice, this hacker stole classified U.S. government military and security information.

One of the largest chip manufacturers released a processor that could not perform mathematics functions properly beyond eight digits. The corporation discovered the defect while the product was being shipped and decided not to inform its distributors or purchasers of the problems with the chip. As a result, at least one large bank in New York was plagued by miscalculations, scientists received incorrect results when making subatomic particle calculations, and many others either experienced problems as a direct result of using the defective chip or replaced or avoided the chip to avoid possible problems. The latter was the case with the Food and Drug Administration when it decided not to purchase the chip for fear of the bad calculations yielding negative consequences in drug testing. Avoiding the purchase of such a chip is not as easy as it might appear when you realize that the manufacturer involved controls approximately 74 percent of the microprocessor market.

What Do All These Cases and Problems Have in Common?

To convict someone of a crime the element of criminal *intent* must be present. As you might expect from reading these brief accounts, most people who are caught in a web of white-collar crime claim that they *did not intend* for those results to occur. When the agent steps beyond the legitimate boundaries of corporate responsibility and professional ethics, that agent may claim that the goals of the corporation, or more specifically the demands of his particular position, required that those steps be taken or they would lose to the competition. Sneaky might claim that he never intended anyone to be deceived by the size or number of lines in their webs any more than if he had placed a unicorn on the web would he be offering a web package that included unicorns. Similarly, the corporation that introduces pesticides into the environment may claim that their intention was to kill insects before they destroy food crops. The graduate student who puts a worm on the web may hope we believe that the goal was merely a bit of, perhaps annoying but harmless, fun into the public domain. Perhaps the hacker would prefer we believe that the true quest is for the perusal of information that should be made accessible to the world at large in the noble name of "freeing" information.

If it is true that these are *unanticipated consequences* then how can these actions be charged as criminal? Unanticipated consequences are those things that happen that you did not expect would happen in the course of accomplishing another intended result. When a college student spends too much time partying with their new friends, the intention is to have fun while the unanticipated consequences, the bad grades, can also occur as a result of those same actions. Similarly in business, the corporation intends to make a profit through selling its product and claims that anyone who was harmed by that product is merely an unanticipated consequence of purchasing, using, or making their product.

These are examples of unanticipated consequence according to Merton's analysis. When we further consider the evidence, however, it is reasonable to make a further distinction in the category of unanticipated consequences. We should differentiate *unanticipated consequences* from *unintended consequences.* Somewhere in the back of the partying college student's mind they "know" that spending time away from studies is likely to result in bad grades. Thus it is more precise to say that while they did not *intend* the bad grade as a result, we cannot say with any accuracy that it was truly unanticipated or unanticipatible. So too it is with the corporation. While they may not *intend* that their product or process harm anyone either through production, release into the environment, or through its use, they seldom can truly say that those results were unanticipatible. This distinction regarding the intent involved is extremely important if you intend to charge someone with a criminal act.

There are four different levels of intent in criminal law. They are recognized by the following terms: *purposely, knowingly, recklessly,* and *negligently. Purposely,* the clearest case of intent, is where one not only has reason to believe that a particular consequence will result from one's actions but that they *intended* that result. When the murderer points the gun at the victim's head and pulls the trigger, the murderer knows that death is likely to result and intends that result. What lies below *purposely* on the intent scale is *knowingly* where one knew or should have known that the actual consequence of the action was likely to occur. When a child dies as a result of a severe beating, we can say that the parent knew or should have known that death or grievous bodily injury was likely to result from such a beating.

While sociologists sometimes refer to unanticipated consequences as unintended consequences, many white-collar crimes point to a distinction between unanticipated and unintended. When Sneaky creates commercials that make the webs appear much larger than they actually are and with double the lines (what spider wouldn't prefer such a web?) we could say that Sneaky's intention is to increase sales while an unintended consequence of the ads is that people think they are buying a more substantial product than they really are. If we examine the situation more closely we find that he does have reason to believe that his actions will defraud the customer and that he undertakes those actions in spite of that knowledge. He has *knowingly* produced ads in which there is a substantial likelihood that the consumer will be defrauded. He not only can anticipate that more consumers will buy their product but he has specifically designed the ad with that intention. What he has not intended, the unintended consequence, is that some people may be harmed in doing so. Criminal law takes the perspective that if the result was foreseeable and the action is undertaken anyway then that result, even if it is not the primary aim, was also intended. Where business activities are concerned, however, there has been and still is a great reluctance to find that a crime has been committed. When a similar action and a similar result occur where legitimate economic business is not concerned, society is quick to recognize that a crime has been committed.

Consider the graduate student who put the worm on the Internet. We might say that this student intended to see if his predictions about the self-replication of his program would actually happen. The Internet was an ideal testing ground for the student because that replication was specifically designed to occur across the network. While the harm that came to other users was an unintended consequence of the experiment, it would be unrealistic to say that it was not anticipated. What might be unanticipated is the rapidity with which the program would actually reproduce itself and the subsequent increased severity of the harm that others would suffer due to the increased consumption of the system resources. When seeking a conviction, however, the prosecutor will likely assert that unauthorized consumption of system resources was part of the program the student wrote and therefore the student knew those results were likely to occur and must have intended the actions that occurred and were capable of being anticipated.

In American culture great attention and rewards are focused on specialization. To the extent that the engineer or scientist is charged with producing the most superior product, her or his incentive may not include much consideration of other consequences of producing such a product. Some, such as Merton (1965), might point to the atomic bomb as a prime example. That orientation of the American culture is mirrored in corporate life, industry, and education. As we advocate the pursuit of ideals we can say at the macrolevel that many unanticipated consequences will result from that noble principle. When we examine the microlevel concerns we find that consequences unanticipated at the macrolevel can be anticipated at the microlevel. Many feel that it is all right to ignore those consequences because the pursuit of the ideal has been privileged as a goal above all else and all other consequences. From the mischievous and criminal antics of the graduate student to the corporate executive to the freedom of information advocate, modern American culture privileges the pursuit of ideals to the exclusion of how actions taken in pursuit of those ideals fit into the more complex social system. Only by carefully analyzing and identifying the real source of the problems can we identify incentives and solutions to further the American dream so that it is not lived as a nightmare for those who fall victim.

References

Been, Vicki, "Market Forces, Not Racist Practices, May Affect the Siting of Locally Undesirable Land Uses," in *Environmental Justice*, Greenhaven Press, 1995.

Bryant, Bunyan, "Issues and Potential Policies and Solutions for Environmental Justice: An Overview," in *Environmental Justice: Issues Policies, and Solutions*, Bunyan Bryant, ed., Island Press, Washington, D.C., 1995.

Bullard, Robert D., *Unequal Protection*, Sierra Club Books, 1994.

Clinard, Marshall B., and Peter C. Yeager, *Corporate Crime*, The Free Press, New York, 1980.

Coleman, James W., *The Criminal Elite*, St. Martin's Press, New York, 1985.

Faith, Karlene, "Institutionalized Violence," *Multicultural Experiences, Multicultural Theories*, Mary F. Rogers, ed., McGraw-Hill, 1996.

Icove, David, et al., *Computer Crime*, O'Reilly & Associates, 1995.

Merton, Robert K., *Social Theory and Social Structure*, The Free Press, New York, 1965.

Mizell, Louis R., *Masters of Deception: The White Collar Crime Crisis & Ways to Protect Yourself*, John Wiley & Sons, 1996.

Mokhiber, Russell, *Corporate Crime and Violence*, Sierra Club Books, 1988.

Reiman, Jeffrey, "A Crime by Any Other Name . . . " in *Sociology: Exploring the Architecture of Everyday Life*, David Newman, ed., Pine Forge Press, 1995.

Ritzer, George, *Classical Sociological Theory*, 2nd ed., McGraw-Hill, 1996.

Small, Gail, "Native Americans Must Fight to Prevent Environmental Injustice on Their Homelands," in *Environmental Justice*, Greenhaven Press, 1995.

Stoll, Clifford, *The Cuckoo's Egg: Tracking a Spy Through the Maze of Computer Espionage*, Pocket Books, 1995.

Sutherland, Edwin H., *White Collar Crime*, Yale University Press, 1983.

Internet Bibliography

Kehoe, Brendan P., *Zen and the Art of the Internet*, 1992.

http://www.cs.indiana.edu/docprroject/zen/zen-1.0_10.html1#SEC91 and related site:

http://fmv.vse.cz/jm/zen/zen-l_l.html

Association of Certified Fraud Examiners, http://www.acfe.org/program.html

National White Collar Crime Center (NWCCC) '97, http://www.iircom/nwccc/nwccc.htm

White Collar Crime Symposium, http://www.ussc.gov/sympo/wc.sumpo.htm

Other fun and interesting sites:

http://ecotopics.com/articles/burrito.htm

http://www.fsu.edu/~crimdo/killers.html

http://www.thelawoffice.com/LLA/FL/bl8.htm

http://www.texlaw.com/news/ttl/5-96_l.htm

http://www.pihome.com/pirc/pirclO.html#slick (click on the White Collar Crime section)

http://www.fbi.gov/academy/itu.htm (FBI Academy)

http://www.oversight-results.com/ifpa.html (Insurance Fraud Prevention Act of 1994)

Article Review Form at end of book.

Do you think that the Midtown Community Court will be effective? Why or why not? Do you think that the assessment interview composed by the Midtown Community Court will be helpful in reducing crime? Why or why not? How can this have an impact on the overall court system? Do you agree with combining punishment and rehabilitation when addressing crime?

The Midtown Community Court Experiment

John Feinblatt and Michele Sviridoff
Midtown Community Court

Located in the busy center of Manhattan, the Midtown Community Court tests new ways for criminal courts to respond to crime—specifically, quality-of-life crimes that take place in Times Square, Clinton, and Chelsea. Although shoplifting, prostitution, turnstile jumping, graffiti, and low-level drug possession may sometimes seem insignificant when compared to murder, robbery, and rape, quality-of-life crimes shape perceptions of justice and pride in neighborhoods and the workplace. In the first year of a three-year experiment, the court is the nation's most ambitious effort to dispense justice on a community level. It draws upon several prominent models: community policing, which builds local partnerships to help solve neighborhood problems; drug courts, like those in Miami, Florida and Oakland, California, which link defendants to substance abuse treatment; and experiments in community-based justice that address prostitution and other offenses of concern to local citizens, like the Neighborhood Court in Hollywood, California.

A Public-Private Partnership

In October 1991, the Unified Court System of the State of New York began an unusual partnership with the City of New York, the Midtown business and residential communities, twenty-nine corporations and foundations, and two dozen social service agencies and civic organizations. The goal of this public-private effort—a first for the New York State courts—was to provide effective and accessible community-based justice for low-level crimes. After a two-year planning period led by the Fund for the City of New York, the Midtown Community Court opened, in October 1993, on West 54th Street. The goals of the court are to make justice constructive, visible, and efficient and to make it responsive and meaningful to victims, defendants, and the community.

Bringing a Court and a Community Closer Together

The decision to establish the Midtown Community Court grew out of a sense that justice had become remote from communities and the people living in them. When the New York City courts were centralized in the early 1960s, gains in efficiency and cost-effectiveness were realized. However, moving the courts out of the communities where the crimes took place had an unforeseen effect—a loss of confidence in the justice system, particularly in neighborhoods where minor offenses are a major part of the daily landscape. Centralized courts, which must focus their limited resources on the most serious crimes, have few resources to devote to quality-of-life offenses. As a consequence, citizens and neighborhood groups lose their incentive to report and prevent crime.

Offenders go unpunished and undeterred from more serious criminal behavior. Police officers view the court as a "revolving door" and lose interest in enforcement efforts. These conditions erode a community's sense of order, leading to more crime and increased frustration about the functioning of criminal courts—a frustration shared by many working inside the criminal justice system.

Nowhere are quality-of-life offenses more concentrated than in Midtown Manhattan. Two midtown precincts—Midtown North and Midtown South—lead the entire city in the volume of misdemeanor arrests each year. Of the twenty-one precincts in Manhattan, the three precincts served by the court account for 43 percent of misdemeanor arrests. A lack of faith in the justice system is a major reason why crime weighs so heavily on the minds of most Americans. Shoplifting, prostitution, or low-level drug possession—the crimes encountered on a daily basis in American cities—are cited most by citizens asked to describe how crime affects their lives. According to studies by the Commonwealth Fund and the Manhattan Institute, 59 percent of people who recently left New York City did so to improve their quality of life. The Midtown Community Court is a response to these expressed frustrations. It exemplifies a growing nationwide interest in using satellite and branch courts to bring court and social services for high-volume, short-duration cases back to the communities in which the crimes occur.

Combining Punishment and Help

Overwhelmed urban courts, which are understandably preoccupied with progressing quickly through large calendars, have little time to address the causes of crime or demonstrate to the injured community that low-level crime has consequences. Policy analysts argue that arrest and case processing, in themselves, have become a common punishment for low-level offenses. Therefore, after engaging in dialogue with the community, social service providers, criminal justice experts, the police, victims, and former defendants, the Midtown Community Court adopted a new agenda, which both punishes and helps defendants. This agenda is based on simple ideas and common sense: if a defendant makes retribution to the community and at the same time receives help in solving the problems that led to his or her involvement in crime, justice, at least in low-level cases, can be both restorative to the community and constructive to the defendant.

Fostering Closer Communication

In its first month, the Midtown Community Court formed a community advisory committee. The members include residents of Clinton and Chelsea, attorneys working at law firms headquartered near the court, administrators of local social services, and officials of quasi-governmental agencies. Meeting every other month, the advisory board keeps the court informed of neighborhood conditions and new and appropriate community service projects. It hears testimony from offenders who have been placed in treatment by the court and reviews strategies for finding additional housing or employment for defendants. Most important, the committee keeps the court in touch with the community, which promotes trust and encourages action.

The court's physical presence in the community has also fostered closer communication with the police. Police officers alert the court's social services staff to recently arrested defendants needing special attention. Officers have even brought in people who are not at risk of arrest but who need services. For example, a mentally retarded woman who lost her money to con artists was reunited with her mother in Ohio as a result of a police referral.

For the first time, patrol officers are receiving information about case outcomes, which gives them a sense that their work reaps results. Additionally, the courthouse is used for meetings between the police and local citizens. A newsletter about the court, published by a neighborhood anticrime group, gives tips to court watchers and information about community service.

Paying Back the Community

Victimless crime is a label often used to describe prostitution, low-level drug possession, illegal vending, and graffiti. However, the communities in which these crimes occur are the real victims and should be paid back for the costs of crime. Nearly two-thirds of convicted offenders at the Midtown Community Court are ordered to work in the harmed neighborhoods—more than twice the rate found in the centralized Manhattan court (64 percent compared to 26 percent). In the court's first year, more than 3,300 sentenced offenders provided nearly $170,000 of labor to the community. Many community service projects are supervised by twelve local organizations—and in fact, a recycling center, the Times Square Business Improvement District and the Horticultural Society have joined the court's effort to improve justice in misdemeanor cases. Many projects have been suggested by local citizens, including an ambitious tree restoration project. Who, after all, knows the eyesores and hot spots of a neighborhood better than the people who live and work there?

While the Midtown Community Court is not the nation's first court to require that defendants perform community service, its insistence on their performing that work in the community where the crimes occurred is unique. Moreover, the work of defendants has had a palpable effect on the streetscape and the community—over 530 tree pits were cleared and maintained, graffiti was removed from nearly 140 walls, and over 740,000 pieces of mail were sorted, stuffed, and labeled free of charge for local nonprofit organizations during the court's first year. Most important, however, members of the community—both law abiding and non-law abiding—who had ceased to believe that committing a crime carries a price, see that indeed crime has consequences: over thirty offenders a day, wearing Midtown Community Court uniforms, work off their sentences in Midtown.

Alternatives with "Teeth"

Contrary to conventional wisdom, many citizens who are frustrated with the criminal justice system support alternative sentences such as community service. However, these programs need "teeth." Compliance rates for community service at the Midtown Community Court, which average 77 percent over the first eleven months, are substantially higher than the 50 percent completion rate in the centralized Manhattan court. The reasons are simple: first, punishment is swift and certain, with most defendants beginning community service on the same day they appear in court or within twenty-four hours. Second, defendants know that the court gets daily feedback about whether a defendant reports for work. Third, the court has developed a range of community service jobs for different sorts of defendants. Those who have had little or no involvement with the criminal justice system are assigned to projects in the community, while defendants with histories of warrants fulfill their obligations in the court building itself, cleaning the courtroom, scrubbing the holding cells, and making sure the courthouse is graffiti free. The immediate sentencing sends a message to defendants and the community: that the Midtown Community Court means business.

Seizing the Moment of Arrest

Moments of crisis provide windows for change, yet only in recent years have courts considered the critical role they could play in linking defendants to social services at a major moment of crisis: arrest. People who commit misdemeanor crimes often have complicated lives, seemingly insoluble problems, and, 70 to 80 percent of the time, some type of dependence on drugs. Thus, it seems natural for courts to use their coercive power at this critical moment to slow the revolving door of drugs and crime.

As the first criminal court in the country to locate social services, health care, education, and drug treatment within the court building itself, the Midtown Community Court is actively rethinking the nature of a court's business. In the past, criminal justice, social service, education, and health care organizations often let bureaucratic divisions hamper or delay access to services. But the Community Court has forged new coalitions by bringing together everyone under one roof—the Department of Health, the Board of Education, the Human Resources Agency, substance abuse treatment providers, vocational programs, homeless outreach workers, and youth service providers. A court is the one place that has physical custody of large numbers of at-risk offenders on a daily basis.

Short-Term Interventions

A hallmark of the Midtown Community Court's system of graduated sanctions are short-term interventions. With many low-level offenders facing little or no jail time and with jail space at a premium, the court has created a set of sanctions that are both productive and appropriate to the defendant's offense and criminal record. For example, since two-thirds of defendants have never received drug treatment, a four-day Treatment Readiness Group introduces defendants without serious records to drug treatment and prepares them for long-term help. In the court's first year, over 1,600 defendants were sentenced to short-term counseling groups for periods ranging from one to four days. As of this writing, nearly 75 percent have completed their sentences. Other short-term interventions include a health education group for both prostitutes and "johns," job readiness training, and a counseling group for youths.

The immediate goals of these short-term interventions are modest. A career prostitute may learn about safe sex or ways out of prostitution or may get advice on how to deal with her pimp's escalating physical abuse, while a person addicted to drugs may meet someone who has kicked his or her own habit for the first time. For these defendants, the services offered at the Court can be a stepping stone toward change and a guide to reducing harm in their lives.

Returning Voluntarily

One unexpected result of the court's under-one-roof approach to service delivery is that many defendants, having been sentenced only to brief interventions, return to the court after completing their sentence. In the court's first year, over 800 did. Some seek results of tuberculosis (TB) or human immunodeficiency virus (HIV) tests or help in preparing a resume or finding a job. Others come to attend classes in English as a second language (ESL) or to earn their general equivalency diploma (GED). Over 100 returned to enroll in longer-term drug treatment, like Beverly, a prostitute who entered residential treatment after completing her participation in the health education group as well as the two days of community service. She has been drug-free for a month and a half. Whatever the reason for their return, however, it seems that many defendants are beginning to see the court, and their own lives, in a new light.

Long-Term Treatment

For defendants facing jail sentences, the court's goals are more ambitious. These defendants, many of whom have extensive criminal careers and lengthy histories of addiction, may be sentenced to long-term treatment as an alternative to jail. It is this population that also poses the greatest risk of failure. Not surprisingly, many fail, and fail quickly. In these instances, it is important that sanctions be imposed on those who drop out. The record at the Midtown Community Court is strong: to date, 79 percent of failures have been rearrested; of these, 84 percent have been sentenced to jail. However, for those who remain in treatment the effects can be far-ranging. When Paul was brought before the court on a shoplifting charge, he was on parole after serving over five years in prison. He had a sixty dollar a day crack cocaine habit and an extensive record of misdemeanor and felony convictions. After assessment by the court's drug treatment staff, he was sentenced to complete a detoxification (detox) program and one year of drug treatment. Shortly after completing detox, and while awaiting admission to long-term treatment, he was arrested again. With the agreement of his parole officer, the judge gave Paul a second chance. However, this time he was held in jail until a treatment bed opened. As of this writing, Paul has been in treatment for the past seven months. He recently enrolled in a local community college and appears each month before the Midtown Community Court judge, who monitors his progress.

The Court as Community Mediator

Many chronic quality-of-life problems in a community never come to the attention of the police or courts. In fact, these divisive issues often do not constitute violations of the law. Today, courts sometimes use mediation and arbitration to help resolve legal disputes, and the Midtown Community Court takes this idea a step further. Mediators at the court hear disputes involving people living and working in Times Square, Clinton, and Chelsea: for example, where to place dog runs, what hours a noisy auto repair shop should be open, and whether a business can be converted to an adult movie house. Although some observers question whether this should be the business of a criminal court, this type of problem solving is consistent with the court's commitment to improving the quality of life within its own community.

A New Way of Conducting Business

New goals require new procedures, technology, staff, and uses of the courthouse. Without the proper coordination of defendants to alternative sanctions or sufficient monitoring, many intermediate sanctions—whether drug treatment or community service—suffer from high "no-show" and dropout rates, which undermine their credibility with defendants and the public. Several procedures being tested at the Midtown Community Court have the potential to build an effective framework for dispensing alternative sanctions, and ensuring they are effective.

Assessment

The Midtown Community Court has developed an assessment interview to gather information about a defendant's background. Interviewers from the Criminal Justice Agency, using hand-held computers, determine whether a defendant has a place to sleep, a history of mental illness, or a substance abuse problem. This information is immediately downloaded to the court computer, making it possible to weigh some of the underlying causes of criminal behavior when fashioning sanctions.

Resource Coordination

A resource coordinator, who is stationed in the courtroom, helps the judge and lawyers match defendants with the right programs. Using the assessment information—which highlights on the computer screen problems such as substance abuse and homelessness—the coordinator reviews each case, enters a recommendation in the computer, presents treatment plans and provides feedback from social service providers about how a defendant is doing. The resource coordinator can tell the judge whether, for example, urine tests are clean or attendance at treatment programs is regular.

On-Site Services

Widely cited as an example of the "courthouse of the future," the Midtown Court building has individual and group counseling rooms, a health care area, and space to perform community service, including a bulk mailing operation for nonprofit organizations. This makes it possible for offenders to begin their sentences in the same neighborhood where they were arrested and arraigned—all on the same day.

Judicial Monitoring

Judges at the Midtown Community Court review the offenders' progress in treatment by requiring them to appear before the court—every two weeks at first, then once a month. Sometimes judges use these appearances to give encouragement or a pat on the back; at other times, they may reiterate their expectations and the consequences of not abiding by the court's orders. Often they do both. This strategy reflects a new approach being tested in innovative courts throughout the country, which uses the authority of the court both to demonstrate interest in the defendant's welfare and to underscore the seriousness of his or her criminal behavior.

Technology

The Midtown Community Court relies on "smart" technology to build a system in which information about a case is gathered electronically from computers around the state. Arrest information, the defendant's criminal record, the complaint prepared by the district attorney, and the color-coded results of the assessment interview are displayed on a single screen in easy-to-understand graphic form. Because all the court's business is conducted on computers, the judges, prosecutors, defense attorneys, and social service staff can work on a case simultaneously and communicate about it electronically. When decisions are reached, they are recorded in the computer from the judge's bench, making it possible for the defendants to commence their sentences immediately. Additionally, large screen terminals located throughout the courthouse display facts about each case—the charges, attorney's name, and disposition—making this information visible to defendants, their families, victims, and members of the public.

Future Directions

The agenda of the Midtown Community Court is ambitious. During the first year, it has dispensed justice that is swift and sensitive to the needs of both the community and the defendant. This has required rethinking many things about how a court does business—about how a courthouse looks, the way in which cases are processed and the technology is utilized, and the relationship between the court and the community.

Since June 1993, even before the community court opened its doors, the National Center for State Courts, the country's leading court research organization, has been serving as the community court's independent evaluator. Center researchers compare the use of intermediate sanctions, compliance rates, and defendant arrest rates at the Midtown Court with those at Manhattan's centralized court. Moreover, focus groups and interviews with community leaders and residents help researchers determine whether the Midtown Community Court is changing community attitudes toward the criminal justice system

The preliminary evidence is encouraging. About 80 percent of all sentences at the Midtown Community Court include orders to perform community service or to enroll in social services or both. Comparisons with sentences at the centralized Manhattan court show that the court has dramatically reduced the extent of nonconstructive sentences, like "time served" in detention before cases are arraigned (1 percent compared to 25 percent at the centralized court). The Midtown Court's emphasis on alternative sanctions has also substantially reduced the extent of costly jail sentences (11 percent compared to 23 percent at the centralized court). The criminal justice process itself—arrest, detention, and arraignment—rarely constitutes the punishment at the Midtown Community Court.

Judges not only have constructive options when they impose sanctions, they do so with confidence that they will be carried out. The compliance rates for community service and short term social services, which range between 72 and 77 percent, demonstrate that immediacy and certainty of sentencing are powerful tools, and also that petty offenders are not, and need not be, "processed" through the system. Compliance rates at the Midtown Court are the highest in New York City. In recognition of these accomplishments, the National Association for Court Management recently awarded the Midtown Community Court the 1994 Justice Achievement Award, which recognizes "exemplary projects and outstanding accomplishments which enhance the administration of justice."

While it is too soon to assess whether all this has affected street conditions in the Midtown community, there is striking evidence that the court's new approach has already had an impact on street-level prostitution. During its first nine months, prostitution arrests in Midtown fell by 31 percent, while they increased by 5 percent in the rest of Manhattan. Given New York City's recent emphasis on increasing arrests for quality-of-life offenses, the decrease in prostitution arrests is particularly noteworthy. This finding in reported crime is underscored by focus group interviews with community leaders, residents, and police officers and with structured observations of street prostitution, all of which indicate that the incidence of street-level prostitution in Midtown has decreased dramatically.

Preliminary research findings also show that community groups—leaders, residents, neighborhood businesses, local police—are increasingly satisfied with the court's performance. Before the court opened, these groups held modest expectations about what could be accomplished. After a year of operations, however, the Midtown court is viewed as "something good that has been done for the community." Community members have shifted from questioning whether the court could affect sentence outcomes or improve community service compliance rates to exploring the Midtown Community Court's implications for the New York City Criminal Court system as a whole.

One question facing researchers is whether a community-based court brings advantages that offset facility costs. The decision to centralize courts in the early 1960s was, in large measure, driven by cost factors—it is less expensive to run one central courthouse than many throughout a borough or a city. There is evidence that the Midtown Court has already produced some cost savings. Substantial reductions in arrest-to-arraignment time translate into more time on the street for police officers: at the Midtown Community Court, cases are heard within seventeen hours of arrest rather than the city-wide average of more than thirty. High compliance rates with community-based sentences (77 percent compared to 50 percent at the centralized court) translate into savings to the police department's warrant squad. Reductions in jail sentences (11 percent compared to 23 percent at the centralized court) cut the costs of incarceration. Of course, an extensive cost-benefit analysis will require ongoing study and must consider the results of court adjournments, drug treatment, health care and community service activity.

However, numbers alone will not tell the whole story of the court. The fear of crime and dissatisfaction with the criminal justice system affect American communities deeply. Over time, they erode people's personal confidence, economic livelihood, and civic pride. Over time, they affect choices about where to live, work and send one's children to school, and it will be over time that the court will be judged. Can the court improve attitudes and perceptions about crime and justice in the community of Midtown Manhattan?

Article Review Form at end of book.

How much religious freedom do you think should be allowed in prison? Where do you draw the line and why? Do you agree with the assessment of prison subculture and with prisoners' adoption of religious practice as a way of coping? What positive implications does religion in prisons have for the prison system? How can religion be controlled to improve the prison system?

Doing Time with God

Maria Tempenis
Vanderbilt University

For much of history, prisons served to punish rather than to correct criminals, thus becoming "human junkheaps" where society's deviants were placed out of sight and out of mind (Johnson 1987: 6). It was not until the nineteenth century that the concept of penitentiaries evolved with the goal of rehabilitating criminals. Today, all branches of the social sciences, as well as criminal justice authorities, struggle to identify those programs and policies that are most effective in the correctional aspect of the justice process. Religious institutions also attempt to recognize their part in the ongoing development of prison reform and the inmate rehabilitation process. Although little research has been done, those who have studied the role of religion in the criminal justice system note an increasing concern with the application of the Constitution's First Amendment rights (regarding religious liberty) to the prison environment. Accordingly, this paper attempts to identify the current status of religion in correctional centers as well as the emerging issues that will eventually demand the attention of government and criminal justice officials.

Evolution of the Penal Institution in America

The treatment of criminals in colonial America branched into two classes, the Puritans and the Quakers. The Puritan belief that humankind was wrought with evil tendencies led to a system of retribution, using public punishments to illustrate the fate for those who yielded to sin and temptation. On the other hand, the Quakers held a more compassionate view toward humanity's sinful nature and practiced a more restitutive system of justice, using penal institutions and workhouses (Bryant 1991). In 1790, the first true penitentiary in America was created, but it was not until the 1820s that the treatment of criminals shifted from local, community-determined punishment to institutionally governed treatment of offenders (Johnson 1987: 17).

From a desire for "civilized" (but painful) punishment, rather than cruel, dehumanizing penalties, the penitentiary or correctional institution emerged. In his 1987 work, Robert Johnson explains that penitentiaries carried the religious appeal of providing a method to bring criminals to God through rational discipline instead of encouraging passionate brutality and violence. He identifies two models of penitentiaries in the early twentieth century. First, the *separate system* involved strict solitary confinement at all times and demanded obedience and manual labor. Second, the *congregate system* allowed inmates to congregate (in silence) for meals and work but to otherwise remain in solitary cells. Furthermore, as Michael Bryant (1991) points out, the earliest penitentiaries appointed ministers as wardens, and the prisoners were placed in cells with Bibles to meditate on the word of God. Eventually, the congregate system became dominant as it proved more efficient in terms of labor production and was analogous in structure to the emerging urban factory subculture.

The penitentiaries soon grew overcrowded, predominantly

with immigrants and the poor (Bryant 1991; Johnson 1987: 34). They returned to functioning as human warehouses with lonely, depressed inmates and violent, harshly disciplinarian prison guards. Then, the mid-twentieth century brought about more lenient and liberal attitudes toward the less fortunate with such programs as the War on Poverty and the Great Society. Similarly, educational, vocational, mental health, and other programs for prison reform were also developed. Even so, by 1974, Andrew Von Hirsch and Robert Marinson each studied the rehabilitation efforts and concluded that prison reform programs had failed, providing a harbinger for the state of correctional institutions today (Bryant 1991).

By 1987, federal parole was abolished and replaced by federal sentencing guidelines. Therefore, inmates now serve longer sentences without parole, resulting in more people entering the system than exiting it. Bryant's research indicates approximately 11 million people filter through American prisons each year, and Johnson reveals that one in twenty American men will serve a prison sentence at some point in their lives. Moreover, Johnson explains that prisons resemble the violence and climate of predation found in urban slums. He traces the "civilization of pain" from its earliest state of public floggings and executions, to the concealed pain of corporal punishment, and more recently, to the prison officials' use of psychological shame to subordinate and control the inmate. Finally, Johnson notes that because solitary confinement and brutality by correctional officers are no longer the norm (although they occasionally occur), the violence and cruelty of today's prisons are a product of misguided prison reform efforts that result in a worsening prison environment.

Key Legislation for the Role of Religion in Prison Reform

Despite the religious influences that permeated the early development of the penal institution in the United States, the role of religion in prisoner rehabilitation has been widely neglected in the latter half of the twentieth century. However, the plurality of religious beliefs found among inmates, coupled with larger society's emphasis on First Amendment rights, are prompting researchers to reconsider the role of religion in the criminal justice system. In the pivotal 1972 case of *Cruz v. Beto*, the Supreme Court held that Texas prison authorities acted improperly by prohibiting a Buddhist inmate from worshipping and proselytizing his faith (DiIulio 1987: 202). The ramifications of this ruling are echoed in a number of cases involving the religious discrimination of prison officials as well as the balancing of religious freedom with the structured regiment of the prison setting.

In 1997, opponents of the *Cruz v. Beto* ruling stressed the latent functions of the Religious Freedom Restoration Act (RFRA). Originally enacted in 1994 to protect religious freedom and customs, RFRA—in the prison setting—yielded several negative effects (Wilson 1996: 21). First, prison religious programs have been curtailed due to equal spending on religions; to avoid paying for lawsuits brought under the RFRA, more states are eliminating religious programs. Second, "structural proselytization" (inmate participation in religious activities for secular benefits) encourages joining religious programs for shallow reasons. Third, the amount of litigation surrounding RFRA cases is mounting, and finally, religions with extreme or dangerous teachings (racism, sacrifice, etc.) can legally obtain negative propaganda. Ironically designed to protect religious liberty, RFRA may reverse the situation and eliminate prison religious policies.

After examining the literature on the religious practices of Muslim, Christian, and Native American inmates, it appears that religion often facilitates rehabilitation and is an integral part of the process of criminal correction for a number of prisoners (see for instance, Haddad 1991; Loux 1987; Grobsmith 1984). However, further research is needed to illustrate the importance of adapting to religious pluralism within penal institutions. Members of many denominations and religious affiliations bring forth lawsuits to preserve their religious freedom, and often, to preserve one of the most essential elements contributing to their well-being in the prison environment. Under the guise of upholding prison safety measures or keeping within budget restraints, prison officials often cater to the religious peculiarities of mainline denominations, but ignore or drastically neglect the requests of inmates with more obscure religious affiliations. Thus, it seems that the problem is not the ineffectiveness of religious programs, but rather, the discriminatory manner in which inmates are restricted from pursuing nonconventional religions.

Native American Inmates

In a 1994 article, Missouri Attorney General Jay Nixon expressed his desire to stop frivolous lawsuits by prison inmates that unnecessarily cluttered the court system. Among the issues he considered most trifling, Nixon equated "the limit on Kool-Aid refills as cruel and unusual punishment" and "the high cost of junk food in the prison commissary" with Native American inmate requests to build a sweat lodge for worship (Seligman 1994: 213). Although the American Civil Liberties Union and a number of appellate courts have ruled in favor of Native American religious liberties in prison, discrimination is not limited to the ill-informed warden or the proselytizing, self-promoting prison guard. The research concerning the role of Native American religion in inmate rehabilitation stresses the need for educating or sensitizing public officials, as well as other members of society, about the practices and belief systems of Native Americans to understand the vital role religion plays in Native American culture (see for instance, Little Rock Reed 1989; Waldram 1994).

Native American Belief Systems

In her work, *Indians in Prison*, Elizabeth Grobsmith (1984) identifies two main types of Indian religious groups in penitentiaries: Pipe Religion and the Native American Church. Pipe Religion revolves around the use of the Sacred Pipe in seven specific rituals, in particular, the sweat lodge ceremonies and the Sun Dance ceremony. The pipe carrier serves as the guardian of the sacred pipe when not in use by keeping it concealed in a ceremonial cloth and protecting it in a ceremonial fashion. The followers of the Native American Church, instead, pray to the Great Spirit through the use of peyote, a hallucinogenic drug believed to communicate the messages of the Great Spirit to the Indians. Clearly, the concealed pipe, sweat lodges, and use of peyote create obstacles in the prison setting.

Consent Decree

The Consent Decree is the legally binding agreement between Nebraska penitentiaries and the Native Americans to aid them in maintaining their cultural identity while in prison. The decree includes provisions for wearing long hair, head bands, participation in the Sun Dance, use of a sacred pipe, consultation of medicine men or spiritual advisors, and the construction of sweat lodges. In addition, the decree does not explicitly rule out the use of peyote (Grobsmith 1984: 40–46). In theory, the decree seems to accommodate Native American religious practices to the prison system. However, a review of the existing research reveals that battles and litigation constantly arise to enforce the decree.

For example, although nearly every correctional facility in Nebraska provides a sweat lodge for Indian inmates, and approximately twenty other states permit inmate use of the lodges, the prisoners are restricted to when and how long the sweat lodges can be used. As a result, Sacred Pipe ceremonies—that normally span several days—cannot be performed. Even more problematic for the prison system is the skin sacrifice of the Sacred Pipe ceremony, where Indians scrape skin from the upper part of their arms; because razors are not permitted for the religious service, the inmates are often forced to share the spiritual leader's knife, thus magnifying the problem of AIDS spreading among the inmate population. The use of peyote is also forbidden in most institutions, forcing many members of the Native American Church to abandon their own religion and turn to the Sacred Pipe practice.

Yet, one of the most discriminatory acts Native American inmates experience involves the treatment of the *canupa waken* or sacred pipe (Little Rock Reed 1989: 403). In an article that addresses aboriginal spirituality among Canadian Indian inmates, James B. Waldrum explains that the Aboriginal Elders endure religious discrimination each time their medicine bundles and sacred pipes are desecrated through searches by prison guards. Unlike Christian priests, permitted to take wine and other religiously significant objects into the prison facilities without question, the Elders are looked upon with suspicion and their holy objects are defiled (by exposure in nonceremonial settings).

Violation after violation of the consent decree occurs, resulting in a multitude of lawsuits including *Tyndall v. Benson*, a 1983 case seeking access to the sweat lodge; *Indian Inmates v. Wolff*, a 1986 suit regarding the use of peyote; and *Dick & Dillon v. Hopkins et al.*, a 1991 court hearing attempting to classify a powwow as a religious service—to name a handful. Since the decree, a few formal rulings in favor of Native American plaintiffs have been awarded, but the struggle continues for transforming the criminal justice system from giving lip service to upholding the American Indian Religious Freedom Act (Little Rock Reed 1989: 409).

Drawing on his own experience as a Native American inmate, Little Rock Reed expresses the foolishness of the prison system in squandering tax money on discrimination litigation when it could use it to accommodate the religious needs of the Indians. Yet, as Ohio state correctional authorities insist, many hold the position that freedom of religion is inferior to the state's interest in maintaining security and order within the prison. Ironically, the violation of institutional rules by Native American inmates usually only takes place when discrimination by officials occurs or when religious services are prohibited. Grobsmith attributes this fear of disorderly conduct with religion to ignorance about Native American religion (p. 159). Part of the problem is found in the lack of understanding and sensitivity to various religious practices. For instance, correctional officers continue to believe peyote is a hedonistic waste when in fact Indians hold the use of peyote outside of proper ceremony as blasphemous. In the words of Little Rock Reed, "We feel that to do less than to help us preserve our traditional ways is no less than forced assimilation. The United Nations General Assembly has a word for that. It's called genocide" (p. 416).

Coping with Religious Discrimination

A number of Native American inmate organizations have been created to provide a social and legal platform for the religious rights of Indian prisoners. For example, the Native American Council of Tribes (NACT) of the Sioux Falls Indians educates people on Native American beliefs, provides language classes, holds at least four family and guest-attended powwows each year, supplies sweat lodge facilities with spiritual leaders, and offers an Alcoholics Anonymous program geared for Native Americans (Grobsmith 1984; Little Rock Reed 1989: 413). The Native Brotherhood is another example of a volunteer organization of inmates who meet to hold religious services and recreational events, such as guest speakers, and discuss social concerns (Waldram 1994: 198).

Another method Native American inmates have adopted to preserve their identity involves the use of seminars and newsletters (Grobsmith 1984: 151). Seminars to educate Indian and non-Indian members of the prison system combined with the circulation of *Iron Horse Drum* and *Journal of Prisoners on Prisons* help to clarify the concerns of Native American inmates. In 1983, Oregon inmates also participated in a film produced by KTCA Public TV in Minneapolis called "The Great Spirit Within the Hole." The seminars, periodicals, and television broadcasts give voice to otherwise silenced religious concerns (Grobsmith: 161).

Finally, the most crucial method to overcome discrimination centers on the effectiveness of the spiritual leaders on the Native American inmates' rehabilitation. Waldram's (1994) research in the Regional Psychiatric Centre in Saskatchewan, an institution operated by the Correctional Service of Canada, combined with his research on other studies of Native American religion in prison systems, has yielded four benefits of Indian spirituality programs. First, aboriginal services provide a mechanism for inmates to cope with the stress of prison life with other inmates or prison officials. Second, Native American inmates are more comfortable with aboriginal Elders as their "therapists" because of their common background. Third, Elders are equipped to handle culture-specific illnesses or mental health problems such as "bad medicine" (supernatural curse by others) and can interpret dreams (an integral part of aboriginal culture as well). Finally, considering that approximately one-third of the Canadian aboriginal inmates lack knowledge of their background, the Elders are able to instill identities in the individuals to build self-esteem and pride in the inmates by teaching them the ways of their ancestors.

Waldram and the Elders he has researched agree that spiritual healing is only part of overall inmate rehabilitation. Even so, dialogue between Native American inmates and spiritual advisors with prison officials and guards is necessary to overcome the ignorance that leads to discrimination (1994: 209). As Grobsmith (1984) suggests, research shows that inmate rehabilitation is improved among Native American criminals when a positive Indian identity is permitted to those who formally had no direction. Rather than an isolated entity, they become a part of a group, with a common religion.

Muslim Inmates

The American Muslim movement was founded by W. D. Fard in a time of racial crisis in our nation. Leadership of the American Muslim movement, however, was soon replaced by Elijah Poole, who became known as the prophet Elijah Muhammed. In

1932, Elijah Muhammed established the Southside Mosque in Chicago, Illinois and proclaimed the Muslim doctrine that Allah is God and Islam is the only true religion. It is not difficult to see, then, how a number of poverty-stricken and racially hated people turned to a religion that held the power to open otherwise unattainable doors. Thus, the Muslim movement in America became equated with a political black rights movement in the minds of many (Jones 1982: 421–423).

Due to its racially segregated start with early black supremacist leaders like Elijah Muhammed and Malcolm X (early teachings), American Muslims have had to overcome the stigma of being racists. More importantly, they have had to struggle to gain an identity as a religion rather than as a political organization. Functioning in a prison within a society of religious pluralism, where Islam is often looked upon as an "unorthodox" religion in America, presents a number of obstacles for inmates to practice Islam.

Religion Versus Politics

To discuss the First Amendment rights of religious freedom for Muslims in the prison setting, it is necessary to understand the legal battle with the definition of Islam as a religion. Fortunately, the courts have ruled that the American Muslim movement is a religion rather than an African-American political movement. The definition of Islam as a religion is based on two grounds. The theistic dimension, to determine if a belief system is a religion by the worshiping of a supreme being, is fulfilled by the Muslim worship of Allah. Also, the "ultimate concern" dimension of the definition of religion is accomplished because regardless of what Muslim doctrine states, it functions and directs the everyday lives of Muslims (Haddad 1991).

Despite having won the battle to gain a religious identity, Muslims must confront the lingering discrimination that remains, especially in the correctional system. As Oliver Jones (1982) points out, many prison administrators still do not perceive American Islam as a religion and subsequently, they ban the Koran (sacred Muslim text) and other religious liberties for Muslims that they consider detrimental to the security of the institution.

Issues of Confrontation

Not without great effort, lawsuits brought forth by African-American Muslims have brought religious rights to inmates in many correctional facilities including the right to assemble for prison worship, consult an Imam, subscribe to religious literature, wear religious medallions, eat special diets, and correspond with their spiritual leaders (Haddad 1991: 139). The most prominent cases center around concerns of diet, dress, and daily prayer.

Islamic doctrine clearly prohibits eating pork. Yet, in the prison system, pork and pork products are frequently served due to their inexpensive price. They are served so often that Muslim inmates who attempt to abstain from pork cannot obtain adequate nourishment without it (Haddad 1991: 144). Furthermore, Muslims are to fast from sunrise to sundown during the month of Ramadan. Prison officials have argued that these special diets would result in costly and inconvenient food plans. However, similar dietary claims by Jews are accommodated. Fortunately, in the case of *Barnett v. Rodgers*, the appellate court ruled that the bare minimum that the Constitution guarantees is one pork-free meal per day (p. 145).

Another area of religious discrimination of Muslim inmates concerns the problem of dress or grooming. Islam teaches its adherents to allow beards and hair to grow long. Inmate regulations, however, demand short hair and clean faces to promote good hygiene and to avoid concealing one's identity. Although courts have been reluctant to permit long hair on Muslims, Native Americans have often been permitted to wear long hair despite prison regulations. One case, however, did grant the right to wear long hair for religious reasons and has set the precedent for several subsequent cases involving Muslims and non-Muslims.

Finally, Muslim inmates confront problems with prayer schedules and Friday night religious services. One of the five pillars of Islam, *salat*, entails praying five times daily at prescribed times. Prison schedules often conflict with the prayer schedule and Muslim inmates have not been supported by the courts in their right to attend Friday night religious services. In a U.S. Supreme Court case, Justice Rehnquist (writing for the majority) stated that Muslim inmates could be prohibited from attending the Friday night religious service when conflicting with the prisons' work schedules on the grounds that inmates may participate in other Muslim services. Haddad (1991) emphasizes that even the Supreme Court will not overrule prison authorities, even where First Amendment rights are concerned.

The courts' decisions in most Muslim inmate cases commonly rule against them, thus upholding the prison's discretion in determining religious "freedom." Considering the difficulties the American Muslim movement encountered to establish itself as a religion rather than a racist political ideology, it is not surprising that the prison officials given the authority to make decisions regarding the Muslim inmates are not always disinterested nor well informed in Islamic doctrine. The result has been arbitrary and often discriminatory treatment of Muslim religious liberty in the correctional system.

Christian Inmates

"Won't you take the time to write a letter of hope?" asks the Penn-Pals Inmate Services Home Page on the Internet. A number of Christian organizations and prison religious groups have brought the religious needs of inmates to the fingertips of web-surfers by providing names and addresses of inmates on death row, homosexual inmates, and even want ads for prisoners to meet members of the opposite sex (http://www.en.com/penn-pals/). The Missing Link, Inc. is a web service that asks Christians to write letters, share scriptures, and encourage inmates to pray; the service will even send the inmate a Bible if needed (http://www.goshen.net/mislink/tips.htm). The Christian concern for the rehabilitation of criminal offenders ranges from prison ministers to lay members of the Christian community who struggle to answer "the call" to save the souls of those gone astray.

There is a substantial amount of information from Catholic and Jesuit ministries; however, most of the research on Christian involvement in the role of religion in prison has focused on evangelical Christians. In *God's Prison Gang*, Chaplain Ray (1977) explains that early societies had no need for elaborate prison systems and criminal rehabilitation programs because the offender suffered swift and severe punishment without "the loopholes of lawyers" (p. 55). With extended litigation, he argues, Christians have the responsibility to teach inmates about Jesus to lead them to repentance and rehabilitation.

Prison Ministries

Unlike the Native American or Muslim condition, research on Christian influences in the prison setting reveals no major obstacles of discrimination. The research seems to neglect and ignore Christian inmates and prison programs. What studies have been conducted are primarily biographies of rehabilitated inmates or reports on types of prison missions that have been established. For example, the Internet again supplies various types of Catholic, Evangelical, and nondenominational Christian ministry programs as well as information on how to hold Bible studies with inmates, offer Christian drug and alcohol counseling, and Prison Ministry Support organizations (http://bonita.gsn.org/jail/).

In May of 1996, Chevy Chase, Maryland, held the sixteenth annual Convocation of Jail and Prison Ministry (Anderson 1996: 8). This five-day gathering of nearly 200 prison chaplains was a racially and ecumenically diverse group seeking methods to achieve "restorative justice instead of the retributive justice that prevails today"(p. 6). Among the speakers was Margaret Moore, Director of Washington D.C.'s Department of Corrections, who was also critical of the status quo in the criminal justice system. Other attendees included the founder of the Murder Victims' Families for Reconciliation (anti-death penalty organization) as well as Rev. George Clements, founder of the One Church, One Inmate ministry.

The research indicates that born-again evangelicals play a central role in Christian prison involvement. In 1876, The Elmira Reformatory of New York was founded by born-again Christian Zebulon Brockway who believed that the spiritual rebirth of criminals could be scientifically attained through the penitentiary. Known as "the college on the hill," this original model for progressive prison reform entailed educational and vocational programs that guaranteed early release for those inmates who rehabilitated themselves. In theory, Brockway sought to encourage offenders to transform themselves into Christians; in reality, Elmira was a brutal system that required absolute conformity or else swift, severe punishment was inflicted (Johnson 1987: 41).

The work of evangelical Christians has been reformed by figures such as Charles Colson, the Nixon aide imprisoned for his role in Watergate who then turned to prison ministry (Talbot 1993: 77). Colson's vision for a prison ministry that would change society through the Christian community's efforts was realized in 1976 by the work of Gordon Loux who established the Prison Fellowship program. *Uncommon Courage*, Loux's (1987) story of Prison

Fellowship explains how this American-based vision to bring Christianity into U.S. prisons expanded into a global concern for inmates, currently in over twenty-eight countries. Known as Prison Fellowship International (PFI), the association attempts to show that the way to change society is from the grass roots level of community participation rather than waiting for new government programs and politics.

The four main characteristics of PFI are: (1) National Leaders and Control (leadership is indigenous to each country rather than controlled by the PF/USA); (2) National Funding (fundraising is also indigenous to the country and each ministry contributes 5 percent of income to the international organization); (3) Regional Caucuses (seven regional caucuses exist, and each national ministry sends one member to its regional caucus; each region sends two people to serve on the PFI Board of Directors), and; (4) Statement of Faith to evangelical Christian doctrine (must be formally accepted with Christ as Redeemer working through the Christian community).

PFI offers a variety of programs to various prison systems throughout the world, according to the needs of the inmates, ranging from marriage counseling for inmates, to playing football, to collecting Christmas gifts for inmates' families, to a number of other related issues. Furthermore, in 1983, PFI president Kathryn Grant brought PFI to the forefront by attaining formal recognition by the United Nations. PFI adheres to its mission of helping other countries through training seminars, networking, providing training materials, motivating the development of indigenous ministries in other countries, and affirming a global concern for justice and righteousness. In the evangelical tradition, scripture shows that many of God's most capable leaders, such as Joseph and Daniel, rose from the ranks of inmate status; therefore, PFI affirms that Christians have a responsibility to uphold this mission.

Evangelical Approach to Rehabilitation

The efforts of Colson and Loux are not new, nor are they alone. Chaplain Ray (1977) has been an evangelical prison minister for forty years encountering and counseling such notorious offenders as members of the Manson Family and an accomplice to Bonnie and Clyde (pp. 33–75). Although he acknowledges that "jailhouse religion" is a cynical device of insincere conversion that some prisoners use to gain secular benefits, Ray argues every capable inmate should be allowed the therapy of work and religion to experience the real possibility of true religious conversion. He finds that the recidivism rate is two-thirds lower among Christian ex-cons than non-Christian ex-cons.

Ray proposes six "steps to Jesus" to help the rehabilitation of offenders—the same process that succeeded in converting Tex Watson and Susan Atkins (Manson Family members). Rehabilitation begins when the inmate repents recognizing that he or she is a sinner. The repentant inmates must then seek the goals and purposes God holds for their lives. Then, they must become examples for others. Next, they must constantly struggle to resist Satan through their faith in God. Finally, they must forgive others and glorify God by making their lives testimonies of God's love.

Role of Religion in the Penitentiary

On any Sunday morning in a Southern Baptist church in South Carolina, there will be those with "every head bowed and every eye closed" silently meditating on the word of God and there will be those with "every head bowed and every eye closed" making up for the sleep they missed having stayed out too late on Saturday night. But South Carolina Southern Baptists are not alone. Every religion is comprised of followers who closely adhere to the tenets of their faith and worship with all the fullness of their spirits—as well as members who belong for more secular benefits like socializing, their parents forcing them to attend, or their children asking too many questions if they do not.

Religious inmates, like the rest of society, also vary in the authenticity with which they practice their beliefs. In a study of two maximum security institutions, Dammer (1992) notes that inmates, like members of larger society, have various levels of religious sincerity that lead to different degrees and types of religious participation. He finds that "sincere" inmates give reasons such as religion bringing meaning to one's life, yet "insincere" inmates offer more utilitarian reasons for being religious such as to avoid heterosexual or homosexual relationships in prison, to obtain food or other goods, or to better appeal to the prison guards. Thus, while recognizing that not every inmate embraces religion with sincerity, this study explores the various "sincere" benefits that religious inmates encounter.

Dammer's study asserts that most inmates who become involved with religious programs during their sentences do so early on as a result of personal reflection, family persuasion, or fellow inmate encouragement to join. In addition to alleviating the austerity of prison life, inmates cite reasons such as the permission to volunteer for setting up altars, doing paperwork, singing in the choir, or assisting chaplains as benefits of involving oneself with religion during a prison sentence. Other inmates welcome the increased respect they receive from guards, staff, and other inmates. Interaction with civilian volunteers from religious organizations also provides positive reinforcement through friendships that develop while writing pen pals, participating in Bible studies, and other related activities. Moreover, Bible studies or prayer meetings encourage inmates to express their feelings and examine their problems in a more intimate setting, as well as provide opportunities for spiritual guidance. Finally, and most widely affirmed in the existing research, inmates find support in religious groups to avoid being absorbed into the prison subculture (Clear et al. 1992; Johnson 1987).

Avoiding the Inmate Subculture

The prison subculture runs counter to the rehabilitation process. It is an atmosphere of looking out for the good of oneself at the expense of others, engaging in further "deviant" behaviors such as homosexuality, drugs, and inmate fights. Thus, research reveals that most inmates seek a way to avoid the prison subculture by isolating themselves from it (Johnson 1987: 66; Dammer 1992).

According to a study by Hans Toch, seven dimensions comprise the prison ecology of what prisoners perceive they need. First, they seek activity for stimulation or distraction from the daily routine of prisons. On the other hand, they also need privacy, a time of quiet to not feel overstimulated. Third, prisoners desire a feeling of safety to minimize the constant fear of needing to stay alert for danger. Fourth, emotional feedback offers inmates a sense of empathy and self-worth. Fifth, prisoners seek tangible support or services to help them improve themselves. Sixth, they also appreciate a structured setting with order and clearly defined rules. Finally, inmates desire some degree of autonomy over their lives (Dammer 1992). Considering the most widely accepted view for handling criminals entails pain, punishment, and total restriction of liberty, these seven "needs" of inmates seem inconceivable. It is not surprising, then, that prisoners establish "niches" within the larger prison setting to preserve their individuality and privacy (Johnson 1987: 103).

Erving Goffman (1959) in *The Presentation of Self in Everyday Life* discusses his concept of "impression management" in relation to his theory of Dramaturgy (constructing one's identity and relationship to others by constantly interacting in a series of dramatic performances with each other). Impression management entails ways in which we attempt to present the most positive view of ourselves to our "audience" by how and what we reveal (Goffman 1959: 15). Goffman expresses this control over our actions as "dramaturgical circumspection" in which we make brief appearances to our audience and limit their access to our private information. As applied to the situation at hand, we see that receding into a religious organization allows inmates more control over their impression management when engaging with other prisoners.

Inmates develop niches to meet a variety of needs, which for some include religion. The niches permit prisoners to avoid the prison subculture and its subsequent implications such as problems with authorities, anxiety, and feelings of inadequacy. More specifically, religious niches propose a coping strategy by teaching and reinforcing the need to "avoid sin" or evil at all times (Johnson 1987: 116). Dammer explains that religion helps convicts to fight the "accepted" notions of how convicts should behave by teaching them to pray or seek spiritual guidance to turn from temptation, as well as by providing them with clear boundaries of what "temptation" and "sin" encompass.

Todd Clear et al.(1992) explains two general ways that inmates adjust to prison via religious programs. First, religious participation assists the inmate in coping with the guilt, self-contempt, and depression that accompany serving time. Second, religious programs can reinforce attitudes and behaviors that help the inmate to evade the traditionally problematic aspects of prison life. Many religious inmates accept a profound responsibility for their crimes or conduct, tend to adhere strictly to religious doctrines, and find a personal sense of peace that provides them with the dignity necessary for them to begin considering how to live outside the prison walls. Inmate participation in religious "niches" through interaction in established programs or with fellow inmates with the same belief system facilitates the rehabilitation process by excluding the prisoner from the negative influences of the prison subculture or from further socialization into criminal deviance.

Potential Implications of Religion in the Penitentiary

Religion in the prison setting promotes other benefits in addition to restraining inmates from further integration into deviance. Inmates must maintain positive relationships with their correctional officers and prison guards to enjoy the prison privilege of following one's religion (Dammer 1992). Negative relations with a guard, for whatever reason, often leads to overt or covert loss of religious privileges (such as neglecting to open the inmates' cells in time for religious services). Thus, prison religion is a social control mechanism within the institution that can carry over into the total rehabilitation process. In this sense, religion functions more as a privilege than as a right, which benefits the inmate and the prison system. Furthermore, Johnson (1987) cites three attributes that inmates encounter in observing religion while imprisoned. He suggests that inmates learn to deal with their problems (with jobs, relationships, etc.) through spiritual guidance or advisors that may, in turn, lower recidivism because the root cause of their situation is uncovered and confronted. Next, inmates learn to avoid the deception and violence evident in the prison environment because they are presented with a different value system, contrary to that of the prison subculture. Finally, they encounter the need to care for others, as well as themselves. Religion promotes rehabilitation in many cases provided it is sincere on the part of the inmate—and offered, without prejudice, on the part of the correctional institution.

Conclusion

In *The Churching of America 1776-1990*, Roger Finke and Rodney Stark elaborate on the church-sect hypothesis. One of the crucial elements, they suggest, in accounting for the success of a sect includes the tension it has with larger society. Furthermore, there are four aspects in their religious economy model that ensure a sect will flourish in its membership: the "sect" must be controlled at the local level allowing for as much democratic participation as possible; the clergy must be a commoner among the members; the message of the sermon must speak antiworldly and sternly against evil; and, the message must be distributed in such a way that the members feel totally engaged and excited (1994: 17). From the discussion thus far, it is clear that the religious groups are in great tension with the prison subculture. Moreover, prison programs provide religious leaders who can reach the prisoners spiritually, teach powerful lessons on religious behavior, and engage the inmates in religious activities.

It follows, then, that religious participation in the prison setting could flourish and have an impact on rehabilitation against the status quo. Finke and Stark acknowledge two conditions that must be met to avoid the "watering down" of religious fervor, however. The prison program would need to remain voluntary to avoid "free riders" or religious participants who join for the benefits without sacrificing for the cause. Finke and Stark also contend that the members must have a high level of participation in the religious action; inmates would then need to be provided as many possible religious interactions for religion to have an impact in the correctional institution.

Johnson concludes his study with several suggestions for correctional institution authorities to consider regarding the role of religion in rehabilitation. For example, he proposes housing inmates based on a common interest, rather than on good or bad behavior toward prison guards. Classifying inmates on interests rather than criminal behavior more closely resembles the conventional world and urges more community-based interaction (1987: 163). In addition, prison workers would be assigned to these "communities" on the basis of their interests to help integrate and monitor their behavior. Finally, Johnson claims inmates should have a part in developing and negotiating a contract with prison authorities, with parole being contingent on their behavior and participation in prison programs; inmates currently "boycott" or "purchase" programs based on how much they choose to ignore or participate (p. 177). This model could easily house inmate groups centered on religion, then further develop cell planning by affiliation. In turn, the prison guard (trained in the particular belief system of the group) would be more aware of the needs of the inmates for rehabilitation through religious programs.

The opportunities for religious programs to influence the rehabilitation process have yet to be fully explored. While this study addresses three main religions within the penitentiaries, other belief systems must be examined. The problems of determining the "sincerity" of the inmates must also be addressed. Dammer's (1992) research hints toward a method of studying sincerity based on inmate responses and observations on the religious inmates' behavior outside of religious services or programs; for example, if an inmate refuses to eat pork due to religious causes, another inmate—due to the tight living confinements—is bound to see if he or she sneaks a ham sandwich into the cell.

Despite the gaps in the existing information regarding religion in correctional facilities, the issues of religious discrimination as well as the role of religion in rehabilitation require further attention. Perhaps assessing the degree of influence religion has on rehabilitating offenders in further research would provide the incentive to reconsider the way legislation and public officials view the role of religion in the penitentiary.

References

Anderson, George M. 1996. "Jail and Prison Ministry." *America* 175(4): 6–8.

Bryant, Michael. 1991. *Catholic Attitudes Toward Criminal Offenders and Related Criminal Justice Issues.* UMI: Ann Arbor.

Chaplain Ray. 1977. *God's Prison Gang.* Felming H. Revell, Co.: New Jersey.

Clear, Todd, Bruce Stout, Harry Dammer, Linda Kelly, Patricia Hardyman, and Carol Shapiro. 1992. "Does Involvement in Religion Help Prisoners Adjust to Prison?" *The National Council on Crime and Delinquency.* Nov. 1–7.

Dammer, Harry R. 1992. *Piety in Prison: An Ethnography of Religion in the Correctional Environment.* UMI: Ann Arbor.

DiIulio, John J., Jr. 1987. *Governing Prisons.* The Free Press: New York.

Finke, Roger, and Rodney Stark. 1994. *The Churching of America 1776–1990.* Rutgers University Press: New Jersey.

Goffmann, Erving. 1959. *The Presentation of Self in Everyday Life.* Anchor Books: New York.

Grobsmith, Elizabeth. 1984. *Indians in Prison.* University of Nebraska Press: Lincoln & London.

Haddad, Yvonne Yazbeck. 1991. *The Muslims of America.* Oxford University Press: New York.

Johnson, Robert. 1987. *Hard Time: Understanding and Reforming the Prison.* Brooks/Cole Publishing: California.

Jones, Oliver, Jr. 1982. "The Black Muslim Movement and the American Constitutional System." *Journal of Black Studies* 13(4): 417–437.

Little Rock Reed. 1989. "The American Indian in the White Man's Prisons: A Story of Genocide." *Humanity & Society* 13(4): 403–419.

Loux, Gordon D. 1987. *Uncommon Courage.* Servant Publications: Ann Arbor.

Lyons, Art. 1996. *Re-Entry Prison and Jail Ministry.* http://bonita.gsn.org/jail/

Missing Link, Inc. 1996. *Tips to Use When Writing Inmates.* http://www.goshen.net/misslink/tips.htm

Prison Inmate Servies Network. 1996. *Penn-Pals.* http://www.en.com/penn-pals/

Seligman, Daniel. 1994. "Great Moments in Religious Freedom." *Fortune* 130(3): 213.

Talbot, Mary. 1993. "Newsmakers." *Newsweek* 121(9): 77.

Waldram, James B. 1994. "Aboriginal Spirituality in Corrections." *American Indian Quarterly* 18(2): 197–211.

Wilson, James C. 1996. "RFRA: More Harm Than Good." *Corrections Today* 58(3): 21.

Article Review Form at end of book.

WiseGuide Wrap-Up

Crime is a multifaceted problem that is not easily understood or resolved. A number of philosophical and practical problems need to be addressed, such as the distinction between street crime and white-collar crime. While the harm and cost of white-collar crime are far greater than all street crimes combined, violent crimes committed by strangers draw the most concern. Our thinking is clouded by media examples of crime, which shape our ideas about public policy concerning crime and prevention steps. The reading by John Fuller about shaping crime as a social problem is a good example. However, while many questions remain unanswered, we are becoming increasingly more insightful about the nature of crime, as well as how to deal with it. John Feinblatt and Michele Sviridoff's reading on the use of technology in processing low-level offenders is one such example. In addition, we are also beginning to understand the causes and consequences of police brutality and the influence of religion among convicted offenders.

R.E.A.L. Sites

This list provides a print preview of typical **coursewise** R.E.A.L. sites. (There are over 100 such sites at the **courselinks**™ site.) The danger in printing URLs is that web sites can change overnight. As we went to press, these sites were functional using the URLs provided. If you come across one that isn't, please let us know via email to: webmaster@coursewise.com. Use your Passport to access the most current list of R.E.A.L. sites at the **courselinks**™ site.

Site name: Peacemaking and Crime

URL: http://www.westga.edu/~jfuller/peace.html

Why is it R.E.A.L.? This is a web site that was created by John Fuller, the author of the reading "The War on Crime as a Social Problem." It provides additional information on and links to the peacemaking model.

Key topics: policing, the administration of justice, informal social control

Site name: Community Courts Case Study

URL: http://www.communitycourts.org/midtown/casestu1.htm

Why is it R.E.A.L.? This link provides additional insight into the Midtown Community Court and even offers a virtual tour of the agency. In addition to reading the article, you will gain a better sense of just what the Midtown Court attempts to accomplish.

Key topics: quality of life crimes, community involvement, certainty and swiftness of punishment

section 2

Learning Objectives

After reading these articles, you should be able to

- Contrast the culture of poverty with the structuralist debate.
- Identify the characteristics of the homeless in the United States.
- Understand the relationship between poverty and health.

Poverty and Inequalities

In 1995, President Clinton introduced the Welfare Reform Act, which was designed to eliminate abuses in the welfare system, reduce governmental dependency, and restore a sense of empowerment to poor people. However, welfare reform remains a topic of considerable debate. Some experts suggest that reform of the system will only exacerbate existing problems for some people and create a host of new ones for others. Advocates of welfare reform contend that a sizable portion of the poor population takes advantage of the assistance provided and loses a sense of work ethic and responsibility in the process.

The readings in this section examine the issue of poverty from a sociological perspective. Some of the readings describe the realities of being poor, while others explain the welfare reform debate.

Renee White's reading on the sociological understanding of the poverty debate is one of the best offered. Not only does she contrast the debate, she offers an explanation of the structural changes in the economy that exacerbated the problems of the poor. In the next reading, Robert McNamara and Maria Tempenis describe the current state of affairs with regard to homelessness in America. Joel Handler then addresses the current welfare reform debate and tries to identify the implications of this new wave of legislation. In another reading, Kristy Maher McNamara discusses links between race, class, and health. She finds that the concepts are clearly connected, and she raises a number of questions about the problems poor minorities have in terms of their quality of life. Finally, Michael Chesser, a service provider, offers a glimpse into the realities of social policy. Removing the abstract concepts and theories, Chesser describes, in humorous and tragic detail, what it means to help the less fortunate.

Questions

Reading 7. Do you agree with the culture of poverty theory that poverty is actually fueled by the culture it creates? How does the structuralist view differ? Do you agree with either of these theories, or would you suggest an alternative theory?

Reading 8. What are the traditional misconceptions of the characteristics of the homeless? How are these different from the true profile? How does the labeling theory explain homelessness? Do you agree?

Reading 9. Do you think that the change in family structure is due to the drop in family income, as the reading suggests? How does the "problem of work" contribute to poverty? Are you surprised that the majority of those on welfare are also working? Do you think that improving the labor market would reduce welfare expenses?

Reading 10. How is the growing inequality in the United States likely to affect the nation's health? While a national health-care program would certainly help uninsured individuals, researchers note that it is not likely to eliminate social class disparities in health. What changes would be necessary to improve the unequal health profile of lower social class individuals? Racial minorities in the United States historically have been disadvantaged in terms of all measures of health. While social class accounts for much of this disparity, what other factors contribute to the poor health of African Americans in the United States?

Reading 11. Do you think that a psychological factor could cause homelessness? Could this explain the lack of cause/effect findings and the low success rates for efficient rehabilitation programs? Considering their overall low success rate, do you think that homeless rehabilitation programs are worth maintaining? Why or why not?

Do you agree with the culture of poverty theory that poverty is actually fueled by the culture it creates? How does the structuralist view differ? Do you agree with either of these theories, or would you suggest an alternative theory?

Race and Poverty

An urban reality?

Renee T. White

Central Connecticut State University

Discussions of the plight of urban areas, whether in the media, during a Congressional session, or in the privacy of a home, frequently turn to the issue of race. Racial and ethnic minorities have become the popular focus of debates concerning social, economic, and political reform. Urban decline and poverty are associated with black and Latino communities. As a result, the identification of social problems in communities, neighborhoods, and cities has become racialist—that is, defined along racial-ethnic lines—particularly during the last four decades of the twentieth century. The images we see of the poor, especially in urban areas, frequently depict blacks and Latinos: Poor urban youth of color are the subjects of the social-policy discourse that casts urban blacks and Latinos as pathological deviates. The 'underclass' literature explains their low wages, declining employment rates, and high unemployment rates as a consequence of cultural pathologies, family breakdown, and bad behavior. Yet often these narratives obliterate discussion of a macroeconomy generating declining earnings and employment rates of a magnitude unprecedented in recent U.S. history (Williams 1993: 83). As Rhonda Williams and others have observed, not only have urban issues been associated with people of color, this association has resulted in the common definition of the poor as deviant.

Understanding this phenomenon requires a brief look at the history of some ethnic groups in the United States, and a discussion of how these histories influence the current situations faced by the poor in this country. Discussing the different experiences of people of color will provide the foundation for a critical assessment of the way race is associated with social class, poverty, and urban issues. Theories of poverty range from ones that consider the way social structure and institutions have affected the composition of the poor to those that address poverty on the level of the individual. Race and ethnicity are relevant to the study of poverty, so it is important to understand whether current poverty theories address race adequately. Therefore, this chapter will include an evaluation of the effectiveness of theories on poverty, the research associated with them, as well as potential alternatives to the traditional debates on poverty.

The Picture of the Poor in the United States

According to the Census Bureau, in 1992 almost 8 million families were living below the poverty line (Statistical Abstract 1994). This constituted 11.7 percent of families in the United States. While most families were white, the proportion of black and Latino families falling below the poverty line exceeded their proportion of the population. Approximately 31 percent (2,435,000) of black families and 26 percent (1,395,000) of "Hispanic origin" families lived below poverty (27.7 percent of Chicano and 30.4 percent of Puerto Rican families live in poverty).[1]

Most poor live in large and medium-sized cities. Fifty-nine percent live in central cities, 13 percent in suburbs, and 27.7 percent in nonmetropolitan areas. Given the disproportionate number of minority poor, and the great likelihood that they will be found in cities, a possible trend begins to emerge. Is there something about cities that lends itself to economic hardship, particularly among blacks and Latinos? Eighty percent of the Latino poor are either Puerto Rican or Chicano (Aponte 1991).

In contrast, 8.9 percent (5,160,000) of white families live in poverty. These percentages differ greatly from the composition of the population. Eighty percent of residents in the United States are white (Statistical Abstract 1992), 9 percent are Latino, and 12.1 percent are black. In terms of median household income, 12.5 percent of white families, 30.5 percent of black families, and 20.4 percent of Latino families reported incomes less than $10,000 (Statistical Abstract 1994).

Answering the previous question involves depicting those factors associated with poverty and low-income status. Educational background, job skills and related training, job market trends, the fit between jobs and wages, industry shifts, demographic trends, and the strength of city economies are associated with economic trends, socioeconomic status (SES), and poverty rates. If blacks and Latinos are disproportionately challenged by these elements, then their representation among the urban poor can be partly explained.

Shifts in Industry Development in Cities

The large cities where most poor are located are also the ones facing much of the industry decline in the United States (Anderson 1991; Gilbert and Kahl 1987; Wilson 1987). What we are seeing is a change in the types of goods companies are producing as well as the types of jobs available to the working public. Traditionally, businesses were industrial and thus factory-based. While management positions existed, most labor was concentrated in entry-level positions that were either semi-skilled or unskilled. These jobs were ones in warehouses, on production lines, and in maintenance. Large cities near major waterways and other key modes of transportation flourished because of the emerging industrial economy (Wilson 1987). During the early part of the twentieth century, as the railroad grew in popularity and the automotive industry was emerging, many cities experienced rapid growth (Gans 1993; Peterson 1985). Ore mining and steel mill production grew in support of the railroad and automotive industries. Large numbers of southern blacks migrated to the Northeast as well as some central states in search of this type of work. Jobs connected with automotive production and steel mills were perceived as vast improvements over the types of potentially exploitative agricultural labor (seasonal migrant work and sharecropping) that was readily available throughout the South (Gutman 1976). Many companies actively recruited black men for these unskilled positions because many black men were willing to relocate in search of stable jobs. Their willingness to relocate also included a willingness to accept low-paying jobs in northern cities. Thus employers considered them "cheap" labor.

The industry growth as well as this active recruitment resulted in an increase in migration starting in Reconstruction and continuing through the Second World War. Large black populations were located in the centers of northern cities by the 1940s. However, after the Second World War, industries started to shift in the items they produced as well as the kinds of skills required for employment. Technological advances, namely automated production, increased factory productivity. As a result, the number of unskilled and semi-skilled workers needed to maintain high levels of production decreased.

Companies moved out of central cities in search of larger, more affordable spaces that could contain their assembly-line production systems. They started relocating to the suburbs, and to parts of the South (what is commonly called the "sunbelt"). Declines in manufacturing plus wholesale and retail trade were primarily located in older cities. As a result, many black and Latino residents found themselves unemployed.

Another factor affected industry development in cities. By the 1960s a new industry had taken hold. Information production and processing was heralded as the wave of the future. Advances in telecommunications and computers enabled companies within expanding industries to improve their access to a range of resources. Financial, legal, consulting, and advertising companies were drawn to the centers of cities, where these resources were most readily available. Employers required a more skilled and specialized work force that could adapt to emerging technology. Service provision, along with food and entertainment industries, grew in response to the increased consumption needs of skilled workers entering many urban work forces.

Although some jobs were available through these service and entertainment industries, they could not absorb the large number of unemployed men and women of color. As John Kasarda observes:

> The transformation of older cities from centers of production and distribution of material goods to centers of information exchange and service consumption has profoundly altered the capacity of these cities to offer employment opportunities for disadvantaged residents. The increments in urban blue-collar jobs spun off by newer service industries employing or catering primarily to higher-income persons have been overwhelmed by central-city job losses in more traditional goods-producing and -distributing industries. Aggravating these blue-collar job losses has been the exodus of middle-income populations and general retail trade and service establishments beyond the central business districts. These movements have combined to further weaken secondary labor markets and isolate disadvantaged groups in economically distressed areas where opportunities for employment are minimal. (Peterson 1985: 43)

Black and Latino semi-skilled and unskilled workers in urban areas found themselves not only unemployed, but also socially, spatially, and economically isolated. This phenomenon, called "spatial-mismatch," creates a vacuum in which there are few employment or mobility opportunities.

Educational Differentials

Though many blacks and Latinos have become poor as a result of these changes in industry and occupational specialization, questions have been raised regarding their educational background and qualifications. Perhaps, it has been argued, many of these outcomes could have been minimized if Latinos and blacks had better educations (Murray 1984; Tienda and Stier 1993; Wilson 1987). The link between employment and education is apparent. Many new types of jobs require a minimum of a college degree. The educational opportunities available to many people of color leave them unprepared to compete in specialized labor markets.

Educational inequality is connected with diminished employment potential and therefore with low wage earnings. Thirty-two percent of blacks over 25 years of age have not completed high school (Statistical Abstract 1993). Among Latinos, 47.4 percent over 25 have not completed high school. This is substantially greater than the 19.1 percent of whites in the same age category who are not high school educated.

In terms of a college education, 6.4 percent of Latinos, 8.8 percent of blacks, and 14.9 percent of whites over 25 years old had a bachelor's degree in 1993 (Statistical Abstract 1994). Most adults of all races and ethnicities have not finished college. Even so, there is an obvious racial difference in finishing education that starts well before high school.

College educated adults are more successful at finding work than ones with less formal education, although even individuals with B.A.'s recorded lower success rates in the 1990s than in previous decades (Jencks 1992). Underemployment and long periods of joblessness are most common among individuals with a high school education or less. Rates of high school completion are lower among blacks and Latinos than among whites; therefore they are more likely to be unemployed at any given time. Furthermore, they remain unemployed for longer periods than whites.

One explanation for the long-term unemployment faced by many blacks and Latinos is suggested by the skills-mismatch hypothesis (Flanagan 1995). Along with the spatial-mismatch hypothesis mentioned, skills-mismatch alludes to the difficulty faced by unskilled and semi-skilled workers who do not have the kinds of occupational training required by growing industries. According to John Kasarda, racial minorities are at a serious structural disadvantage in central cities losing entry-level industry jobs because substantially larger proportions of city minority residents lack the formal schooling to take advantage of information-processing jobs that are expanding in the cities (Peterson 1985: 53).

As jobs become more specialized, those without college educations continue to be shut out from entry-level positions and are thus unable to secure positions with on-the-job training or promotion potential. Again, as Latinos and blacks are overrepresented among the undereducated, they are at greater risk of either unemployment or working in positions without the potential for advancement.

As a result of geographic isolation, low rates of college completion, and a lack of skills, the rates of unemployment are either maintained or increased among people of color (Mead 1992). Without adequate employment to at least maintain their standard of living, more black and Latino working-class families find themselves slipping into poverty than white working poor.

Occupational Status and Wage Inequality

In addition to occupational and educational differences, blacks and Latinos are also affected by differences in wages (Tienda and Stier 1993). Two different sets of factors shed light on this claim. First, racial discrimination (and gender discrimination) in the workplace maintains differences in salaries. Second, the continued presence of a large unskilled working population of color results in their placement in low-skilled, and thus, low-paying positions:

> [O]ccupations with above-average wages grew about 20 percent faster than those with average or below-average wages between 1973 and 1982. High-wage occupations almost always require more education than low-wage occupations. It seems likely, therefore, that occupations with above-average educational requirements are growing faster than occupations that require little or no formal education. (Jencks 1992: 126)

The poor face a double bind of sorts. They are not acquiring the level of education that enables them to seek well-paying and prestigious positions and they need strong job and educational skills to compete for positions with mobility. There are fewer entry-level jobs in larger cities, and therefore more people compete for these positions. Entry-level jobs offer lower wages than other employment. Occupational mobility and competitive wages appear out of reach.

Although the subject of this chapter is the urban poor, racial differences in wages exist at all levels of employment. Regardless of occupational status and prestige, black and Latino labor force participants are paid less than their white counterparts, even when they have the same educational background.

In her analysis of reported occupational gains among black Americans, K. Sue Jewell (1988) notes that "the mere fact that blacks are categorized, for census purposes, in white-collar positions does not mean that they have white-collar incomes" (p. 77). Her observation is also true for most Latinos as well. The racial gap in median earnings for adults over 25 years old is clear. According to the 1990 census, a white adult's median earnings is $20,233; for blacks and Latinos median earnings are $15,764 and $11,954 respectively.

Mean annual earnings for any college-educated individual is $50,879. When racial groups are compared, differences emerge; whites earn $51,669, Latinos $46,163, and blacks $37,700 (Statistical Abstract 1990). According to these census data, the mean income for whites with some high school education is $22,759 while Latinos and blacks earn $19,860 and $14,112 respectively. Racial differences in salary are found regardless of educational background or job title. The effects are arguably most detrimental to low-income workers who often live paycheck-to-paycheck.

Accounting for Racial Inequality and Poverty

The racial differences in educational, employment and occupational outcomes is a real phenomenon. To what extent do these differences relate to the racial distribution of the poor? Evidence of racial inequality does not explain why it exists. In the debates over poverty in the United States, a broad spectrum of voices have been heard. Although many of the names of the participants have changed over time, as have the statistical facts, what has remained surprisingly constant are many of the theoretical perspectives and philosophical assumptions in the discussion.

Early Labor History of Poor Blacks and Latinos in the U.S.

Although the current debate in the arenas of social science research, public policy, and public opinion is heated, the topic of poverty has been a long-standing source of concern. Social classes, and the accompanying social stratification, have long been fixtures in the United States. Economic shifts and industry trends influence the composition and stability of social classes. Before the Industrial Revolution, most white families depended on agriculture for subsistence and thus were relatively independent.

In the case of blacks' and Latinos' early history in the United States, independence and control over employment was a luxury rather than a reality. The plantation economy, and the system of slavery that supplied the manual labor, exploited rather than nurtured the labor potential of blacks of African, Caribbean, and South American descent (Blassingame 1972; Gutman 1976; Herskovits 1970). Even during the period of Reconstruction, blacks' participation in farming was largely as sharecroppers who did not own their property; a leasing fee was paid the property owners, as were fees for the use of heavy equipment for harvesting.

Latino workers' early labor history in the United States was also agrarian. Some were employed in railroad construction, but agriculture remained the main employer of Chicano immigrants (Dinnerstein, Nichols, and Reimers 1979). Most of these early immigrants were migrants from Mexico. Due to the nature of farming and agriculture, Chicanos were usually hired as migrant workers and seasonal farm laborers—as such, their employment status was erratic (Aguirre and Turner 1995). They hired out as farm hands, so very few owned their own property and few experienced the same transition from a farm-based to industrial economy that was faced by white Americans. Additional Latino immigration into this country did not occur until the 1950s; most of the Puerto Rican and Cuban migration to the United States started after World War II (Aponte 1991).[2] By then, the importance of agriculture for subsistence had diminished.

In terms of the emergence and continuing presence of poverty, then, there have always been poor blacks and Latinos, along with many whites. The Colonial Poor Laws of the 17th Century are reportedly the earliest antipoverty legislation in the United States (Murray 1984; Sidel 1986). Early antipoverty laws recognized the role of government in providing for the indigent. The laws provided institutional care for the mentally ill, apprenticeships for the "able-bodied," room and board for the homeless through the creation of almshouses and poorhouses, and financial aid for poor families having trouble keeping their homes. In spite of these early efforts, the bulk of theorizing and policy analysis regarding poverty has emerged within a relatively contemporary, and short, period of history.

During the Depression, the Social Security Act of 1935 and related federal programs were created in response to the growing population of poor (Skocpol, in Jencks and Peterson 1991). Federal intervention, public assistance, and poverty were thus linked through the passage of social policy. At this point, poverty was defined as a social problem when it affected mothers and their children (especially widows), as well as disabled war veterans and the elderly. The popular perception was that men who were wounded in service of their country had earned the right to be supported by able-bodied citizens. Furthermore, women with children, who could not be expected to find work (which would remove them from their caretaking responsibilities in the home) should also be supported until they found an adult male to assume responsibility for their financial survival. Ironically, as Theda Skocpol (in Jencks and Peterson 1991) and others (Sidel 1986) have noted, early antipoverty initiatives targeted more white recipients than people of color. Whites were identified as more deserving and morally-sound than people of color (most of whom were, at this time, black).[3] The distinction between the deserving and undeserving poor emerges in criticisms of product consumption of poor blacks and Latinos, described later in this chapter.

The Current Poverty Debate in Review

The most common contemporary signifier of research on poverty is the "War on Poverty," initiated by the Kennedy administration in the early 1960s. During that decade, concern over the number of single women with children continued to grow. Too many women seemed to be depending on Aid to Families with Dependent Children (AFDC) and other aid to help alleviate the financial strain of raising their families. Furthermore, most of these young women seen in the public eye—through the media—were never married and were black. As Charles Murray (1984) observes:

> [T]he *Atlantic Monthly*, a sober-minded and liberally oriented magazine, ran a story in its April 1960 issue describing in muckraking detail the cases of 'Charlotte' with fourteen children and 'Maude' with nine (several of whom were fathered, it was reported, by an illiterate mental defective), and others who were portrayed as mindlessly accumulating children, neglecting them, and producing generations that would come back to haunt us in the decades to come. (p. 19)

As the media attention to the "typical" welfare mother increased, the poverty debate started to shift. No longer was the issue the provision of temporary federal support for widows and public servants, but the issue became the presence of "minorities" on the welfare rolls who indefinitely depended on federal aid. The battle turned into a full-fledged war.

The shift in the perception of the poor represented a number of political and ideological shifts that occurred after World War II (Gans 1993; Gilbert and Kahl 1987; Wilson 1987). First, the suburban middle class had grown. This middle class, though constituting less than a majority of families in the United States, provided the template for idealized social and economic behavior. White war veterans and their families were able to benefit from federal support. Smaller cities were growing, and thus also sought new families as well as veterans and their families, for residential developments. As a result, sociologist Herbert Gans observes:

> After the war, as prosperity and the subsidies of the Federal Housing Administration enabled the white lower class and working-class population to become homeowners in suburbia, the city increasingly became

the residence of a small number of rich people, a still large but declining middle-income population, and a rapidly rising number of poor nonwhite residents. (1993: 131)

At the same time, technology was developing rapidly, while businesses were made more efficient, consumers were also provided more products for leisure-time activity (the most common being television). These two factors created a social climate in which consumerism and hard work were associated. Those people with gainful work, responsible in their family lives, were encouraged to reward themselves with quality leisure goods. More of those families eligible for the "American Dream" were white rather than Latino or black.

Also at the same time, the civil rights movement gained strength. Social movement for racial equality and antibias legislation was sought through the federal government. The Supreme Court desegregated public schools and other public spaces in the 1954 *Brown v. Board of Education* decision. Economic discrimination, whether through poor education, employer bias, different wages, or inaccessible job training, were targeted through the courts (Jencks 1992). In fact, "[d]uring the 1960s the revolutionary position of the federal government in planning, developing, and monitoring social programs to facilitate self-reliance and economic independence for black and poor families was more pronounced than in the Roosevelt administration" (Jewell 1988: 49).

In the midst of the struggle for racial equality, the Kennedy administration also committed itself to the containment of poverty. The link between race, racial inequality and discrimination, and social class was cemented. As Jewell (1988) further observes, "blacks were defined as victims of slavery and racial inequities that had created structures and patterns of functioning, which, if not corrected, would continue to manifest social anomalies" (pp. 49–50). This is why the image of the poor shifted so dramatically during the 1960s.

Considering Race and Poverty Since the 1960s

What emerged during this period were political, social, and moral tensions. The connection between race-based politics and poverty programs was debated; the role of federal, state, local, and individual intervention was challenged; the link between past oppression and current circumstance was questioned. How much of a family's economic and material conditions were due to changes in industries, housing, technology and other institutional factors, and how much was caused by the choices made by the adults in the family?

These contemporary poverty debates have taken on different perspectives (Piven and Cloward 1971; Ryan 1981). Some are oriented toward problem-solving, and thus concern social policy innovation. Others address the sources or causes of poverty. The factors associated with some families' descent into poverty may be different from the factors affecting other families' continuing poverty status. In addition, the racial distribution of the poor had to be explained, because the proportion of black and Latino poor was so great. Last, the effects of poverty were often addressed, particularly by those interested in developing interventions that would allay some of the challenges the poor faced.

In most cases, theory addressed a combination of these questions, often attempting to identify what keeps a family in poverty to find effective long-term preventive measures as well as temporary or "stop-gap" measures. Opinions regarding "what to do with the poor," particularly during the last three decades of the twentieth century, could be broadly defined as either focusing on institutions or on individual behavior. Thus, theories identified within the poverty debate are often separated into two categories—the culture of poverty and structuralist.

The Culture of Poverty and Individual Responsibility

Daniel Patrick Moynihan (1965) and Oscar Lewis (1966) were at the forefront of the culture of poverty debate in the 1960s. In *The Negro Family: The Case for National Action*, Moynihan seeks to understand the existence of nontraditional family structures and behavior within the black community. He views single female-headed households, crime rates in certain black communities, and substance abuse as indigenous to poor blacks. Thus, he locates the cause of these tendencies in black culture and value systems.

In his study of Latino families, cultural anthropologist Oscar Lewis (1966) proposes that poor children are socialized into a value system that reduces their motivation to enter the labor market and become self-sufficient adults (Jencks and Peterson 1991; Wilson 1987). He acknowledged the effects of structural factors such as unemployment, plus social, economic, and educational isolation on the poor (Flanagan 1995). At the same time, though, he argued that structural elements only explain the initial slip into poverty.

Lewis believed that continual poverty, whether defined as long-term or multigenerational, can only be understood by making a cultural argument. As the author of the concept "culture of poverty," he proposed that a series of values and moral systems emerge from the poor, ones unique to poor families. These adaptive elements become internalized and are passed from one generation to another. If social values and culture reinforce behaviors that keep one in poverty, then social policy initiatives will not work. This is because the cultural rewards of poverty-related behavior are perceived as greater than the rewards for engaging in traditional, mainstream behavior.

These views of poverty, often labeled conservative, focus on the interconnection between cultural traditions, family history, and individual character. Specific cultural traits emerge from existing in poverty, but would still influence the behavior of the poor even if they were offered improved opportunities for social mobility. Behaviors result from a system of internalized values and beliefs that exist within the "ghetto subculture":

> A series of special adaptations to existential circumstances, including a sense of resignation and passivity because of enduring poverty; a present-time orientation because of the pressures of day-to-day survival; feelings of fatalism and powerlessness because of separation . . . low aspirations because of the lack of opportunity; feelings of inferiority because of the larger society's contempt and aversion for the poor; and the creation of female-headed households because of the inability of poor men to be adequate breadwinners. (Wilson 1987: 182)

Beliefs and attitudes developed in association with the economic realities faced during any decade result in social behaviors (for example, drug and alcohol use, teen pregnancy, illicit economic activity, and low marriage rates) identified as pathological and destructive. These "pathological" behaviors are seen as creating boundaries that minimize people's chances to transcend poverty. Prior values determine how people react to structural change, so the ability to adapt to any given social reality is dependent on culture as well as value systems.

A second school of thought that is associated with the culture of poverty argues that welfare creates poverty. Charles Murray, in *Losing Ground* (1984), claims that the poor see no need to care for themselves because they know that the state will care for them.[4] He identifies welfare dependency as a social policy problem along racial terms. During the "Great Experiment" of civil rights policy development in the 1960s the rules were changed:

> Until 1965, the principles of equal treatment and a fair shake did not compete. They created no tension. Their application to racial policy was simple: make the nation color blind. People were to be judged on their merits. But then the elite wisdom changed. Blacks were to be helped to catch up . . . Before the 1960s we had a black underclass that was held down because blacks were systematically treated differently from whites. Now, we have a black underclass that is held down for the same generic reason—because blacks are systematically treated differently from whites, by whites. . . . Whites began to tolerate and make excuses for behavior among blacks that whites would disdain in themselves or their children. (pp.221–223)

As a result of these policies, poor blacks (and Latinos) behave in ways considered socially unacceptable by the mainstream. "By permitting low-income people to expect that they need never work . . . [there is] a class of people who remain poor because they feel no obligation to contribute to the larger society and who exhibit high rates of out-of-wedlock births, teen pregnancy, long term unemployment, criminality and drug use" (Jencks and Peterson 1991: p. 343). Poor people, according to this view, choose their "lifestyle" because doing otherwise would require working hard and participating in mainstream culture. They opt for leisure activities and remain unconcerned with the ramifications. Social and institutional structures cannot account for the inequities in people's lives because, by this argument, each individual is personally responsible for improving his or her opportunities in life through modifying behavior.

In proof of the claim that the dysfunctional poor engage in inappropriate leisure activities, critics like Murray often point to the purchasing practices of some poor families (Gans 1993; Gilbert and Kahl 1987; Sidel 1986). In critiquing welfare, conservative scholars argue that poor blacks and Latinos own too many leisure items like clothes, electronic goods, and cars. The distinctions between the "deserving" and "undeserving" poor are thus made by evaluating consumption behavior. Those who buy leisure items are seen as wasteful, not thankful for the federal support they receive, not forward-thinking with their financial planning, and therefore uninterested in changing their poverty status. Those who only buy the basic necessities are characterized as committed to changing their poverty status because they "appreciate the value of the dollar."

What is interesting about this evaluation of the poor is that it does not account for the general socially-recognized consumerist climate. One is to show financial and social success through owning visible, high-value items. A counterinterpretation of the critique of purchasing behavior of the poor is that they are merely attempting to attain part of the "American Dream" through what they own.[5] As such, they too are maintaining popular mainstream values, but using available means to do so.

Many of the visible poor who live in urban areas are black and Latino, so there is an additional danger in the culture of poverty literature in making a conceptual leap from associating poverty with certain characteristics to connecting poverty to blacks and Latinos. The intersection of race and class, as we have seen, is real. However, there is a tendency among culture of poverty theorists to argue that there is a causal relationship between culture, ethnicity, and destructive behaviors. They are not as concerned with how structural factors unique to poverty influence behavior.

Structural Determinants and Government Responsibility

Structuralists critique culture of poverty theorists for being reductionist in viewing the poor as intrinsically pathological (Jencks 1992; Sidel 1986; Zinn 1989). Instead, structuralists argue that while institutional barriers limit social mobility and result in poverty, the poor still share values and aspirations associated with the "mainstream." Whatever behaviors and attitudes the poor display will change when opportunities and access to resources improve. What appears to be negative and destructive behavior might be rational responses to the range of options available to young women (Anderson 1991; Hayward, Grady and Billy 1992). Critiques of culture of poverty theories highlight that there is little room for considering the importance of agency. People are not actively choosing to behave in ways that are immersing them in poverty. Instead, structuralists see individuals as victims of malevolent institutions who have little control over their situations because many of their problems have an institutional basis.

Liberal critics consider the crisis of the poor to be largely created and maintained through institutional causes. There are three approaches used in structuralist accounts of poverty (Aponte 1991; Greenstone, in Jencks and Peterson 1991; Santiago and Wilder 1991; Zinn 1989). In the mismatch hypothesis popularized by John Kasarda (Peterson 1985) and William Julius Wilson (1987), among others, shifts in the geographic location of manufacturing has resulted in the isolation of working class communities of color in urban areas. This population is removed from the kinds of employment they usually seek; furthermore, the movement of middle-class and some lower-class populations out of the inner city compromises the economic base of these communities. The remaining residents find themselves cut off from important social, economic, and political networks because of these two types of shifts.

The second model focuses on labor market segmentation. The racial distribution of jobs is unbalanced. Blacks and Latinos are more likely to be in the secondary labor market in positions requiring manual labor. The secondary labor market is largely unstable, so people of color face more horizontal than vertical job mobility; they are paid less, and have little chance of job advancement or job training. A number of social scientists have illustrated the role of employer discrimination in the job placement of Chicanos, Puerto Ricans, and blacks. In their essay on racial bias in employer decision making, Joleen Kirschenman and Kathryn Neckerman (in Jencks and Peterson 1991) note that for many Chicago-based employers,

> [C]haracterizations of inner-city workers mirrored many descriptions of the underclass by social scientists. Common among the traits listed were that workers were unskilled, uneducated, illiterate, dishonest, lacking initiative, unmotivated, involved with drugs and gangs, did not understand work, had no personal charm, were unstable, lacked a work ethic, and had no family life or role models . . . race was important in part because it signalled class and inner city residence, which are less easy to observe directly. (pp. 208–209)

Race became a proxy for job skills, and thus determined the kinds of employment made available to blacks and Latinos.

In the case of race, structuralists identify the ways discrimination and bias operate to exclude people of color from the resources widely available to whites. While employment discrimination is one factor, another is education. As the census data show, Latinos and blacks record lower rates of college completion and are likely to drop out of high school. In considering opportunity structures, some critics have argued that lower quality schools are often found in low-income communities because the public school system is based on property taxes from the community. As a result, schools in these communities have problems competing with private schools and suburban public schools for teachers, equipment, and other important resources (Gans 1993; Piven and Cloward 1971). The children ultimately suffer and are thus less likely to be prepared for college (Jiobu 1990). The social stratification within communities excludes some from opportunity while continuing to protect the opportunities already held by the privileged. Structural critics such as Frances Fox Piven, Richard Cloward, and William Ryan look to the ways inequities are replicated from one generation to the next through the way social institutions continue to function. They consider behavior associated with the poor to be the outcome, not the cause, of poverty. Culture has to be defined with qualifiers, as its conceptualization often implies that individuals have chosen to engage in certain behaviors. Many have accused conservative, culture of poverty theorists of "blaming the victim" for his or her poverty.

In criticizing culture-based explanations of poverty, structuralists have argued that such perspectives are reactionary—they are responding to the small fraction of people who chose to be out of work (often referred to as the nonworking poor or nonparticipant labor force). Most poor retain the same values identified with the middle class (the mainstream). What is different is that they do not have the same mechanisms with which to realize their goals. Elijah Anderson (1991) has described the frustration felt by black residents of a northeastern city who watch the jobs leave their neighborhoods and their communities decline:

> With rising unemployment, brought on in part by increasing 'deindustrialization' and the exodus of major corporations, the local black community suffered. The employment lives of its members are further complicated by continuing racial prejudice and discrimination, which often frustrate efforts to make effective adjustments to these changes and the emerging reality. (p. x)

The same psychological and emotional states defined as influencing destructive behaviors associated with poverty, namely despair, frustration, and cynicism, are seen by structural critics as a by product of continued efforts to escape poverty despite structural barriers. For them, the solution to persistent poverty lies in the *system*, not the individual. Social policy that addresses racial discrimination, inequality, and stratification is the only way poverty can be alleviated. Black and Latino poor are subjected to inordinately challenging oppression because of the way race operates within the social structures of the United States. Race and poverty are associated, but this association cannot be explained by looking at race without considering the effects of racism.

New Perspectives on Race and Poverty

What we see have seen in this debate is how race and culture have been closely associated with poverty. The current discussions on this topic appear to be taking a surprising turn. There are those social scientists and policy analysts who keep the culture-structure debate alive. There are others, though, who have begun to approach the intersection of race and social class from values-based vantage points. Still others have embraced the importance of culture, but in a way that differs from the "culture" addressed by the culture of poverty.

Conservative critics such as Arthur Schlesinger, Jr., and Allan Bloom mourn the demise of "traditional" American life. For them, the Great Society and other progressive measures geared toward the poor and otherwise disadvantaged (whether citizens or immigrants) has resulted in something unexpected and unwanted—the loss of American culture. Efforts to redress the effects of racial bias for blacks has resulted, in Blooms' opinion, in the following:

> Blacks are not sharing a special positive intellectual or moral experience; they partake fully in the common culture, with the same goals and tastes as everyone else, but they are doing it by themselves. They continue to have the inward sentiments of separateness when it no longer effectively exists. The heat is under the pot, but they do not melt as have *all* other groups. (1987: 93)

In his view, multicultural reform, immersion schools, bilingual education, targeted job training programs, and other initiatives are not making the underserved "more equal." These efforts merely weaken the quality of the preparation available to young men and women who want to enter the work force. They fragment American society into a set of individual groups rather than unify them under the banner of American.

In their debate in *Mother Jones* in early 1993, Roger Wilkins, former Director of the Justice Department's Community Relations Service, and Shelby Steele, professor of English at San Jose State University and social commentator, discuss the relative effects of race-based policies (Steele and Wilkins 1993). They figure among the current voices in this debate. For Steele, poverty among blacks is mostly a function of the self-defeatism he believes is part of programs such as affirmative action. Federal programs merely reinforce feelings of powerlessness by focusing on racial inequality. As a result, whites become the "enemy"; they represent privilege and racism.

Wilkins sees poverty and race as interconnected. As such, they must be redressed for poor people of color to survive poverty. This means confronting the structural influences on poverty while realizing the unique ways race affects how poverty is experienced, and which solutions will be effective.

This new discussion may be policy oriented at times, but it also concerns broad social, moral, and philosophical questions. What responsibility do the successful have to those who are among the poor and working class? What does race mean in today's social world; does it explain the persistence of poverty among people of color? Do targeted programs, which benefit certain categories of people, do more good than harm? Do they reinforce the race inequality and poverty they aim to eradicate?

In response, other social critics have claimed that the only way people can be judged by "the content of their character" is if social institutions allow them access on this basis (merits), rather than constraining opportunities through the maintenance of race, class, and gender-based barriers. In other words, people's differences must be considered in relation to institutions—that is, the way race affects poverty status. By acknowledging these effects on economic and social opportunity, poor blacks and Latinos may have better chances for advancement. In terms of the future of poverty research and reform, this would mean developing what Paul Peterson (1985) calls a "nonurban policy for urban America"; continuing to address in specific ways how people of color survive poverty.

Notes

1. Cuban-American families are the least likely of Hispanic families to live in poverty. Most Cuban-American adults are employed in managerial and technical positions. This is because they are either older Cuban exiles (many of whom come from the former Cuban elite) or are U.S. born children of Cuban elites. Furthermore, the U.S. government developed resettlement programs for Cuban refugees that provided housing, job training, and financial assistance. These advantages have resulted in a decades-long gap in the achievements of Cuban-Americans and other Latinos (Aguirre and Turner 1995).
2. Scholars have argued for a more detailed analysis of Latinos by ethnicity because of the differences in the occupational, educational, and economic outcomes for Latinos (Santiago and Wilder 1991; Zinn 1989). For example, Cuban Americans, and some Central and South Americans, are more likely to be high school and college educated than other Latinos. One common criticism has been that research on poverty focuses on blacks. While there are some factors common to the black and Latino poor, there are differences that render some findings and subsequent policy developments inaccurate. Cultural differences due to ethnic heritage, along with others, should be recognized when studying poverty in Latino communities.
3. This racial-ethnic difference holds true for current recipients of in-kind cash receipts and other forms of federal aid. Skocpol and Sidel note that most people on welfare are white, not black or Latino.
4. Murray and the late Richard J. Herrnstein (1994) are coauthors of the controversial book *The Bell Curve: Intelligence and Class Structure in American Life* (New York: The Free Press), in which they argue that there are significant racial differences in I.Q. tests that can only be explained in terms of culture and other "natural" traits. It is an example of the way the "nature vs. nurture" debate is surfacing in social science discussions of class and poverty.
5. See author's discussion of middle-class consumption.

References

Aguirre, Adalberto, and Jonathan H. Turner. 1995. *American Ethnicity*. New York: McGraw-Hill.

Anderson, Elijah. 1991. *Streetwise: Race, Class and Change in an Urban City*. Chicago: University of Chicago.

Aponte, Robert. 1991. "Urban Hispanic Poverty: Disaggregations and Explanations." *Social Problems* 38(4): 516–28.

Blassingame, John. 1972. *The Slave Community*. New York: Oxford University Press.

Bloom, Allan. 1987. *The Closing of the American Mind*. New York: Touchstone.

Cloward, Richard A., and Frances Fox Piven. 1975. *The Politics of Turmoil: Poverty, Race, and the Urban Crisis*. New York: Vintage Books.

Dinnerstein, Leonard, Roger Nichols, and David M. Reimers. 1979. *Natives and Strangers*. New York: Oxford.

Flanagan, William B. 1995. *Urban Sociology: Images and Structure*. Needham Heights, MA: Allyn and Bacon.

Gans, Herbert J. 1993. *People, Plans, and Policies*. New York: Columbia University Press.

Gilbert, Dennis, and Joseph A. Kahl. 1987. *The New American Class Structure*. Chicago: The Dorsey Press.

Gutman, Herbert. 1976. *The Black Family in Slavery and Freedom*. New York: Pantheon.

Hayward, Mark D., William R. Grady, and John O. G. Billy. 1992. "The Influence of Socioeconomic Status on Adolescent Pregnancy." *Social Science Quarterly* 73(4): 750–72.

Hernandez, Jose. 1990. "Latino Alternatives to the Underclass Concept." In Richard C. Monk (ed.), *Taking Sides*, pp. 32–40. Guilford, CT: Dushkin.
Herskovits, Melville. 1970. *The Myth of the Negro Past*. Boston, MA: Beacon Press.
Jencks, Christopher. 1992. *Rethinking Social Policy: Race, Poverty, and the Underclass*. Cambridge, MA: Harvard University Press.
Jencks, Christopher, and Paul E. Peterson. 1991. *The Urban Underclass*. Washington, D.C.: Brookings Institution.
Jewell, K. Sue. 1988. *Survival of the Black Family*. Westport, CT: Praeger.
Jiobu, Robert Masao. 1990. *Ethnicity and Inequality*. New York: SUNY Press.
Lewis, Oscar. 1966. *La Vida: A Puerto Rican Family in the Culture of Poverty*. New York: Random House.
Mead, Lawrence. 1992. *The New Politics of Poverty*. New York: Basic Books.
Moynihan, Daniel Patrick. 1965. *The Negro Family: The Case for National Action*. Washington, DC: Office of Policy Planning and Research, U.S. Department of Labor.
Murray, Charles. 1984. *Losing Ground: American Social Policy 1950-1980*. New York: Basic Books.
Murray, C., and R. J. Herrnstein. 1994. *The Bell Curve: Intelligence and Class Structure in American Life*. New York: The Free Press.
Peterson, Paul E. 1985. *The New Urban Reality*. Washington, DC: Brookings Institution.
Piven, Frances, and Richard Cloward. 1971. *Regulating the Poor: The Functions of Public Welfare*. New York: Vintage.
Ryan, William. 1981. *Equality*. New York: Pantheon Books.
Santiago, Anne M., and Margaret G. Wilder. 1991. "Residential Segregation and Links to Minority Poverty: The Case of Latinos in the United States." *Social Problems* 38(4): 492–515.
Sidel, Ruth. 1986. *Women and Children Last*. New York: Penguin Books.
Statistical Abstract of the United States. 1994. Washington, DC: US Bureau of the Census.
Statistical Abstract of the United States. 1993. Washington, DC: U.S. Bureau of the Census.
Statistical Abstract of the United States. 1992. Washington, DC: U.S. Bureau of the Census.
Statistical Abstract of the United States. 1990. Washington, DC: U.S. Bureau of the Census.
Steele, Shelby, and Roger Wilkins. 1993. "Backtalk." *Mother Jones*, 17: January/February.
Tienda, Marta, and Hagda Stier. 1993. "Color and Employment Opportunity in Chicago's Inner City." In *Immigration, Race and Ethnicity in America: Historical and Contemporary Perspectives*. Belmont, CA: Wadsworth Press.
Williams, Rhonda. 1993. "Accumulation as Evisceration: Urban Rebellion and the New Growth Dynamics." In *Reading Rodney King, Reading Urban Uprising*, by Robert Gooding-Williams (ed.). New York: Routledge.
Wilson, William Julius. 1987. *The Truly Disadvantaged*. Chicago, IL: University of Chicago Press.
Zinn, Maxine Baca. 1989. "Family, Race, and Poverty in the Eighties." *Signs* 14(4): 856–874.

Article Review Form at end of book.

What are the traditional misconceptions of the characteristics of the homeless? How are these different from the true profile? How does the labeling theory explain homelessness? Do you agree?

The Nature of Homelessness in America

Robert P. McNamara
Furman University

Maria Tempenis
Vanderbilt University

Homelessness. It has become one of the most visible scenes of American life and in some ways, too visible. While interest in this population has spanned decades and involved a host of different individuals and groups, from researchers to churches, to missionaries of various sorts, the public has become too accustomed to the presence of this population. Also, like many social problems in our society, we have relied on stereotypical images to understand this diverse group of people and our observations of the most extreme forms of homelessness only underscore that simplistic understanding. Coupled with this are some of the commonly understood reasons why and how one becomes homeless. Perhaps more troubling is the way we deal with the problem. To most people, homelessness is an abstract phenomenon to be discussed at cocktail parties, in classrooms, or in settings that remove us from the realities of the situation. This is true despite the fact that we are much closer to homelessness than we realize: we are about two or three steps away from being homeless at any point in our lives. A devastating illness or tragedy, or a sudden catastrophe to a relative, and we could find ourselves faced with one of the most serious problems of our time.

One of the main reasons this particular social problem remains in the minds of many Americans has been its visibility. While always a part of the American social fabric, until recently homelessness has been confined to a certain segment of our society and to certain sections of our cities and towns. It has only been since the 1990s that Americans have been forced to confront the plight of this group of people in any substantial way. At the same time, however, this visibility has made us uncomfortable with the topic and, in some ways, we have attempted to conceal or minimize its significance, thereby exacerbating the problem (Blau 1992). There are a variety of ways in which this minimization is accomplished. One way is to incorporate homelessness into another social problem. That is, many have equated homelessness with poverty. Many people think that if we were to take steps to alleviate poverty, we would also ameliorate the homeless situation as well. While there is a relationship between the two social problems, solving one does not necessarily eliminate the other. The complexities and issues of homelessness are many and transcend a number of problems the poor encounter.

Definitional Matters: Who Are the Homeless?

Part of the difficulty in dealing with homelessness is related to how it is defined. In the 1970s, Mitch Snyder argued that a million Americans were homeless. In 1982, he and Mary Ellen Hombs, in their report *Homelessness in America: A Forced March to Nowhere* estimated the population at between two and three million. Interestingly, in the absence of official statistics, advocates for the homeless, policy makers, and a host of other people, began using this figure. In response, in 1984 the Reagan administration directed the U.S. Department of Housing and Urban Development (HUD) to study the homeless population and to produce its own estimate.

HUD contacted the most knowledgeable people it could find in each large American city and asked them to estimate the number of homeless people in their metropolitan area. The Department then selected a number near the middle of the range for each area. From this, HUD's best estimate of the homeless population was between 250,000 and 350,000 (Jencks 1995).

In response to the dramatic differences between Snyder and Hombs's and HUD's estimations, Snyder publicly admitted that he had no basis for their calculation, except that the number was large enough to warrant national attention on the problem. This playing of the "numbers game" has been, and continues to be, a pervasive problem in addressing the needs of the homeless. In his book *Rude Awakenings,* White (1992) echoes this point and describes the inflation of the size of the population as an attempt to secure additional funding to account for those individuals who are typically ignored in the definition of homelessness. He refers to this process as "lying for justice."

In his analysis of defining the problem, Jencks (1995) begins by defining the homeless into two groups: those who sleep in free shelters (what he calls the *shelter homeless*) and those who sleep in public places (e.g., bus stations, automobiles, doorways). These he refers to as the *street homeless*. While this definition works at a given point in time, it fails to identify the homeless over time. This is especially true because many studies have shown that the homeless select different locations on different nights. Jencks contends that identifying these individuals as homeless is relatively easy. The problem becomes more complicated when a family lives in welfare hotels. These are places welfare departments send families with children when no shelter space is available. The rooms, while not at all lavish, do constitute privacy for the individuals and give them control over access to that area. If a family paid its own rent in one of these places, Jencks argues, we would not call them homeless. In addition to this problem, he says, we fail to make an adequate distinction between welfare hotels and subsidized housing. In both of these cases, the government pays the rent, yet we still classify one homeless and not the other. In criticizing advocates of the homeless, who want to include these individuals in their definition of the homeless, Jencks contends they are playing the numbers game.

Jencks also takes issue with those who wish to include individuals doubled up in someone else's home. This is said to represent a large portion of the homeless population as well as being the most difficult to count. Jencks argues that this group cannot be included because it is nearly impossible to parcel out those who have no money and nowhere else to go as well as people who live with others by choice. For Jencks, the definition of homelessness are those who slept in a public place or a shelter during a given week and welfare hotels are considered a form of shelters. In short, what he and others like him identify as homeless are those who are the most visible—those in the most desperate of situations. However, despite the problems with defining homelessness, some evidence suggests that at least 700,000 people live in the street and shelters in the United States at any one time (Wright and Devine 1995).

This absence of shared definitions is also a major obstacle to the accumulation of knowledge about this population. As Blau (1992) points out, the absence of shared definitions naturally reinforces the tendency toward counting. However, the problems of accurately obtaining a count are as problematic as adequately defining the population.

Counting the Homeless

There are only a limited number of options to choose from to obtain a census of the population. The first is what is sometimes known as *a point in time* study. This is a one-time survey of shelters, institutions, and the areas on the street where the homeless are likely to be found. This method is considered the most accurate of the two, but it is also the most expensive. It is also likely to identify the most visible portion of the population. The second method is to ask individuals if they have ever spent any time homeless. This tends to depart from the government's definition, as well as studies like HUD, which ask about homelessness on any given night rather than at any other time (Jencks 1995).

A Profile of the Homeless

There is much greater consensus on the characteristics of the homeless than there is on its size. While no study has been accepted as the seminal work on the subject, especially since regional differences have been discovered, there are some fairly consistent themes that run through this population. The research suggests that the homeless population is younger than their historical counterparts (see for instance City of New York 1984, 1982; State of Ohio 1985; Pilivian, Sosin and Westerfelt

1988) and consists of about 50 percent minorities. Also, families are the fastest growing group of the homeless and an increasingly large number are part of the working poor who have full-time jobs. This is such a rough sketch of the population; therefore each of these and other topics will be explored at greater length.

With regard to age, most studies place the average age of the adult homeless at about thirty-five years old (an exception to this general trend is that homeless women tend to be younger) (Institute of Medicine 1988). Part of the explanation for this trend has to do with the changes in the economy. As the United States made the transition from an industrial to a service economy, many manufacturing jobs were moved to other countries. This meant that many members of the urban poor, who had few technical skills to begin with, were excluded from those job opportunities, and eventually forced into the shelters and the streets.

The homeless population is also made up of mostly men, and single men make up slightly more than 51 percent of the total homeless population. Probably the most striking trend in the characteristics of the homeless has been the increase in the number of families. The research suggests that families make up anywhere between 30–55 percent of the homeless population. For instance, one study estimates that during a four-year period, the number of families using shelters increased fourfold. Moreover, there is increasing evidence that children are becoming a common feature of the homeless (see for instance Bassuk and Rubin 1987; Institute of Medicine 1988).

The HUD survey, as well as a study by the Urban Institute and the Robert Wood Johnson Foundation, have found that a little over half of the homeless population are people of color. This makes sense if one recognizes that minorities have long represented a disproportionate percentage of people in poverty. Other variables, such as substance abuse and mental illness, two of the most common characteristics of the stereotypical homeless person, account for approximately one-fourth to one-third of the population. With regard to drug and alcohol abuse, there remains a considerable amount of debate whether this should be considered a cause or a consequence of homelessness. With regard to mental illness, there are many problems with estimating this figure. First, defining mental illness, as well as which types of disorders are included in any given study, need to be identified. Second, the subjective nature of assessing mental illness must also be taken into account. A clinical diagnosis is not always the definitive way of identifying a disorder. Third, few studies have compared the incidence of mental illness among the general population. Therefore, it is difficult to determine how extensive severe mental disorders are among the homeless as compared to disorders for the rest of the population.

Another common misperception of the homeless is that they are primarily veterans of military service. However, there have been several studies (see for instance Schutt 1988) that indicate veterans make up about one-third of the homeless male population. Of those, up to 40 percent of these individuals served in Vietnam. Also in contrast to conventional wisdom, a significant portion of the homeless are employed. In a 1993 study by the U.S. Conference of Mayors, almost a quarter of the population were engaged in some type of work, typically casual labor. The study also shows that requests for emergency food assistance increased by 13 percent from 1992 with families, not individuals, accounting for two-thirds of that aid. Additionally, 30 percent of the adults seeking food assistance were employed (Silverstein 1994). The study also showed that requests for emergency shelter increased by 10 percent from the previous year and requests by homeless families by 13 percent. This came at a time when the number of emergency shelter beds rose 4 percent, traditional housing units by 20 percent, and single-room occupancy units by 16 percent. What is particularly interesting is that about 25 percent of the requests by homeless individuals and 29 percent of those by homeless families go unanswered (Silverstein 1994).

Another interesting finding is that the homeless population in a given community or city is usually comprised of people who are from that particular area. Approximately 76 percent of the sheltered population have lived for more than one year in the area where the facility was located (Blau 1992). There are a number of regional differences, with some cities having a much higher percentage, but overall the research shows that homelessness is a *home-grown* phenomenon. This calls into question much of what is proposed in the so-called *magnet theory* of homelessness, explained in greater detail in another section.

The length of time one stays in a shelter can be misinterpreted to imply that homelessness is a short-term problem. This is especially true when the data reveals that the range of time is between thirty-four days and eleven months (Blau 1992). The U.S. Conference of Mayors study estimated that the average homeless experience lasted seven months, with single men and families with children comprising 43 percent of the homeless population and children accounting for 30 percent of the total (Silverstein 1994).

Finally, AIDS and homelessness are related. The relationship between these two variables, like substance abuse, is not exactly clear. There are people who are already homeless who contract AIDS, and some people with AIDS become homeless because they cannot support themselves any longer. In any event, the problems encountered by the homeless, the methods by which some homeless people cope with their situations, and the social policy concerning the treatment of AIDS patients (as well as those who are also homeless) are likely to result in an increase in this segment of the population (Kifner 1991).

The Sociological Study of the Homeless

The sociological research on the homeless is vast and has uncovered quite a bit in terms of our understanding of this phenomenon. It has also helped to demystify much of the popular notions that pervade our thinking about the subject. For instance, Snow and Anderson (1995) provide one of the most comprehensive field studies of the homeless. Situated in Austin, Texas, Snow and Anderson offer perhaps the most elaborate typology of the homeless, which includes the following three categories: the recently dislocated, the straddlers, and the outsiders.

The Recently Dislocated

These are made up primarily of individuals new to the plight of the homeless in that they have entered a world that is as foreign as anything they have encountered. They do not know the rules, the expectations, or if they will survive. As a result of what Merton (1953) referred to as an *anomic* state, these individuals tend to gravitate toward local service providers that provide food and shelter. There is also a reaction from this group to exaggerate their past lives. There is a strong desire to return to that world and much of their conversations with people include talk of how and in what ways they will get off the street.

The Straddlers

As the recently dislocated person becomes acclimated to the problems and consequences of being homeless, the fears associated with being on the street begin to lessen. This is especially true for those who make friends and find assistance. As the memories of the past begin to fade, the images and experiences of the present begin to take on a new level of importance. There becomes a disconnectedness between the past and the present, as well as with the present and the future. In other words, while the person does not positively identify with others on the streets, there is a recognition of the similarities between them and one's self. Snow and Anderson (1995) identify two types of straddlers: the *regular straddlers* and the *institutionally adapted straddlers.*

The regular straddlers are those individuals who will, in time, either find a way off the streets or drift into a life-style that results in their becoming a permanent addition to the street scene. The institutionally adapted straddler is in a transitional state, but finds himself or herself assigned to different roles and is able to link their activities to the service organizations that are available. While this group will go through periods of homelessness, their experiences in the street, longer than the traditional straddler, tend to make the pains of homelessness easier as well as reducing the problems of role conflict.

The Outsiders

The term *outsider* carries with it a host of social connotations. For the homeless, this is the group that has imposed a form of isolation on itself and for whom street life has become taken for granted. These are not individuals experiencing periods of adversity, but rather see themselves in terms of their street identities. As Snow and Anderson (1995) describe, "They are people for whom the past and the future have collapsed into the present" (p. 58). This is also the group that is most often thought of when one thinks of the homeless. Within this category, there are four subtypes. One, labeled *tramps,* includes the hoboes as well as those people who were active in the hippie movement and who never left the counterculture mentality. A second type of outsider are the *bums,* which comes closest to approximating the image of the skid-row alcoholic. This group is relatively immobile and engages in sporadic or periodic employment. This is due in part to their addiction to alcohol, but also because their physical limitations preclude full-time permanent jobs. As a result, individuals who fit into this category are likely to panhandle, sell plasma, or beg to acquire funds. This is also a group that is very territorial of the areas they outline as their own, can be gang-like in their associations, and are prone to violence.

This discrete categorization of the homeless population has been duplicated elsewhere and seen in various forms. However, what this typology does is to provide a framework of understanding of the nature of life on the streets as well as the different ways homeless people adapt to and cope with their problems.

Kozol (1988) makes another important contribution to the literature on the homeless. In this study in New York City, he describes the inequities and paradoxes homeless people typically encounter in rich and textured detail. He describes, from a structuralist perspective, how the system exacerbates the problem and encourages a form of self-defeatism for those who would otherwise like to overcome the various obstacles that led to their current situation.

For instance, Kozol describes how a family is often placed in temporary hotels if there is insufficient room for them in a shelter. In one instance, the city of New York was paying almost two thousand dollars per month (sixty-five dollars per night) for a woman and her children to live in a single room. Contingent upon them staying in this hotel was the stipulations that the mother attempt to find permanent housing. Her rent subsidy by the city was limited to $270, yet virtually all the apartments she inspected cost at least one hundred dollars more than that. If the mother wanted to move into an apartment and become more self-sufficient, the difference between the rent and her housing subsidy would have to be absorbed either in food, clothing, or some other necessity. This was not possible, so the mother chose to stay in the hotel (p. 43).

The difference in cost between an affordable apartment and the price of keeping them in a hotel room is startling, especially when one considers the price of any housing in New York City. Yet, argues Kozol, policy makers lament of a dependency on the system and how we often enable women to be in the system for an extended period of time. In addition to a moving and emotional description of life as a homeless person, Kozol's contribution is to show that the system is organized in such a way that perpetuates, rather than alleviates, the problem.

Besides identifying the characteristics of the homeless, much of the research has focused on the causes that resulted in the increase in the size and composition of the population. Most of the research on homelessness identifies four main causal factors: a shift in the economy; the lack of affordable housing, such as the destruction of Single Room Occupancy (SRO) units through urban renewal efforts; the deinstitutionalization of the mentally ill; and drug and alcohol abuse. While there remains serious debate over which of these is most significant, there is substantial evidence to suggest they all play a part in the problem. Rossi (1989), for instance, has argued that the primary cause of homelessness is the lack of affordable housing for many people. In his analysis of the problem in Chicago, Rossi concludes that the decline in SROs and other forms of inexpensive housing has forced many poor Chicago residents to either spend a very large proportion of their income on housing, which perpetuates their impoverished status, or to resort to the shelters or the street. He goes on to argue that a major factor in explaining the decline of SRO housing units is the shrinkage of the casual labor market in many urban economies in the 1960s and 1970s. As he describes it,

> In earlier decades, urban employers needing muscle power to wrestle cargo apparently put up with the low productivity of the Skid Row inhabitants because they could hire them as needed for low pay. Apparently, material-handling equipment such as forklifts put both the homeless and Skid Row out of business. Cause and effect are almost hopelessly muddled here. As Skid Row populations declined, employers may have been motivated to invest in equipment that lowered their need for casual labor, and at the same time the lowered need for such labor meant that Skid Rows were populated more and more by persons out of the labor force (e.g. pensioners either retired or disabled). (p. 132)

For Rossi then, the problems of urban renewal, coupled with the rising cost of existing housing, and the declining value of welfare for the poor, is perhaps the best explanation of today's homeless.

Similarly, Blau (1992) attempts to explain the causes of homelessness. This analysis incorporates not only a relevant discussion of the shift to a service-oriented economy, which resulted in the decline of well-paying job opportunities for the poor, but also how this current trend has been occurring since the post-World War II era. As he and others explain it, when American corporations lost their competitive edge, which was exacerbated by the U.S. military build-up, as well as the loss of access to a supply of natural resources, attempts were made to restore the country's economic prosperity in other ways. The most noted of these was the deregulation of the environment so that corporations would regain their foothold in the marketplace. An additional strategy was to offset the costs of production. Corporate America found that because of the high price of American labor, their profit margins were constantly being strangled. As a result, executives discovered that they could reduce their costs of production, and by extension increase their profits, by moving assembly lines overseas (see also Wilson 1987). Blau argues that while this helps the corporation's bottom line, the impact it has on its workers is devastatingly real. For many of those workers whose plant was closed, it is a short step from living in a shelter or living on the streets. Exacerbating this was the social deregulation that took place during the Reagan administration, whereby many of the programs designed to help the poor, such as food stamps, AFDC, CETA, and others were eliminated, scaled back, or witnessed drastic changes in criteria, which affected the eligibility of hundreds of thousands of people.

While these events are not the only way people become homeless, Blau contends that this has become an all-too-familiar scene of American life. Like Rossi (1989), he contends that a fundamental part of the problem has to do with inadequate housing. If one were to examine the number of SRO units demolished and to compare them with the number of new affordable units that were built, the difference is startling.

A third factor used to explain the rise of homelessness has been the deinstitutionalization of the mentally ill. Recall that about one-third of today's homeless suffer from some type of diagnosed mental disorder. One explanation for this has been that deinstitutionalization caused homelessness. As Blau (1992) contends, this argument has lost much of its validity since it was first heard in the 1980s. As he argues,

> Sixty-five percent of the decline in the hospital census had already occurred before 1975. Deinstitutionalization therefore cannot explain very much about the spread of homelessness one decade later. By the early 1990s, when 40 percent of the homeless consist of families and upwards of 100,000 children were without shelter, even federal agencies such as the National Institute of Mental Health were reporting to Congress that deinstitutionalization had played a comparatively small role. (p. 85)

The problem, then, is not that deinstitutionalization caused homelessness, but rather that the problems of mental illness compound the marketability of those seeking jobs at a time when those jobs are scarce. Thus, Blau asserts that the cause and effect relationship is not at all clear: it may be that the consequences of being homeless may lead to various types of mental disorders. He states,

> But at a time when families are the fastest growing segment among the homeless, and the great majority of homeless people do not, *prior to their homelessness*, behave in notably bizarre or unusual ways, the label of "mental illness" tars the entire population with a very broad brush. (p. 77)

Jencks (1995) makes yet another important contribution to our understanding of the homeless problem. He attempts to synthesize much of what has been discussed and learned about this population. In this analysis, Jencks tries to show that the most common reasons cited for the increases in homelessness, specifically the deinstitutionalization of the mentally ill, the lack of adequate housing, and the shift in the economy, all have had a limited effect in explaining the rise in the homeless population. Rather, he argues, the role of drugs and alcohol are more important factors in understanding the nature of the problem.

Jencks echoes Blau's point on deinstitutionalization of the mentally ill as a causal factor in the growth of the homeless population, but does so in a more elaborate way. As he argues, the hospitalization rates for mental illness began to fall in the late 1950s not the late 1970s or early 1980s. It seems unlikely that it would have the kind of impact many people think it had. In reality, he contends, deinstitutionalization was not a single policy but a series of them, all of which tried to reduce the number of hospitalized patients and accomplished this by moving patients to different places. Jencks argues that the policies implemented before 1975 worked, the ones after that did not.

Prior to 1975, a number of programs and events took place that led to the release of many formerly institutionalized patients. These changes include a recognition on the part of the psychiatric community that hospitalization was a counterproductive measure. This resulted in the release of any patient that could be cared for as an out-patient and if a patient was hospitalized, they were to be released as soon as possible. The second event was the development of drugs to treat schizophrenia, specifically Thorazine. These drugs made it much easier to treat patients outside the institution rather than in it.

The third event was the creation of several federally funded programs that gave patients the economic resources to survive as out-patients, specifically Medicaid and Supplemental Security Income (SSI). Medicaid paid for outpatient treatment but not hospitalization, and SSI was available for those who were incapable of holding a job because of a physical or mental disability. These programs led to the release of many people suffering from mental disorders but provided them with a means by which to continue their treatment and to maintain their economic viability without being hospitalized.

Jencks argues that after 1975 advocates of deinstitutionalization set out to end the use of involuntary commitment by hospitals. Focusing on the subjectivity of diagnoses as well as the legal authority of physicians to commit anyone to an institution, many sought legal avenues to end what they thought was a rather arbitrary practice. Many politicians pressured state hospitals to reduce their budgets due to an overall concern about rising taxes. As a result, most hospitals closed their psychiatric wards and discharged the remaining chronic patients. States compounded the problem by cutting their benefits to the mentally ill. Then the Reagan administration tightened the eligibility standards for disability benefits. The cumulative effect of these events was that many individuals who suffered from serious mental disorders were left to the street without adequate funds to support themselves.

Another important point Jencks identifies is the introduction of crack cocaine into the homelessness equation. While alcohol abuse has been, and continues to be, a pervasive feature of homelessness, crack became the newest and most problematic coping mechanism for the homeless: it was cheap and produced an intense high. Crack made dealing with the problems of being homeless less painful and could be accomplished more cheaply than even a half-pint of whiskey. While few researchers will argue that crack has not made a significant impact on the population, the debate begins when some contend that addiction to the drug causes homelessness. As with the problems relating to mental illness, drug use can be viewed as a cause or a consequence of homelessness. Homeless people could be using crack because they are homeless or the other way around. While Jencks does not conclusively state this, the implication is that heavy drug use causes homelessness, although indirectly. By being addicted to crack, for example, he argues that the person is less employable, uses money earmarked for other expenses, and causes their friends and relatives to be less inclined to provide them with a place to stay. Jencks also seems to be saying that while we may not have the definitive answer about its causal properties, he does contend that crack use perpetuates a person's homeless status.

Finally, Congress recently passed a Welfare Reform bill, which, among other things, curtails the length of time a person (or family) is eligible for benefits and prohibits teenage mothers from receiving them at all. Many service providers, advocates for the homeless, and experts on homelessness, have expressed grave concern about these changes in that they could push many individuals and families, who are on the brink of being homeless, into the shelters or the streets. Many agencies are already witnessing evidence of this prediction. While the evidence is preliminary and far from conclusive, somewhat ironically, one of the newest causes of homelessness may be a policy designed to alleviate dependency on the government.

While the causes of homelessness, as well as their solutions, will remain controversial, there are a few studies that focus on some of the more important, but obscure aspects of homelessness. Liebow (1993) for instance, has examined the struggles of homeless women. While not empirically rigorous, this study, building on the sociological traditions of symbolic interactionism, attempts to document the particular difficulties homeless women encounter, as well as the ways in which they cope with those problems. In chronicling the lives of these women, Liebow captures the essence of the boredom many of them wrestle with; the practical problems of survival, such as storing one's possessions, meeting one's health care needs, especially since many of them suffer from various ailments; and obtaining adequate sleep without being victimized by others. Liebow refers to these daily struggles as the "little murders of everyday life." Other problems include obtaining and keeping a job, transportation, and the sentiment that life is much easier on welfare. This is especially true because the jobs for which they are eligible usually do not have any medical or retirement benefits. This says nothing about trying to keep their families intact. It is a moving and, at the same time, chilling account of the lives of a forgotten people.

While the research on the problems and causes of homelessness continue, we must also attempt to understand how and in what ways the homeless are perceived by the majority of society. From a sociological point of view, one way to grasp the implications of this is to view homelessness as a form of deviance. The explanation of homelessness then, in many ways, can be found in the literature on deviance, specifically the labeling perspective. In sum, the societal reaction to this group as a stigmatized segment of our society leads to numerous problems for these individuals and, at the same time, offers us a glimpse of the future of this population and their role in American society.

The Labeling Perspective and Homelessness

The essence of the labeling perspective is that deviance does not exist independent of the negative reaction of people who condemn it. Behaviors are never weird, bad, sick, or deviant in themselves. They are deviant only because someone or some group responds to them in this fashion. In his classic text *The Outsiders*, Howard Becker (1963) states,"Deviance is not a quality of the act a person commits but rather a consequence of the application by others of rules and sanctions to an offender. The deviant is one to whom the label has successfully been applied; deviant behavior is behavior that people so label" (p. 9).

Labeling theory has a different focus from the variety of theoretical explanations of deviance. Labeling theorists are not interested in the causal factors that lead an individual to commit a deviant or criminal act. Rather, labeling theory has pursued three interrelated concerns: the social historical development of deviant labels; the application of labels to certain types of people in specific times and places; and the symbolic and practical consequences of the labeling process.

The Roots of the Labeling Perspective

Although it was not until the 1960s that this perspective of deviance emerged as a major theoretical tradition, its intellectual origins can be traced to a 1928 essay by George Herbert Mead in "The Psychology of Punitive Justice." In it he says that the labeling process sets boundaries between those who are acceptable and those who are condemned. This essay describes the ways in which labels are applied. In a similar vein, in 1938 Frank Tannenbaum used the term "tagging" to describe a like process in his book *Crime and the Community*. He says,

> The process of making the criminal is a process of tagging, defining, identifying, segregating, describing, emphasizing, making conscious and self-conscious; it becomes a way of stimulating, suggesting, emphasizing, and evoking the very traits that are complained of. The person becomes the thing he is described as being. Nor does it seem to matter whether the valuation is made by those who would punish or by those who would reform. In either case, the emphasis is upon the conduct that is disapproved of. The parents or the policeman, the older brother or the court, the probation officer or the juvenile institution, insofar as they rest on the thing complained of, rest upon a false ground. Their very enthusiasm defeats their aim. The harder they work to reform the evil, the greater the evil grows under their hands. The persistent suggestion, with whatever good intentions, works mischief, because it leads to bringing out the bad behavior it would suppress. The way out is through a refusal to dramatize evil. The less said about it the better. (pp. 19–20)

Therefore, according to Tannenbaum, the stigma accompanying the deviant label may drive people deeply into the realm of nonconformity.

The early ideas of Mead and Tannenbaum were elaborated by Edwin Lemert in his 1951 classic *Social Pathology*. Lemert argued that other perspectives of deviance failed to examine the implications of being labeled. He argued that deviance should be seen "as behavior which is effectively disapproved of in social interaction" (p. 17). Perhaps most important, Lemert is responsible for the development of one of the most fundamental distinctions made by the labeling perspective: primary and secondary deviance. He states,

> Primary deviation is assumed to arise in a wide variety of social, cultural, and psychological contexts, and at best has only marginal implication for the psychic structure of the individual; it does not lead to symbolic reorganization at the level of self-regarding attitudes and social roles. Secondary deviation is deviant behavior or social roles based upon it, which becomes a means of defense, attack or adaptation to the overt and covert problems created by the societal reaction to primary deviation. (p. 17)

For Lemert, primary deviance is the type of deviant behavior that is trivial, explained away, or otherwise dealt with as part of a socially acceptable role. Should this change, the person may step into a deviant role. This role and the definition of oneself are affected by several factors: how much deviance the person engages in, how visible such acts are to the community, and how aware the deviant is of their reaction. If the answers to these questions are positive, then the person will see himself or herself very differently and will have difficulty holding onto his or her past self-image.

The person will have to choose new roles that may be more deviant. This is what is referred to as patterned or *secondary deviance*. Lemert sees this as an outgrowth of a long process, a relationship between the person's behavior and the society's reaction to it. Thus, while people may initially deviate for any number of reasons, once one is caught and labeled, the reaction to deviance may cause further problems for that individual.

The Application of Labels

According to the labeling perspective, the most crucial step in the development of a stable pattern of deviant behavior is usually the experience of being caught and publicly labeled deviant. Whether this happens to a person depends not so much on what the person does but on what other people do. Erikson (1966) expands on this. He states:

> The community's decision to bring deviant sanctions against the individual . . . is a sharp rite of transition at once moving him out of his normal position in society and transferring him into a distinctive deviant role. The ceremonies which accomplish this change of status, ordinarily, have three related phases. They provide a formal confrontation between the deviant suspect and representatives of his community (as in the criminal trial or psychiatric case conference); they announce some judgment about the nature of his deviancy (a verdict or diagnosis for example); and they perform an act of social placement, assigning him to a special role (like that of a prisoner or patient) which redefines his position in society. (p. 43)

Once a person is stigmatized by being labeled a deviant, a self-fulfilling prophecy occurs, with others perceiving and responding to the person as a deviant. Further, once people are publicly processed as deviants, they are typically forced into a deviant group. As Lemert (1951) contends, once this happens the larger community will anticipate the worst from the person and will take steps to protect itself. This will make it difficult for the individual to reintegrate himself or herself into society.

Labeling theory also describes how deviance becomes a person's master status. While people have many statuses, the master status is the one that dominates and plays an important part in a person's social identity. In our society, one's occupation usually serves as the master status. However, once people are labeled, this changes and the stigma becomes their dominant status and they may encounter serious obstacles with other people.

Labeling Physical Characteristics as Deviant

The writings of Erving Goffman liken social interaction to the performance of theatrical roles. Like actors on a stage, people are said to carefully manage social cues that enable them to create and sustain an impression of who they are and what they are up to. Some people, however, are cast into roles that constrain their abilities to manage positive impressions of themselves. Such persons are stigmatized, the bearers of what Goffman (1963) describes as a "spoiled identity."

Goffman parallels the stigmatized problems of labeled deviants to the plight of physically or mentally handicapped persons. He extends the scope of the labeling perspective to people who are negatively labeled for how they appear in addition to how they may act. The threat of stigmatization does not, however, eliminate a person's capacity for "impression management." Stigmatized persons who are savvy may restrict the flow of information about themselves to others they can trust.

Goffman's work raises an interesting point: whether they are successful in managing stigma, labeled deviants are confronted with social problems not faced by the "straight" world. This underscores a central theme of the labeling perspective: a full sociological understanding of deviance requires us to identify the dynamic between people who condemn nonconformity and those who commit it. We take for granted that appearances represent something deeper, that they tell us about who the person is and why the person is behaving in a particular way. This allows us to neatly package an individual into a stereotype that is reflective of their current label. Moreover, we are then able to assess the individual's past, present, and future behavior in light of this new label. This is something Edwin Schur (1971) refers to as *retrospective interpretation.*

In summary, the labeling perspective has focused its attention on the societal attributes of those who react and those who are reacted against to explain why certain persons and not others are labeled as deviant. They argue that once a person has been labeled a deviant, and particularly if that person has passed through a *status degradation ceremony* (Garfinkel 1956) and forced to become a member of a deviant group, the person experiences a profound and often irreversible change. He or she has not only acquired an inferior status, but has also developed a deviant world view and the knowledge and skills that go with it.

Consequences of Labeling

One of the more interesting questions regarding the labeling perspective is whether or not a deviant label can be removed. Theoretically, once individuals have paid their debt to society, the label is removed. However, in practice, these individuals are still presented with a host of obstacles that limit their ability to navigate the social landscape. While removal of the label depends to some extent on the seriousness of the offense, the long term consequences cannot be minimized. Some sociologists argue that the label can never be removed, at best it can be transformed or minimized.

For instance, some people might contend that the deviant can relocate and begin a new life with a new identity. This argument fails to appreciate that the label can reassert itself if the deviant is recognized in his or her new environment. It is at this point that the consequences and problems return. Others contend that a label can be removed based on what the individual does after being labeled. This has sometimes been referred to as "legitimating the ex-status." In other words, the individual uses the label to help others (as in the case of a drug addict who gives lectures to elementary school children about the evils of drug use or who becomes a rehabilitation counselor at a drug treatment facility).

Still others contend that if society changes its view on the particular behavior, then the label is removed. For instance, if a certain type of behavior is viewed as a medical problem or disease, such as alcoholism, then the person's responsibility for committing those acts is diminished. This is often referred to as the *medicalization of deviance* (Conrad and Schneider 1980). Another example occurs when society alters its moral compass and no longer looks on the behavior as deviant. However, in each of these examples the label is not removed, it is transformed. A change in morality is highly unlikely and even in those instances in which it has occurred (e.g., Prohibition), individuals who were considered criminal are still viewed in that way.

Some sociologists contend that while removal may not be possible, recovery from the label can occur. The following factors are said to be most important in determining whether an individual can recover from the label: the seriousness of the act, the more serious the less likely they are able to recover; temporal factors, how much time has passed between committing the act and the current situation; and behavioral factors (e.g., what the individual has done since committing the act) (see for instance McNamara, Ramey, and Henry 1994). However, even this strategy has its limitations. In short, it seems unlikely that a deviant label can be removed once it is affixed.

The labeling process has profound consequences for individuals. Our society tends to be rather unforgiving in its treatment of deviants irrespective of what they do to reintegrate themselves into society. We tend to be quick to affix labels, so it is easy to see how problematic this can become for certain segments of our society.

Labeling and Homelessness

The labeling perspective offers a compelling explanation of homelessness in American society. Becoming homeless is a clearly stigmatized status and the consequences, or the societal reaction to this label, are found not only in the reactions of individuals on the street and their attitudes toward this group of people, but in the increasing number of laws that attempt to curtail the behavior of the homeless as well. For instance, some cities have tried to eliminate the homeless problem by providing one-way plane or bus tickets out of town (see for instance Johnson 1988). Other cities have passed laws against sleeping outdoors, on beaches, benches, or other public property (National Law Center 1995), while still others have made rummaging through garbage a criminal offense (National Law Center). There are other, more subtle instances of keeping the homeless at length. While police crackdowns are a normal strategy to rid the homeless from a particular area, especially during highly publicized events (see for instance McNamara 1994b, 1994c), in 1991, long before the refurbishing and stepped up law enforcement efforts inside, the custodial staff used chemicals such as ammonia on the floor of Grand Central Terminal to prevent the homeless from sleeping there (Stein 1988; Kifner 1991).

One of the best examples of the labeling effect of the homeless was a study conducted by the National Law Center in 1994 and 1995. In *No Homeless People Allowed* (National Law Center 1994) the Center identified instances of local government actions designed to target the homeless population in forty-two cities. These laws included restrictions on the use of public spaces, prohibitions or limits on begging, and selectiveness in enforcing local ordinances against the homeless. Santa Monica, California's ordinances prohibit sleeping in public spaces and are designed to force the homeless out of the city. Similarly, Seattle attempts to keep the homeless away from its downtown area by not allowing homeless people to sit in public places. This was accomplished through a liberal interpretation of its laws on trespassing. In 1996, in anticipation of the summer Olympics, Atlanta used a variety of ordinances against the homeless to "clean" the streets, such as a ban on "remaining" in a parking lot for an extended period of time (National Law Center 1995).

Other municipalities have attempted to rid themselves of the homeless by limiting organizations and agencies that provide services to this population. For instance, Roseville, California refused to open its armory as a shelter during the winter as it had for the previous six years although there would be no cost charged to the city. At the same time, the city issued citations to individuals living in public places. Finally, the city made a concerted effort to discard the property and eject homeless people from informal camps (National Law Center 1995). Other cities, such as Huntsville, Alabama and Cleveland, Ohio, have used zoning laws to prevent shelters or single room occupancy hotels from being established or built.

This latter strategy has become so pervasive that the National Law Center (1995) has conducted another study in thirty-six jurisdictions across the country of governmental opposition to service providers for the homeless. In this study, sixty-one examples of such action were cited including the termination of some proposed projects, closing existing facilities, or requiring existing operations to relocate. The study cites that the most common means by which cities attempt to exclude the homeless from their communities is through zoning and building code changes. In approximately half of the cases analyzed, changes were made in zoning regulations to exclude a particular provider.

This trend of communities not wanting to accept responsibility for the homeless population in their area is sometimes referred to as *Nimbyism* (Not-In-My-Backyard). Proponents of Nimbyism contend that shelters and other facilities may attract homeless people from other jurisdictions (sometimes referred to as the *magnet theory*); cause property values and business activity to decline, resulting in an increase in crime, especially those considered nuisance crimes (see for instance McNamara 1994a); and contribute to an overall decline in the quality of life in a given community (National Law Center 1995). While much of these assertions are inaccurate or typically do not have this intended effect, particularly the magnet theory, the public's perception of the problem remains unwavering.

Although Nimbyism occurs on the local level, there is widespread support for this perspective. There are a number of bills before Congress that could support these local efforts (National Law Center 1995). For instance, there is a House-Senate Budget Reconciliation Bill that would completely repeal an essential element of the Stewart B. McKinney Homeless Assistance Act (National Law Center).

The societal reaction to the homeless is increasingly becoming negative and there is a clearly defined stigmatization to this segment of our population. Consequently, the issues and ideas raised by the labeling perspective offer us a more thorough understanding of the problems encountered by this group as well as the ways in which the construction of rules influences the identification and subsequent treatment of a deviant group in our society.

References

Bassuk, E., and L. Rubin. 1987. "Homeless Children: A Neglected Population." *American Journal of Orthopsychiatry* 57(2): 279–286.

Becker, H. 1963. *The Outsiders.* New York: The Free Press.

Blau, J. 1992. *The Visible Poor.* New York: Oxford University Press.

City of New York: Human Resources Administration. 1984. Report: *The Homeless in New York City Shelters.*

———. 1982. Report: *Chronic and Situational Dependency.*

Conrad, P., and J. W. Schneider. 1980. *Deviance and Medicalization: From Madness to Sickness.* St. Louis, MO: C.V. Mosby.

Erikson, K. 1966. *Wayward Puritans.* New York: MacMillan.

Garfinkel, H. 1956. "Conditions of Successful Degradation Ceremonies." *American Journal of Sociology* 61: 420–424.

Goffman, E. 1963. *Stigma: Notes on the Management of a Spoiled Identity.* New York: Simon and Schuster.

Hombs, M. E., and M. Snyder. 1982. *Homelessness in America: A Forced March to Nowhere.* Washington, D.C.: Community on Creative Non-Violence.

Institute of Medicine. 1988. *Homelessness, Health, and Human Needs.* Washington, D.C.: National Academy Press.

Jencks, C. 1995. *The Homeless.* Cambridge, MA: Harvard University Press.

Johnson, S. 1988. "Homeless Get Tickets to Leave." *New York Times,* November 20.

Kifner, J. 1991. "New York Closes Park to Homeless." *New York Times,* June 4.

Kozol, J. 1988. *Rachel and Her Children.* New York: Crown.

Lemert, E. 1951. *Social Pathology.* New York: McGraw-Hill.

Liebow, E. 1993. *Tell Them Who I Am.* New York: Penguin.

McNamara, R. P., D. Ramey, and L. Henry (eds.). 1994. *Managing a Deviant Status: Field Research and the Labeling Perspective.* New York: Cummings and Hathaway.

———. 1994a. "Urban Redevelopment and the Social Ecology of New York City's Times Square." In Kristy M. McNamara and Robert McNamara (eds.), *The Urban Landscape: Selected Readings.* New York: University Press of America, pp. 211–230.

——— (eds.). 1994b. *Crime Displacement: The Other Side of Prevention.* New York: Cummings and Hathaway.

———. 1994c. *The Times Square Hustler: Male Prostitution in New York City.* Westport, CT: Praeger.

Mead, G. H. 1928. "The Psychology of Punitive Justice." *American Journal of Sociology* 23: 577–602.

Merton, R. K. 1953. *Social Theory and Social Structure.* Glencoe, New York: The Free Press.

National Law Center. 1994. *No Homeless People Allowed.* Washington, D.C.: National Law Center.

National Law Center. 1995. *No Room for the Inn.* Washington, D.C.: National Law Center on Homelessness and Poverty.

Pilivian, I., M. Sosin, and H. Westerfelt. 1988. *Conditions Contributing to Long-Term Homelessness—An Exploratory Study.* Madison, WI: University of Wisconsin Institute for Research on Poverty.

Rossi, P. 1989. *Down and Out in America.* Chicago: University of Chicago Press.

Schur, E. 1971. *Labeling Deviant Behavior: Its Sociological Implications.* New York: Harper and Row.

Schutt, R. 1988. *Boston's Homeless.* Boston, MA: University of Massachusetts Press.

Silverstein, K. 1994. "Homelessness Commands Attention." *American City and County*, p. 10.

Snow, D., and L. Anderson. 1995. *Down on Their Luck.* Belmont, CA: University of California Press.

State of Ohio: Department of Mental Health. 1985. *Homeless in Ohio: A Study of People in Need.*

Stein, S. 1988. "Bypass Beggars, Koch Urges." *New York Newsday*, August 10.

Tannenbaum, F. 1938. *Crime and the Community.* New York: McGraw-Hill.

White, R. 1992. *Rude Awakenings: What the Homeless Crisis Tells Us.* San Francisco, CA: Institute for Contemporary Studies.

Wilson, W. J. 1987. *The Truly Disadvantaged.* Chicago: University of Chicago Press.

Wright, J., and J. Devine. 1995. "Housing Dynamics of the Homeless: Implications for a Count." *American Journal of Orthopsychiatry* 65(3): 320–328.

Article Review Form at end of book.

Do you think that the change in family structure is due to the drop in family income, as the reading suggests? How does the "problem of work" contribute to poverty? Are you surprised that the majority of those on welfare are also working? Do you think that improving the labor market would reduce welfare expenses?

The Problem of Poverty, the Problem of Work

Joel F. Handler
University of California at Los Angeles

Joel F. Handler argues that trying to solve the problem of welfare dependency by requiring that welfare mothers go to work is doomed to failure. Structural changes in the economy have reduced the number of low-skill jobs, as well as their salaries. Job-training programs have a notorious record of failure, and the availability and costs of childcare are problems that those wanting welfare mothers to work usually ignore. Rising poverty rates are not a function of rising welfare rolls, rather it is the other way around. As a society, we should be concentrating our efforts on how to reduce poverty, not welfare benefits.

The contemporary consensus on work as the solution to welfare dependency was forced when the liberals switched positions recently. Liberals have consistently argued that welfare mothers should be treated the same as nonwelfare mothers, and now that the majority of nonwelfare mothers are in the paid labor force, they argue that it is reasonable to expect welfare mothers to do the same.

There are a number of problems with the new liberal position. First, nonwelfare mothers work by choice and can choose to be man-dependent; although this may seem a little curious today, there is no stigma or sanction. Welfare recipients do not have this choice. Second, we know from twenty-five years' experience that setting the poor to work is expensive and extremely problematic administratively; this should give us pause before we embrace another "new solution." Third, given child care problems, health care issues, school problems, bad neighborhoods, and so forth, it is questionable how young children and adolescents will fare when their mothers have to work enough hours to achieve self-sufficiency. As with nonwelfare mothers, these decisions should be left to the individual families. Related, and fourth, perhaps we ought to rethink the value of mother-provided child care and concentrate on better ways of supporting families so that they can make decisions based on their needs.

Although I think that these are important arguments and will return to them shortly. I wish to make a different one: The way the debate is framed is "welfare" as contrasted with "work" is obsolete and counterproductive . . .

The Problem of Poverty

Concerns about welfare dependency cluster around two issues—family values and the work ethic. Included in discussions of family values are concerns that men aren't supporting mothers and children; mothers aren't marrying; and children aren't cared for—they suffer from ill health, poor nutrition, bad parenting, and dangerous neighborhoods. Children growing up in these families fail to make successful transitions to adulthood, and the cycle is repeated. The standard euphemism is "counter-culture poverty." The image, often unspoken, is the black ghetto "underclass."

These concerns are real. Large numbers of children and youth are suffering and are at great risk of not becoming successful adults. But the root problem is poverty, and this is much

Joel F. Handler, "The Problem of Poverty, the Problem of Work" from *The Poverty of Welfare Reform* (New Haven: Yale University Press, 1995), pp. 32–35. Footnotes have been deleted.

larger than welfare. To discuss this, we need some numbers. The most convenient way to talk about poverty is to use the federal poverty line. The poverty line, established in 1955, is calculated on what a family would need to spend on a minimally adequate diet and then multiplied by three. It was, and is, an austere budget. The dollar amount is adjusted for inflation but does not include noncash benefits, such as food stamps, housing subsidies, and Medicaid. In 1993, the poverty line for a family of four was $14,763.

The federal poverty line is controversial. Conservatives argue that noncash benefits ought to be included, thus lowering the line; liberals claim that housing costs now take a far larger share of a family's budget and that the line should be raised. Although it is still convenient to use the official line—which will be used here—it must be recognized that it is very low. Most Americans, according to a Gallup poll conducted in 1989, think that a family of four needs about $16,000 a year to get by.

According to the official poverty line, more than 39 million Americans live in poverty. In 1989, moreover, 38 percent of the poor, or 14 million Americans, reported income of less than *one-half* the poverty line. Now, it is true that this is *reported* income, but still, 14 million people are very poor. The poverty line is an arbitrary cut-off; by definition, it excludes millions of people whose incomes are technically above the line but who nevertheless live on the margin—the "near poor." They lack education and training and work at insecure jobs without health insurance or other benefits. There is insufficient quality day care. At about 150 percent of the poverty line, roughly $21,000 for a family of four, there are more than 30 million people, including 6 million full-time and 5.5 million part-time workers. At this income level there is barely enough for the lowest-cost necessities such as food, housing, clothing, transportation, and medical care, and nothing at all for what better-off Americans take for granted—meals out, vacations, child-care, lessons or allowances for children, haircuts, and so on.

Whatever figures one uses—the near poor or the official poor—the welfare population is considerably smaller. The number of people on welfare in 1993 stood at 13.6 million. This is a lot of people, but it is only about a third of the poverty population. Another way, of looking at relative size is to consider child poverty. The 13.6 million on welfare includes 9.2 million children. But almost 22 percent of all children, or 14.3 million, are living in families below the poverty line, and this is an increase of nearly 1 million since 1990.

The reason for these large and increasing numbers of poor people is that family income has deteriorated significantly. Between 1973 and 1990, the median income declined almost a third for families headed by parents under age thirty. Although the problem is most acute for single-parent families, most two-parent families have been able to maintain their relative position only if both parents work. In fact, there is a growing trend for one of these two earners to now hold two jobs. Seven million Americans, or 6 percent of the work force, hold 15 million jobs. Most multiple job holders are married, and, increasingly, as many of them are women as are men. No other country approaches these numbers of multiple jobholders. The reason, according to Richard Freeman, is that wages from one job are sufficient in other countries. Today, the majority (61 percent) of children have mothers who are in the paid labor force; moreover, these mothers are working longer hours—over 30 percent more than a decade ago.

Family structure has changed dramatically during the past two decades. Although most children still live in two-parent families, the number of single-parent households, mostly female-headed, has grown significantly, and they now account for about 25 percent of all children. Single-parent households are much more likely to be poor than two-parent households. Although female-headed households represent about 10 percent of the population, they account for more than a third of the poverty population and more than half of the increase in poverty since 1990. Almost three-quarters of all children in single-parent households will experience at least some poverty while they are growing up. For African-American children, the poverty spell will be extended. Because almost all of these single parents are women, gender discrimination limits their ability to earn a living. In spite of women's participation in the labor market, the economic circumstances of a family decline after divorce primarily because of a lack of child support. It is thus no surprise that single parents are twice as likely as married couples to be worried about, "making ends meet" and concerned that their children will "get beat up," "get pregnant," "not get a job," or "drop out of school."

Two-parent households will not necessarily escape poverty. In most poor households, there is only partial employment or unemployment, but even in families with two wage earners, a fifth remain poor. In these poor households, fewer than half of the unemployed workers receive unemployment compensation, and jobs found after unemployment usually pay, on average, about a third less than previous jobs. David Ellwood thinks that because many of the full-time working poor families fail to qualify for benefits, such as Medicaid, they may be actually the poorest of the poor.

Although low income is not the exclusive cause of family behavior, the fact remains that poverty is the most powerful predictor of the harmful behavioral consequences we ascribe to welfare families. As Sara McLanahan and Gary Sandefur [note], low income or income loss is the single most important factor in accounting for the lower achievement of children in single-parent families. It accounts for half of the difference in educational achievement, weak labor force attachment, and early childbearing. Not surprisingly, parents in these families suffer more emotionally and are more anxious about their children's future than better-off parents. Poor families are more likely to disintegrate and become single-parent households, and single parents, in turn, are less likely to engage in "good" parenting practices. Even allowing for the problems of official reporting, the highest incidence of child neglect and abuse and the most severe injuries to children occur in the poorest families. Economic instability and hardship and social stress among adults is related to marital conflict and harsh and inconsistent punishment, rejection, and noninvolvement. Brain dysfunctions, caused by exposure to lead, injuries from abuse, or mothers' substance abuse—all highly correlated with poverty—interfere with language and cognitive development resulting in learning and social problems at school. Early school failure, in turn, is one of the strongest predictors of adolescent problems, including violent behavior. It is not surprising that children growing up in poor families are more likely to suffer from poor physical and mental health problems, do poorly at school, and compromise successful development by early sex, pregnancy, substance abuse, delinquency, and crime.

Education is a crucial determinant of future employment, and low income (income less than 150 percent of the poverty line) seriously affects educational achievement. Poor children attend schools of inferior quality; they cannot afford after-school enrichment activities; and their parents are both likely to have lower expectations and less likely to be involved with their schooling and to invest in themselves. When income is controlled, school dropout rates are fairly similar regardless of race. Approximately the same percentages of white, black, and Latino students will have neither a high school diploma nor a general equivalency diploma by the time they reach twenty-four. And people without a high school degree or its equivalent are severely disadvantaged in an already difficult job market.

Because there is such a high correlation between poverty and single-parent households, it is hard to separate out the effects of each disadvantage. It's a case of double jeopardy, for both the parents and the children. As Uri Bronfenbrenner summarizes it, the developmental risks associated with a one-parent family structure are relatively small in comparison with those involved in two other types of environmental contexts. The first and most destructive of these is poverty. Because many single-parent families are also poor, parents and their children are in double jeopardy. But even when two parents are present, in households living under stressful economic and social conditions, processes of parent-child interaction and environmentally oriented child activity are more difficult to initiate and sustain.

To be sure, when the mother, or some other adult committed to the child's well-being, does manage to establish and maintain a pattern of progressive reciprocal interaction, the disruptive impact of poverty on development is significantly reduced. But, among the poor, the proportion of parents who, despite their stressful life circumstances, are able to provide quality care is, under present circumstances, not very large. And even for this minority, the parents' buffering power begins to decline sharply by the time children are five or six years old and exposed to impoverished and disruptive settings outside the home.

One important risk for adolescent deviant behavior is parents leaving kids alone. Understandably, overloaded single parents are more likely to give their children more autonomy. It is estimated that the average parent spends eleven fewer hours per week with his or her children than in 1960; less than 5 percent of families have another adult, such as a grandparent, living in the house to relieve the burden. As a result, children are increasingly on their own. The National Commission on Children estimated in 1991 that 1.3 million children aged five to fourteen are on their own after school. This is important to bear in mind when employment and work requirements are being discussed.

The risk of a poor outcome is increased when the parent is a teenager. The children of these parents are even more likely to do poorly in school and to engage in compromising behaviors. Again, it is hard to separate the effects of teen parenting from low income. There are some differences between white and black teenage mothers. Whereas white teenage mothers are more likely to marry, black teenage mothers are more likely to live in an extended household. Although black teenage mothers stay longer on welfare, they are also more likely to graduate from high school.

A recent synthesis of research on adolescents at risk conducted by a panel of the National Research Council concluded [that] the combination of financial insecurity for an increasing proportion of families, increased work effort by parents seeking to maintain their living standard, and the demographic changes that have so dramatically increased the number of children and adolescents living in single-parent households result in increasing numbers of adolescents who do not receive the nurturance necessary for positive development. The consequences are not inescapably negative. Indeed, the majority of adolescents—even those from poor and single parent homes—do succeed despite the obstacles. However, the adverse outcomes—the failure rates—are unacceptably and unnecessarily high.

The problems attributed to welfare are, in reality, the problems of poverty. Large numbers of parents are working yet not escaping poverty. This is especially true for the growing number of single parents. Why is this happening and what implications does this have for moving single mothers from welfare to work?

The Problem of Work

If the problem is poverty, and the vast majority of the poor are working and not on welfare, then what is the problem of work? Several studies on the growing inequality of earnings have all reached a similar conclusion—namely, that the real earnings of the less skilled, less educated workers have declined substantially since 1973. This decline, moreover, occurred during a period of economic expansion and aggregate growth in employment. In 1973, men with one to three years of high school had a median income of $24,079 (in 1989 dollars); in 1989, the median was $14,439. Men with a high school diploma saw income drop from $30,252 to $21,650. In 1973, women with one to three years of high school had a median income of $7,920; by 1989, the median was $6,752. Women with a high school degree had a median income of $11,087 in 1973 and $10,439 in 1989. Furthermore, the decline in income was not because of the shift in jobs from manufacturing to service; real wages declined in both sectors.

Overall, wages for less skilled women have not declined as men's wages. The primary reason, according to Rebecca Blank, is that less skilled women are in occupations and industries that have not suffered such severe wage declines. However, although men's and women's wages are now closer, women still earn substantially less. For example, women who have not graduated from high school earn less than 60 percent of similarly situated men.

With the decline in real wages, the poverty rate of full-time workers is increasing. According to the latest figures, in 1992, 18 percent of full-time workers earned less than the poverty line, which is a 50 percent increase over the past thirteen years. The poverty rate of full-time workers increased for both men and women but was particularly steep for those without a high school degree. For men without a high school degree, the poverty rate rose from 15 percent in 1979 to 32 percent in 1992—and this is for full-time workers. It is not surprising that over the past two decades, there has been a steady decline in work among men in families in the bottom fifth of the income distribution (earning less than $12,497 in 1989). Although the expansion of low-wage (below poverty-level) jobs affected all workers, it was greatest for minorities. Between 1979 and 1987, the proportion of African Americans in these jobs increased from 33.9 to 40.6 percent, for Latinos from 31.7 to 42.1 percent, and for whites from 24.3 to 29.3 percent

Not only have earnings declined, but so has employment for both high school graduates and dropouts. Although the unemployment rate for all workers was roughly the same in 1974 as it was in 1988, it doubled for these two groups. It is this combination—declining real earnings and rising unemployment—that has resulted in increasing poverty among these young families. They simply cannot work their way out of poverty.

The low-income employment rates of married women increased over these two decades. It is important to note, however, that higher proportions of single women, even with children, work more than married women, with or without children. Almost half (48.3 percent) of poor, single mothers work, as compared to 29.8 percent of married women without children and 39.9 percent with children. But the most important point is that earnings for these groups has fallen because real wages have declined.

The future does not look good for the less-skilled worker. First, sectoral shifts in employment have meant a decline in manufacturing opportunities for this group. Wages in the service sector are lower, but skill levels are higher. Second, although unemployment rates in general have stabilized, younger, less educated, and especially black workers are the last to be hired and the first to be fired. For both men and women, unemployment rates are considerably higher for people of color than for whites. Third, although the impact of immigration varies throughout the nation, there has been a large overall increase in less educated immigrants, which has contributed to the shrinking labor market for high school dropouts.

A decline in union membership has meant a loss of higher wage jobs. The minimum wage has declined significantly in real terms. At $4.25 per hour (the rate in 1995), a full-time worker supporting a family of four has earnings that are only two-thirds of the poverty line. Almost 5 million workers are stuck in minimum wage jobs.

Other factors contributing to the bleak picture for the less skilled worker include what is called the "spacial mismatch"—the fact that jobs continue to leave the inner cities for the suburbs. There continues to be discrimination against men and women of color. Empirical research has shown strong prejudices against African Americans who are associated with the culture of the inner cities.

On the supply side, it is often argued that a decline in basic reading and math skills accounts for the decreased earnings of the less educated. Yet earnings for African Americans fell while their test scores and academic achievement rose, and earnings of less educated cohorts fell as they aged. The more likely explanation is that academic skills have not kept pace with job requirements.

Crime, of course, affects employment. It not only provides an attractive alternative for the less educated, especially in the drug trade, but is also a disqualification for legitimate employment. In any event, as we know, the number of young, less educated—especially African-American—males who are involved in the criminal justice system is staggering.

Continued levels of unemployment exacerbate the problems of the less educated worker. Of the workers who lost their jobs in 1988, 78 percent were re-employed by 1990. However, 60 percent had been jobless for five or more weeks, almost 10 percent were still unemployed, and just over 12 percent were no longer in the work force. Many displaced workers suffered earnings losses when they were rehired. A worker's likelihood of being employed depended on the length of time with the previous employer, number of years of school completed, age, gender, and the local unemployment rate. High school dropouts, older workers, women, and minorities were less likely to be re-employed.

Earnings opportunities are seriously affected by household composition. In 1960, about a quarter of female-headed families were poor, now it is more than half (53 percent in 1992). These families are poor because there is typically only one earner, they usually have child care expenses, and women earn less than men, even when they work the same number of hours.

Not only is there the spread of low-wage jobs, but the nature of employment is shifting from full-time work for a single employer to various forms of "contingent" work. Many workers are employed in part-time, temporary, contract, or other types of flexible work arrangements that lack job security. The General Accounting Office estimated that in 1988 there were 32 million contingent workers, accounting for almost a quarter of the work force. The contingent work force grew rapidly in the 1980s and is expected to increase again because new jobs are expected to be almost entirely in the service sector, where contingent employment is most likely to occur. According to the Bureau of Labor Statistics, almost two-thirds of new entrants into the labor force by the year 2000 will be women, and they are more likely than men to hold part-time and temporary jobs. Although most part-time workers are women, men now account for a significant fraction. It is estimated that by the turn of the century, 40 percent of jobs could be part-time.

Part-time work has both positive and negative aspects. At its worst, it is a disguised form of unemployment. It can be good for some workers: it provides additional income, flexible hours, and continued attachment to the labor force for those workers who pursue other activities. With the rapid growth of nontraditional families, many workers are interested in part-time work. This would be true for both single parents and two-earner families with children. In any event, in the 1980s, *involuntary* part-time work grew 13 percent, but 45 percent during the 1980–83 recession. In contrast, voluntary part-time work grew by 19 percent during the decade. More than three-quarters of part-time workers say that they voluntarily choose this status. It is not clear what "voluntary" means as measured by the Bureau of Labor Statistics. The data do not reveal why part-time workers look only for part-time work—for example, child care, transportation, and health costs may operate as constraints. Further, if female heads of households are more constrained than male heads to work part-time, income inequality (and poverty) will increase as the sex distribution of family heads continues to change.

More than a quarter of women work part-time, making them one and a half times more likely to be so employed than the average worker. While women are more likely to *choose* part-time work, they are also more likely to be *stuck* in part-time jobs against their will. The female rate of involuntary part-time work is 44 percent greater than that for men. In any event the real growth in part-time employment has been in involuntary part-time jobs, indicating that employer, not employee, preferences are predominating.

Part-time jobs are more likely to be deadend. Part-time workers keep their jobs for shorter periods than full-time workers. The average job tenure for a part-time worker is 3.4 years, as compared to 5.7 years for full-time working women and 8.1 years for full-time working men. Not only do part-time workers often lack health and pension benefits, but they also receive a lower hourly wage. Controlling for education, gender, and age, part-time workers receive about 40 percent less per hour than full-time workers in the same jobs. Part-time workers are disproportionately in the low-wage distribution, and these workers constitute 65 percent of all people working at or below minimum wage. As a result, families headed by part-time workers are four times more likely to be below the poverty line as compared to families headed by full-time workers. A fifth of families headed by part-time workers are in poverty, and 12 percent also received welfare, as compared to 2 percent of families headed by full-time workers. Again, single-parent families were worse off—40 percent of these families were poor, and 26 percent were on welfare.

The significant portion of employees in part-time work, and the expected proportional growth of this form of employment, indicate that underemployment will continue to be a concern. Hugh Heclo [observes] the [following] effect of low-wages and poverty: In 1990, of the 2 million married couples with children living below the official poverty line, 63 percent of the adults were working at least some of the year, and over a third had work levels approaching the equivalent of full-time work all year. Likewise, half of the 3.7 million poor, single mothers with children worked some of the year, and almost a fifth were in, or close to, full-time, full-year employment. If anything, the adults in such poor families with children were working more in 1990 than in 1975. To define the poverty problem as simply a matter of unmotivated, unfunctional people who need government's tough love to make them seize the opportunities surrounding them is absurd.

This, then, is the labor market for the population we are concerned with—the less educated mother of young children, disproportionately of color: overall declining real wages, increasing education and skill requirements (even more than high school) for the better jobs, and increasing low-wage, part-time jobs without benefits. How does the welfare population match the labor market?

The Welfare Population

The popular stereotype or myth is that welfare is composed primarily of young black women who have lots of children, are long-term dependent, and pass on this dependency from generation to generation. On examination, we find that most welfare recipients are not African American; that few are teenagers, especially young teenagers; that welfare families have about the same number of children or fewer than nonwelfare families; that most are on welfare for relatively short periods; but that most remain quite poor, and this probably accounts for their children being more likely to have welfare spells when they are older as compared to children whose parents did not experience welfare. When we then examine how welfare recipients survive, we find that a great many are most likely already working. They may be working off the books, but they are working. And most work their way off welfare.

In 1993, the total AFDC bill for assistance payments was $22.3 billion; the federal share was $12.2

billion. Although this is not a trivial amount, it is well to keep in mind that AFDC is a small program, in terms of both recipients and budget dollars. The federal Food Stamps program, for example, is twice as big—26.6 million people (10.4 percent of the U.S. population), costing $23 billion in federal funds. The really big programs are the Social Security Retirement and Disability programs, with costs in 1993 of about $419 billion; Medicare, about $143 billion; and Medicaid, $132 billion [see Figure 1].

In 1993, the average monthly family enrollment in AFDC was 5 million, of which 359,000 were in the unemployed parent program. This number is an all-time high and is projected to increase steadily, though at a slower pace, to 5.5 million in 1999. The 5 million families translates into 13,626,000 recipients, of which 9,225,000 were children. This represents about 63 percent of the children in poverty. Adjusting for inflation, the average grant per AFDC recipient in 1970 was $676 per month and $373 in 1993—a 45 percent reduction.

The greatest increases in the AFDC population occurred between 1988 and 1992, when the number of recipients grew from 10.9 million to 13.6 million. Although unemployment rates are clearly responsible for a portion of the increase, they are not the only factor. In some states, unemployment rates declined while AFDC rates rose. In spite of the recent increases, AFDC recipient rates for the total population actually declined by 4.8 percent between 1975 and 1992.

Who are the AFDC recipients?

Most (45 percent) mothers have never married; less than a third (30 percent) are divorced or separated.

Between 1969 and 1992, the average AFDC family size decreased from 4.0 persons to 2.9. In 72.7 percent of the families, there are one or two children. Another 15.5 percent have three children. And there are four or more children in 10.1 percent of the families. The average AFDC family is either about the same size or slightly smaller than the average non-AFDC family.

Very few AFDC mothers are teenagers [see Figure 2]. Teen mothers, of course, are of special concern. Of the 7.6 percent of AFDC recipients who are teen mothers, more than half are 19, more than 80 percent are over 18, more than 90 percent are over 17, and less than 2 percent are 15 or younger. In fact, the rate of teen births was much higher in the Eisenhower years than it is today. What has changed is that the teens are not getting married. Teen pregnancy became a social problem in the 1970s when attention began to be paid to the harmful effects of teen motherhood.

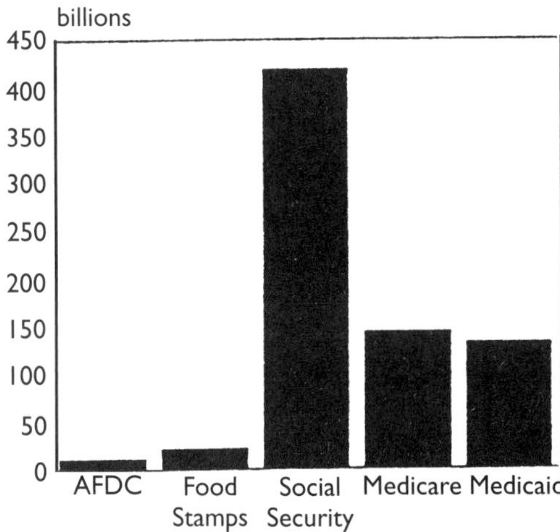

Figure 1. Federal welfare expenditures, 1993.

Whites account for 38.9 percent of the AFDC population, African Americans 37.2 percent, and Latinos 17.8 percent [see Figure 3].

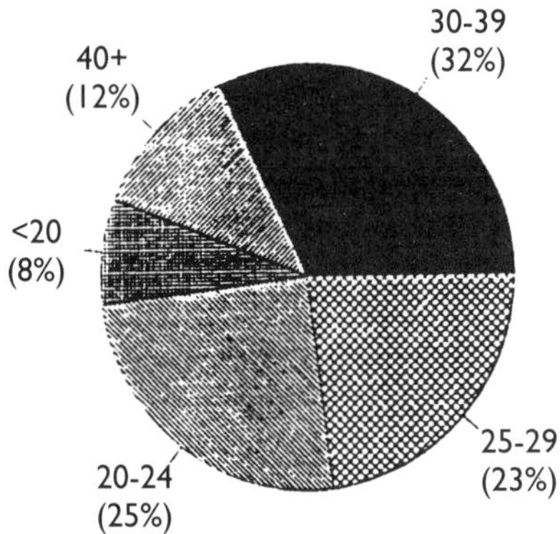

Figure 2. Age of AFDC mothers, 1993.

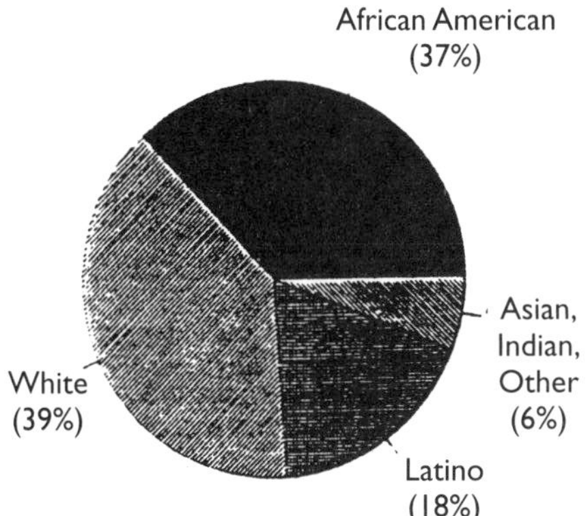

Figure 3. Race of AFDC population, 1993.

About half of the children are younger than six; a quarter are younger than three.

At this point, we have established that AFDC parents are mixed racially, are for the most part in their twenties or thirties, and have about two children, about half of them preschoolers. We turn now to education and welfare spells.

About half of the mothers have not graduated from high school. Only about 10 percent have attended post-secondary school. Only about 1 percent have graduated from college. And most score in the bottom quarter on standardized tests of general aptitude and ability.

How long on welfare? The stereotype behind the current debates on welfare reform is that although some recipients are on welfare for a short time, for most, welfare becomes a "way of life." This commonly held view is perpetuated in part because most empirical studies of AFDC are based on annual data—that is, they seek to answer the question of whether a particular person was on AFDC at some particular point during the year. Even so, based on annual data, half are on welfare for two years or less and 62 percent are on welfare for four years or less. For whites, 44 percent of welfare spells last only one year and 22.8 percent last an additional year; for blacks, the corresponding numbers are 33.7 percent and 16.2 percent [see Figure 4].

Length of time on welfare is only a part of the story. Research based on *monthly* data shows a very dynamic welfare population. Not only do people go on and off welfare, but a significant fraction (about one-third) have more than one spell. It is estimated that during the first year of welfare, half the recipients exit AFDC within one year and about three quarters leave within two years. But many women who leave welfare rapidly also return within the first year. The longer a woman can stay off welfare, the less likely she is to return. Even counting multiple spells, 30 percent are on welfare less than 2 years, and 50 percent are on welfare less than 4 years. Only about 15 percent stay on welfare continuously for five years. The overall picture is that one group receives welfare for short periods of time and never return. A middle group cycles on and off, some for short periods and others for longer periods, but again, not for five *continuous* years. And a third, but quite small group stays on welfare for long periods of time.

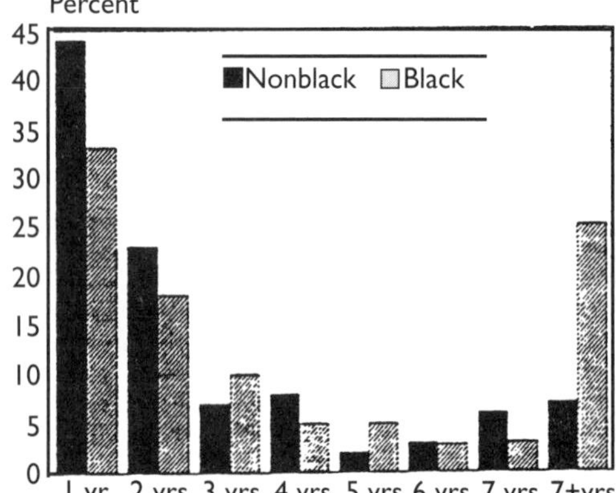

Figure 4. Length of stay on AFDC, by race (1974–1987).

What, then, accounts for the commonly held view of the long-term welfare recipient? Even though most welfare spells are relatively short, at any one time a majority (65 percent) of persons enrolled are in the midst of what will be long periods of receiving welfare benefits. This is because the probability of being on welfare at any given time is necessarily higher for longer-term recipients than for those who have shorter welfare spells. Thus, even though the typical recipient is a short-term user, the welfare population at any point in time is composed predominantly of long-term recipients. The example that the House of Representatives Ways and Means Committee uses to illustrate this point is as follows: Consider a 13-bed hospital in which 12 beds are occupied for an entire year by 12 chronically ill patients, while the other bed is used by 52 patients, each of whom stays exactly 1 week. On any given day, a hospital census would find that about 85 percent of the patients (12/13) were in the midst of long spells of hospitalization. Nevertheless, viewed over the course of a year, short-term use clearly dominates: out of 64 patients using hospital services, about 80 percent (52/64) spent only 1 week in the hospital.

The most powerful predictor of long-term welfare receipt is the young, never-married woman. She is usually disadvantaged at least threefold: no high school diploma, no significant employment experience, and a very young child. She is probably also a minority. But even among this group, no more than a third will be on welfare for as long as ten years. As Mary Jo Bane and David Ellwood [observe], long-term welfare is still very much the exception.

Several studies have now documented that the most common route out of AFDC is through work. Many recipients attempt to exit via work but for a variety of reasons—lack of health care, a breakdown in child care, low wages, and jobs that do not last—return to welfare. Still, by the end of six years, more than 40 percent will have left to enter the labor force. Of those who leave welfare through earned income, about 40 percent remained poor after their exit. The picture that emerges from the studies of welfare spells and exits is that for most recipients, welfare is a safety net rather than a "way of life."

Generational welfare is also a myth. A significant majority (80 percent) of daughters who grew up in highly dependent homes (defined as receiving at least 25 percent of average family income as welfare payments) do not become dependent themselves. Only 20 percent were themselves highly dependent on AFDC in their early twenties; and 64 percent of daughters with welfare backgrounds received no AFDC. However, there is a higher likelihood that women with welfare backgrounds will receive welfare. The fraction of daughters from highly dependent homes who themselves become highly dependent (20 percent) is much greater than the fraction of daughters from nonwelfare families who become highly dependent (3 percent). And although more than three-fifths of the daughters who grew up in AFDC-dependent homes received no AFDC themselves, more than nine-tenths of those who grew up in nonrecipient families received no AFDC in their early adult years.

There is a relation between intergenerational welfare, but there is no solid evidence that welfare *causes* welfare dependency in the next generation. The powerful effects of poverty and single parenthood probably make it more likely that daughters growing up in these conditions will be poor themselves. As Peter Gottschalk, Sara McLanahan, and Gary Sandefur [observe]: because families receiving welfare are poor—-indeed, poverty is a condition of welfare receipt—we would expect children from welfare families to have higher rates of poverty and welfare use as adults than children from nonpoor, nonwelfare families. Intergenerational correlation, therefore, does not necessarily indicate a causal relationship. Daughters and their mothers may simply share characteristics that increase the probability of their both receiving assistance. For example, if both mother and daughter grow up in neighborhoods with poor-quality schools, both will be more likely to have lower earnings and, hence, a greater need for income assistance. Changing the quality of the school the daughter attends will raise her income and, in turn, lower the probability that she receives public assistance.

We have seen that most welfare recipients are neither teenagers nor long-term dependents nor having lots of children. What about dependency, or, more specifically, what about the work ethic of welfare mothers? Is it true that welfare saps the work ethic?

Both qualitative and quantitative data address the work ethic of welfare recipients. A recent study by Kathryn Edin and Christopher Jencks examined empirically the economic position of AFDC recipients in Chicago. They found an extensive amount of work for the simple reason that single mothers on welfare cannot pay their bills on welfare alone; they have to obtain additional income, often without telling the welfare department. The authors based their conclusions on a study of the Illinois welfare system between 1988 and 1990. At that time, a single mother with one child, counting both the welfare grant and food stamps, received $399 per month, or $4,800 per year. Benefits rose per additional child, to $9,300 if she had four, but were still only 60 to 75 percent of the poverty line. Edin interviewed fifty welfare families in Chicago and the suburbs to see how they got along.

Almost all of the recipients obtained additional income, both legal and illegal, to cover their expenses, by work, by receiving money from friends and relatives, or by someone else paying expenses. Recipients had to obtain this income because unless they lived in subsidized housing the AFDC check would not even cover rent and utilities. For those living in unsubsidized housing, rent and utilities came to $37 more per month than the welfare check; those living in subsidized housing had $197 extra—still not enough to get through the month. Food stamps helped, but again, very few were able to feed their family for the entire month on food stamps alone. Taking the sample as a whole, recipients spent $314 a month for food, rent, and utilities. This left only $10 for everything else—clothing, laundry, cleaning supplies, school supplies, transportation, and so forth. Edin calculated that her sample spent about a third of what the average mother in the Midwest spends on these items. Still, it amounted to $351 in excess of the welfare grant, and almost all of this came from unreported income.

Almost half of the extra money needed to live was earned but not reported. Jobs varied. Some held regular jobs under another name and earned $5 per hour. Others worked off the books (bartending, catering, baby-sitting, sewing), earning an average of $3 per hour. A small number sold drugs but earned very little ($3–5 per hour). The only high earners ($40 per hour) were occasional prostitutes (in the sample, five).

The families' expenses were about $1,000 per month. The federal poverty line in 1990 was a little less than $10,000. This meant that the recipients consumed $2,000 above the poverty line. As previously discussed, the poverty line is low, and most Americans think it should be considerably higher. Edin estimated that the public would put the figure for her sample at about $16,000, or $4,000 higher than the recipients were presently consuming. Almost all of the sample (88 percent), to varying degrees, lacked basic necessities and material comforts. Edin reported that they lived in bad neighborhoods in rundown apartments, often without heat and hot water. Roofs and windows leaked. The sample had no telephones or money for entertainment. They could not afford fresh fruits or vegetables. There were some small "extravagances," such as renting a video, eating at McDonald's, and purchasing cigarettes and alcohol, but these amounts were just 6 percent of the sample's expenditures. Half of the sample could have cut expenses if they were willing to move into Chicago's worst neighborhoods or the large public housing projects, but they considered these areas too dangerous.

The Chicago results have been replicated in Cambridge, Charleston, and San Antonio. Urban welfare mothers need about $11,000 per year to live on, which they get from work, family, male friends, and absent fathers. Working mothers need even more money to pay for transportation, clothing, and child care. These mothers typically spent between $12,000 and $15,000 per year.

Circumstantial evidence, Edin and Jencks argued, suggests that their findings can be generalized. Both rent and living necessities appear to vary little across major metropolitan areas. If these estimates are only reasonably accurate, then in no major American city can welfare recipients get by on their grants. Furthermore, in several states, grants are less than $200 per month for a family of three, and no family can get by on that small sum.

Edin and Jencks compared their results with the Consumer Expenditure Survey for 1984–85. Although that survey is problematic, over 80 percent of the single adult welfare families report outside income. The average is about 40 percent in excess of AFDC and food stamps, consistent with Edin's findings.

If these mothers are so willing to work, why, then, are they also on welfare? According to Edin and Jencks, single mothers do not turn to welfare because they are pathologically dependent on handouts or unusually reluctant to work—they do so because they cannot get jobs that pay better than welfare. This conclusion is supported by recent quantitative research that examined the dynamics of work and welfare. As stated, most recipients leave welfare for work. Moreover, a great many (more than half) leave during the first year. The problem is that many also return, and then try again and again. There is significant movement between welfare and work. At least one-half work for at least some of the time that they are on welfare. Although there is some variation depending on the survey, significant numbers—as high as two-thirds—of welfare exits occur when the mother finds a job or continuously works until she leaves welfare. The failure to make a successful exit from welfare is not because of a failure of the work ethic—these women say they prefer to work *and they validate their attitudes by their behavior.* They simply cannot make it in the labor market. Not surprisingly, those who are the most disadvantaged in terms of employability are the least successful. As Gary Burtless notes, even if welfare recipients had no young children to care for—and almost half have children under six—most face severe problems finding and holding good jobs. Limited schooling and poor academic achievement doom most AFDC mothers to low-wage, deadend jobs. Nevertheless, in spite of these odds, work is much more common in poor single mothers' lives than previously thought, in spite of their very low wages, risk of losing medical care provisions, and child-care constraints.

Contrary to myth, most welfare mothers are adults, they have few children, and they are not long-term welfare recipients. Furthermore, there is no problem about their work ethic. Most either work or try to work while on welfare, and most leave welfare via work. The "problem" of welfare dependency is not the recipients. Rather, the problems are the job market and the conditions of work. In addition to poorly paying, unsteady, increasingly part-time work, are the difficulties of a lack of benefits, especially critical health insurance, and child care.

Nevertheless, welfare policy insists on putting the poor to work by concentrating on the individual rather than on the labor market.

Article Review Form at end of book.

How is the growing inequality in the United States likely to affect the nation's health? While a national health-care program would certainly help uninsured individuals, researchers note that it is not likely to eliminate social class disparities in health. What changes would be necessary to improve the unequal health profile of lower social class individuals? Racial minorities in the United States historically have been disadvantaged in terms of all measures of health. While social class accounts for much of this disparity, what other factors contribute to the poor health of African Americans in the United States?

Race, Class and Health

Kristy Maher McNamara
Furman University

One of the most consistent patterns documented in the field of medical sociology is the relationship between social class and health. Study after study illustrates a consistent relationship: the lower one's social class standing, the poorer their health (Williams 1990; Marmot 1996; Wilkinson 1996). Regardless of what country they live in, what type of health insurance they have, and the amount of health care they receive, people at the bottom of society have the worst health of all (Cockerham 1998: 53). This pattern is true inside and outside of the United States. In a study of health in Finland, Denmark, Sweden, Norway, Hungary, and England and Wales, Lahelma and Valkonen (1990) found that persons with less education had the highest mortality statistics.

This paper begins by examining the available data on the relationship between social class and health in the United States. After describing the nature of this relationship, it continues by discussing the numerous social factors that play a role in the health and well-being of people living in poverty. Using the "Cycle of Poverty and Pathology" proposed initially by Starfield in 1984, the available research is extended in an attempt to illuminate the explanatory power of this model. By exploring the various variables and their relationships to each other in this model, the hope is to untangle the complex interrelationship of factors that affect health in our society. Once this model is explained the focus will turn to the difficult question of the relationship between race and health. Both sides of the debate are discussed in an effort to answer the following question: are the negative health profiles of minority groups in America the result of their overrepresentation in the poverty sector of society or a reflection of racism and prejudice that still plagues American culture? Finally, recent research suggesting that it is the amount of inequality in a society that is the most important factor relating to health is discussed. This research raises challenging questions about the future of race, class, and health in America.

The Relationship Between Social Class and Health

"The inescapable conclusion is that class influences one's chances of staying alive."
Antonovsky (1972: 28)

In America, as in other places in the world, socioeconomic status is one of the strongest and most consistent predictors of a person's health and life expectancy (Williams 1990; Marmot 1996; Wilkinson 1996). Studies have shown that as social class standing increases, rates of mortality and morbidity decrease. A robust inverse relationship between social class and health status dates back to our earliest records and exists in all countries where it has been examined (Williams 1995). At each age, those in the upper social classes have lower rates of illness and death (Feinstein 1993;

Navarro 1990). This finding persists across the life span and for all diseases with few exceptions (Winkleby et al. 1992). This is evident even at the earliest stages of life. For example, infant mortality is significantly higher among those born to poor women (Nersesian 1988).

One of the most difficult concepts to measure sociologically speaking is social class. How does one accurately assess a person's standing in the stratification system of society? Sociologists use a term called socioeconomic status (SES) to measure social class. SES consists of measures of income, education, and occupational prestige. Although interconnected, each of these measures reflects different dimensions of a person's position in the stratification system of a society. In studies of health and illness, *income* reflects spending power, housing, diet, and medical care; *education* is indicative of a person's skills for acquiring positive social, psychological, and economic resources; and *occupation* measures status, responsibility, physical activity, and health risks associated with work (Winkleby et al. 1992: 816). While income and occupational status are important, the strongest single predictor of good health appears to be education (Liberatos, Link, and Kelsey 1988). Well-educated people are generally the best informed about the merits of a healthy life-style and the advantages of seeking preventive care or medical treatment for health problems when they need it. The impact of education on health gets stronger over the life course as less-educated persons have increasingly more sickness and disability, and die sooner than the well-educated (Arber 1993; Pappas et al. 1993; Ross and Wu 1996).

This relationship between socioeconomic status and health occurs at every level of the social hierarchy. Marmot and his colleagues (1991) explain by stating that the upper social class was found to live longer than the upper-middle class who live longer than the lower-middle class and so on—until the lower class is reached having the lowest life expectancy of all. In this way, health differences are found not only between the rich and the poor, but at every step along the social class ladder.

For several decades medical sociologists have explored this relationship between social class and health. A variety of variables can be used to measure health (e.g., mortality, longevity, and morbidity). A classic study in this area was authored by Antonovsky in 1972. This well-known study conducted statistical analyses on approximately thirty studies of mortality in the United States and Europe. Antonovsky concluded that the upper social classes were favored in all dimensions of life expectancy. He emphasized the importance of this relationship by suggesting that on every measure, social class position influences one's opportunity for longevity. Other, more recent, studies have demonstrated that socioeconomic status is one of the strongest and most consistent predictors of a person's health and life expectancy (Link and Phelan 1995; Marmot 1996).

Health profiles can also be examined by looking at morbidity or sickness. Arber (1993) examined chronic illness at a variety of different ages and found that by the time lower-class men and women reached old age, they were significantly less healthy than better educated and more affluent elderly people. Arber also found that the highest levels of chronic illness were among unskilled workers and the lowest among higher professionals. Class differences in health were smaller below age twenty-five, but increased thereafter. Finally, this research shows that the lower class also experienced greater physical disability and the differences became especially pronounced among the elderly.

Morbidity is often measured by looking at acute (short term) and chronic (long term) illnesses. On both measures those in the lowest socioeconomic groups fair poorly. Coronary heart disease, while traditionally seen as a "yuppy" or white-collar disease, is concentrated among the poor (Gatchel, Baum, and Krantz 1989; Polednak 1989). While rates of coronary heart disease have declined dramatically in the past twenty-five years for Americans, the decline has been greatest among the upper and middle classes.

The poor also suffer from diseases of past human existence that we as a society have, for the most part, controlled for years. For example, tuberculosis was extremely rare in the United States until the late 1980s and early 1990s when it resurfaced with greatest concentration among the poor. Lead poisoning, influenza, and pneumonia are also more prevalent among the lower class. This higher rate of communicable diseases may be linked with the unhealthy living situations in which many poor people live.

The negative health profile of the poor has been documented consistently with regards to mortality and a variety of acute, infectious, and chronic illnesses. The question can be raised, "Why do people who are poor become ill more often and die younger than their wealthier peers?" The answer to this question, like the answer to most questions involving social problems, is not simple. For example, the direction of the causal relationship is sometimes questioned. While most sociological studies focus on the effect of one's social class standing on his or her health, other studies argue that a "drift" process may be responsible. This "drift" hypothesis argues that it is the person's poor health that causes their lower social class position. To address this issue, longitudinal data must be examined. Several cohort studies suggest that despite that health-driven downward social mobility does occur, it contributes only a minor amount to the social class differences in health (Wilkinson 1986; Power et al. 1990).

The Cycle of Poverty and Pathology

At the most fundamental level, poverty and illness are linked by underlying social conditions. Several factors play a role in the relationship between social class and health. There is more to health than the availability of medical care. Environmental factors, life-style choices, stress, and social isolation play a role in determining one's health status. A healthy life-style includes enough sleep; an adequate amount of exercise; and avoiding such practices as smoking, abusing alcohol, and taking drugs. The type of life-style that promotes a healthy existence, however, is more typical of the upper and middle classes, who have the financial and social resources to support it. One of the most important factors affecting the relationship between social class and health is the way in which social class influences the opportunities a person has for a healthy life.

The poor face many combined forces that decrease their life chances. They have greater exposure to physical (crowding, poor sanitation), chemical and biochemical (diet, pollution, smoking, alcohol and drug abuse), biological (bacteria, viruses), and psychological (stress) risk factors that produce ill health. One of the most comprehensive conceptual models designed to explain the relationship between social factors and health is called "The Cycle of Poverty and Pathology." This model, developed by Starfield in 1984, portrays various factors that appear to reinforce and perpetuate the cycle of poverty and illness (see Figure 1).

Environmental Conditions

One of the most obvious problems faced by lower-class individuals is adverse environmental conditions at home and at work. Poor neighborhoods are characterized by overcrowding, substandard housing, air pollution, noise, violence, rodents, insects, fires, and filth. While all of these conditions combine to create a stressful environment, which has a direct effect on health as discussed in the upcoming section, these environmental conditions at times are solely responsible for ill health effects. Air pollution, for example, has been linked to higher rates of respiratory disease and increased hospitalization (Whittemore 1981). National data show that lead poisoning occurs more often among lower income and minority children. This is likely because of their exposure to chips of lead based paint historically used in public housing projects (Mahaffey et al. 1982). Exposure to constant noise can also produce physiological changes similar to a generalized stress response. Studies have shown that children living in a noisy environment suffered from a variety of cognitive, behavioral, and physiological (blood pressure abnormalities and unusually high pulse rates) problems (Starfield 1984).

Substandard housing conditions may also present a variety of threats to the occupants' health: rats, poisons, tires, inadequate heating and plumbing, faulty electrical wiring, overcrowding, and deteriorating structures (Rainwater 1966). Exposure to toxic waste in residential areas may also play a role. The Commission on Racial Justice (1987) found that the treatment, storage, and disposal of hazardous waste sites were disproportionately located in areas where the surrounding residents were poor and black.

Environmental conditions at work may also have an adverse effect on health. Lower status jobs are often more hazardous, physically taxing, and menial. People from lower social classes are more likely to be employed in settings where there is a greater risk of exposure to toxic substances and bad working conditions. Exposure to occupational hazards such as toxic chemicals, dust, and fumes is more common among blacks than whites (Sterling and Weinkam 1989). Bad working conditions (e.g., daily contact with poisons, dust, smoke, acid, explosives, vibration) were found to be the major source of socioeconomic differences in physical illness (Lundberg 1991).

In addition to the environmental hazards at work that many lower social class individuals face, these jobs also tend to be less rewarding financially and emotionally. Ross and Wu (1996) found that well-educated people, in comparison to people with less education, are more likely to have fulfilling and rewarding jobs.

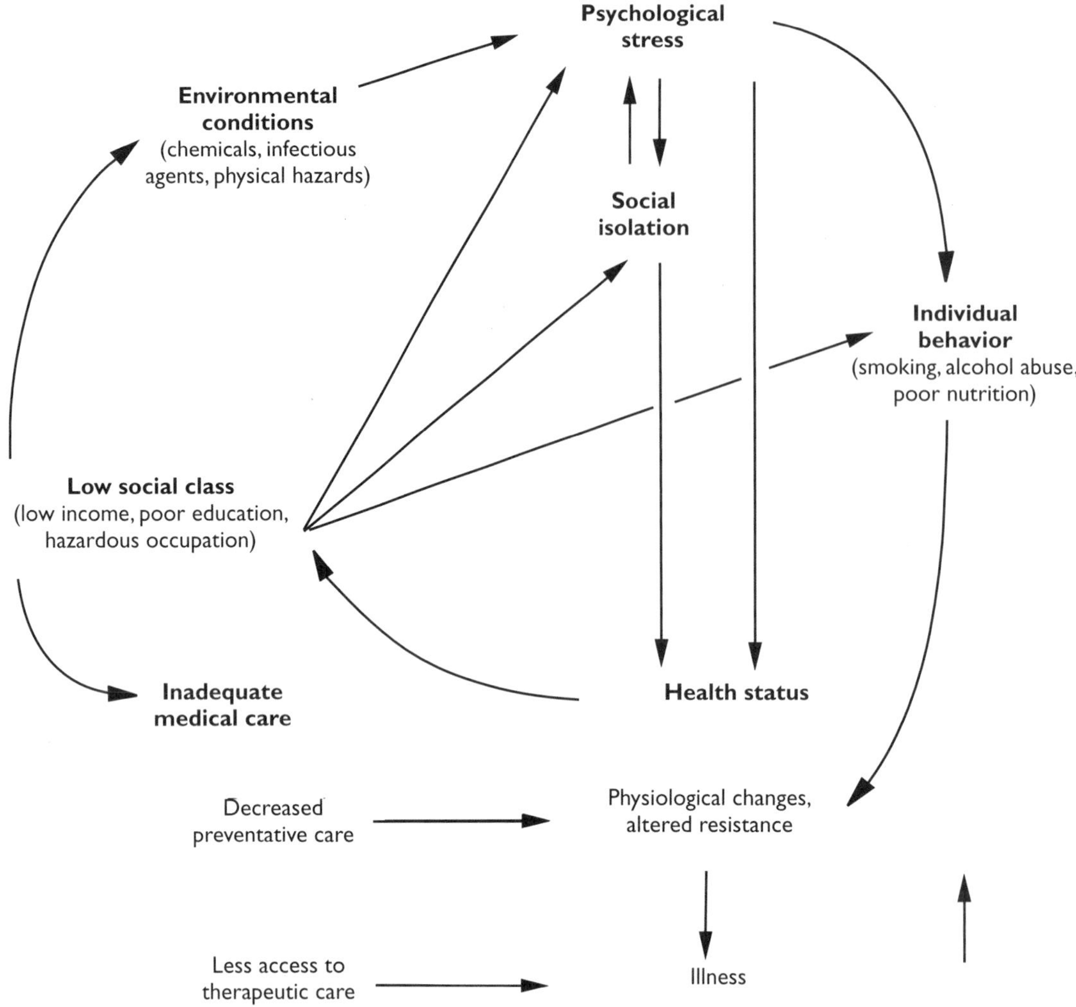

Figure 1. The cycle of poverty and pathology. (*Source:* Adapted from Starfield 1984.)

One's social class standing can also affect workers' ability to improve the conditions in which they work. Brenner (1995) argues that blue-collar workers are less able to affect the development of occupational safety and health codes because of their lack of knowledge about occupational health risks and lack of political influence to change their work environments. This lack of knowledge and political clout is likely to be a factor in their neighborhoods as well. As such, the environmental risks faced by the poor at home and at work are not likely to be rectified without governmental intervention.

Psychological Stress and Social Isolation

While people living in poverty are not the only ones to suffer from stress, they certainly experience more than their fair share of stressors. The chronic stress that can accompany living in poverty presents a relatively constant strain that creates problems in the daily lives of poor people. Some medical sociologists have argued that people's relative status in the social hierarchy has a critical impact on health. Namely, being "on the bottom" of any hierarchy involves not only physical hardships, but also the humiliation and stigmatization that accompanies this low status (Lindheim and Syme 1983).

The lower class is characterized as being subject to the most stress and having the fewest resources to cope with it (Adler et al. 1994; Evans, Barer, and Marmor 1994). Evans (1994) argues that social rank is correlated with the ability to handle stress. The higher one's social standing, the better one's ability to deal with stressful situations. This advantage decreases proportionally the lower one goes down the social ladder. Evans and his colleagues (1994) suggest that stress is the primary cause of the social class gradient in mortality. They argue that the levels of stress experienced, the amount of resources available to cope with stress, and the degree of control over one's life situation vary by social class position.

One of the mechanisms used to cope with stress is social support. This term refers to contacts with other people (family, friends, coworkers) who can provide emotional support in times of trouble. The protective function of social supports has been documented as early as the late 1800s in the classic piece by Emile Durkheim called *Suicide* (1897; trans. 1951). More recent studies have documented the positive function that social support plays in promoting health. Moss (1973) was one of the first to emphasize the advantages of group membership in providing social support for the individual. He states that subjective feelings of belonging, acceptance, and feeling needed have been shown to develop positive feelings of well-being and to relieve stress. Many others conclude that the social support rendered by families and groups helps reduce the potentially harmful effects of stress on the body and the mind (Matt and Dean 1993; Thoits 1995).

Without adequate social support one can find themselves in a position of social isolation. In a classic study on mortality, Berkman and Syme (1979) found that the age-adjusted relative risk of the most isolated individuals was more than double that of the least isolated, independent of initial health status, medical care, personal health practices, and socioeconomic status. In other words, social support serves as a buffer against disease. This protective buffer of social support was found to be unevenly distributed by social class. Those individuals with the lowest income were less likely than the more affluent to have a large number of social contacts.

Health Behaviors

The term "health behaviors" is used to describe a variety of daily activities that people engage in that have an impact on health (e.g., diet, exercise, smoking, drinking alcohol). As Figure 1 indicates, socioeconomic status and stress have a direct impact on lifestyle choices and these behaviors affect health status. Cigarette smoking, for example, is responsible for approximately one in six deaths annually in the United States (Chen 1993). Smoking is disproportionately concentrated in the lowest social classes. Also, alcohol consumption tends to be higher among lower social classes. These activities may be seen as ways to cope with the stresses of a life of poverty.

Poor people are also more likely to have an inferior diet. Data from the National Health and Nutrition Examination Survey shows that poor children are consistently more likely to suffer from protein deficiencies. About one-half of low-income children were below nutritional standards for vitamins A and C, one-fourth were deficient in calcium and 95 percent were deficient in iron (Rice and Danchik 1979). These deficiencies are likely to be the result of poor eating habits and diets. Poor and minority children, for example, were more likely to have diets that included candy, sweetened beverages, and salty snacks. These dietary habits may result from a lack of information about a proper diet, limited income, and stress.

Exploring the other end of the social hierarchy, a more affluent life-style typically involves more leisure-time physical exercise and less obesity. The well-educated are less likely to smoke and more likely to exercise, get checkups from physicians, and drink alcohol moderately (Ross and Wu 1996).

Inadequate Medical Care

Differences between social class groups in access, use, and quality of care also affect the overall health outcome for poor individuals. The United States is the only developed country in the world without national health insurance (Cockerham 1998). This creates particular difficulties for those not eligible for Medicaid, for public health insurance for the poor, and for those who do not have private insurance through their place of employment. According to the National Center for Health Statistics, 17.8 percent of the American population under the age of 65 had no health insurance in 1994 (NCHS 1995). This statistic marks an increase in the proportion of people without health insurance (1989–13.4%; 1980–11.6%). The uninsured are typically people working in low-income jobs whose employers do not provide health insurance benefits for their employees. These are "near poor" individuals, who make enough money to disqualify them from welfare programs like Medicaid but they cannot afford private insurance because it is too expensive.

Another issue of importance is use of health care. Many years ago it was believed that persons of the lower social class backgrounds tended to underuse health services because of the financial costs. More recent studies, however, confirm that this assumption is inaccurate. As the effects of Medicare and Medicaid (passed in 1965) became more apparent, the use of physician services by lower class individuals increased to the point that the significance of the relationship between income and use was greatly diminished. By 1970, the poor had higher rates of physician use than any other income group (Andersen and Anderson 1979). When actual need for health services is taken into account, however, low-income persons appear to use fewer services relative to their needs (Dutton 1986; Sudman and Freeman 1989). These studies find that the poor have more sickness and, despite their greater use of services, they still do not obtain as much health care as they need. While the lower class visits physicians more frequently than members of other socioeconomic groups, their need for care is much greater because of their relatively poorer health and underuse of preventive care. Preventive medical care, appropriate early intervention during the course of an illness, and management of a chronic illness are important factors that affect health. Higher mortality rates may result from later initial diagnosis, delays in treatment, or lack of adequate follow-up care.

Research documents that the poor are the least likely to use preventive care (Dutton 1986). Wilkinson (1996) points out that women with low incomes receive less prenatal care, low-income children are more likely to have never had a routine physical examination, and other measures such as breast exams and childhood immunizations are considered less common among the poor. One of the main reasons for this situation is that low-income persons tend not to have a regular source of care. Also, the costs not covered by health insurance, which must be paid out-of-pocket, can be a significant barrier in visiting the doctor when one is not feeling well. This is most notably the case for those Americans without any health insurance. For the uninsured, preventive health care may be an unaffordable luxury. For these reasons, it can be argued that preventive care is found most often among the upper and middle social classes.

Access and use are only part of the picture in discussing medical care. The quality of care is also important. Government sponsored programs, such as Medicaid and Medicare, have resulted in more frequent visits to doctors, but the poor are still treated within the context of a type of "welfare medicine." Differences between social classes in terms of where they seek medical care are obvious and consistent. According to data from the National Center for Health Statistics (1996), higher income people were more likely than those with lower incomes to receive care in private doctors' offices and group practices or over the telephone. People with lower incomes, on the other hand, were more likely to contact hospital outpatient clinics or emergency rooms. In these settings of "public medicine," patients often receive poorer quality medical care. For example, they spend more time waiting to be seen by the doctor and they have less continuity of care (i.e., they do not have a personal physician).

While inadequate medical care is an important feature affecting the health of the poor, recent reviews of the literature argue that the role of medicine is frequently overstated. Specifically, they state that removal of economic barriers alone will not eliminate social disparities in health care use (Adler et al. 1993).

In sum, Starfield's "Cycle of Poverty and Pathology" visually depicts the multiplicity of factors involved in the association between lower social class and poor health status. Low social class, as measured by income, education, and occupational prestige, contributes directly to environmental conditions at home and at work; psychological stress and social isolation; individual health behaviors (e.g., smoking, drinking, poor nutrition); and inadequate medical care (i.e., decreased preventive care and reduced access). This model also highlights the interconnectedness of the variables noting, for example, the effect of stress on health behaviors, social isolation, and health status. It also documents, with the feedback loop from health status to low social class, the possible "drift" process that may occur when sickness contributes to social class standing. In short, this "Cycle of Poverty and Pathology" attempts to include the variety of variables that interact to create this unbreakable cycle that results in the poor health profile of people living in poverty.

The Relationship Between Race and Health

". . . the life expectancy of blacks in Harlem is lower than that of persons in Bangladesh, one of the poorest countries in the world."

McCord and Freeman (1990)

There are clear and unmistakable differences in the health profiles of racial groups in the United States. The infant mortality rates for blacks, for example, are twice that of whites. The 1993 data show an infant mortality rate of 16.5 for blacks versus 6.8 for whites (NCHS 1994a). Moreover, the age-adjusted death rate for the black population is higher than that of whites (NCHS 1994a). The gap in life expectancy between blacks and whites widened between 1980 and 1991, from 6.9 years to 8.3 years for males and from 5.6 years to 5.8 years for females (NCHS 1994b). This disparity in life expectancy is due to a number of factors. First, one of the chief contributors to this widening racial gap is a slower rate of decline among blacks than whites for heart disease (Kochanek, Maurer, and Rosenberg 1994). Also, HIV infection, homicide, diabetes, and pneumonia are major causes of decreasing life expectancy for blacks.

A more careful examination of the causes of death documents that under the age of 70, infant mortality, cancer, and cardiovascular disease account for 50 percent of the excess deaths for black males and 63 percent of those for black females (NCHS 1994b). Homicide accounts for 19 percent of the excess deaths for black males and 6 percent for black females. In 1993 Cooper pointed out that black-white health inequality among men was at an all-time high for the twentieth century.

These comparisons, however, mask the true story behind race differences in health. While the tragic picture described documents the clear racial disparity in health, it does not explain why it occurs. While some attempt to argue that genetics plays the primary role in explaining racial differences in health, diseases that have a clear genetic component (like sickle-cell anemia) account for only a miniscule amount of the racial disparities in health (Cooper 1984). Also, biological explanations tend to divert attention from social factors that influence the health status of minority racial groups.

Social class differences between racial groups are primarily responsible for the observed patterns of racial disparities in health. Many studies have concluded that social class affects the health of infants, children, and adults at least as much, if not more than race or ethnicity (Baquet et al. 1991; Navarro 1990; Otten et al. 1990). This is largely because race is so strongly correlated with social class in American society. For example, in 1996, while 11 percent of whites were poor, 28 percent of blacks fell below the poverty line (Statistical Abstract of the United States 1997). Researchers often find that controlling for SES differences substantially reduces the racial disparities in health. In some cases (see, for example, Baquet et al. 1991 and Rogers 1992), the racial disparity disappears when adjusted for SES. More frequently, however, it is found that adjusting for social class differences substantially reduces, but does not eliminate, racial disparities in health (Cooper 1993; Krieger and Fee 1994).

When comparisons are made within socioeconomic levels (e.g., comparing middle-class blacks to middle-class whites) blacks have worse health status than whites. For example, one study found higher infant mortality rates among college educated black women than among comparably educated whites (Schoendorf et al. 1992). Even more surprising is the finding that the black-white mortality ratio increases as social class standing increases. That is to say, the black-white gap is narrowest at the lower socioeconomic levels and highest at higher social class levels. Krieger and colleagues (1993) found, for example, that the black-white gap in infant mortality rates was narrowest among women who had graduated from high school and highest among women with a college education.

There is no simple or universally accepted explanation for this finding. Many studies suggest that racism plays a key role in the residual effect that race has on health (Cooper 1993; Krieger et al. 1993; King and Williams 1995). Racism, or negative attitudes and beliefs toward racial groups and the consequent discrimination that occurs at the individual and institutional levels, can affect health in a variety of ways. First, race can alter the relationship between SES variables. Take for instance the racial differences in average incomes based on the number of years of education. Whites receive higher income returns from education than blacks. For example, the median income for white males with a college degree was $38,263; while black males with a college degree earned on average $30,532 (U.S. Bureau of the Census 1991). In this way, education does not fully capture the economic status differences between black and white households. Several studies have also found that the purchasing power of a given level of income varies by race (Cooper 1984; King and Williams 1995). This research has found that blacks pay higher prices than whites for a variety of goods and services including food and housing.

Racism can also produce greater stress that, as discussed, may have a negative impact on physical and mental health. The impact on health may also be indirect, through a greater likelihood to engage in violence and negative health behaviors like drug/alcohol addictions. Finally, racism may result in restricted access to health care. A study by the Council on Ethical and Judicial Affairs (1990) found that blacks were less likely to receive a wide range of medical services than whites even after adjusting for severity of illness, SES, and/or insurance status. As we witnessed the twenty-fifth anniversary of the uncovering of the Tuskegee Syphilis Experiment, it was hard to deny the role that racism played in the history of medicine.

Growing Inequalities: A Forecast of More Trouble to Come

"In the developed world, it is not the richest countries which have the best health, but the most egalitarian."

Wilkinson (1996: 3)

A cross-cultural examination of the relationship between social class and health raises interesting questions. While one might assume that it is the location at the bottom of the stratification system that has the most negative impact on health, research questions this assumption. Some researchers argue that it is not only the location at the bottom of the social stratification system that is an important determinant of health, but the overall level of social and economic inequality in the society as a whole that affects health. Wilkinson (1996), after reviewing numerous international studies, determined that the more egalitarian a society is, the better its overall health level.

The key variable appears to be the degree of social and economic equality within the population. If there is a significant gap in income, education, and living conditions between the wealthiest and poorest members of a society, then large-scale health inequalities will exist within the society. If the gap is narrow, those health inequalities will significantly diminish. For example, the overall levels of health and life expectancy are higher in countries such as Japan and Sweden, where social class differences are smaller, than in countries with significant gaps between the rich and the poor, such as the United States and Britain.

This is especially disturbing given the widening inequalities found in American society. For example, wealth has become more highly concentrated in the hands of a few at the top of our stratification system. According to Hurst and colleagues (1996), the richest fifth of the United States holds more than 75 percent of the wealth of the country. Since the mid-1970s there has been an increase in income inequality in the United States. According to Pearlstein (1995), the richest fifth earns 49 percent of the income.

Changes in the economic structure, namely postindustrialization, with its decline in the number of manufacturing or blue-collar jobs and increase in service sector and white-collar jobs, has contributed to a polarization of the income distribution. Consequently, the majority of households in the 1980s experienced a deterioration in their standard of living (Danziger and Gottschalk 1993). In the 1980s, for every seven families in the United States that rose from the middle to the upper class, nine families declined from the middle to the lower class (Bradsher 1995). Additionally, the gains in economic status of blacks relative to that of whites have stagnated, primarily as a result of the increasing income inequality in America (Smith and Welch 1989).

The impact of this growing inequality is reflected in health studies that look longitudinally at social class and health outcomes. For example, Feldman and colleagues (1989) found that mortality differentials by education increased substantially for white men between 1960 and 1984. A similar comparison of mortality statistics between 1960 and the late 1980s found evidence documenting an increase in socioeconomic disparity (Pappas et al. 1993). It is precisely this increase in economic inequality that appears to be the driving force behind widening health disparities.

Conclusion

This paper has examined the complex interrelationship between social class, race, and health. The available data clearly document the disparities in health by social class. "The Cycle of Poverty and Pathology" allows the reader to explore how environmental conditions, psychological stress, social isolation, health behaviors, and inadequate medical care contribute to the poor health of the economically disadvantaged. After reviewing this literature, the unmistakable conclusion is that health and illness are unequally distributed in our society and that people in poverty have more than their fair share of illness.

An examination of the health profile of blacks in this country shows a disturbing racial disparity in health as well. Although social class affects morbidity and mortality more than race, the latter continues to play an important and independent factor in predicting health status. The differentials in health status associated with race, however, are smaller than those associated with socioeconomic status. This raises difficult questions about the role that racism plays in the health care arena.

While greater access to health care is an essential part of the solution to improving the disparity in health statuses between the rich and the poor, poor people face a plethora of social problems that contribute to ill health. If the pattern of growing economic inequalities in the United States continues with its corresponding gap between the rich and the poor, the forecast for our nation's overall health is stormy at best.

References

Adler, Nancy E., Thomas Boyce, Margaret A. Chesney, Sheldon Cohen, Susan Folkman, Robert L. Kahn, and S. Leonard Syme. 1994. "Socioeconomic status and health." *American Psychologist* 49: 15–24.

Adler, Nancy E., Thomas Boyce, Margaret A. Chesney, Susan Folkman, and S. Leonard Syme. 1993."Socioeconomic inequalities in health: no easy solution." *Journal of the American Medical Association* 269: 3140–45.

Andersen, Ronald, and Odin W. Anderson. 1979. "Trends in the use of health services," pp. 371–91 in *Handbook of medical sociology,* 3rd ed., H. Freeman, S. Levine, and L. Reeder (eds.). Englewood Cliffs, N.J.: Prentice Hall.

Antonovsky, Aaron. 1972. "Social class, life expectancy and overall mortality," pp. 5–30 in *Patients, physicians and illness,* 2nd ed., E. Gartly Jaco (ed.). New York: The Free Press.

Arber, Sara. 1993. "Chronic illness over the life course: Class inequalities among men and women in Britain," pp. 39–64 in *Medical Sociology: Research on chronic illness,* T. Abel, S. Geyer, U. Gerhardt, J. Siegrist, and W. van den Heuvel (eds.). Bonn: Informationszentrum Sozialwissenschaften.

Baquet, C. R., J. W. Horm, T. Gibbs, and P. Greenwald. 1991. "Socioeconomic factors and cancer incidence among blacks and whites." *Journal of the National Cancer Institute* 83: 551–57.

Berkman, Lisa F., and S. Leonard Syme. 1979. "Social networks, host resistance, and mortality: A nine-year follow-up study of Alameda County residents." *American Journal of Epidemiology* 109(2): 186–204.

Bradsher, Keith. 1995. "America's Opportunity Gap." *New York Times* (June 4), p. E4.

Brenner, M. H. 1995. "Economy, society, and health: theoretical links and empirical relations." In *Society and health: Foundation for a nation.* S. Levin, D.C. Walsh, B. C. Amick, A. R. Tarlov (eds.). New York: Oxford University Press.

Chen, V. W. 1993. "Smoking and the health gap of minorities." *Annals of Epidemiology* 3: 159–64.

Cockerham, William C. 1998. *Medical Sociology.* 7th ed. New Jersey: Prentice Hall.

Commission on Racial Justice. 1987. *Toxic Wastes and Race in the United States: A National Report on the Racial and Socioeconomic Characteristics of Communities with Hazardous Waste Sites.* New York: United Church of Christ.

Cooper, R. S. 1984. "A note on the biological concept of race and its application in epidemiologic research." *American Heart Journal* 108: 715–23.

Cooper, R. S. 1993. "Health and the social status of blacks in the United States." *Annals of Epidemiology* 3: 137–44.

Council on Ethical and Judicial Affairs. American Medical Association. 1990. "Black-white disparities in health care." *Journal of the American Medical Association* 263: 2344–46.

Danziger, S., and P. Gottschalk (eds.). 1993. *Uneven Tides: Rising Inequality in America.* New York: Russell Sage.

Durkheim, Emile. 1951. *Suicide.* New York: The Free Press.

Dutton, Diana B. 1986. "Social class, health and illness," pp. 31–62 in *Applications of social science to clinical medicine and health policy,* L. Aiken and D. Mechanic (eds.). New Brunswick, N.J.: Rutgers University Press.

Evans, Robert G. 1994. "Introduction," pp. 3–26 in *Why are some people healthy and others not? The determinants of the health of populations,* R. Evans, M. Barer, and T. Marmor (eds.). New York: Aldine de Gruyter.

Evans, Robert G., Morris L. Barer, and Theodore R. Marmor (eds.). 1994. *Why are some people healthy and others not? The determinants of the health of populations.* New York: Aldine de Gruyter.

Feinstein, J. S. 1993. "The relationship between socioeconomic status and health." *Milbank Quarterly* 71: 279–322.

Feldman, J. J., D. M. Makuc, J. C. Kleinman, and J. Cornoni-Huntley. 1989. "National trends in educational differentials in mortality." *American Journal of Epidemiology* 129: 919–33.

Gatchel, Robert J., Andrew Baum, and David S. Krantz. 1989. *An introduction to health psychology.* New York: Random House.

Hurst, Erik, Ming Ching Luoh, and Frank P. Stafford. 1996. "Wealth Dynamics of American Families, 1984–1994." Unpublished paper, Institute for Social Research, University of Michigan, Ann Arbor, Michigan.

King, G., and D. R. Williams. 1995. "Race and health: a multi-dimensional approach to African American health." In *Society and Health: Foundation for a Nation,* S. Levine, D. C. Walsh, B.C. Amick, and A. R. Tarlov (eds.). New York: Oxford University Press.

Kochanek, K. D., J. D. Maurer, and H. M. Rosenberg. 1994. "Why did black life expectancy decline from 1984 through 1989 in the United States?" *American Journal of Public Health* 84: 938–44.

Krieger, N., and E. Fee. 1994. "Social class: the missing link in U.S. health data." *Journal of Health Services* 24: 25–44.

Krieger, N., D. L. Rowley, A. A. Herman, B. Avery, and M.T. Phillips. 1993. "Racism, sexism, and social class: implications for studies of health, disease, and well-being." *American Journal of Preventive Medicine* 9(supp.): 82–122.

Lahelma, Eero, and Tapani Valkonen. 1990. "Health and social inequities in Finland and elsewhere." *Social Science and Medicine* 31: 257–266.

Liberatos, P., B. G. Link, and J. L. Kelsey. 1988. "The measurement of social class in epidemiology." *Epidemiology Review* 10: 87–121.

Lindheim, Roslyn, and S. Leonard Syme. 1983. "Environments, people, and health." *Annual Review of the Public Health* 4: 335–359.

Link, Bruce G., and Jo Phelan. 1995. "Social conditions as fundamental causes of disease." *Journal of Health and Social Behavior* extra issue: 80–94.

Lundberg, O. 1991. "Causal explanations for class inequality in health—an empirical analysis." *Social Science and Medicine* 32: 385–93.

Mahaffey, Kathryn R., Joseph L. Annest, Jean Roberts, and Robert S. Murphy.

1982. "National estimates of blood lead levels: United States, 1976–1980." *New England Journal of Medicine* 307(10): 573–79.

Marmot, Michael. 1996. "The social pattern of health and disease," pp. 42–70 in *Health and Social Organization,* D. Blane, E. Brunner, and R. Wilkinson (eds.). London: Routledge.

Marmot, Michael G., George Davey Smith, Stephen Stansfeld, Chandra Patel, Fiona North, Jenny Head, Ian White, Eric Brunner, and Amanda Feeney. 1991. "Health inequalities among British civil servants: the Whitehall II study." *Lancet* 337: 1387–92.

Matt, George, and Alfred Dean. 1993. "Social support from friends and psychological distress among elderly persons: Moderator effects of age." *Journal of Health and Social Behavior* 34: 187–200.

McCord, C., and H. P. Freeman. 1990. "Excess mortality in Harlem." *New England Journal of Medicine* 322: 173–77.

Moss, Gordon E. 1973. *Illness, immunity, and social interaction.* New York: John Wiley.

National Center for Health Statistics. 1994a. *Health United States 1993.* Washington, D.C.: Government Printing Office.

National Center for Health Statistics. 1994b. *Excess Deaths and Other Mortality Measures for the Black Population: 1979–1981 and 1991.* Hyattsville, M.D.: Publication Health Service.

National Center for Health Statistics. 1995. *Health United States 1994.* Washington, D.C.: Government Printing Office.

National Center for Health Statistics. 1996. *Health United States 1995.* Washington, D.C.: Government Printing Office.

Navarro, Vincente. 1990. "Race or class versus race and class: mortality differentials in the United States." *Lancet* 336: 1238–40.

Nersesian, William S. 1988. "Infant mortality in socially vulnerable populations." *Annual Review of Public Health* 9: 361–77.

Otten, M. C., S. M. Teutsch, D. F. Williamson, and J. S. Marks. 1990. "The effect of known risk factors on the excess mortality of black adults in the United States." *Journal of the American Medical Association* 263: 845–50.

Pappas, Gregory, Susan Queen, Wilbur Hadden, and Gail Fisher. 1993. "The increasing disparity in mortality between socioeconomic groups in the United States, 1960 and 1986." *New England Journal of Medicine* 329: 103–109.

Pearlstein, Steven. 1995. "The winners are taking all." *Washington Post National Weekly Edition* 13 (December 11): 6–8.

Polednak, Anthony P. 1989. *Racial and ethnic differences in disease.* New York: Oxford University Press.

Power, C., O. Manor, A. J. Fox, and K. Fogelman. 1990. "Health in childhood and social inequalities in health in young adults." *Journal of the Royal Statistical Society* 153 Part 1: 17–28.

Rainwater, Lee. 1966. "Fear and the house-as-haven in the lower class." *Journal of the American Institute of Planning* 32: 23–31.

Rice, Dorothy, and Kathleen Danchik. 1979. "Changing needs of children: Disease, disability, and access to care." Paper presented at Institute of Medicine Annual Meeting, Washington, D.C.

Rogers, R. G., 1992. "Living and dying in the U.S.A.: sociodemographic determinants of death among blacks and whites." *Demography* 29: 287–303.

Ross, Catherine E., and Chia-ling Wu. 1996. "Education, age, and the cumulative advantage in health." *Journal of Health and Social Behavior* 37: 104–120.

Schoendorf, K. C., C. J. R. Hogue, J. C. Kleinman, and D. Rowley. 1992. "Mortality among infants of black as compared with white college-educated parents." *New England Journal of Medicine* 326: 1522–26.

Smith, J. P., and F. R. Welch. 1989. "Black economic progress after Myrdal." *Journal of Economic Literature* XXVII: 519–64.

Starfield, Barbara 1984. "Social factors in child health," pp. 12–18 in *Ambulatory Pediatrics III,* Morris Green and Robert J. Haggerty (eds.). Philadelphia: W. B. Saunders.

Statistical Abstract of the United States. 1997. Washington, D.C.: U.S. Bureau of the Census.

Sterling, T. D., and J. J. Weinkam. 1989. "Comparison of smoking-related risk factors among black and white males." *American Journal of Industrial Medicine* 15: 319–33.

Sudman, Seymour, and Howard E. Freeman. 1989. "Access to health care services in the U.S.A.: Results and methods," pp. 177–96 in *Health and illness in America and Germany,* G. Luschen, W. Cockerham, and G. Kunz (eds.). Munich: Oldenbourg.

Thoits, Peggy A. 1995. "Stress, coping, and social support processes: Where are we? What next?" *Journal of Health and Social Behavior* extra issue: 53–79.

U.S. Bureau of the Census, Current Population Reports, Series P-60, No. 174. 1991. *Money Income of Households, Families and Persons in the United States.* Washington, D.C.: USGPO.

Whittemore, Alice S. 1981 "Air pollution and respiratory disease." *Annual Review of Public Health* 2: 397–429.

Wilkinson, Richard G. 1986. *Class and health.* London: Tavistock.

Wilkinson, Richard G. 1996. *Unhealthy societies.* London: Routledge.

Williams, David R. 1990. "Socioeconomic differentials in health: a review and redirection." *Social Psychology Quarterly* 53: 81–99.

Williams, David R. 1995. "U.S. socioeconomic and racial differences in health: patterns and explanations," pp. 5–43 in *Perspectives in medical sociology,* 2nd ed., Phil Brown (ed.). Prospect Heights, IL: Waveland Press, Inc.

Winkleby, Marilyn A., Darius E. Jatulis, Erica Frank, and Stephen P. Fortmann. 1992. "Socioeconomic status and health: How education, income, and occupation contribute to risk factors for cardiovascular disease." *American Journal of Public Health* 82: 816–820.

Article Review Form at end of book.

Do you think that a psychological factor could cause homelessness? Could this explain the lack of cause/effect findings and the low success rates for efficient rehabilitation programs? Considering their overall low success rate, do you think that homeless rehabilitation programs are worth maintaining? Why or why not?

The Best of Times, the Worst of Times

Reflections of a service provider

Michael Chesser

Sunbelt Human Advancement Resources, Inc.

Winter, 1995. The house meeting had just started with the usual banter among the men in the Transitional Housing Program. As the group settled in, the common complaint seemed to be how tired everyone was—tired of work or tired from work, tired of the daily cares—just, well, tired. As usual, being tired, like many other things, got related to religion. Ronnie said he was ready for the Lord to come back and set up his new heaven and new earth. Anthony said it wouldn't be a new heaven and new earth—he said our perception would change and the old heaven and the old earth would still be around, we'd see it differently. Erwin was adamant—hopeful of a new heaven and a new earth—it had to be so he insisted—it just had to be because as he told us, "he wasn't doing so well in this heaven and this earth."

Homeless people not doing well in this heaven and earth? How can that be what with all the money we spend and the programs we have to assist homeless people? Let's see.

What Does It Mean to Be Homeless?

I doubt if home always carries fond memories for any of us. Surely, home can be the place of great joy and great sorrow. Such, though, is to be expected, for home is the place where we grow up and there is always great joy and great sorrow in growing up. Home is never idyllic; but then neither is life and home is part of life. Home is home, more than house less than Eden.

Whenever I ask a homeless person what they want most, the answer is, invariably "a place of my own." That, of course, is home. A place of my own: a place where, for a few hours a day, we can close the door on the world. It is a place where we rule, that is ordered by our thoughts and priorities and values. It is a place of safety and security. It is a place where we learn to get along, to resolve conflict, to be responsible, to honor our obligations, to serve, to love and to be loved, and be served. It is the place where our holiday traditions and rituals are established and perpetuated. It is the place of familiarity where the rules of living are known and that creates a sense of security and belonging, connectedness, and meaning.

These are precisely the things a homeless person does not have. These are precisely the things a homeless child does not experience. Homeless means being disconnected, not belonging, being insecure, and unsure. It means following the rules, values, and priorities of others—it means being unfree, a captive, a stranger in the land. The unfree, by definition, are dependent. In dependency, honor, integrity, and one's sense of worth are forfeited.

What does it mean to be homeless? It means there is no meaning to life. It means life is a series of disconnected, transient events held together by the occasional hot shower and the daily meal at the local soup kitchen.

What Are the Causes of Homelessness?

If we are honest, I do not think we know why people become homeless. What we do know is twofold. First, homelessness is not a career choice for 99 percent of homeless people (we do not address the one percent for whom it is). Second, the things we label as causes are no more than contributing factors. There is not "a cause" of homelessness.

We would like to say that the root cause of homelessness is poverty. Even that is not the cause. While it is true that many homeless people grew up in poverty, many, nay most, people experiencing poverty are permanently housed. Also, a good number of homeless people grew up in the middle class. Economic class is not the cause of homelessness.

We would like to say that the lack of a good, marketable education is the cause of homelessness. Again, it is true that many homeless people lack good education, read and spell poorly, and are dismal failures at arithmetic, but then, that is also true of a lot of college graduates. I have worked with homeless men who hold Ph.D.'s and/or Masters degrees in engineering, economics, and other disciplines. It is not unusual to find the college graduate among the homeless. Lack of education is not *the* cause of homelessness.

This exercise with economic class and education has a point. In every discipline, we have fallen in love with the cause and effect relationship. If we can identify the cause and know the effect, surely we can provide the solution. That fable permits us to reduce human life to the mechanical. That will not change lives. We want to hold on to the cause and effect relationship because it is simple, because we do not really want to think, because we really do not want to engage the whole person. We want the cause and effect relationship to hold because it is neat and clean. However, life is messy and sometimes, even sordid. Life is confusing and mysterious and, far more than we want to admit, beyond our control.

We want the cause and effect relationship to hold, we use the mechanistic, resort to reductionism, and fail to engage the whole homeless person for a reason. We do that so we do not have to examine our own lives. To engage the wholeness of another, we must also engage our own humanness. That can be a fearsome task.

The training of our new case managers engages these notions. Our task is to create in the new case manager a sense of humility—a lost virtue in our society. Without humility, a case manager can never truly be a catalyst for change.

If there is no "cause" of homelessness, what are the contributing factors? There are the obvious: poor education, lack of job skills and work experience, chemical dependency, lack of coping skills, lack of stress management techniques, lack of personal discipline, lack of a developed sense of responsibility, poor credit history, lack of direction and goals, poor decision-making skills, inability to see the likely consequences of an action, domestic abuse, poverty—well, you get the picture. The contributing factor is—life. How does one live in a complex, modern, technological, "aspiritual" society? Most of us live in it because we do not think about it. In working with the homeless, we must get them to think about it.

Transitional Housing

It is not reasonable to expect a homeless person to address the issues of living *and* make the effort to hold together body and soul. Our transitional housing program is designed to permit a person to deal with the issues in their life without having to work. We pay the rent, the utilities, the telephone bill, and provide child care and a host of other supportive services. The homeless person's full-time job is to resolve the difficulties that have led to their homeless status.

Our folks come to us by referral from other human service agencies: the Drug and Alcohol Commission, emergency shelters, halfway houses, mental health agencies, outreach teams, departments of social services, and others. Once referred, we begin a rather lengthy assessment period. We require a psychological evaluation; a physical examination; and, if there is a history of chemical dependency, a drug and alcohol (D&A) assessment. While these are being done, we gather a social history and assess their educational background, work experience and history, and job skills. These assessment tools are coordinated by a case manager. During the assessment period, the case manager will assign the homeless person several small tasks: arrange transportation to the medical exam, call for an appointment to establish food stamp eligibility, and the like. The homeless person's actions in these tasks will often demonstrate their level of commitment. If they are not willing to do these small tasks, their chances of self-sufficiency are limited.

Once the assessment is complete, the case manager determines if the program will benefit the homeless person. While many are needy, not all will benefit. Once accepted into the program, a case plan is developed in conjunction with the homeless person. Goals are established with appropriate time frames and the game is on. Please be aware that while housing is provided, ours is not a housing program. We provide housing SO THAT a person has an opportunity to develop the skills and resolve their personal issues to become self-determining. To do that, we may work with a person for as long as two years.

The Reality of the Work

Transitional Housing Programs exist so homeless people may gain the skills necessary to be self-determining. The ultimate goal is that the homeless person will become permanently housed. This is accomplished through intensive case management; our case managers have a small case load, usually around ten persons/families. Case managers are required to make daily contact and have at least one in-home visit per week. The case manager's task is to coordinate the services the assigned client needs to fulfill the case plan: arrange transportation, establish interview times for, say, psychotherapy, and a host of other duties.

In the first days, all generally goes well. Clients keep appointments, are cooperative, and have the best of intentions. By about the sixth week of residency, things begin to unravel: work is missed, appointments are broken, plans change abruptly without notifying the case manager, and program rules are violated. I really do not know why this occurs. I suspect it has to do with the first attempts by the homeless person to assert themselves—to live by their own rules, values, and priorities. Surely, that is a positive step—the desire to be independent emerges. It is negative in that the homeless person isn't ready to embrace that freedom.

One might think a homeless person would be appreciative and grateful for the opportunity they have been given, that they would be compliant, eager to make the necessary changes in their lives. That is not the case. The problem of change has been an issue among theologians, psychologists, sociologists, governments, and revolutionaries for ages.

Change is a fearsome thing. The goals for which change is made are often too far away. To go from being homeless on the street to a responsible, permanently housed person is a huge leap. Change, of course, means doing things differently. Doing things differently means a change in the rules; it means living in the unfamiliar; it means not really knowing the outcome. Change is hard work. We would rather live in chaotic familiarity than serene uncertainty.

Change must occur for the homeless person. They must face their fear, overcome anxiety, and be willing to fail. At this point, the case manager becomes a cheerleader. A small success, for example setting up a payment plan on a long overdue bill, is saluted and hailed as a major accomplishment.

In these types of programs, the general rule is failure not success—at least not meaningful, lasting success. Most homeless folks cannot sustain the force for change and resort to the familiar comfortable ways of the past. Failure is the rule and not the exception; therefore it raises some interesting problems. Case managers, in very real ways, foster failure. Not intentionally of course, but as an outgrowth of their jobs and misguided societal norms. Homeless people are notoriously impatient; they want what they want when they want it. Case managers are also notoriously impatient; they want immediate success for their clients. Society is notoriously impatient and demonstrates what Kahn has referred to as *the brown butterfly syndrome*—ease and comfort without effort, right now. So case managers must be patient.

Patience though is problematic. When does patience become indifference and tolerance license? Traditionally, transitional housing programs have a maximum stay of two years. A forty-year-old single mom with two children has to reorder forty years of experience and alter forty years of perception in two. Case managers are under the gun—hurry up because the clock's ticking. Hurry up, but do not be impatient. Yeah, right!! Consequently, case managers often face the prospect of becoming cynical and calling into question the meaningfulness of what they do. We call it burn-out.

The question becomes "Am I doing these folks any good?" It would seem, on the surface, to be a rhetorical question. However, the issue is far deeper. First, compliance from the client is often only conditionally forthcoming—to remain in the program. No real learning occurs. Second, what the client receives from the program is, in most cases, more than they will be able to maintain on their own. They receive housing, utilities, telephone, medical, dental and psychological care, child care, transportation, and more. With the exception of psychological care, these are the necessities of life. They cannot be sustained in a job that pays seven dollars per hour. Perhaps as telling is the philosophy. What are we teaching them that has lasting value and meaning?

We preach freedom and responsible choice, and, equally important, we teach the acceptance of the consequence of choice. Only in decision and the acceptance of the consequence of decision is there freedom. If we have, own, possess stuff (houses, cars, washers, TV's, etc.) these soon become the master of our lives. We must repair the car; we must have the car to get to work, church, play, get the kids, and so on. The same is true of the stuff we accumulate—we forfeit our freedom. It is not a choice. Without an automobile (especially true in our community, which lacks an effective public transportation system), one cannot engage the life of the community or expand one's life beyond walking distance.

The question is: "Are we, in an effort to prepare homeless people to be self-sufficient, in effect setting them up for failure or at best, to be second-class citizens?" We often talk of these things among ourselves. We make an effort at self-condolence by suggesting that we offer an opportunity—in reality that's what we do. We offer homeless people an opportunity to partially correct the consequences of the past, to relearn, to change perceptions. We want this opportunity to provide hope for a better future. Privately, we wonder if the opportunity is an opportunity and if the hope is not false.

An Excursus: Economic Reform

I am not trained in economics, but in theology. However, the practical experience of working with the homeless people I am called to serve has led me to see the need for a reallocation of our nation's economic resources.Welfare was in need of reform, of that there is no doubt. The reports we are getting lead us to believe the success of reform. I have my doubts, but that is another story. Our efforts at welfare reform do nothing to attack poverty. If programs such as ours are to be successful we need, as a nation, to provide the necessities of modern living to the poor. We need to do so at little or no cost to them.

We briefly addressed the transportation crunch. I love my car. I love the drive to and from work, my coffee, cigar, and NPR. I love the thirty minutes of "aloneness." However, it is a most ineffective way to get to and from work and it (the private auto) is not available to the poor. In my community, many higher paying jobs are in suburban industrial parks. Our local transportation system maintains sporadic, first-shift hours to these jobs. They are not accessible to the poor, especially on off-shifts.

Services needed by the homeless are located in the inner city—the Department of Social Services (DSS), D & A, free medical clinics, community health centers, and the like. Low-income housing (which is all a program like ours can afford) is located in or near the city. Rare is the grocery or the pharmacy or the doctor or the library located near low-income housing—the neighborhoods have the wrong image. If we are to address poverty, if we are to offer homeless people real hope and opportunity, we need a public transportation system that effectively matches the advantages of the private auto. Public transportation needs to be readily available (no more than thirty minutes between pick-ups) and serve the job market on all shifts.

The same is true of child care. Single parents could afford to work at lower paying jobs if child care was available at nominal or no cost. They could afford to work the off-shift if off-shift child care was available. If we want to provide people with an opportunity to be self-sufficient, we need to provide the services to make that possible. Certainly, we have the resources to do this. Whether we have the will and courage to do that is another question.

A Miscellany of Problems

One thing we learned early on in our adventure, is, in addition to the normal problems our folks bring with them, there are always special individual problems. These "out of the ordinary" situations bring groans and variety to our work. Working with recently released prisoners is difficult. Working with the illegal alien raises lots of groans: like the homeless man who spoke only Polish, had no green card, was present in the United States on a tourist visa that had expired eight years earlier, well, that was fun. Finding an interpreter to communicate with him only took three weeks. Working with the pedophile brought special dangers and liabilities. Having homeless clients sell illegal drugs from one of your homeless shelters is always interesting. Having a former drug abuser relapse and sell the furniture from the homeless shelter always adds to the variety of daily life. Working with the pregnant thirty-seven year old illiterate female who had five children and no work history or skills was most challenging.

You get the point. There is no such thing as the routine homeless case. They all bring special problems and concerns to our desks. A case manager must be all things to all people—equipped to deal with the most "routine" problem and have the imagination to handle off-the-wall problems.

The Best of Times

The work can be, often is, depressing, frustrating, and tedious. Service providers must be able to survive on a minimum of success. However, the joys are real and the pleasure intense and the fullness of being human is present when . . .

Sherry got her teeth fixed and came by to give me one of the most beautiful smiles I have ever seen. Her self-confidence soared. . . .

John finally trusted me enough to sit sobbing in the park and tell me how afraid of life he was. . . .

Peter, aged twenty, got his first full-time job working with a landscaping company. He was finally "like all men should be."

Latoya, aged six, Latrissa's daughter, got her first puppy. . . .

Joanne took into her small two-bedroom home a stray full grown St. Bernard. The homeless sheltering the homeless.

Our folks do succeed—life does flourish. From time to time, there is even peace.

The Other Side

The fun part of working with the homeless is being a case manager. Despite the sorrow and frustration, the short lived success, this is where the action is. We do not pay case managers much, so if human services is to be the career that allows us to live the life we see on TV, one must become an **ADMINISTRATOR** (spell that Bureaucrat). Overnight—effective with the day of "promotion"—one becomes resident expert in all things, great and small. The administrator knows the answers, knows where the land mines are hidden, knows every person of influence in town, knows every applicable public law, is expert in double-entry accrual accounting (as well as CFDA 14.235), and has grown the eternal smile. Human life as lived by the lesser mortals has been left behind. The work day is now congruent with the massive pay raise—sixteen hours is a good start and dreams (off duty of course) should lead to new methods of fund-raising. Arrogance and disdain are job requirements—never let someone know you do not know someone or some law or some new initiative. Never! Administrators are drawn from the ranks of the criminally insane and are returned (average life span—five years) to the pool of serial killers. Other than that, it's a fun job—especially if you take yourself seriously.

Grant Writing

This is always fun—it's more fun for the masochist, less fun for the obsessive-compulsive, no fun for the anal-retentive. The fun is really to be had by the administrator's boss. Writing a grant is like shooting in the dark. Grant writers write for grant readers. The language used is specialized jargon like "human services delivery system" (where to go for help), "seamless system" (all the bases are covered) and "Continuum of Care" (we have involved everyone we could think of in this project). Language, which used to be a method of communicating an idea clearly, has no place in grant writing. Know the jargon. Cloak the project in language acceptable to the reader (whom you have never met). Close reading of the NOFA (Notice Of Funding Availability) or RFP (Request For Proposal) can supply the writer with language clues.

NOFA's usually arrive at one's office three days before the application deadline. By the time the mail has been date-stamped (an essential agency action: it verifies that the NOFA is real) and finally gets to the grant writer's desk, two days are left before the application deadline. Reading the NOFA takes half a day. Contacting the grantor for clarification takes half a day, if they can be reached (grant readers, in anticipation of all that reading, usually take a vacation the week before application deadlines).

At this point, experienced grant writers have a distinct advantage. They can determine what past application in their barrel of dead applications most nearly approaches the existing NOFA. With a few changes of words (not language), voila!—instant application. The novice, however, must actually write. The novice does not understand grant writing reality. The novice does not actually know that the computer will intentionally eat the application file. The novice has not yet learned that the computer will tell the printer "print every third word." The novice does not know that the computer will coerce the copier to jam during a long series of duplex instructions. The novice *really* thinks the application can be written in one day. The novice does not yet know UPS will go on strike the night the application is scheduled for delivery. There are no novice grant writers living today.

Developing the budget to bring the project to reality, if funded, is always an adventure. Grant writers know that cost effectiveness is critical to being funded. They also know grantor's rarely fund at the requested level. This makes an interesting game. Grant writer: how much can I pad the budget and still be cost-effective? Grantor: how much have they padded the budget and given the appearance of being cost-effective? Usually the grantor wins. What is funded is rarely enough to do the work.

Most funding cuts are directed at staff salaries. Do with less people. However, human services work is labor intensive. Most program participants, or recipients, or clients, or customers (yes, customers—relevance you know) need close, directive support. Case loads need to be restricted so that the case manager can actively, daily, follow the customer (isn't that word awful?). The cost of one case manager runs between fifty and sixty thousand dollars a year. What's included? Salary, fringe, travel, training, office space, supplies, telephone, and supervision.

The next place cuts are made is in the area of supportive services. In homeless programs, supportive services are essential. Affordable housing and living-wage jobs are important. Unless supportive services are available, however, the homeless person is destined to remain in or return to their homeless state.

Here's an example. In my community, services are available to a single person free of charge if their annual income is less than $8,400. That's about $190 a week, gross. After taxes, it is about $152. If a single homeless person seeks D & A treatment and makes more than $190 a week they must pay for the service. Now a homeless person seeking D & A help is probably actively using. They are not going to have the resources to pay for treatment. They aren't going to have $50 up front for assessment, orientation, and staffing. On the other hand, D & A treatment centers must pay staff and operating expenses. They cannot afford to provide pro bono for all who are in need. In this example, the sad part is that those who suffer D & A problems rarely become sober, rarely abstain the first time treatment is provided. They are simply not ready. One strike and you're out is punitive—three strikes and you're out is better, but in some cases still inadequate.

It is not that grantors are ignorant of the problem. Their responsibility is to fund as many programs (especially where national competitions are concerned) as possible. HUD has recently drawn fire for continuing to provide supportive services as an eligible activity for its national Supportive Housing Programs (SHP) competition. The criticism is that supportive services, if funded at all, should be funded by Health and Human Services. HUD should be concerned with housing. At least HUD, for all its flaws and missteps, understands the issue. If such legislation is passed, many good, sound, effective homeless programs will die. Why? Housing is, as I have repeatedly emphasized, critical, but not the overriding issue. Their objective is addressing and resolving the contributing factors of D & A abuse, education, job training, transportation, and child care. So if one applies to HUD for housing, one must also apply to HHS for services. Twice the work. HUD may fund; HHS may not; or vice versa. So an agency may be left with a housing program and no services or a host of services and no housing. Sometimes, it seems, we step over quarters to pick up nickels.

Working with Other Agencies

The trend is to involve as many agencies as possible in a given project. Grantors love to see a page (typed, single spaced in six point Helve) of involved agencies as part of this application. This is called concerted community involvement. What it really is, is a group grope. Remember the qualifications for being an administrator—resident expert on all things. Concerted community involvement brings together in one room many, many resident experts who are very, very important and very, very busy and indispensable. A one o'clock meeting usually convenes by one-thirty. Such meetings are well-attended. The need to establish one's importance and visibility is essential. Without fail, the one person who truly knows something is being important and visible at a meeting about which he/she knows nothing. The meeting is usually convened by the most senior administrator present with something like "While we wait for Jane/John, let's rehearse the known parameters of the population this Continuum intends to bring into the delivery system under the HUD SHP initiative delineated by this NOFA." This is immediately followed by some important, highly, visible person's cell phone ringing. Everyone waits sharing knowing smiles using the time to consult their Daytimers.

It is easy to poke fun at the egos that make up these community building meetings. The truth is they are necessary—the egos and the meetings. Funders are pleased when the involvement in a project appears to cover a broad spectrum of the community: human service providers, business, banking, religious organizations, volunteers, and government. The concept is good; the reality is something less. Usually, the bulk of the work falls to a few people, generally those who are most concerned and most knowledgeable about the project underway. These meetings do create new ventures, more cooperation among a wide variety of enterprises, and keep people informed. This can lead to a reduction in duplication of services and programs.

Duplication of services and the elimination of such is a key issue in the human services arena. It is a false issue. Duplication of services exists when the service supplied exceeds the demand. When the demand for a service is equal to or exceeds the supply, duplication does not exist. To mandate that a service be consolidated under one provider may be justified, but often is not feasible. A given agency may not have space or staff to meet the need. The agency may not want to expand for reasons of mission or limiting their service areas. What may be advantageous in consolidation is decreasing overhead and supervisory staff.

What is needed is a universal (at least a community wide) criterion for access to services, waiting periods before a person may reenter the system in the event of noncompliance, common in-take forms, and general access to this information. If homeless people knew that every agency and religious organization in town operated under the same regulations, procedures, and waiting periods there would be less effort to "beat" the system. Duplication is not the issue; having a universal system is. Why isn't such a system in place? It calls for change.

Let's get back to those meetings. Every program, existing, proposed, or planned, is fraught with political considerations. Who works well with whom? Who should be invited? Who should convene? What is the relationship between the convening agency and those who need to be present? Who is sensitive to criticism? Who are the "idea" people, "the policy-makers," the "worker bees," and the "drones"? Who will block the proposal or support it? As much maneuvering occurs at these meetings as in the back rooms of Congress. If one wants to see their project succeed, one must be cognizant of these considerations and careful in one's planning. It is emotionally exhausting and frustrating because it involves "turf." Turf is not so much protecting one's agency's programs as it is survival and image. Propose something or say something that threatens either of these icons and the fight is on—serious blood-letting and the choosing up of sides. The proposal that may be needed and necessary or the truth of the statement matter little. Funding does (survival). To be funded, one needs a good image.

Some wag once paraphrased the Gospel according to John, chapter three, verse sixteen: "For God so loved the world, he didn't send a committee." The problem with committees is accountability and responsibility. Committee decisions are made by majority vote—who's responsible and who's accountable? Committee decisions are often made under time constraints—people cannot stay long enough to think their way through a problem, they must hurry off to another meeting. As a result, decisions made must be amended as flaws are discovered that will call for another meeting. In essence, there is too much to be done, by too few people in too short a time. Even workshops are not effective. Administrators have worries on the homefront, reports to get out, fences to mend, and contrary to popular belief, private lives and families. Concentration levels are short and attention spans are easily broken. For all the difficulties, amazingly and encouragingly, work does get done.

Working with Funders

The life-blood of any human service project is funding. Show me the money! As public contributions are only a fraction of what is needed, most agencies rely on government and foundations. Funders do not fund what they are not interested in. In that respect, working with funders is easy—there exists common ground and common goals.

Some funders set their regulations in place, provide technical assistance for compliance, audit once a year or so, and leave you to do the work. HUD is an example of this. It is a pleasure to work with the local field office of CPD/HUD. They want your program to succeed and often find ways to enhance program directions. Personal relationships based on common objectives are built and support is received. Unless one does something stupid or attempts to deceive, one can enjoy these relationships.

Other funders, far too many, want to micromanage the program. They delve into program criteria, attempt to set limits on duration of services, limit services to "acceptable" persons (no homosexuals for example), even want to reshape management techniques. They often visit program sites several times a year and do so *en masse*—five or six people in the party. No program has been known to satisfy these funders. Why bother with them? Show me the money! Without money, nothing gets done. It is a fact of human services life, unescapable, mandatory. Consequently, keeping funders happy is essential. Keeping funders happy may be a matter of personality or doing things their way or "politics."

Administrators often feel like hypocrites. It is hard to be open and honest, to maintain personal integrity and honor when one must be all things to all people. It is a constant strain having to choose language that will not offend, cloak answers in half-truths, be aware of the personal agendas of those with whom one speaks, be aware of their hot buttons and areas where they feel threatened. Adult people are fragile, egos are easily dented, feelings are hurt—our "touchy-feely," yet radically "bottom line" society has made it so.

So we are wary of funders, yet play the game. Why? In those "dark nights of the soul" one doesn't know. It seems senseless and more profoundly, meaningless. Being itself is called into question. No answer, no ideal satisfies in those nights. There are too many people in need of so much, with too few resources and too many "hoops" to make the work worthwhile. However, from time to time, one hears again the call—people are worth the effort. The call may revisit us as a spiritual confirmation, or a sense of human dignity, or the stark realization that one must work to eat. I think, though, for the most part, people want to help people. The need is there—endless, eternal, and some step in the breach and make the effort. The trick is to know that you are not defined by success or failure or the necessary hypocrisy. The trick is to know you must play the game—the trick is to admit the games one plays. Devastation and loss of one's person happens when we come to believe we are not playing a game.

Reporting

Every funder requires program reports. These are not bad in themselves as funders need information and programs need to know where they stand. Reports are necessary and valuable even if they are, and they definitely are, time consuming to generate. From an agency standpoint, the problem is that all funders want different information. A problem is that reporting periods differ from funder to funder—some monthly, quarterly, or annually. Some want quantitative reports while others want qualitative reports while still others want both. No one wants a verbal report.

The information necessary to generate a report begins at the intake and case management level. These people must gather data, assess, staff, and plan—and keep score. Keeping score is a low priority (rightly so, I think) for them, but a high priority for administrators. Administrators cannot get enough information. A natural conflict exists between administrators and case managers. A good case manager has more to do than they can accomplish; yet, they can provide good, accurate information. So we try to schedule office days—days for paperwork and the compiling of information. Usually, case managers are sick on these days. Threats to their personal well-being are effective cures. Information is amassed, usually in illegible form—only doctors have worse handwriting. Colleagues will help colleagues and the information is gained (always late). The task is to put it in the form the funder requests. Formats differ, information requested differs, time of submission differs. An administrator could spend their life generating reports—that is why there are administrative assistants.

Let me address one critical area of reporting. In this age of accountability, funders are requiring outcome based goals as part of the application. An outcome based goal for a homeless program might be something like this: Fifty percent of all people who complete their case plan will become permanently housed for at least one year. Sounds good, professional, and certain. The funder needs to have some assurance some good will come from their money. Programs need some objective ways to measure productivity and effectiveness.

However, the premise of outcome based goals is wrongheaded. It assumes one can control and predict outcome, which one cannot do. The old, time-worn adage, "You can lead a horse to water, but you can't make it drink," has special relevance here. We can provide the services—arrange D & A treatment, mental health intervention, job training, child care, life skills courses, and more—but we cannot make it "take." That is beyond our control. To require accountability where one has no control is akin to making one responsible to see that a task is done, but granting no authority to get it done. It is senseless.

What is possible are input goals. Such a goal might read: 100 percent of homeless persons enrolled in the program will receive at least ten hours of instruction in the South Carolina Landlord-Tenant Act. Such instruction will be given during the first three months in residency. This is a measurable goal. This can be controlled. If a person does not receive the necessary instruction within the mandated time, administration/management can determine why and it is hoped, rectify the error.

Working with Local Government

This is the black hole of human services work. Local government does not trust service providers who, in turn, do not trust local government. This quality relationship stifles productive work. Local government does not have the resources to determine the areas of need within the community or the intensity of the problem. They rely on service providers to inform them. They know service providers need money, so government has a tendency to view the information provided askance. Government believes agencies inflate the need and over dramatize its intensity. There is some truth to that, especially as there is no effective way to present numbers in an unduplicated manner.

Agencies may provide service to the same person. Each agency counts that as a person served and that, of course, inflates the number. What government needs to understand is there is no intentional attempt to deceive. Inflated numbers grow out of requested reports. Such numbers do, however, put us on notice with regard to the intensity of the problem. The problem for those who are homeless is probably greater than we understand if they are seeking services from so many agencies.

There is not a good method to determine the number of homeless people in a given community. How many homeless people are there? A lot. Is that a good enough answer—probably not. Providing numbers isn't either. Numbers are either too high or too low. Numbers, at best, are only approximate: even good, well-thought out, methodologically sound surveys won't provide complete accuracy.

The natural conflict between service providers and local government officials sets the stage for the more serious problem. Distrusting the information given by service providers, local officials rely on their personal opinion of homeless needs, problems, and solutions. These are, at least in our community, ill-informed and stereotypical: The homeless are hoboes and tramps, lazy beggars who could take care of themselves if they'd quit drinking or drugging or conning. Consequently, public policy is developed and public funds expended based on the local officials, usually, uninformed opinion. This is why service providers distrust local government officials.

Accurate information is necessary. An understanding of the problem is essential. The admission that a socially unacceptable problem (homelessness) exists is critical. We need the support of local government to assist us in these areas. A good start would be for units of local government (ULG) to meet and develop uniform reporting criteria and time frames. Then meet for a frank discussion of the problem. Then determine which ULG will assume responsibility for a certain portion of the problem, for example, housing or transportation or services. Perhaps then, we could get on with it.

Conclusion

There are real joys, heartaches, frustration, and success in working with the homeless. It is not easy work. It requires some expertise in a wide arena of subjects: programs, politics, time-management, funding, administration, human relations, accounting, and management.

From a program standpoint, I don't think we know what works. If the homeless person is truly motivated, most any program will be of benefit. If not, probably none will. How to motivate people, especially those who are oppressed by poverty and their own poor choices, is critical. I am not intelligent or wise enough to know, universally, what works. Some things work with some people, some of the time. Is that acceptable? You must decide.

This raises our final consideration. What does the public, you, have a right to expect from the expenditure of public monies on homeless programs? Let me suggest a realistic expectation. Perhaps 25 percent of homeless people will go on to be self-sufficient and permanently housed. Perhaps. Most will become permanently housed for six months or so and then become homeless or precariously housed again. It is unreasonable to expect that everyone can live effectively in a society as complex as ours. I am not so sure that those who can are better for it. What I think justifies such programs as ours and the huge monetary expense, is our national belief that everyone deserves an opportunity and, often, several. In reality, that's what we are about—we offer, with your money, an opportunity to people who have failed, to people who may not even know how to take advantage of an opportunity. Programs like ours say a lot about the kind of nation, and, consequently, the kind of people we are.

Will we continue to fund such programs or not? I don't know. What's important—the bottom line or people? You must decide and the choice will be painful.

So are homeless people doing well in this heaven and this earth?

Article Review Form at end of book.

WiseGuide Wrap-Up

The problems of the poor are chronic, and like crime, they show few signs of ever being eliminated completely. Issues relating to poverty, such as homelessness, urban redevelopment, and welfare reform, are often obscured by popular conceptions, media images, and common stereotypical thinking. In addition, a solid sociological perspective on these issues requires us to examine the problem pragmatically. Far too many people deal with poverty as though it were an abstract intellectual exercise. The readings in this section have shown the more realistic side of the poor and called attention to the distortion effect that clouds our thinking. Joel Handler's review of welfare reform is one of the best descriptions of what we have done with regard to poverty, while Renee White's reading is perhaps the best synthesis of the data on the poverty debate within sociology. Further, Maria Tempenis and Robert McNamara presented concrete information about the homeless in the United States.

R.E.A.L. Sites

This list provides a print preview of typical **coursewise** R.E.A.L. sites. (There are over 100 such sites at the **courselinks**™ site.) The danger in printing URLs is that web sites can change overnight. As we went to press, these sites were functional using the URLs provided. If you come across one that isn't, please let us know via email to: webmaster@coursewise.com. Use your Passport to access the most current list of R.E.A.L. sites at the **courselinks**™ site.

Site name: Homes for the Homeless

URL: http://www.opendoor.com/hfh/opendoor.html

Why is it R.E.A.L.? This site provides an in-depth look at Homes for the Homeless, one of New York's largest shelters. It provides information on the nature of homelessness as well as data on a promising program called American Family Inns.

Key topics: homelessness, poverty, foster care, self-empowerment

Site name: Institute on Race and Poverty

URL: http://www.umn.edu/irp/

Why is it R.E.A.L.? This is the Institute on Race and Poverty's home page. In addition to providing some of the most up-to-date research information on the links between poverty and race, the IRP also provides avenues for the poor if they need legal advice, housing information, or other social services.

Key topics: research on poverty, single-parent families, social service programs

Site name: U.S. Census Bureau

URL: http://www.census.gov/

Why is it R.E.A.L.? Of all the sites available to learn more about poverty, the Census Bureau is one of the most comprehensive. Those who visit this site can easily obtain a litany of information on poverty as the government defines it.

Key topics: the Poverty Line, eligibility requirements, trend analysis on poverty

section 3

Learning Objectives

After reading these articles, you should be able to

- Define what is meant by race and ethnicity.
- Discuss the trends and problems associated with interracial marriages.
- Describe the "model minority" myth.

Racial Inequalities

Racism is a social problem of particular interest to many people. The problems our society has experienced with regard to race date back almost as far as American society itself. Moreover, the problems, while they may appear to be subsiding, have not really abated to any significant degree. In fact, one of the problems surrounding racism in American society is the perception that it is an issue of declining importance.

The readings in this section attempt to show that a number of racial problems remain in our society. Brian Siegel does an excellent job of describing the problems of defining race in our society. Drawing from the anthropological literature, he concludes that race is an inappropriate term for classifying groups. In their reading on the nature of black/white relationships, Robert McNamara, Maria Tempenis, and Beth Walton review the literature and find that the number of interracial marriages has increased and that opposition to these types of relationships has generally declined. In their discussion of white racism, Joel Fegin and Hernon Vera describe two examples of this type of discrimination involving the Denny's and Shoney's restaurant chains. Finally, Jieli Li discusses the problems and issues surrounding Asian Americans in our society.

Questions

Reading 12. According to evolutionary biologists, what are the three main biological problems with the concept of race? Do you agree that evidence is sufficient to refute the need for racial categories? Why do anthropologists prefer the term *ethnic group* to *race*? Do you agree with the dangers of using the term *race* to describe a group of people?

Reading 13. Do you think that the poor success rate of interracial couples will improve if their numbers continue to grow? Do you think that the growing number of interracial couples will positively or negatively affect race relations in society?

Reading 14. Have you observed racial inequality in restaurants today? Do you think that the publicity over the discrimination in large restaurant chains will affect the overall food industry's treatment of discrimination?

Reading 15. Do you agree that the myth of the model Asian is contributing to discrimination in the labor market? Do you agree that the myth of the model Asian is interfering with Asians' assimilation of American culture?

According to evolutionary biologists, what are the three main biological problems with the concept of race? Do you agree that evidence is sufficient to refute the need for racial categories? Why do anthropologists prefer the term *ethnic group* to *race*? Do you agree with the dangers of using the term *race* to describe a group of people?

Anthropology and the Science of "Race"

Brian Siegel
Furman University

The fixity of a habit is generally in direct proportion to its absurdity.
Marcel Proust,
Remembrance of Things Past

"Race" is not a black or white issue in anthropology, certainly not for the last sixty years. Most anthropologists deny the existence of "biological races," but they all acknowledge the reality of "social races" and the tendency for people to deal with one another in terms of socially and culturally constructed racial categories. Forensic anthropologists, for example, measure bones to identify the race of unidentified skeletons, but their racial attributions are statistical inferences drawn from comparative skeletons of known social races. Such classifications vary across time and space, so American forensic anthropologists are best at identifying the social races recognized in America. Social races are as often distinguished on the basis of their cultural as physical features, so anthropologist Ashley Montagu (1942) has long insisted that races should properly be called "ethnic groups."

The racial categories used by the federal Census Bureau are examples of "social races." While often based on perceived physical differences, such perceptions have changed over time. The 1890 census was the only one that attempted to distinguish between mulattos (one-half), quadroons (one-quarter), and octoroons (one-eighth black). The 1920 census was the last one to distinguish mulattos from Negroes. The people who had once occupied these categories were still around, but the Bureau abandoned them as subjective and, in the case of mulattos, irrelevant, having decided that about 75 percent of the Negroes were of mixed origins anyway (Williamson 1980: 112–14, 118). Similarly, Asian Indians have been classified as the Hindu race from 1920–40, as White from 1950–70, and as Asian or Pacific Islander since 1977, when the 1970 Hispanic racial category was dropped, and Spanish-speakers were tabulated separately under "Hispanic Origin (of any race)" (Wright 1994: 50–52).

The racial categories used by the federal government were set in 1977 by the Office of Management and Budget's Statistical Directive 15. It offers a choice of five broad racial categories: White (for people who are mostly pink); Black (for people who are mostly brown); American Indian, Eskimo, or Aleut (the Native American category); Asian or Pacific Islander (a uniquely American racial category); and Other (largely claimed by Latin Americans who reject the Black/White alternatives). These classifications are far from perfect, and the House Subcommittee that oversees the system is under pressure to change it. The Arab American Institute would like a new, nonwhite category for Middle Easterners, and native Hawaiians want to be moved from the Asian/Pacific Islander to the Native American category. Most contentious of all is the movement to create a new Multiracial category for the children of interracial marriages. This, by undermining the current classification system, might pose serious problems for the apportionment of congressional districts, and for affirmative action and civil rights regulatory programs. Clearly, the Census Bureau's racial categories are socially and culturally defined and are as much about politics and money as about personal identity issues (Wright 1994).

A characteristic feature of social races is their arbitrariness. America used to recognize, as South Africa and most Latin American countries still do, a mixed (mulatto) race category of *Coloreds* or *Creoles;* and such people had substantial communities in Charleston and New Orleans. However, under the racism and miscegenation fears of the late nineteenth century, mulattos had to either "pass" as whites or join with the Negroes. Many states then adopted the South's *one-drop rule,* meaning that a person with any African ancestry was defined as black, although most "blacks" by then were brown (Davis 1991; Williamson 1980). The one-drop rule only applies to African Americans and has never made a Native American out of someone with a Cherokee great-grandmother (even a princess). All this is peculiar to America. So is the case of the Mississippi Chinese studied by James Loewen (1988), who were classified as blacks in the 1870s, and gradually became whites in the 1940s and 1950s.

The racial categories used in American society take different forms in other countries (Davis 1991: 81–122). A white from the Dominican Republic is considered Colored in Jamaica, and black in America. A Mexican Indian who wears Indian clothes and speaks an Indian language is an Indian, but one who opts for European clothes and speaking Spanish is a Ladino (mestizo). Brazil, like America, is a color-conscious society with a history of plantation slavery. While Brazilians have some three dozen racial categories, and can assign the same person to different categories from day to day, their massive lower class tends to be populated with darker-skinned people. However, their system of racial classification is not entirely color bound. "Money whitens," the Brazilians say, and a wealthy, dark-skinned person is a white. None of this makes any biological sense. Social races operate on the basis of sociocultural criteria rather than on biological facts. They justify self-perpetuating differences in social rank and livelihood opportunities as if they were predetermined facts of nature. This is because these socioculturally constituted categories are grounded in the ideology of distinct biological races.

That most anthropologists—about 50 percent of the physical and 70 percent of the cultural anthropologists, according to a 1989 survey reported in *Newsweek* (Begley 1995: 67)—no longer accept "race" as a valid biological category is interesting in and of itself. It is even more interesting, though, when contrasted with the fact that nineteenth century anthropology all but invented the idea of "race" (Cunningham 1908; Stocking 1968). Most of our current racial folklore derives from the "scientific racism" and armchair evolutionism of the nineteenth century anthropologists. However, most of their twentieth century counterparts reject the idea of biological race(s), and even those who want to retain it seem uncertain about what to do with it. What happened here? What is the history of the biological notion of race, and why is that notion now generally rejected?

Apart from Antarctica, our human ancestors had populated every continent on earth well before the end of the last Ice Age. Few species are as widely distributed across the globe. As with any widely distributed species, natural selection (or environmental adaptation), random genetic drift (the tendency for the gene frequencies in small, isolated populations—for no adaptive reason—to rapidly diverge from those of their parental stock), and sexual selection ("survival of the chicest," or preferential mating for attractive traits) combined to make us a widely varied species. Though these human differences are all based on nonobservable genotypic variations, such as the ones for the sickle-cell trait and the various blood groups, we more often interact on the basis of such observable, phenotypic variations as size, shape, and color differences.

Humans have long been aware of phenotypic differences, but what they did with them varied from place to place. The *Rig-Veda* from about 3000 B.C., for example, suggests that color prejudice is no recent invention, for it tells how the Aryan invaders conquered and slew the dark-skinned and "flat-nosed barbarians" of the Indus River Valley. The ancient Egyptians were also color-conscious, for tomb paintings from as early as 1350 B.C. represent the Egyptians in red (though occasionally, black), and the Middle Easterners, Northerners (i.e., Europeans) and Nubians in yellow, white, and black (Gossett 1963: 3–4). The Egyptians, though, ordinarily referred to these peoples by geographical or political names, rather than by color. Recognizing physical differences does not require racial labels. Neither does it necessarily entail "racism," the belief that such differences make some people innately inferior or superior to others.

The biological meaning of "race" has changed over time. The word seems to have entered English around 1500 from one of the romance languages—probably French (*race*) or Spanish (*raza*)—to denote a breed, variety, nation, or descent-related line of creatures. Thus a dog or horse "of race" was a pedigree or thoroughbred creature, while "the race and stock of Abraham" meant the Jews or ancient Hebrews (Banton 1987: 1–2).

This same, varietal sense of race was applied to humans in the tenth edition of Carolus Linnaeus's (1707–78) *Systema Naturae* (System of Nature, 1758), the Swedish taxonomist's binomial catalogue of plant and animal life. Apart from two fanciful categories of humanity—the "wild" children abandoned in the forests and a jumble of early ape lore and legendary men with tails—he identified four geographical varieties of *Homo sapiens*: the red (Native) Americans, white Europeans, pale Asians, and black Africans. Though his brief, one and two word descriptions of each variety's temperament, posture, and governance hint at unflattering stereotypes, Linnaeus offered a largely descriptive, nonhierarchical account of four geographical varieties of the human species.

There were contrasting views of human differences by the late eighteenth century, when the debate began over just how different these human varieties were, and whether they were best explained in terms of one or separate creations (monogenesis vs. polygenesis). While the monogenists explained human varieties in terms of their divergent experiences since the time of creation, the polygenists considered them distinctly different species, each the product of its own separate (and unbiblical) creation. Some sense of these contrasting views is captured by comparing the ideas and attitudes of two contemporary monogenists, Johann Friedrich Blumenbach, a German medical professor and the father of physical anthropology, and Baron Georges Cuvier, the eminent French naturalist and the father of comparative anatomy and paleontology.

The third edition of Blumenbach's (1752–1840) *Generis Humani Varietate Nativa* (*On the Native Varieties of the Human Genus* 1795) was a particularly influential discussion of human varieties. He, "the least racist and most genial of all Enlightenment thinkers" (Gould 1994b: 67), rejected the polygenists' claim of separate creations and argued, instead, that his five human varieties were generated after people left their common origin place and adapted to different environments. Moreover, he saw the geographical distribution of human physical differences—he had tried and rejected hair forms and facial angles (Gossett 1963: 70, 80)—as being so gradual in nature as to defy any demarcation of discrete racial types. Thus, Blumenbach claimed, the very traits that many viewed as markers of blacks' inferiority also exist, to varying degrees, among other human varieties. To rebut the claim that blacks were innately less intelligent than whites, he wrote about Benjamin Banneker, the African American mathematical genius, and of his particular fondness, within his own special library of black authors, for the poetry of Phillis Wheatley.

It is ironic, then, that Blumenbach imposed hierarchy upon the study of human varieties. Convinced that his Europeans were the most handsome and, thus, the original human variety, he renamed them "Caucasians" after the handsomest skull in his collection, that of a women from near Mt. Caucasus on the Georgian-Russian border. The other human varieties, through migration and environmental adaptation, were "degenerations" (meaning "derivations") from that original white stock. There were, he reasoned, two main and two subsequent derivations, for a total of five varieties: one Caucasian line went off to become the brown Malays (including Australian aborigines, Melanesians, and Polynesians), who gave rise to the black Ethiopians (Africans); another went off to become the red Americans, who later gave rise to the yellow Mongoloids (Asians). Thus while Blumenbach rejected the notion of separate biological races, his hierarchical, pseudoevolutionary scheme implied that some varieties were purer, more original and handsome, than others (Gould 1994b; Banton 1987: 5–6; Gossett 1963: 37–39). His scheme was easily misrepresented during this age of the trans-Atlantic slave trade and growing color prejudice, as evidenced in Thomas Jefferson's *Notes on Virginia* (1786).

Baron Cuvier (1769–1832), on the other hand, viewed such varieties or races as fixed and distinct physical types. An opponent of early evolutionary thought, the mutability of species, Cuvier invented *catastrophism* to reconcile the extinctions documented in the geological strata with his belief in fixed, unalterable species. The earth, he said, had experienced a long series of natural "revolutions" or catastrophic environmental changes, after which the surviving members of the species in a given region left and were replaced by new, immigrant species.

Just such a catastrophe, Cuvier believed, had driven Adam and Eve's descendants off into different, mutually isolated regions, resulting in a hierarchy of three fixed human types—the Caucasians on top, Mongoloids in the middle, and Ethiopians on the bottom—each with its own distinctive cultural and mental traits. Thus, Cuvier divided the human species into fixed geographical types and used their physical differences to explain their cultural and (alleged) intellectual differences (Banton 1987: 28–32). The race scientists of the nineteenth century shared Cuvier's belief in a hierarchy of fixed racial types. However, they sought measurable data to demonstrate it and, in their search, invented *anthropometry*, the measurement of living humans, and *craniometry*, the measurement of human heads and skulls.

One of the earliest contributors to this "scientific racism" of the nineteenth century was the Philadelphia physician and paleontologist, Samuel George Morton (1799–1851). Morton was convinced that black and white Americans represented different, unalterable species, and that the blacks had been predestined for slavery since the days of ancient Egypt (Lorimer 1978: 136). Given the mulatto presence in America, he was forced to temper the long-held polygenist claim that mulattos, like mules, were infertile. Separate species, Morton said, could indeed propagate fertile offspring, but the resulting racial hybrids suffer such diminished fertility that they eventually become extinct (Gossett 1963: 59; Lorimer 1978: 132–33, 139–40; Stanton 1960: 66–68; Williamson 1980: 73, 95).

Seduced by the fallacious belief that brain or skull size was an index of the capacity for civilization, Morton used pepper seed, lead shot, and calibrated cylinders on 256 skulls from his collection to determine the average cranial capacity for each of Blumenbach's five "races." His results, reported in an often copied, final footnote to his *Crania Americana* (1839), seemed to confirm the notion of a racial hierarchy of intelligence: Caucasians had the largest skulls; Mongolians, Americans, and Malays had middle-sized ones; and Ethiopians had the smallest (Banton 1987: 34–37; Gossett 1963: 73–74; Gould 1981: 50–69; Stanton 1960: 24–44). Upon Morton's death, his two disciples, Josiah Clark Nott and George Robin Gliddon, gave even wider currency to the Euroamerican cause of polygenesist white supremacy with at least nine editions of their 800 page *Types of Mankind* (1854) (Banton 1987: 37–45; Gossett 1963: 64–65; Stanton 1960: 45–53, 161–73).

Apart from the fact that cranial capacity is a direct function of body size (males tend to have larger skulls than females; and Neanderthals had 10 percent larger crania than modern humans), Morton's results were predetermined by the skulls he selected for his sample. As his footnote clearly states, fourteen of his seventeen Hindu skulls and all of his Mexican and Peruvian skulls were omitted from the Caucasian and American subsets because of their small size. He only obtained an acceptable American figure by including a number of Iroquois specimens, which were, on average, 4.5 cubic inches larger than the average Caucasian skull. He reported the range of variation found within each of his racial categories, but was so focused upon the interracial differences that he ignored that his reported intraracial differences (14 to 40 cubic inches) were far greater than those between racial categories (1 to 9 cubic inches).

Harvard biologist Stephen Jay Gould has since reexamined Morton's skulls, remeasured his sample, and recalculated his figures. It turns out that Morton's Caucasians did not have a monopoly on the largest skulls, and that there was no significant difference (4 cubic inches, or 65.5 cubic centimeters) between his racial categories. Morton was wrong. He made no attempt to cover up his errors, so he cannot be accused of fraud. Gould, instead, finds him guilty of "an *a priori* conviction about racial ranking so powerful that it directed his tabulations along preestablished lines" (Gould 1981: 69, 50–69; Banton 1987: 34–37).

By 1850, European and American ideas about human varieties assumed the existence of a hierarchy of fixed types based on heritable physical and cultural traits. Such ideas were all but universal in the 1870s and 1880s. This change cannot be traced to the influence of any single racial theory or theorist, for, as historian Douglas Lorimer (1978) argues, the race scientists were following, rather than leading, popular opinion. Discussions about race in mid-Victorian England were very political, focusing on social class and class mobility, and the question of white-nonwhite equality made little sense when few thought that poor whites, the Irish, or the Jews, much less women, merited equal treatment. Citing anthropologist Ruth Benedict (1943), Lorimer concludes that the pattern of intense racial determinism and nationalism then found across Europe "was a common reaction to the increasingly antagonistic international climate and to the threatening political and social environment posed by the advance towards a more fully industrial, urban, and democratic order" (Lorimer 1978: 209). Factor in the apologies for slavery and the attacks on immigration, and the same conclusion applies to America (Fredrickson 1988; Williamson 1980: 61–109).

Most nineteenth century scholars, then, viewed races as pure and fixed human types, if not as separate species. Charles Darwin's (1809–1882) *The Descent of Man* (1871) was a partial exception, for while comfortable with the cultural distinction between "savage" and "civilized" peoples, and with the idea of racial extinctions and progression, Darwin generally used "race" in terms of a nonhierarchical series of varieties produced by sexual selection, and he saw no point in giving names to things he could not define. By arguing that all people were descended from the apes, he and Alfred Russell Wallace (1823–1913) made hash of the old monogenesis-polygenesis debate. However, their approach did not satisfy most of their readers, who wanted to know which race had derived from which ape, or which among the races was the most or least ape-like (Lorimer 1978: 142–45; Stepan 1982: 56–82; Stocking 1968: 110–32).

These scientific racists were not only convinced that an evolutionary hierarchy of fixed racial types existed in nature, but that Darwin's own natural selection (or Herbert Spencer's "survival of the fittest") had created it. As scientists, however, they went in search of measurable data to prove it. They studied skin color, hair forms, facial angles, the ratio of lower to upper arm length, autopsied brains, racial species of body lice, and, by the end of the century, over 5,000 measurements on the skull alone (Gossett 1963: 69–83). However, if pure and fixed racial types did exist in nature, such differences proved frustratingly difficult to measure.

Measurements were also used by the critics of scientific racism. While British and American scholars of this period celebrated the Anglo-Saxon race and the Teutonic origins of democracy (Gossett 1963: 84–122, 310–38), the Germans were captivated with the myth of Aryan (national) purity. Attempting to discredit Aryanism and a French anthropologist's claim that the Prussians were an alien, Slavo-Finnish race, the German pathologist and statesman Rudolph Virchow (1821–1902) arranged an anthropometric survey of 6.7 million German school children. His results, published in 1886, found that they fell short of the Aryan ideal. Real German children seemed to be of mixed origins, for they were not predominately blonde, blue-eyed, or fair-skinned. Virchow's results had little impact upon the Aryan ideology (Shipman 1994: 99–100; Stepan 1982: 101).

One of Virchow's former students, anthropologist Franz Boas (1858–1942) arranged a similar 1908-10 anthropometric survey for the U.S. Immigration Commission, then concerned with the hordes of "inferior" immigrant types from Southern and Eastern Europe who threatened to overwhelm the more refined, but less prolific, "Native Americans" (i.e., Nordic types) from Northwestern Europe. Such concerns, later popularized in at least eight editions of Madison Grant's *The Passing of the Great Race* (1916), were also shared by supporters of Charles B. Davenport's influential American eugenics (literally "good breeding") movement, and were substantially similar to those of its German counterpart, the ominously entitled *Society for Racial Hygiene* (Shipman 1994: 122–30; Shanklin 1994: 82–89).

Boas surveyed nearly 18,000 recent immigrants and their children, and measured, among other things, head length and breadth. Head form was then considered a fixed racial trait, but Boas reported in 1911 that each successive American child born to round-headed, Russian Jewish immigrants was progressively more long-headed, while those born to long-headed Southern Italian immigrants became progressively more round-headed. Boas concluded that if such a supposedly fixed racial trait could change in a single generation, "we must speak of a plasticity (as opposed to a permanence) of types" (Boas 1940: 71; Stocking 1968: 175–82). In other words, his measurements contradicted the usual view of immigrants as fixed racial types.

Boas had as much influence upon the preconceived ideas of the eugenicists and the Immigration Commission as Virchow had on the German notion of Aryan purity. Madison Grant accused Boas, a secular Jew from Germany, of leading a Jewish conspiracy to discredit the scientific fact of fixed racial types (Shanklin 1994: 82). Grant and Davenport soon dominated the National Research Council's Committee on Anthropology, and, disturbed by Boas's professionalization of anthropology, together founded the Galton Society for the study of "racial anthropology" by "Native Americans, who are anthropologically, socially, and politically sound, no Bolsheviki [i.e., Jews] need apply" (Shanklin 1994: 87; Stocking 1968: 287–90). Given the prevailing social climate and the sensational findings of the Army intelligence tests, the Immigration Restriction Act passed in 1924.

Bad ideas never die, and American racism was given a new lease on life in 1916 with the perfection of the Stanford-Binet intelligence scale. It purported to offer an objective means of measuring innate intelligence, and, with the testing of 1.75 million Army inductees in 1917, soon yielded data confirming the popular suspicion that nonwhite and foreign-born Americans were less intelligent, and that immigration restrictions were badly overdue (Benedict 1963: 363–69; Gould 1981: 146–234).

Nearly fifty years later, inspired by Sir Cyril Burt's bogus studies of twins (Kamin 1974; Stepan 1982: 181–88), psychologist Arthur R. Jensen (1969) argued that the lower average IQ score of black Americans is an accurate reflection of a hereditary (i.e., racial) trait. One obvious problem with his thesis is the unstated assumption that black Americans, 20 to 30 percent of whose genes came from European and Native American populations, are a discrete biological population. His other problematic assumptions—that intelligence is largely fixed by birth, that IQ tests accurately measure intelligence, and that one can use an explanation of IQ differences among whites to explain IQ differences between blacks and whites—are examined at greater length by Stephen Jay Gould (1977: 243–47; 1981: 156–57, 320–24). These same erroneous, if unstated, assumptions have reappeared in Richard J. Herrnstein and Charles Murray's *The Bell Curve* (1994), which argues that race and class differences are genetically determined and immutable (Gould 1994a).

By the 1930s, it had become increasingly awkward for American anthropologists to talk about human diversity in terms of the nineteenth century concept of race, racial hierarchies, and racial determinism. By the end of World War II it was nearly impossible. Boas had examined these issues in his *The Mind of Primitive Man* (1911)—or *Kultur und Rasse* (1914) in the German edition—and concluded that the physical features used to define fixed racial types are not fixed and do not in any way correlate with such socially acquired habits as culture, language, or styles of thought. Except at Harvard and the Smithsonian, Boas dominated academic anthropology in America, but the debunking of race and racial determinism then was as much a part of British biology as of American cultural anthropology (Barkan 1992; Stepan 1982: 140–81). So the physical anthropologists who still insisted that race meant something fell back on the idea of races as major geographical stocks.

There were at least three such major stocks: the Caucasoids (Europeans), Mongoloids (Asians and Native Americans), and the Negroids (Africans). The main problem with this approach is the interesting anomalies it creates, peoples who do not conveniently fit into the available categories, such as the Australian aborigines —tall, dark-skinned (a Negroid trait) peoples with some high frequencies (50 to 100 percent) of wavy blonde hair (a Caucasoid trait); the Ainus of northern Japan—short, light-skinned people with (Caucasoid) beak-like noses and abundant facial hair; and the San ("Bushmen") of the Kalahari Desert—short, yellow to copper-colored people with peppercorn curls of head hair, and (Mongoloid) wide cheek bones and epicanthic eye folds ("almond-shaped" eyes). These and other anomalous peoples were usually explained away in terms of the migration and mixings of the major geographical stocks. Thus, the Australian aborigines presumably represented some crossing between the Negroid and Caucasoid stocks. However, in none of these cases was there any other evidence for these supposed migrations and mixings.

Stanley Garn (1969) tried to rescue this approach by marrying it to populational genetics. He defined a race as a Mendelian breeding population, one that thus differs from other populations in its frequency of one or more genetic traits. His resulting scheme of nested racial divisions—nine geographical races broken down into a host of local races and their constituent, neighborhood micro races—is as arbitrary as, if much more complicated than, any other system of racial classification.

Finally, by 1950, the evolutionary biologists joined the anthropological attack on race, arguing that subspecies categories are categories of convenience rather than facts of nature (Gould 1977: 231–36). The three main biological problems with the concept of race are as follows:

1. Races are arbitrarily defined. There is no agreement on which or how many traits best define a race. The more traits one selects to define a given race, the smaller that race becomes; and, as Stanley Garn's work suggests, the fewer people included in a given race, the greater number of races one needs to define.

2. No supposed racial category has exclusive possession of a given genetic trait. That we are a single species means that humans have always mated with their neighbors, and they with theirs. Thus, as Blumenbach and Darwin had anticipated, the form or frequency of any given genetic trait is gradually distributed over the face of the earth in what biologists call a *cline*. Humans have always mated with their neighbors to produce these clinal variations; therefore pure, fixed racial types have never existed among modern humans—at least not outside people's minds.

   None of us would have any difficulty distinguishing between native Swedes and Japanese. They appear to be distinct racial types. However, if one looks at the peoples who live between them, it is not clear where a European-Asian boundary line should be drawn, nor why one would want to draw such a line. Consider this comparison of people with dogs. Both are domesticated species with worldwide distributions and both come in all sorts of sizes, shapes, and colors. Just as the ordinary dogs of the world are mutts, rather than the distinct breeds that humans have artificially created, people do not come prepackaged in pure, distinct racial types.

3. Human genetic traits are distributed in clines, so the range of genetic variation *within* a supposed racial category is greater than those *between* supposed racial categories. Though he was blind to the fact, Samuel Morton's data on racial cranial capacities demonstrated this in 1839. Indeed, a classic study by Harvard geneticist Richard Lewontin (1972) examined the distribution of seventeen polymorphic traits, like those for blood group types, among the equivalent of seven geographical races and found that only 6 percent of these variations were distributed along racial lines. In other words, 94 percent of the variations he studied did not sort themselves out into neat, discrete geographical races. This is why the scientific racists of the nineteenth century were never able to find measurable data that would yield objective racial types.

   Human beings are a geographically variable species. That is a fact of nature, while "races" are not (Gould 1977: 231–36). Biological races are descriptive representations of human physical diversity. They are, at best, rough approximations of that reality, for the static categories of distinct racial types can never capture the dynamic realities of human sizes, shapes, and colors. Using racial categories to represent these dynamic realities is like using a box of crayons to capture the wide range of color hues, saturations, and intensities found in nature. Why bother naming races at all?

The concept of race conveys little or no information that could not be expressed in terms of the distribution of individual traits among populations. Furthermore, racial classification can interfere with the objective study of variation. It can create a mental set in which evolutionary theories for which there is little justification are uncritically accepted. It can also cause people to waste time finding pseudosolutions to nonproblems—ways to make this or that population "fit"—while ignoring real problems, such as why a given variation shows the variation that it does. It is possible that there really are major divisions of humankind, distinguishable on the basis of unbiased estimates of generalized genetic distance among populations. As yet, however, the existence of such groupings has not been satisfactorily demonstrated. Until it is, we would do best to avoid "racial" classifications of all kinds (Jolly & Plog 1982: 411).

Still, a lot of people believe the self-evident physical differences between humans require a word like "race" to describe them. Although anthropologists have tried debunking the concept of race for more than sixty years, racial labels are a social fact. Biological races, I have argued, cannot be defined and do not exist. However misleading and harmful, social races remain a convenient way to order the complexity of social life. Most of the racial labels used today refer to ethnicity and are best understood as such. For a social race is not a primordial social fact, but a situationally defined, collective social identity; an historically grounded sense of peoplehood based on insiders' and outsiders' interpretations of subjective boundary markers. In short, a social race is an ethnic group.

Relatively little harm is done when "race" is used as a descriptive device—a way to tell where a person's ancestors came from, or what she or he looks like. The real danger lies in using "race" as an explanatory device in assuming that a person thinks, feels, or acts in a certain way because of where his or her ancestors came from, or because of what she/he looks like, for that hearkens back to the erroneous nineteenth century view of fixed racial types and racially determined behavioral traits. I would prefer that we abandon the hopelessly misleading word "race." Meanwhile, we had best be careful about how that word is used.

References

Banton, Michael. 1987. *Racial Theories*. Cambridge: Cambridge University Press.

Barkan, Elazar. 1992. *The Retreat of Scientific Racism: Changing Concepts of Race in Britain and the United States Between the World Wars*. Cambridge: Cambridge University Press.

Begley, Sharon. 1995. "Three is not enough: surprising new lessons from the controversial science of race," *Newsweek* 125/7 (February 13): 67–69.

Benedict, Ruth. 1943 (orig. 1940). *Race: Science and Politics* (2nd ed.). New York: Viking Press.

Boas, Franz. 1911. *The Mind of Primitive Man*. New York: Macmillan.

———. 1940 (orig. 1912). "Changes in bodily form of descendants of immigrants," in his *Race, Language and Culture*. New York: The Free Press, pp. 60–75.

Cunningham, D. J. 1908. "Anthropology in the Eighteenth Century," *Journal of the Royal Anthropological Institute* 38: 10–35.

Davis, F. James. 1991. *Who Is Black? One Nation's Definition*. University Park, PA: Pennsylvania State University Press.

Fredrickson, George M. 1988 (orig. 1971). "Social origins of American racism," in his *The Arrogance of Race: Historical Perspectives on Slavery, Racism, and Social Inequality*. Hanover, NH: Wesleyan University Press, pp. 189–205.

Garn, Stanley M. 1969. *Human Races*. Springfield, IL: Charles C Thomas.

Gossett, Thomas F. 1963. *Race: The History of an Idea in America*. Dallas, TX: Southern Methodist University Press.

Gould, Stephen Jay. 1977. *Ever Since Darwin: Reflections in Natural History*. New York: W. W. Norton.

———. 1981. *The Mismeasure of Man*. New York: W. W. Norton.

———. 1994a. "Curveball," *The New Yorker* 70/39: 139–49.

———. 1994b. "The geometer of race," *Discover* 15/11: 65–69.

Jensen, Arthur R. 1969. "How much can we boost IQ and scholastic achievement?" *Harvard Educational Review* 39: 1–123.

Jolly, Clifford J., and Fred Plog. 1982. *Physical Anthropology and Archeology* (3rd ed.). New York: Alfred A. Knopf.

Kamin, Leon J. 1974. *The Science and Politics of IQ*. New York: John Wiley & Sons.

Lewontin, Richard C. 1972. "The apportionment of human diversity," in Theodosius Dobzhansky, et al. (eds.), *Evolutionary Biology*, vol. 6. New York: Plenum, pp. 381–98.

Loewen, James W. 1988 (orig. 1971). *The Mississippi Chinese: Between Black and White* (2nd ed.). Prospect Heights, IL: Waveland Press.

Lorimer, Douglas A. 1978. *Colour, Class and the Victorians: English Attitudes to the Negro in the mid-Nineteenth Century*. New York: Holmes & Meier.

Montagu, M. F. Ashley. 1942. *Man's Most Dangerous Myth: The Fallacy of Race*. New York: Columbia University Press.

Shanklin, Eugenia. 1994. *Anthropology and Race*. Belmont, CA: Wadsworth.

Shipman, Pat. 1994. *The Evolution of Racism: Human Differences and the Use and Abuse of Science*. New York: Simon & Schuster.

Stanton, William. 1960. *The Leopard's Spots: Scientific Attitudes Toward Race in America, 1815–59*. Chicago: University of Chicago Press.

Stepan, Nancy. 1982. *The Idea of Race in Science: Great Britain, 1800–1960*. Hamden, CT: Archon Books.

Stocking, George W., Jr. 1968. *Race, Culture, and Evolution: Essays in the History of Anthropology*. New York: The Free Press.

Williamson, Joel. 1980. *New People: Miscegenation and Mulattoes in the United States*. New York: The Free Press.

Wright, Lawrence. 1994. "One drop of blood," *The New Yorker* 70/22 (July 25): 46–55.

Article Review Form at end of book.

Do you think that the poor success rate of interracial couples will improve if their numbers continue to grow? Do you think that the growing number of interracial couples will positively or negatively affect race relations in society?

The Nature of Black/White Relationships

Robert P. McNamara, Maria Tempenis, and Beth Walton
Furman University

Interracial couples. The term evokes powerful emotions in many people. In others, it causes confusion or concern. In essence, the issues surrounding interracial couples are a reflection of the ways in which race operates in American society. The problems and difficulties many interracial couples experience only underscore the legacy of slavery and mistreatment of minority groups.

On the surface, race seems to be a simple concept. It can be defined as those physical characteristics that distinguish one group of people from another. It is also simple in the sense that there are essentially only three categories of racial groups (Caucasian, black, Asian). However, there are a host of problems with the meaning of race. Many sociologists point to the ways in which these physical characteristics come to be defined—what is referred to as *the social construction of race*. Others take issue with the purity of the concept: it is virtually impossible to distinguish where one race ends and the next begins. As a result of these and other issues, some scholars have argued that we abandon the term (see for instance Siegel 1998).

Thus, the concept of race is actually quite complex and the issues surrounding it become much clearer (and problematic) when individuals from different races become involved in intimate relationships (dating and/or marriage). For our purposes, we define an interracial couple as consisting of an African American and a white partner. It not only avoids confusion regarding what we mean by interracial, but it also avoids the seemingly endless debate over whether race is the appropriate term to use. As mentioned, this issue has been controversial in many disciplines, and rather than adding fuel to the debate, we chose to define our group in a way that most people could easily identify.

Attitudes about Interracial Couples

At first glance, it would seem that the United States, with its history and heterogeneous population, would be tolerant of intimate relationships between people of different races. However, while it is true that the number of interracial marriages has been increasing in this country, there is considerable debate over whether they are considered acceptable. In their study of college campuses, Stimson and Stimson (1979) found that one of every three white girls and one of every three black girls were willing to date members of another race. They also found that 67 percent of black males and 43 percent of white males were willing to date members of another race. The authors concluded that as Americans' negative attitudes toward interracial marriage declined, there would be a greater willingness to tolerate not only interracial dating, but marriage as well. This, in turn, would improve race relations across all groups. More recently, Rosenblatt, Karis, and Powell (1995) contend that the significant increase in the number of interracial marriages and dating indicates a greater tolerance toward relationships between people of different races. This is also interpreted to mean that racism in America is declining.

On the other hand, some researchers have suggested the number of couples, although increasing, has remained small in part because of a lack of societal acceptance (see for instance Johnson and Warren 1994; Staples and Johnson 1993). In other words, many experts have argued that Americans are strongly opposed to interracial relationships, particularly between African Americans and whites. The reasons for this vary, but part of the explanation is found in stereotypical images of African Americans as well as the reasons why they intermarry with whites.

Popular Conceptions about Interracial Couples

There is a great deal of misinformation concerning interracial couples, especially why individuals would want to become involved in this type of relationship. While these explanations can be applied to virtually any minority group, they are most clearly seen with black and white couples. Perhaps the most often cited reason is that African Americans date and marry whites to escape their current financial and social situation. That is, when an African American marries a white, it is a step toward upward social mobility.

Mills (1996) argues that while largely inaccurate, there is an element of truth to this statement. From an economic standpoint, if an African American female marries a white male, there exists the possibility of upward social and economic mobility due to the fact that white men earn, on average, more than African American men. However, because the vast majority of black/white relationships involve African American men and white women, and because white women earn substantially less, on average, than men in general, this type of relationship does not benefit the African American. This pattern, particularly among African American males and white females led to a theoretical explanation of interracial marriages. Often referred to as a "hypogamy" theory, it was postulated by Robert K. Merton as well as Kingsley Davis and given some support by Robert Staples. This explanation essentially states that African American males are attracted to white females because this type of relationship improves the social standing of the male. The same is true of white women who are attracted to higher status African American males. In short, the parties are "marrying up" (Billingsley 1992). Davis and Merton's theory is based on a pair of assumptions. First, it assumes that the choice of marriage partner is based on quantifiable factors such as income and education. Second, it is also based on the assumption that most, if not all, black men want to marry white women but do not possess the means to do so. The real problem with the theory, as Spickard (1989) notes, is that it does not provide an adequate explanation of interracial marriage.

Another popular conception concerning interracial couples involves those individuals who strike out against their families by becoming involved with someone from a different race. Again, this may have some basis if a person's family is racist and would clearly oppose this type of relationship. However, in those instances where the families support the couple, the rebellion argument loses much of its validity.

A related explanation suggests that people who become involved in multiracial relationships are either traitors of their own race or are incapable of making a reasonable decision. Many people argue that blacks who marry whites are diluting their racial identity. Parenthetically, Mills (1996) contends that this suggests a dislike of themselves or a lack of reasoning ability. A similar argument is used to explain the behavior of whites. It is often implied that a white who marries a black is considered mentally ill for doing so (Frankenburg 1993). Thus, the white partner is considered unstable and the black has demonstrated a lack of loyalty to African American culture, is selfish, and lacks a complete understanding of his or her behavior.

A fourth perception about interracial couples implies that the basis of the relationship is sexual. That is, the reason for the union has more to do with a preoccupation with what Staples (1994) defines as the "forbidden fruit." This applies especially to white women and black men. Here the historical connotations linger: during slavery, blacks were forbidden to have intimate relationships with white women. Somehow, Mills (1996) argues, this preoccupation of centuries ago has manifested itself in black males' desire for white women in contemporary society. The same historical logic is used to explain the attraction of white men to black women. That is, during slavery, it was a relatively common practice for white males to become sexually involved with black females. This sexual allure of black women continues today when white males act on their fascination and develop relationships with African American women.

Finally, and somewhat related to many of these explanations, it is believed that many interracial couples, particularly those who are public figures, flaunt their relationship for the shock value or to engage in exhibitionism. However, in reality, public figures tend to be very concerned about their image and are careful not to damage their public persona. Additionally, other studies have shown that, in general, many multiracial couples tend to avoid drawing attention to themselves and are often unwilling to participate in research on the subject for fear of being labeled and stigmatized (Kerwin et al. 1993; Rosenblatt, Karis, and Powell 1995).

In general then, there is some element of truth to the reasons why people from different races marry. However, it is one thing to suggest that individuals marry for economic and social benefits, to punish or rebel against their parents, because of some internal mechanism of self-loathing, or who do so for the shock value; it is quite another to suggest that these motivations are the exclusive domain of interracial couples. Every reason cited, as well as others not mentioned, can be used to describe the motivations for all types of marriages. There is a double standard applied to interracial couples.

For example, women who marry affluent men of the same race are considered to have "married well." It is considered socially acceptable. Others who marry for convenience or because they are iconoclastic in their beliefs are praised as self-directed individualists who "march to the beat of a different drummer." When this same logic is applied to people of different racial backgrounds, they are considered promiscuous, immoral, or irrational.

Tucker and Mitchell-Kernan (1990) challenge many of these perceptions, particularly the upward mobility argument. In their study, they did not find significant differences in the characteristics of African Americans who married whites. Intermarriage seems most likely to occur among middle-class partners, among more African American men than women, more in the Western states than the South, and finally, there exists a greater age difference between partners.

Interracial Relationships Today

While the subject of race is one of the most frequently discussed in the sociological literature, and while there is ample research concerning intermarriage among Europeans and other ethnic and religious groups (see for example Healey 1995; Kivisto 1995; Feagin and Feagin 1993; Marger 1994), surprisingly little attention has been given to intermarriage between African Americans and Caucasians (see for instance Rosenblatt, Karis, and Powell 1995; Mathabane and Mathabane 1992; Stuart and Abt 1975). Part of the reason for this may be the small number of cases and how the data is collected on interracial couples. While the information collected on interracial couples is not comprehensive or, in some cases, systematic (Porterfield 1982), the U.S. Bureau of Census provides perhaps the best tool with which to quantitatively measure this population. According to the Census Bureau, there were 65,000 black-white married couples in 1970 and 246,000 in 1992. This represented about one-tenth of 1 percent of married couples (Staples 1994).

As Table 1 indicates, interracial marriages increased from 65,000 in 1970 to 167,000 by 1980, roughly a 125 percent increase. By 1990, the number rose to 211,000 followed by another jump in 1995 to 326,000.

While the number of black/white marriages makes up a very small percentage of the estimated 55 million marriages in this country, a careful reading of this data shows that the number of black/white married couples tripled from 1970 to 1990 and increased another fifteen percent from 1990 to 1992. Thus, although still small in absolute numbers, black/white marriages are increasingly becoming a common feature of the social landscape (Staples 1994; Nakao 1993). Additionally, the proportion of black men married to white women has increased even more, quintupling from 1960 to 1990. The trend is even clearer if

Table 1 Ten-Year Trends in Interracial Couples: 1970 to 1995 (in thousands)

Race	1970	1980	1990	1995
Interracial couples—all races	310	651	964	1,392
Black/white	65	167	211	326
Black husband/white wife	41	122	150	204
White husband/black wife	24	45	61	122
White/other race	233	450	720	988
Black/other race	12	34	33	76

Source: *Statistical Abstract of the United States, 1996*; U.S. Department of Commerce, Bureau of Census, *Current Population Reports*, pp. 20–450.

Table 2 Changes in Interracial Marriages 1970–1995 (in thousands)

Type of Couple	1970	1984	1986	1988	1990	1995
Black husband/white wife	41	111	136	149	150	204
White husband/black wife	24	45	64	45	61	122

Source: U.S. Bureau of Census, *Current Population Reports, Population Characteristics, Household and Family Characteristics, March 1984, 1986, 1988, 1990.*

one examines new marriages. In 1993, about 9 percent of black men who married that year married a white woman.

For African American women, the rate was slightly less than half that but it is increasing dramatically (Besharov and Sullivan 1996). Thus, the most common black/white marriage involves a black male and a white female. Table 2 elaborates on Table 1 by showing incremental changes in the number of black husbands and white wives. It shows an increase from 41,000 in 1970 to 111,000 in 1984. The number increased to 136,000 in 1986 to 149,000 in 1988 and to 150,000 in 1990 (Billingsley 1992). Among black wives with white husbands, the numbers are distinctly smaller: from 24,000 in 1970 to 45,000 in 1980, 64,000 in 1986 and 45,000 in 1988. In 1990, the number rose to 61,000 and jumped again to 122,000 in 1995. The census data also suggests that the overwhelming majority of blacks who get married do so to other blacks: the proportion is approximately 95 percent and has been declining as the proportion of interracial marriages increases (Billingsley 1992).

In an attempt to answer the question of why the rate for African American women is only half that of African American men, Behsarov and Sullivan (1996) offer a couple of possible explanations. First, according to M. Belinda Tucker at the UCLA Center for African American Studies, women are more likely to select a spouse on the basis of earning capacity or ambition, while men are more likely to choose on the basis of physical attraction.

Another reason for the lower number of black women marrying white men has to do with children. A woman with children is much less appealing to a male, irrespective of her race. Additionally, the data clearly shows that African American females are more than twice as likely as whites to have had a baby out of wedlock.

Still another trend in interracial marriages is that, unlike in the past when they occurred later in life, often as second marriages, today's interracial couple tends to marry earlier (Besharov and Sullivan 1996). Interestingly, for many white women, the interracial marriage is often their first. Besharov and Sullivan (1996) estimate the proportion of second marriages for whites to a black man was 33 percent in 1985, but only 22 percent by 1990, a decrease of one-third.

As Besharov and Sullivan (1996) suggest in their study of data from the National Center for Health Statistics, African Americans are substantially less likely to marry whites than are Hispanics, Asians, or Native Americans. However, the increase in the number of couples could lead one to conclude that interpersonal racism is declining and that African Americans are increasingly becoming attractive to other racial groups as potential mates. As African Americans continue to make strides in education and employment markets, their overall "marriageability" to other African Americans as well as to those from other races, improves.

Region of the Country

According to the 1990 Census, the five states with the most interracial couples are California, Florida, Oklahoma, Texas, and Washington. California for example had 26 percent of all interracial couples. As mentioned, although the data on this issue is not comprehensive, interracial marriages are unevenly distributed to different parts of the country, with the West having the largest number of interracial couples. Tucker and Mitchell-Kernan (1990) offer an interesting explanation to explain this trend.

In explaining these trends, they offer a version of social control theory. The reason for the increase in interracial marriages is not so much due to status enhancement, although that may be part of it. Rather, the reason, especially for the higher incidence in the West than other parts of the county, has more to do with a weakened socialization from the various societal institutions (family, schools, and peers) as people move away from their families of origin as well as their hometowns. In other words, the old social networks that operated to regulate a person's behavior no longer carry the same influence when they move away or change the groups to which they affiliate. In their study in Los Angeles for example, they found that most of the people involved in interracial marriages were not born or raised in the city: they usually came from other parts of the country, most notably the Northeast, and from other parts of the world. In trying to explain not only the regional differences, but also why couples chose someone from another racial group, the authors state:

> Systems of social control that discourage racial intermarriage, in particular, may exert greater influence on mate selection for first marriages than for subsequent marriages . . . the role of geographic mobility in this scheme is a function of one's social network. Moving usually means leaving behind relatives and friends, and establishing new relationships. (p. 215)

Stability of Interracial Marriages

In terms of other demographic variables, the research is fairly consistent: most interracial couples tend to be similar in social, educational, and occupational characteristics. Interracial couples also tend to be middle- or upper-class individuals. Additionally, in terms of housing, a factor in determining social class, the race of the husband determines where the couple lives. For instance, white husbands typically resulted in the couple living in a white neighborhood and black husbands typically bring their spouses to a black neighborhood (see for instance Porterfield 1978; Billingsley 1992).

Related in some ways to socioeconomic status is the stability of the interracial marriage. Many who oppose these types of relationships believe them to be less stable than other, more conventional marriages. As Billingsley points out, the prevailing view in the literature is that this perspective has some validity: that these marriages are less stable than marriages of, say, two African American partners. Billingsley (1992) also contends that interracial marriages are at least three times less likely to succeed than single race families. Over twenty-five years ago, McDowell (1971) suggested that the problem lies in the legacy of discrimination and racism in our society and is particularly problematic for interracial couples. The result is that many are incapable of withstanding the stress that accompanies it. This point is echoed by others (see for instance Staples 1992; Billingsley 1992; Besharov and Sullivan 1996). As Staples (1992) states:

> The 78 percent increase in divorce for whites during the past decade obviously indicates that they are encountering their share of problems with each other. Add to that the fact that intraracial marriages have a considerably higher dissolution rate, it is clear that marrying across racial lines is no quick solution to the intractable problems of male-female conflict. (p. 147)

On the other hand, there is some evidence that suggests interracial marriages, depending on how they are defined, may be as stable as marriages with two black partners, although they are less stable than marriages with two white partners (see for instance Monahan 1966; Mehta 1978). Unfortunately, the evidence on this subject is dated and the absence of recent research suggests that interest in this topic has waned.

While the relationship between marital stability and education is well known, meaning the higher the educational level of the partners, the higher the probability the marriage will survive for a long time, an interesting question is whether the same holds true for interracial couples. Billingsley (1992) finds that education is a key factor in the stability of interracial marriages. Where husbands went beyond high school, the survival rate is so high among black husband-wife couples that it is virtually equal to the survival of white couples at the same educational level. Further, looking just at husbands with a college education, black married couples (with husbands' education at the college level and beyond) had the highest survival rate, followed by black husbands with white wives, while white husbands with black wives had the lowest survival rate at this level of education.

Families

One of the most difficult aspects of participating in an interracial relationship is the reaction by each partner's family. This can either place a tremendous strain on the couple or provide a haven of understanding and support. Tizard and Phoenix (1993) as well as Johnson and Warren (1994) found that members of the immediate families of white partners were either hostile or fearful of the interracial relationship. Johnson and Warren (1994) also found that members of a white partner's family typically tried to conceal the relationship from their friends, neighbors, and other family members.

One explanation offered for this was that the members may have been concerned about racism or perhaps they were concerned about the dilution of the all-white family. Johnson and Warren (1994) speculate that, at some level, family members were concerned about losing their status or standing with other whites who considered this type of relationship unacceptable. In sociological terms, this concealing was a form of face saving and impression management (see Goffman 1969). The implications of this problem are far reaching and can easily serve to isolate the white partner from the immediate and extended family. While feelings of rejection are understandable, especially if they are from one's immediate family, isolating oneself from the entire family precludes the possibility of any member accepting them.

There also seems to be what Frankenberg (1993) referred to as a "standardized discourse" against interracial relationships. Frankenberg describes five categories of reasons that seem to characterize whites' opposition to interracial marriages. They are societal, community, neighborhood, or family disapproval; issues of safety and well-being; alleged clannishness of African Americans; problems relating to the children; and the likelihood of a poor economic future. Additionally, some white parents viewed the choice of a black partner as an indication that they were somehow inadequate in raising that child.

Finally, there is evidence to suggest that another type of opposition to or reaction by the person's family is to disown them should they enter into an interracial relationship (Rosenblatt, Karis, and Powell 1995). This is the strongest reaction, but it does reflect how severe a threat the introduction of an African American is to the integrity of the white family. By disowning their family member, whites are able to avoid the stigma of becoming related, even parenthetically, to a minority. Thus, the underlying reason explaining white families' rejection of interracial relationships is due to a fear of losing status and the concern about racism from associates and friends (Rosenblatt, Karis, and Powell).

Fortunately, it appears that in those cases where there is opposition, there also seems to be a tendency for it to subside. That is, while there may be one or more family members who would not initially accept the relationship, over time, they became more tolerant and accepting of the African American partner (see for instance Kouri and Lasswell 1993; Tizard and Phoenix 1993; Rosenblatt, Karis, and Powell 1995). A good indicator of this acceptance was the willingness of the family member(s) to publicly acknowledge the relationship.

On the other hand, many black families, for a variety of reasons, seem to be more accepting of interracial relationships. Part of the reason relates to the structure of the African American family, which can be very different than white families. As described by Rosenblatt, Karis, and Powell (1995) and supported by Staples (1994), mothers seem to be much more central to the family structure for African Americans. Additionally, given that many African American families do not consist of both parents, they have a greater understanding of familial diversity. Consequently, African Americans encounter fewer problems with interracial relationships. This acceptance has been documented in other studies of interracial relationships as well (see for instance Kouri and Lasswell 1993; Porterfield 1978; Golden 1954). Golden, for instance, found that, compared to white families, the families of African American partners in interracial relationships were much more able to see the white partner as a person rather than to react to him or her as a member of a group. Further, the relationship between the white partner and the African American's family tended to be much more lasting. While Golden's research is dated, more recent research underscores many of his initial findings (see for instance Frankenberg 1993; Rosenblatt, Karis, and Powell 1995).

In those cases where there was opposition by the African American partner's family to the white spouse, the reasons stem largely from the fear and pain of being connected with a representative of their societal oppressor (Rosenblatt, Karis, and Powell 1995). Like their white counterparts, some family members opposed the relationship, but over time a period of accommodation was reached. However, there is some suggestion in the literature that this tolerance or acceptance is less complete than it is with white families (Tizard and Phoenix 1993). Thus, one way to interpret the reaction of families to the relationship is that initially, white families reject the African American partner, only to accept them to some degree as time passes (especially if the couple begins to raise a family). African American families tend to be more accepting of interracial couples in general, but of those that reject them, feelings of hostility tend to linger for longer periods of time (Kouri and Lasswell 1993).

It may well be that the deleterious effects of family opposition to interracial relationships is that the couple faces particular and somewhat unique stressors from each other. This could, in part, explain why interracial marriages are less stable than intraracial ones. That is, the couple already faces problems from society when they decide to enter into this type of relationship. Adding the family opposition may result in a situation where the two individuals are unable to resolve the related issues. While a certain amount of discord among in-laws is found in all types of families, it is particularly problematic for interracial ones given how race and racism are such fundamental parts of our society.

In some ways, family opposition to interracial relationships can become a self-fulfilling prophecy: initially the families oppose the relationship for fear it will not last, as well as the racism the couple will face, only to contribute to the eventual demise of the marriage by their behavior and attitudes toward the member's partner. When the marriage does fail, the members then have some validation of their initial prediction.

Children

As mentioned, one of the tempering mechanisms to family opposition, and, at the same time, a reason to oppose interracial relationships, has to do with children. How many mixed racial children are there? This is difficult to determine. For instance, many states no longer require that the parents' races be recorded on birth certificates. The Census Bureau estimates that in 1990, nearly 2 million children resided in homes where the primary adults were of different races (Besharov and Sullivan 1996). That is about 4.1 percent of the children who lived in two-parent households, about double the number since 1980, and four times the number in 1970. While this is only a rough estimate, we must also take into account those children who were adopted or are from a previous marriage. However it is calculated, there has been a significant increase in the number of interracial children in much the same way that there has been an increase in the number of interracial marriages.

In general, the problems that are identified as relating to children of interracial relationships have to do with conflicts relating to social and self identity. That is, one of the major issues for interracial families is identifying, preserving, and explaining the cultural heritage to their children. Researchers have often conjectured that biracial children are at risk for developing a variety of problems (see for instance Adler 1987; Brandell 1988, Kerwin et al. 1993). Some researchers contend that the biracial child should identify themselves as African American because society will inevitably place them in that category. Others argue that a child should accept African American as his or her identity because it is based on the notion that they will likely adopt the norms, attitudes, and beliefs associated with that group (see for instance Sebring 1985). Kerwin et al. (1993) in their study of black/white biracial children, found that, in contrast to other research, children did not perceive themselves as marginal and demonstrated, as did the adults, strong feelings of sensitivity to the views, values, and culture of black and white communities.

Still, problems can and do emerge for biracial children. According to Ladner (1984), the issue of social identity among biracial children is dealt with in one of three ways. Parents may deny that race is an issue; they may promote minority identity in their children; or they may attempt to raise their children to understand the meaning and significance of a biracial identity.

Second, and perhaps more important, are the ways in which parents deal with the problems their multiracial children face, during childhood and later as young adults. All of these things can cause conflicts within the child in terms of his or her identity. McRoy and Freeman (1986) have found that many biracial individuals have a particularly difficult time during adolescence, in part due to the lack of a clearly defined social identity.

Clearly, while much has been learned, there remain numerous questions about the critical issues associated with biracial children, particularly as it relates to their sense of self-identity. Herring (1992) notes five identity conflicts. First, there are issues surrounding the child's biracial identity. By definition, there is some ambiguity. Are they African American, white, a combination, what? Typically, racially mixed children will be somewhat ambivalent toward their parents' ethnic or racial backgrounds (see Sebring 1985). However, when one child identifies with a particular parent's heritage, it is usually at the expense of the other's. It is at this point that conflicts emerge.

A second type of conflict relates to the child's feeling of social marginality. Instead of the basic question being "Who Am I?" the question becomes "Where Do I Fit?" While this is not especially problematic in elementary school, as the child enters high school, where one's identity begins to take a particular shape, and the person begins dating, it is easy to see how this can lead to difficulties for biracial children. Their physical appearance is different and their families are considered unusual; therefore many peer groups reject them.

A third type of conflict relates to sexuality. This issue becomes important in older children, particularly those in high school or just beyond. Here the problem stems from which type of partner the child should select. They do not fit into a traditional category, and because our attitudes about interracial relationships remain complex, biracial females may feel that their choice of sexual partners, as well as their patterns of sexual behavior, may be limited only to minority men. Similarly, biracial males may be leery of white women for fear of rejection (Herring 1992). While this may be a common problem for all males in interpersonal relationships, Herring argues that it can be especially troubling for biracial ones. These conflicts may lead children and young adults to perceive their situation as dichotomous: that they must choose one race or the other in terms of their interpersonal relationships. Moreover, as Gibbs and Huang (1990) point out, these patterns can develop early and translate into perceptions and attitudes as an adult.

Fourth are conflicts relating to separation from the child's parents. This involves the typical distance between adolescents and their parents. The question here is "Who controls my life?" Herring (1992) argues that biracial parents tend to be either overly protective of their children or ambivalent about the race issue. Depending on which approach is taken, the children may become more dependent on their parents or more rebellious. The problem is that these normal adolescent attempts at autonomy usually occur earlier in biracial children, largely due to the way the parents respond to their multiracial family structure.

Finally, biracial children often experience conflicts relating to their future careers. This conflict centers around their attitudes toward achievement and upward mobility. Here stereotypes about racial and ethnic groups permeate the child's thinking about career choices. While they may not seem significant at an early age, Herring (1992) has found some evidence that these early thoughts about what types of people perform certain types of jobs begin early and can have a long-lasting effect on the child's motivation, worldview, and level of determination.

Until this point, we have been describing the issues as they relate to biracial children that are biologically related to their parents. While little research has been done on this (see for instance Baptiste 1994), identity issues and problems may be exacerbated in what are sometimes referred to as *blended interracial families*: those that involve stepparents (Wardle 1995). The child has already had an identity established only to have that questioned when their mother or father marry someone from another race. It can become even more confusing when, say, the new father wishes to adopt the child.

As a way of dealing with many of the issues relating to biracial children, a national interracial movement is occurring. As Wardle (1995) describes it:

> The interracial movement now boasts several national publications, many local newsletters, over sixty local education and affiliation groups, and scholarly seminars. We are also becoming more militant about the need for a category on forms—school, federal, Census Bureau, Head Start, birth certificates—that accurately reflects the racial, national and ethnic identity of our children; and we insist our children are Biracial, normal, and potentially very successful. (p. 109)

Problems Encountered by Interracial Couples

Despite what can be generally referred to as an increased acknowledgement of interracial couples, problems, some quite serious, remain. Perhaps one of the most common problems relates to members of the African American community. A great deal has been written about the concerns of African American women about African American men and white women (see for instance Staples and Johnson 1993; Collins 1990). As mentioned, because many African American males have not had successful attempts at the American Dream, which makes them less viable as marriage partners for African American women, there remains an image that African American males are being taken away from them.

Many African Americans feel that if a male member of their race marries a white, he is "selling out" his culture, his heritage, and his people. Others view this as a rejection of black women's beauty (Rosenblatt, Karis, and Powell 1995). Others feel African American males who marry white women are trying to gain economic and social standing through affiliation with the dominant group in society. In some cases, the attention is focused on white women "stealing" their men from them. Whether this is an accurate depiction, the realities of the situation mean that interracial couples involving a black man and a white woman must somehow come to terms with the resentment from African American females.

Other members of the African American community feel that any interracial marriage is unacceptable, but especially to whites. The rationale behind this is the feeling that it is unacceptable to choose a partner that belongs to a group that has historically and currently, exploited and denied opportunities to African Americans in general (Rosenblatt, Karis, and Powell 1995).

Other problems relate to discrimination and prejudicial behavior in public. This can consist of poor service at restaurants and motels, hostile stares, the loss of promotional opportunities in the workplace, or even dismissal for being involved in an interracial relationship. At the other extreme are the outright physical and verbal attacks, receiving hate mail, death threats, or the burning of churches that welcome interracial couples. There is also anecdotal evidence of a fear of institutional racism operating: many couples are leery of revealing the nature of their relationship to government agencies. For example Welborn (1994) discovered that many interracial couples do not list their race on marriage licenses.

Thus, the nature of the problems experienced by interracial couples are vast and range from stares to attacks against them. While there is still a great deal to learn about this topic, and while it appears that our sensitivity as a society toward interracial couples seems to be improving, as evidenced by the increase in numbers of couples, there remain a number of unexplained circumstances and unresolved conflicts.

References

Adler, A. J. 1987. "Children and Biracial Identity" in A. Thomas and J. Grimes (eds.) *Children's Needs: Psychological Perspectives*. Washington, D.C.: National Association of School Psychologists.

Baptiste, D. A. 1994. "Marital and Family Therapy with Racially/Culturally Intermarried Stepfamilies: Issues and Guidelines," *Family Relations* 33: 373–380.

Besharov, D. J., and T. S. Sullivan. 1996. "America is Experiencing an Unprecedented Increase in Black-White Intermarriage," *The New Democrat*, July/August, pp. 19–21.

Billingsley, A. 1992. *Climbing Jacob's Ladder*. New York: Simon and Schuster.

Brandell, J. R. 1988. "Treatment of the biracial child: Theoretical and Clinical Issues," *Journal of Multicultural Counseling and Development* 16: 176–187.

Collins, P. H. 1990. *Black Feminist Thought*. New York: Routledge.

Feagin, J., and C. Feagin. 1993. *Race and Ethnic Relations*. Clifton-Hills, NJ: Prentice Hall.

Frankenberg, R. 1993. *White Women, Race Matters: The Social Construction of Whiteness*. Minneapolis, MN: The University of Minnesota Press.

Gibbs, J. T., and L. N. Huang. (eds.) 1990. *Children of Color*. San Francisco: Josey-Bass.

Goffman, E. 1969. *The Presentation of Self in Everyday Life*. New York: Anchor.

Golden, J. 1954. "Patterns of Negro-White Intermarriage," *American Sociological Review* 19: 144–147.

Healy, J. F. 1995. *Race, Ethnicity, Gender and Class*. Thousand Oaks, CA: Pine Forge.

Herring, R. D. 1992. "Biracial Children: an Increasing Concern for Elementary and Middle School Counselors," *Elementary School Guidance and Counseling* 27: 123–130.

Johnson, W. R., and D. M. Warren (eds.) 1994. *Inside the Mixed Marriage*. Lanham, MD: University Press of America.

Kerwin, C., J. Ponterotto, B. Jackson, and A. Harris. 1993. "Racial Identity in Biracial Children: A Qualitative Investigation." *Journal of Counseling Psychology* 40(2): 221–231.

Kivisto, Peter. 1995. *Americans All*. Belmont, CA: Wadsworth.

Kouri, K. M., and M. Lasswell. 1993. Black-White Marriages: Social Change and Intergenerational Mobility." *Marriage and Family Review* 19(3/4): 241–55.

Ladner, J. 1984. "Providing a Healthy Environment for Interracial Children." *Interracial Books for Children Bulletin* 15: 7–8.

Marger, M. N. 1994. *Race and Ethnic Relations*. 3rd edition. Belmont, CA: Wadsworth.

Mathabane, M., and G. Mathabane. 1992. *Love in Black and White*. New York: HarperPerennial.

McDowell, S. F. 1971. "Black-White Intermarriage in the United States." *International Journal of the Family* 1: 57.

McRoy, R. G., and E. Freeman. 1986. "Racial Identity Issues Among Mixed-Race Children." *Social Work in Education* 8: 164–174.

Mehta, S. K. 1978. "The Stability of Black-White vs. Racially Homogamous Marriages in the United States 1960–1970." *Journal of Social and Behavioral Science* 24: 133.

Mills, C. 1996. "Interracial Marriage is Identical to Same-Race Marriage" in Bonnie Szumski (ed.), *Interracial America: Opposing Viewpoints*, pp. 210–215. San Diego, CA: Greenhaven Press.

Monahan, T. 1966. "Interracial Marriage and Divorce in Kansas and the Question of Instability of Mixed Marriages." *Journal of Comparative Family Studies*, Spring, 119.

Nakao, A. 1993. "Interracial Marriages on the Rise in State, US" *The San Francisco Examiner*, February 12, p. A1.

Porterfield, E. 1978. *Black and White Mixed Marriages*. Chicago: Nelson-Hall.

—. 1982. "Black-American Intermarriage in the United States." *Marriage and Family Review* 5(1): 17–34.

Rosenblatt, P. C., T. A. Karis, and R. D. Powell. 1995. *Multiracial Couples*. Thousand Oaks, CA: Sage.

Sebring, D. L. 1985. "Considerations in Counseling Interracial Children." *Journal of Non-White Concerns in Personnel and Guidance* 13: 3–9.

Siegel, B. 1998. "Anthropology and the Science of Race" in Robert P. McNamara (ed.), *Perspectives in Social Problems*. Boulder, CO: **coursewise publishing**.

Spickard, P. R. 1989. *Mixed Blood: Intermarriage and Ethnic Identity in Twentieth-Century America.* Madison, WI: University of Wisconsin Press.

Staples, R. 1992. "Black and White: Love and Marriage" in R. Staples, *The Black Family: Essays and Studies.* Belmont, CA: Wadsworth.

Staples, R. 1994. *The Black Family: Essays and Studies.* Belmont, CA: Wadsworth.

Staples, R., and L. B. Johnson. 1993. *Black Families at the Crossroads: Challenges and Prospects.* San Francisco: Jossey-Bass.

Stimson, A., and J. Stimson. 1979. "Interracial Dating: Willingness to Violate a Changing Norm," *Journal of Social and Behavioral Sciences* 25: 36–44.

Stuart, I. R., and L. E. Abt. 1975. *Interracial Marriage.* New York: Grossman.

Tizard, B., and A. Phoenix. 1993. *Black, White, or Mixed Race? Race and Racism in the Lives of Young People of Mixed Parentage.* New York: Routledge.

Tucker, B., and C. Mitchell-Kernan. 1990. "New Trends in Black American Interracial Marriage: The Social Structural Context." *Journal of Marriage and the Family* 52: 209–218.

Wardle, F. 1995. "Children of Mixed-Race Unions Should be Raised Biracially" in Bonnie Szumski (ed.), *Interracial America: Opposing Viewpoints*, pp. 210–215. San Diego, CA: Greenhaven Press.

Welborn, M. 1994. Black-White Couples: Social and Psychological Factors That Influence the Initiation, Development, and Continuance of their Relationship. Unpublished doctoral dissertation, University of Minnesota.

Article Review Form at end of book.

Have you observed racial inequality in restaurants today? Do you think that the publicity over the discrimination in large restaurant chains will affect the overall food industry's treatment of discrimination?

A Tale of Two Restaurant Chains

Racial discrimination lawsuits

Joel Fegin and Hernon Vera

University of Florida

On February 1, 1960, four African American college students sat down at a Woolworth lunch counter in Greensboro, North Carolina. Although black patrons could purchase items in other areas of the store, they were not served at the food counter. In a later interview one white employee said that she would have served the black students, but her managers would not allow her to do so. The next day, as word got around, more than two dozen black students occupied the counter, doing schoolwork when they were refused service. As their numbers grew over the next few days, a few whites joined the students, but most whites heckled them. Whites across the nation verbally assaulted the student demonstrators for transgressing the color line. The protest spread to the rest of Greensboro's lunch counters, all of which were quickly closed. The spontaneous actions of these black students protesting racial discrimination in public accommodations marked the beginning of the modern sit-in movement.[1]

The Reverend Martin Luther King, Jr., told the black student leaders "not to forget that the struggle was justice versus injustice, not black versus white."[2] The efforts of black customers to be treated fairly in white-owned restaurants are but one example in the long history of African Americans' struggle to overcome injustice. The sit-ins were not just about gaining access to food counters. The rituals of racism at lunch counters or family restaurants, as well as in other public accommodations, proclaim a message of exclusion from the national society that few other acts of discrimination can deliver with as much force. For black Americans today, encounters with discrimination in public accommodations summon up this collective memory of past degradation. For black and white Americans, discrimination of this type is yet another marker of the racialized geography of American towns and cities.

Eating out is often a meaningful social event and is a frequent activity for many families. The restaurant industry is one with which most Americans, white and black, have repeated contact. Yet, even though African Americans spend a quarter of their food budgets eating away from home, some segments of the restaurant industry, including some "family restaurants," still discriminate against black customers.

The idea of the family-restaurant chain originated in the United States, then spread around the globe. Conrad P. Kottack has noted the behavioral uniformity one finds at such restaurants: people "know how to behave, what to expect, what they will eat, and what they will pay."[3] The racial uniformity imposed by whites at public eating places like lunch counters, was obvious during the days of legal segregation. It was not by chance that these public eating places were selected by civil rights activists in the 1960s as major targets for desegregation. This chapter examines the continuing reports of racial discrimination in America's family restaurants, first in employment and then against black customers.

Discrimination in Employment

The restaurant industry is the largest employer of service workers, white and black, in the United States. This institutional arena is filled with opportunities for whites with racist inclinations to victimize blacks. In some cases it is white customers who create problems for black employees, but most publicized complaints in recent years have been against management. Restaurants across the nation have been charged with discrimination against black employees.

Although black workers make up a tenth of all those employed in the United States, they constitute 13 percent of those in food service jobs. Sixteen percent of kitchen workers and 19 percent of cooks are black, compared with only 5 percent of waiters and waitresses and less than 3 percent of bartenders. Black workers are more likely to be in the back of a restaurant than in the front. The food service industry hires more black employees than all other major industries, but few are found in the ranks of the industry's management or as owners of franchises.[4] In the District of Columbia in 1993 the lack of black workers in customer contact jobs precipitated organized protests that brought increased opportunities for black workers. The district's 1,500 restaurants employed 30,000 workers, but a 1993 survey found that many of the district's best restaurants employed no black servers or bartenders. Black workers were buspersons or kitchen workers. As a result of the protests, numerous restaurants improved the representation of minority workers in their better-paying jobs.[5]

Very few black entrepreneurs have been able to secure franchises in major family-restaurant chains. Black entrepreneurs have also had great difficulty obtaining bank loans to start restaurants, either on their own or as part of a franchise arrangement. One black businessperson in Los Angeles recently noted that when a black person deals with banks, "a definite barrier [is] set up." In 1992 this man started a Denny's franchise in Watts, a black community in Los Angeles. Until then, no one had succeeded in obtaining money for a new full-service restaurant in the area since the major 1965 Watts riot. In the early 1990s this was the only Denny's owned by an African American.[6]

Shoney's Inc., and Charges of Employment Discrimination

Headquartered in Nashville, Tennessee, the Shoney's family restaurant is one of the largest in the United States. In 1993 it included 1,800 restaurants (under several names) with 30,000 employees in 36 states. During the 1980s a number of individual lawsuits were filed against Shoney's charging employment discrimination, and the federal Equal Employment Opportunity Commission (EEOC) reportedly received hundreds of discrimination complaints involving the firm's hiring practices. In 1989 the national image was damaged when a number of black job applicants along with black employees and former employees, with the aid of NAACP Legal Defense Fund attorneys, filed a class-action job discrimination suit against the company. This case involved the largest number of employees and employment locations of any class-action suit in the history of such workplace litigation.[7]

The suit charged that Shoney's, had "turned away black applicants and relegated the few it hired to kitchen chores."[8] Black employees stated that they were assigned the least desirable hours. Even some white supervisors reported that they were fired or threatened with demotion if they refused to obey instructions to restrict black employment in the company. A former assistant manager reported that she was told to darken the "O" in the Shoney's logo on job application forms to indicate that an applicant was black.[9]

According to some reports antiblack attitudes and policies had been common in the company from its beginning. Depositions from job applicants, employees, and managers at all levels of the company implicated numerous restaurant managers, supervisors, and executives in discrimination in hiring, firing, and promotions. A number of executives have described the racial views of Raymond L. Danner, Shoney's cofounder and chair of its board. Former chief executive officer, (CEO) Dave Wachtel said Danner's negative views of African Americans were widely known and that Danner had even said that he would match donations by his executives to the Ku Klux Klan.[10] A former personnel director stated, "Danner would say that no one would want to eat at a restaurant where 'a bunch of niggers' were working." A vice president said that Danner believed "Blacks were not qualified to run a store" and that "Blacks should not be employed in any position where they would be seen by customers."[11] Danner was also charged with instructing his managers to fire black employees when they became too numerous and with using racial slurs when talking about his black employees.[12] During lawsuit depositions, Danner himself admitted to having used the "nigger" epithet and also that he had discussed one store's "possible problem area" being the presence of "too many black employees" relative to the "racial mix" in the store's geographical area.[13] In an important investigative report in the *Nation* Steve Watkins noted that Danner had once put into a letter his personal concern over too many black workers at one of his southern restaurants.[14]

The negative views of blacks were not just those of the company's founder. Watkins also reported that the views of some restaurant managers at Shoney's reflected the perspective attributed to Danner. Among the numerous racist code words reportedly used by some managers were "Arnold Schwarzenigger" for a muscular black man; "re-nigging" for rehiring blacks in a restaurant; and "nigger stores" for those in black communities.[15] It seems likely that the opinions attributed to Danner and some of his associates are not unique. The view that white customers dislike black servers, or at least too many black servers, has been found among other whites in the restaurant industry. Black cooks in the kitchen may be acceptable, but blacks in customer contact positions sometimes are not.[16]

Prior to the class-action suit, less than 2 percent of the managerial and supervisory positions were filled by black employees. Only one of the sixty-eight division directors, and not one of the top executives, was black. The majority of black employees were in positions that did not involve regular contact with customers.[17] The chain's position that the restaurants needed only a small number of black workers, even in the low-wage positions, brings to mind Sidney Willhelm's argument that much black labor is no longer needed by a U S. economy that is restructuring to take advantage of low-wage immigrants and workers overseas. Corporate disinvestment in the U.S. economy has also created a large group of whites seeking jobs, including lower-wage service jobs that might otherwise have become available to minority Americans.

Henry and Billie Elliott, the white supervisors of a Captain D's restaurant in Florida, part of the Shoney's chain, said that they were dismissed for refusing to terminate black workers and put whites in their place. The Elliotts filed suit to recover lost wages. They and their attorney, Tommy Warren, compiled 200 boxes of company records that reportedly reveal racial discrimination in the Shoney's empire. Eventually the Elliotts, who had taken jobs driving school buses, won their private legal struggle and received a substantial monetary settlement.[18] The Elliotts' experience signals a very important aspect of contemporary racial relations—that whites too can be victims if they stand against what they feel to be unfair racial discrimination.

Lawsuits Bring Changes at Shoney's

The lawsuits and related publicity had a major impact on the corporation. White corporate executives usually do worry about the images of their companies, and a steady drumbeat of bad publicity can force them to take action whatever their own personal inclinations may be. The fact is especially true for an industry where an image presented in the media can affect everyday business. In 1989 Shoney's executives made an agreement with the Southern Christian Leadership Conference (SCLC) to hire and promote more black workers and to increase opportunities for blacks to secure business franchises. By the end of 1992 the firm had reportedly spent more than $120 million in black communities as a result of its agreement with the SCLC. Moreover, in the summer of 1993 the SCLC signed another agreement with Shoney's new head, Taylor Henry, Jr., who commented that he had "never seen any other covenant of this type in our industry." This second agreement committed the corporation to spending $60 million over several years to help black entrepreneurs buy land for business franchises and to establish black-owned businesses to supply Shoney's restaurants.[19]

By 1992 Shoney's had also increased its number of black employees, including managers and executives, significantly. Some black applicants were hired at Shoney's Nashville, Tennessee, headquarters. In 1989 a woman hired as vice president of corporate and community relations became the first black senior executive. A half dozen others were subsequently employed at the home office. Shoney's had begun to change its image and was making one of the most aggressive moves to hire minorities in the restaurant industry. By 1992 the firm had also substantially increased its business with black suppliers.[20] Disagreement within the firm arose, however, over the aggressive action of the remedial and affirmative action plans. In December 1992 Leonard Roberts, the chair and chief executive hired in 1989 to deal with the charges of racism and affirmative action, resigned his position. Three other top managers working on the remedial plans were fired. According to some sources, Roberts was forced to resign because of his aggressive approach to affirmative action, although company representatives denied this charge. Roberts was replaced with Taylor Henry, Jr. late in December 1992.[21]

In November 1992, the restaurant chain's executives agreed to settle the major class-action lawsuit out of court. This action did not require that the firm's executives admit to discrimination, and they were also able to avoid the negative publicity of a major court trial. Shoney's agreed to pay $105 million between 1993 and 2000 to the many former and present black employees who had charged the company with discrimination and to some white employees who were fired for protesting what they saw as discriminatory company actions. Although this amount was far less than the $350 million in back pay and $180 million in punitive and compensatory damages that the litigants had originally sought, it was the largest settlement ever in a job discrimination case. The firm also agreed to hire more black local managers and regional directors.[22] Taylor Henry, Jr. stated that the lawsuit had focused the company's "priorities on doing what is right. We are a changed company, and we regret any mistakes we made in the past."[23] After the settlements, Danner resigned from the board charging that the firm had not dealt with him fairly.

The $105 million Shoney's settlement has been discussed in the mass media as an indicator of the high cost of persisting racial discrimination. In a February 7, 1993 column titled "Paying the Price of Racism," columnist Clarence Page made this point and noted that the Shoney's case, among others, shows "how racism is alive and well in America" even in a society with "sweeping anti-discrimination laws."[24] In a restaurant industry publication one writer spoke candidly of "recent discrimination scandals involving the Denny's and Shoney's chains." The writer continued with a lengthy discussion of the "disturbing and costly problems" of racial discrimination "still dogging the restaurant industry."[25]

Remedial responses to reported discrimination such as those made at Shoney's are particularly important because of the difficulty individual victims have in dealing with government enforcement agencies. Employment discrimination in the United States is a major problem for African American workers in all income groups, but U.S antidiscrimination laws are weakly enforced, and government-aided remedies usually come slowly if at all. The 1964 Civil Rights Act and later amendments officially prohibit racial discrimination in employment: the EEOC was created to enforce the act by investigating complaints, seeking conciliation, and filing suits to end discrimination. For a time, the federal courts and the EEOC played a major role in reducing racial barriers, but under the conservative Reagan and Bush administrations in the 1980s and early 1990s, the number of broad, institutionally focused investigations of discrimination conducted by the agency declined sharply.[26] As reported by the EEOC, black complaints of job discrimination grew from 112,000 in 1990 to 124,000 in 1992, and the pace of resolving complaints was usually slow. As a result, many black victims of discrimination turned to the NAACP for help. The chair of Howard University's Afro-American Studies Department noted: "Folks are turning to them [local NAACP chapters] on the assumption they have the manpower to handle the problems they are talking about, but many branches are just discussion groups.[27] The NAACP's small legal staff has become overwhelmed; this organization cannot replace governmental agencies whose mandates include the eradication of discrimination in employment across the nation.

During their terms Presidents Ronald Reagan and George Bush appointed several conservative justices to the U.S. Supreme Court, which subsequently handed down a number of restrictive decisions that made it more difficult for workers to bring and win discrimination suits.[28] As a result of the court backtracking on enforcement, it became more difficult for the victims of employment discrimination to win in court. An Urban research study that sent matched white and black applicants to the same employers found that a significant proportion of the black applicants suffered discrimination in the hiring process. In addition, the overwhelming majority of black respondents in a late 1980s national survey felt that if an equally qualified black and white were competing for the same job, the black applicant would be likely to suffer racial discrimination.[29]

Family Restaurants and Black Customers

The problems African Americans face at family restaurants extend beyond employment to a variety of customer service issues. Indeed, the degrading racial images used by some restaurant chains have caused black customer boycotts and protests. For example, in the late 1970s some critics targeted the Sambo's family restaurant chain, a California-based firm with one thousand locations across the nation, because of the stereotypic "Little Black Sambo" story its name suggested and because some restaurants used that story's cartoon-type character as a logo. Complaints were filed against the firm with the Rhode Island Commission on Human Rights, which ruled that the name made black customers feel unwelcome and ordered the name of Sambo's restaurants in that state to be changed. Subsequently, Sambo's restaurants in a number of states changed their name to Sam's or A Place Like Sam's, although the company denied that these changes were made because of charges of racism. By 1981 the chain was losing millions of dollars and had closed half of its restaurants. By the mid-1980s all of its restaurants were closed or sold.[30] The name controversy and declining black patronage were likely contributors to the chain's demise. Here again black families were major victims of symbolic violence, but they were not the only ones to pay a price. The cost of racial insensitivity for the whites involved was very substantial.

In recent years, the Denny's family restaurant chain has faced numerous charges of racial discrimination against black customers. In the early 1990s this firm had nearly 1,500 restaurants across the nation. About 70 percent were company owned: the rest were mostly white-owned franchises. Denny's parent firm, Flagstar Companies, Inc., of Spartanburg, South Carolina, with 120,000 employees, is one of the largest corporations in the nation. In the early 1990s Denny's reportedly faced more than 4,300 complaints of racial discrimination by black customers. One report from Denny's management noted that among the restaurants under the Flagstar umbrella the Denny's chain had the fewest patrons from black and other minority groups.[31] A lawyer for one group of black plaintiffs who filed a class-action suit against Denny's in the spring of 1993 noted the direct historical connection between the student sit-ins of the 1960s and the discrimination recently reported at Denny's restaurants: "It evokes the memory of segregated lunch counters in the Deep South in the 1950s. And it's appalling to see this kind of 'Jim Crow' discrimination occurring in a California restaurant in the 1990s."[32]

In March 1993, one U.S. Department of Justice lawsuit against the company was resolved by a consent decree in which Denny's acknowledged no discrimination but agreed to conduct sensitivity training for all employees and to place notices in each restaurant indicating that patrons of all racial and ethnic groups would receive good service. The suit had alleged that the firm had a "pattern . . . of discrimination" that included such practices as requiring black customers, and not white customers, to prepay for their orders, demanding special identification, and excluding black patrons.[33] In various interviews about the charges of racial discrimination at Denny' s, corporate officials denied that there was a company policy of discrimination but did admit that some Denny's restaurants had been the scene of "isolated" or "individual" instances of racial discrimination from time to time.[34]

In response to the many complaints of discrimination, Jerome J. Richardson, Flagstar's CEO, took an aggressive approach to remedying Denny's racial problems. Richardson met with Benjamin Chavis, NAACP executive director, late in May 1993 to discuss a "fair-share" agreement. Typically, such agreements are privately negotiated and oblige firms to take positive action to address black and other minority concerns. Fair-share agreements between civil rights organizations and businesses have sometimes been effective in channeling investments into minority communities. One NAACP analysis of forty fair-share agreements made by U.S. firms between 1988 and 1993 found that the companies had invested no less than $47 billion in minority employment, service companies, and franchises.[35]

In the summer of 1993, Richardson made a broad agreement with the NAACP that included aggressive minority recruitment, more minority franchises, and more use of minority service and support firms, including insurance and law firms. The agreement also included outside monitoring of the fairness of service at Denny's restaurants.[36] Denny's parent company agreed to invest $1 billion in black- and other minority-owned franchises and restaurant support firms and to place minority workers in 325 new management jobs in its restaurants by the year 2000.[37] The company agreed to substantially increase its purchasing from minority suppliers in this same period.[38] Television ads asserting the company's new image ran in forty-one cities.[39] Impressed by the extent of Richardson's actions, Chavis commented, "In my 30 years in the civil rights movement, I've never seen the commitments made by this CEO today."[40] Richardson said the agreement was "tangible evidence" of Flagstar's intention to end discrimination in its operations.[41] In addition to the NAACP agreement, some Flagstar executives and other representatives made highly visible appearances at NAACP and Urban League conventions, and newspapers reported that the company planned to arrange meetings with minority community groups.[42]

Significantly, however, the company's official position was that it had *not* fostered racial discrimination in its operations in the past or the present. While it is common for employers to refuse to admit past guilt when reaching a settlement, Denny's explicit denial had negative implications for the general public, both black and nonblack. Such a denial reduces the amount of media coverage and public discussion of the reality of discrimination in business settings. In addition, the settlements imply that the problem of antiblack discrimination is not basic to the U.S. economy by suggesting that a few short-range programs will solve whatever racism remains.

A California Class-Action Lawsuit

About the same time that Denny's executives agreed to the aforementioned consent decree with the Justice Department, a class-action suit against Denny's was filed in a California federal court. Thirty-two black plaintiffs alleged that they had faced discrimination at Denny's restaurants,[43] charging that white personnel at Denny's restaurants had discriminated against them in a number of ways.[44] They decided to pursue their case even though the consent decree had dealt with some of the general racial complaints against the firm.

The class-action suit focused on alleged incidents of racial discrimination in several California cities. Several incidents cited in the lawsuit involved prepayment for meals or special cover charges not applied to white patrons. A middle-class black couple had been required to prepay for their meals in a San Diego Denny's. The white manager of a San Jose Denny's had refused to seat a group of eighteen black high school and college students—who entered the restaurant after attending a symposium on what college life was like for black students—unless they paid a cover charge and prepaid their meals. Reportedly white students sitting nearby had not been required to prepay. The black students decided to leave, and the incident made the local news.[45] One of the young people said that the incident made him "embarrassed. I was mad that it was happening." Reflecting on the lawsuit, his father added that "We are not concerned with money. We just want to be able to go to a restaurant and order a meal like everyone else."[46]

Another incident cited in the lawsuit involved a free birthday meal. Seeking a pleasant family outing, a black couple had taken their children to a Denny's restaurant to celebrate their daughter's birthday, but the restaurant refused to honor the girl's baptismal certificate as proof and denied her the birthday meal. At a news conference on the events at the restaurant the mother stated, "I felt violated, humiliated and embarrassed, so we didn't eat there. I can't adequately describe the pain that you feel to see this happen to your child."[47] The daughter also reported great embarrassment: "They acted like we were begging for a meal. Everyone was angry after that and it wrecked my birthday night."[48] The goal of these black complainants is clear: to be treated fairly and equally. The cost of the humiliation for the black targets is also evident in their words: pain, frustration, and embarrassment.

The documents provided to the court indicated a range of racial problems. In an affidavit attached to the class-action suit, one Denny's employee documented "repeated instances of racial prejudice" in which employees treated black customers badly or differently from white customers. *Blackout* was used as a code word for too many black customers in a Denny's at one time; managers were expected to prevent these so-called blackouts.[49] In a statement for the media, a Denny's manager in California said his superiors had taught him "to avoid blackouts by requiring black customers to pay for their meals in advance or simply close the restaurant for a few hours." He added that when he objected to such action, his supervisor told him they would have to get another manager.[50]

These events reveal certain important aspects of white thought about black Americans in everyday situations. The code word *blackout* for too many black customers in a store may have originated as an attempt at humor, but the term has significance beyond racist joking. Like the electric blackout for which it is likely named, it represents a loss of proper functioning. White feelings and fears about African Americans can prevent whites from functioning in normal human ways. Concern over the presence of too many blacks relative to the number of whites is common among white Americans in many social settings. The racial geography we noted earlier has its own territorial imperative. Whites are often uncomfortable if the proportion of blacks in a given group—a residential neighborhood, for example—exceeds a modest percentage, perhaps 5–10 percent. One famous Detroit survey in the 1970s found that the proportion of white respondents who said they would be unwilling to move into a hypothetical neighborhood with black families increased as the black proportion increased. If the neighborhood were 8 percent black, just over one-quarter said that they would be unwilling to move in. But if the neighborhood were 36 percent black, three-quarters of the whites expressed an unwillingness to live there.[51] It is probably still true that a majority of whites would refuse to move into a substantially black community if they were faced with that possibility.

Indeed, many whites are uncomfortable with the presence of *any* black people in what they view as white territory, such as historically white restaurants. Why are so many whites uneasy in the presence of black people? One answer may be that these whites reject black people because they project certain fears onto the dark otherness. We noted in chapter 1* the work of Joel Kovei and others who suggest that these antiblack fears and impulses are irrational and that they are rooted in the world of the unconscious. For some whites "blackouts" may symbolize dirt, danger, even the unknown—symbols rooted deeply in the white unconscious. Such reactions mark a breakdown in understanding across the color line.

Because of the consent decree Denny's made with the Justice Department, the firm's lawyers argued that the California class-action lawsuit should be set aside. However, lawyers for the black plaintiffs countered that the many charges of discrimination at Denny's restaurants across the United States provided ample reason to continue the private lawsuit.[52] Referring to Denny's persisting discrimination after the decree, a lawyer for the Washington Lawyers' Committee for Civil Rights and Urban Affairs contended that the U.S. Department of Justice should hold Denny's "in contempt of court for violating the terms of the consent decree."[53]

A Politicized Incident

On April 1, 1993, Dan Rather opened the CBS evening news with a statement about black Secret Service agents. As a Flagstar executive remembered it, Rather said, "They put their lives on the line every day, but they can't get served at Denny's."[54] The six black Secret Service agents had received what they viewed as discriminatory service at a Denny's restaurant in Annapolis, Maryland. They waited for about an hour while fifteen white agents, as well as white customers who entered the restaurant after they did, received speedy and repeated service. The agents made several attempts to get their waitress to serve them, then sought the manager, who did not come out immediately. Both the black and the white agents were in the same section of the restaurant, and all were dressed the same way.[55] This account suggests that any African American, regardless of his or her economic status, can be the victim of discrimination in public accommodations.

One of the black agents later remarked, "I was somewhat invisible that day."[56] He explained that he and the other black agents, like many black Americans, were reluctant to seek redress: "It was very difficult for us to come forth with this information. The question that went through our minds was, 'If not us, who? If not now, when?' And we answered that if we are about social responsibility as well as the Secret Service, we had to step forth."[57] These Secret Service agents felt a responsibility to confront discrimination on behalf of the black community. Denny's officials said that the problem that day was not discrimination but a backup in the kitchen. The manager was fired, but only for not reporting the incident. This well-publicized incident encouraged other black customers of Denny's to complain openly. Within a few months the agents' lawyers had received 250 reports of racial discrimination in service at a number of Denny's restaurants.[58]

The discrimination charges involving Denny's received widespread, albeit brief national attention. Newspapers and television news shows carried editorials condemning the poor treatment of the agents. At the Annapolis restaurant civil rights organizations held a protest demonstration reminiscent of the 1960s lunch counter protest. Even the White House responded. Bill Clinton's communications director stated that the president "is strongly against discriminatory practices against anyone. Discrimination against

*Does not appear in this publication.

black Secret Service agents would be a very serious problem."[59]

Late in May 1994 both the California class-action suit and another class-action suit brought on behalf of the black Secret Service agents were resolved by a consent decree in which Flagstar agreed to pay damages of $46 million to the victims of discrimination as well as $9 million in lawyers fees.[60] In its report on the court settlement *Business Week* noted that Flagstar had "apologized for apparent racism" in some of its operations.[61] The head of Flagstar, Jerome Richardson, stated that the firm settled in part to show that Denny's wants black customers: "We deeply regret these individuals feel they were not treated fairly at Denny's. We invite any customers who have perceived discrimination at Denny's to give us another opportunity to serve them."[62] He also indicated that some employees had been terminated because of the discrimination lawsuits.

In a news conference regarding the settlement Assistant Attorney General Deval Patrick stated that the Denny's decree was one type of solution for illegal discrimination in public accommodations: "There will be a high price to pay for unlawful indignities, and the Justice Department will exact that price whenever the law is violated.[63] Patrick indicated that the decree required Denny's to hire an independent monitor to watch over its implementation, the first time such a monitoring requirement had been agreed upon. He noted that in addition to the payment of monetary awards, the settlement required Denny's to advertise nationally that patrons from all racial and ethnic groups were welcome and "to conduct random testing to determine whether black patrons continue to be treated differently, because this testing helps to uncover this particular subtle form of racism.[64] This major U.S. Department of Justice involvement in racial discrimination lawsuits in the early Clinton administration was a clear break from the policies of the previous Reagan and Bush administrations and a hopeful indicator of renewed federal efforts to enforce existing civil rights laws in the area of public accommodations.

Problems at Other Restaurants

Shoney's and Denny's are not unique. Other family and fast-food restaurants have faced charges of racial and ethic discrimination. Some are small and local and receive little media attention. A bar in Champaign, Illinois, that refused to admit black customers until compelled to do so by the Justice Department is but one example.[65] Most incidents that have received national media coverage have involved restaurant chains. In the late 1980s, after a number of complaints from potential patrons who represented a number of racial and ethnic groups, the California Department of Alcoholic Beverage Control ruled that the Red Onion chain had discriminated against minority patrons as part of company policy. The firm denied the charge of discrimination, but in the late 1980s it agreed to pay more than two hundred thousand dollars to twenty-nine people of color who charged they had been unfairly denied entry.[66]

In January 1993 another major chain, the International House of Pancakes (IHOP), with more than five hundred restaurants nationwide, agreed to pay $185,000 in settlement of a discrimination lawsuit.[67] The lawsuit charged that the white manager of an IHOP in Milwaukee refused entrance to a group of black college students when the restaurant locked its doors to several groups of black youth on December 28, 1991. The fifteen black plaintiffs, who had just attended a party hosted by Howard University alumni, reported that the IHOP manager and staff told them the twenty-four-hour restaurant was closed, although white customers were being admitted.[68]

Executives at family-restaurant chains, like those at other major U.S. businesses, have reportedly viewed racial and multicultural issues as diversions from their major business goals. Consequently, as some industry analysts have noted, racial and ethnic matters have often been approached in a superficial or too-bureaucratic manner. Company officials may address such issues on paper, but until they are confronted with a crisis most take little significant action. A *Business Week* report concluded that top officials at Flagstar, as well as those at other large firms, "depend too heavily on policy statements instead of active monitoring and training to avoid discrimination complaints."[69] According to the head of Denny's Franchisee Advisory Council, until the late 1980s only ten to twenty minutes of the month-long training provided to franchisees involved learning about problems of discrimination.[70] One analyst of corporate responses to interracial problems has noted that written policies are not the same thing as "the way people really behave." He added that corporate cultures "reflect the behaviors and values that are rewarded."[71]

For a time, the national publicity of the Denny's and Shoney's lawsuits forced the restaurant industry to pay more attention to persisting problems of racial and ethnic discrimination. These two companies and other major chains began to require more racial and ethnic sensitivity training for their employees. It remains to be seen, however, how long this emphasis on multicultural training will last.

Conclusion

Why is the family restaurant sometimes a site of racial rituals? Is there something especially significant about such places for white Americans? At first glance contacts between white diners and black employees or diners appear to be fleeting, making restaurants unlikely settings for interracial friction. Yet there is more to consider. The preparation and sharing of food in the United States have long had socioreligious meaning. Since biblical times, Jews and Christians have celebrated some of their most important religious traditions around a table. Certain meals or foods have special commemorative value. In Christianity, Jesus' last supper with his apostles remains a crucial religious symbol, and the act of sharing food in communion is thought to be a celebration of the union of the communicant with the person of their Christ. This ceremony is one of the powerful symbols of communal solidarity in Western religion.[72]

The importance of food-centered communion can also be seen in other religious celebrations. The Massachusetts pilgrims blessed and shared food at a special thanksgiving ritual that over time has become a part of American civil religion. Ironically, this yearly celebration of familial and national solidarity commemorates a supper that the seventeenth-century pilgrims shared with aboriginal Americans who had played a critical role in the European immigrants' survival. Yet the native peoples with whom the meal was shared would soon be dispossessed of life and land by their dinner-table companions. The commemorative act of Thanksgiving, repeated yearly by generation after generation of Americans, sometimes at family restaurants, signals an acceptance of a social order and values that transcend the sharing of food per se. Collective consumption can symbolize a common destiny—the "we" feelings that theoretically bind families, groups, and the nation together.

Not surprisingly, then, the racial rituals carried out by some whites in the food service industry have serious consequences beyond the victimization of black customers and workers. These consequences are symbolic as well as material, and they are destructive of the social fabric. Although certain costs of this discrimination are directly borne by black customers and workers, other costs are paid by the society as a whole. Paul Claudel has written about European social stratification in earning arrangements, which he calls "an eternal class struggle" in food fashions. In Europe the nicer restaurants represent very clear and privileged markers of social class differences. Food fashions reflect and reinforce social class differences "that nothing can compensate for."[73] While class stratification does exist in the U.S. restaurant industry, the distinctive U.S. family restaurant chains have become great equalizers that break Claudel's rule. Internationally, the U.S. chain restaurant has become an unintentional symbol of class equality.

Yet the reported attempts by some white owners, managers, and employees to exclude or restrict African American access to family restaurants strike another blow at the fundamental values of equality and democracy. Many white Americans seem to regard the family as their particular province, perhaps in part because many whites believe, erroneously, that African Americans have weak families and poor family values. For many black and white Americans the word *family*, whether in "family values" or "family restaurant," has often become a ritualistic code word for *white*. As a result, most black customers who enter family restaurants across the nation doubtless do so with caution or the expectation that they may be unwelcome or unwanted. The 1964 Civil Rights Act, perhaps the major civil rights legislation of the twentieth century, officially banned discrimination in all places of public accommodations. However, thirty years later this nation is not close to eradicating discrimination in restaurants or many other types of public accommodations.

Still, the reactions of Shoney's and Denny's top executives to the racial discrimination lawsuits are encouraging. While it took a number of lawsuits to bring major changes, it is clear that among the nine major cases of racial problems examined in this book, the most substantive remedial actions have been taken in the cases of Shoney's and Denny's restaurants. Some newspaper reports and editorials celebrated the resolution of the lawsuits with strong headlines such as this one in the *Chicago Sun Times:* "Denny's Pact Combats Racism."[74] We agree with these editorials and with civil rights observers who have been complimentary to Denny's and Shoney's for compensating the black plaintiffs in response to the discrimination lawsuits, for bringing greater racial diversity through their employment and purchasing policies, and for working to eliminate future discrimination in their operations. Yet some observers have taken a watchful attitude toward these ongoing corporate changes, hoping for continuing improvements but aware that retrogression is possible. Some civil rights advocates with whom we have spoken have expressed concern that the major remedies taken as a result of the many charges of racial discrimination and several lawsuits have been linked to consent decrees in which the companies publicly deny that there is racial discrimination in their operations. This public denial by influential corporate officials of what seems obvious to many Americans, especially African Americans, contributes to the impression common among white Americans that racism is no longer a serious problem in the United States.

Notes

1. David J. Carrow, *Bearing the Cross: Martin Luther King, Jr., and the Southern Christian Leadership Conference* (New York: Vintage Books, 1986), p. 127.
2. Carrow, *Bearing the Cross*, p. 128.
3. Conrad P. Kottack, "Rituals at McDonald's," *Natural History* 87 (1978): 75.
4. Richard Martin, "Foodservice's Changing Face: Still Grappling with Diversity," *Nation's Restaurant News*, September 20, 1993, p. 1.
5. Calvin W. Rolark, "Let's Talk: Restaurant Justice Is Needed," *Washington Informer*, July 28, 1993, p. 12.
6. Martin, "Foodservice's Changing Face," p. 1.
7. New York Times News Service, "Transformation: Settlement Commits Shoney's to Top-to-bottom Restructuring," *Dallas Morning News*, February 1, 1993, p. D1; Joan Oleck, "Shoney's Angles for Settlement," *Restaurant Business*, September 20, 1992, p. 26.
8. Darryl Fears, "Shoney's Agrees to Extend Minority Business Investments," *The Atlanta Journal and Constitution*, June 3, 1993, p. G1.
9. Fears, "Shoney's Agrees to Extend Minority Business Investments," p. 1; New York Times News Service, "Transformation," p. D1.
10. Oleck, "Shoney's Angles for Settlement," p. 26.
11. Quoted in Steve Watkins, "Racism Du Jour at Shoney's," *Nation*, October 18, 1993, pp. 426–427.
12. Martin Dyckman, "Lawyers Can Be Heros Too," *St. Petersburg Times*, April 11, 1993, p. 3D.
13. "Shoney's Co. Founder Quits Board, Sells Stock After Multimillion Bias Decision," *Jet*, March 29, 1993, p. 4; Ronald Smothers, "$105 Million Poorer Now, Chain Mends Race Policies," *New York Times*, January 31, 1993, Section 1, p. 16.
14. Watkins, "Racism Du Jour at Shoney's," pp. 426–427.
15. Watkins, "Racism Du Jour at Shoney's," pp. 426–427.
16. See Blair S. Walker and Judith Schroer, "Paralyzing Prejudice: Minority Customers Still Shut Out," *USA Today*, June 11, 1993, p. B1.
17. Watkins, "Racism Du Jour at Shoney's," p. 427.
18. Dyckman, "Lawyers Can Be Heros Too," p. 3D.
19. Fears, "Shoney's Agrees to Extend Minority Business Investments," p. 1.
20. Fears, "Shoney's Agrees to Extend Minority Business Investments," p. 1.
21. Chicago Tribune wireservice, "Shoney's Stock Falls on News of Shakeup," *Chicago Tribune*, December 22, 1992, p. C3.
22. New York Times News Service, "Transformation," p. D1.
23. New York Times News Service, "Transformation," p. D1; "Shoney's Ex-chairman Dannet Quits Board," Reuters Limited, BC Cycle, June 30, 1993.
24. Clarence Page, "Paying the Price for Racism," *Chicago Tribune*, February 7, 1993, p. C3.
25. Martin, "Foodservice's Changing Face," p. 1.
26. Joe R. Feagin and Clairece B. Feagin, *Racial and Ethnic Relations*, fourth ed. (Englewood Cliffs, N.J.: Prentice Hall, 1993), pp. 232–233.
27. Jerry Thomas, "NAACP's Army Thins as Its Battles Multiply," *Chicago Tribune*, September 27, 1993, Zone N, p. 1.
28. The 1991 Civil Rights Act was designed to countermand these Supreme Court decisions. Congress was more liberal than the court and President Bush.
29. Margery Austin Turner, Michael Fix, and Raymond J. Struyk, *Opportunities Denied: Discrimination in Hiring* (Washington, D.C.: Urban Institute, 1991); James E. Ellis, "The Black Middle Class," *Business Week*, March 14, 1988, p. 65.
30. "Restaurants Ordered to Change Name," UPI, March 18, 1981, BC cycle; Cheryl Devall, "African-Americans Still Suffer Bias When Eating Out," *Weekend Edition*, National Public Radio, May 29, 1993.
31. Calvin Sims, "Giving Denny's a Menu for Change," *New York Times*, January 1, 1994, Section 1, p. 43; Jim Doyle, "32 Blacks Sue Denny's for Bias," *San Francisco Chronicle*, March 25, 1993, p. A17.
32. Doyle, "32 Blacks Sue Denny's for Bias," p. A17.
33. James Victini, "Denny's Restaurants Settles Race-Bias Charges," *Reuters Asia-Pacific Business Report*, March 26, 1993, BC cycle.
34. Sims, "Giving Denny's a Menu for Change," Section 1, p. 43; Robin Schatz, "Denny's and Others Stumble on Racism Charges," *Newsday*, August 8, 1993, p. 84.
35. Schatz, "Denny's and Others Stumble on Racism Charges," p. 84.
36. Jay Mathews, "Denny's Tackles a Stained Image: Fighting Bias Charges, Chairman Forges Links with Rights Leaders," *Washington Post*, August 1, 1993, p. H1.
37. Susan Christian, "Denny's Hires San Diego Consultant for Civil Rights Job, Liaison," *Los Angles Times*, July 28, 1993, p. D1.
38. Mark J. McGarry, "Denny's to Spend $1 Billion to Do the Right Thing," *Newsday*, July 2, 1993, p. 47.
39. Mathews, "Denny's Tackles a Stained Image," p. H1.
40. Quoted in Andrea Adelson, "Denny's Parent Vows Larger Role for Blacks," *New York Times*, July 2, 1993, p. D2.
41. Adelson, "Denny's Parent Vows Larger Role for Blacks," p. D2.
42. Sandra Clark, "Denny's Campaigns to Counter Charges," *Plain Dealer*, July 20, 1993, p. F2.
43. Bruce Vielmetti, "More Saying Denny's Discriminates," *St. Petersburg Times*, June 17, 1993, p.A1.

44. Robert L. Jackson, "Denny's Breaks Bias Vow on Day of Accord," *Los Angeles Times*, May 22, 1993, p. A1; Doyle, "32 Blacks Sue Denny's for Bias," p. A17.
45. "Not Yet Free from Racism," *Metro Reporter*, January 26, 1992, p. 3; Chuck Hawkins, "Denny's: The Stain That Isn't Coming Out," *Business Week*, June 28, 1993, p. 98; "New Race Bias Charges Against Denny's Restaurants," *San Francisco Chronicle*, June 17, 1993, p. A19.
46. Quoted in William D. Murray, "Denny's Charged with Discriminating Against Blacks," UPI, BC cycle, March 24, 1993.
47. Quoted in Calvin Sims, "Restaurant Chain Settles Charges of Racial Bias," *New York Times*, March 26, 1993, p. A14.
48. Quoted in Murray, "Denny's Charged with Discriminating Against Blacks."
49. "Class Action Suit," *Sacramento Observer*, March 31, 1993, p. F1.
50. Quoted in Mathews, "Denny's Tackles a Stained Image," p. H1.
51. Reynolds Farley, Howard Schuman, Suzanne Blanchi, Diane Colasanto, and Shirley Hatchett, "Chocolate City, Vanilla Suburbs," *Sociology and Social Research* 7 (1978): 335–336.
52. Washington Post wire services, "Turning Up Heat on Denny's," *Houston Chronicle*, June 17, 1993, p. A10.
53. "New Race Bias Charges Against Denny's Restaurants," p. A19.
54. Quoted in Mathews, "Denny's Tackles a Stained Image," p. H1.
55. Jerry Thomas, " 'Invisible' Patrons Demand to Be Seen," *Chicago Tribune*, June 10, 1993, Zone N, p. 1; Mathews, "Denny's Tackles a Stained Image," p. H1.
56. Quoted in Thomas, " 'Invisible' Patrons Demand to Be Seen," Zone N, p. 1.
57. Quoted in Devall, "African-Americans Still Suffer Bias When Eating Out."
58. Schatz, "Denny's and Others Stumble on Racism Charges," p. 84.
59. Quoted in Jackson, "Denny's Breaks Bias Vow on Day of Accord," p. A1.
60. Bureau of National Affairs, "Discrimination: Denny's Restaurants to Pay $46 Million, Provide 'Sensitivity' Training to Employees," BNA Management Brief, May 26, 1994.
61. "Denny's Does Some of the Right Things," *Business Week*, June 6, 1994, p. 42.
62. "Denny's, Blacks Settle Suits: Company to Pay $54.7 Million," *Orlando Sentinel*, May 25, 1994, p. A1.
63. Rupert Cornwell, "Rocketing Cost of Race Bias in the U.S.," *The Independent*, May 28, 1994, p. 8.
64. "Justice Department News Conference with Deval Patrick, Assistant Attorney General, Civil Rights Division," Federal News Service, May 24, 1994.
65. Thomas, " 'Invisible' Patrons Demand to be Seen," Zone N, p. 1.
66. Walker and Schroer, "Paralyzing Prejudice: Minority Customers Still Shut Out," p. B1.
67. Bill Carlino, "IHOP OKs Settlement in Racial Bias Suit," *Nation's Restaurant News*, January 18, 1993, p. 3.
68. Joan Oleck, "Hearings Set in IHOP Discrimination Suit," *Restaurant Business*, October 10, 1992, p. 22.
69. Hawkins, "Denny's: The Stain That Isn't Coming Out," p. 98.
70. Hawkins, "Denny's: The Stain That Isn't Coming Out," p. 98.
71. Quoted in Schatz, "Denny's and Others Stumble on Racism Charges," p. 84.
72. Paul Claudel, *The Structures of Everyday Life* (New York: Harper & Row, 1981), p. 208.
73. Claudel, *The Structures of Everyday Life*, p. 186.
74. "Denny's Pact Combats Racism," *Chicago Sun Times*, May 30, 1994, p. 17.

Article Review Form at end of book.

Do you agree that the myth of the model Asian is contributing to discrimination in the labor market? Do you agree that the myth of the model Asian is interfering with Asians' assimilation of American culture?

Exploring Asian Americans

The myth of the "model minority" and the reality of their lives

Jieli Li

Ohio University

There is a myth revolving around Asian Americans in the United States. Many Americans are led to believe that Asian Americans fare well as higher achievers in education and social status. The myth of the "model minority" first surfaced in the mid-1960s when William Petersen published his article "Success Story, Japanese American Style" in *New York Times Magazine* on January 9, 1966. By the early 1980s, the myth became more entrenched in American society as *Newsweek* (6 December 1982) had a cover story to applaud Asian Americans as a "Model Minority" that have achieved success despite the suffering from prejudice and discrimination. The author wrote, "Asian Americans now enjoy the nation's highest median family income: $22,075 a year compared with $20,840 for whites, and . . . the industrious Asians believe they are contributing a needed shot of some vanishing American values: thrift, strong family ties, sacrifice for the children" (p. 39). *Time* (31 August 1987) continued to praise Asian American businessmen as successful entrepreneurs, and Asian American youths as academic "whiz kids," especially in math and sciences.

The image of model minority created by the media has generated a popular belief that Asian Americans are no longer the disadvantaged who appear to be well integrated into mainstream American system, and the discrimination and prejudice are things of the past. While Asian Americans' relative accomplishments should not be denied by any means, the myth associated with the "model minority" thesis is questionable in its validity. In short, it is misleading in many ways that do not reflect the reality of Asian American lives.

Myth 1: "Asian Americans as an ethnic group are generally faring well."

It has been a long tradition in American society that the people of Asian descent are referred to as "Asian Americans." As such, they tend to be labeled indiscriminately as "all faring well." Lowe (1991) and Trueba et al. (1993) argue that it is misleading to lump together Asians as a single homogeneous ethnic group, for Asian immigrants came from different parts of Asia such as Mainland China, Japan, Taiwan, Hong Kong, Singapore, the Philippines, Korea, Thailand, Vietnam, Laos, Indonesia, Malaysia, and so on. These groups are a collection of diverse people with distinct linguistic, cultural, and social backgrounds. For example, Asian Indians come from different cultural traditions than Chinese, Japanese, and Koreans.

Southeastern Asian cultures can also be distinguished in many ways from those of East Asia. In addition, the Asian population in the United States varies substantially in terms of region of residence, educational levels, occupational levels, generations in the United States, recency of immigration, and proficiency of English.

The 1993 U.S. Bureau of the Census data indicate that there is a wide variation in education attainment among American Asian groups with Asian Indians the highest and Southeast Asian among the lowest. Thus, Asian Americans vary accordingly in socioeconomic status, with some occupying high-paying jobs and some low-paying jobs. However, statistics on family earnings can be misleading if not differentiated between native-born and foreign-born Asians. Socioeconomic differences are found to exist between native-born Asians and foreign-born Asians. For example, there is a big earnings gap between Japanese Americans, almost three-quarters native born and Vietnamese, recently new arrivals (Hsia 1988, p.180). Chinese Americans are similarly polarized into two groups, with the native-born more established and newcomers struggling at the bottom of society. Even for the new arrivals, the Asian immigrants range from well-educated professionals and business people to poorly educated and penniless refugees. Barringer et al. (1993) found that there is a huge difference in terms of human and economic resources between the Taiwanese and Hmong immigrants. The former are mostly well-educated professionals while the latter are refugees. Hence, the myth about the homogeneity of Asian Americans is a misperception that largely overlooks cultural and socioeconomic differences that exist among Asian American groups.

Myth 2: "Asian Americans have reached and even surpassed educational and earnings parities with whites."

What consistently favors the "model minority" thesis is the statistical data on higher educational attainment among Asian Americans—the percentage of educational level is higher for Asian Americans than those for whites and other minority groups. The 1994 U.S. Census indicates that the percentage of Asian Americans having graduated from college (42%) is well above that of whites (23%). Two factors may contribute to this high percentage. First, as compared to other Asian subgroups, native-born Japanese and Chinese Americans are more educated and professional, and the data that were used to support the model minority thesis were primarily collected from these two groups (Lyman 1974, p. 119). Second, there has been a constant influx of immigrants from Asia since 1965, generally viewed as a "brain drain." Most of the Asian immigrants, especially those from East Asian countries and Asian India, were either educated professionals in their home countries or students who came to the United States for advanced degrees and later decided to stay permanently. For example, between 1988 and 1990, Asians accounted for over half the number of professional immigrants admitted to the United States from all over the world (Kanjanapan 1995). This demographic movement reversed the pre-1965 pattern of older Asian immigrants, who generally had low educational attainment and low socioeconomic status.

However, statistics focusing only on educational level without taking into account economic returns to education is misleading. Although Asian Americans have higher educational attainments, the economic returns to their education are low. Asian professionals are overrepresented in technical careers such as engineering, and underrepresented in law, medicine, teaching, and administration. Even in the same industries, Asian immigrants received earnings far below those of whites (Chan 1991). When they have a comparable income, they usually earned it by acquiring more education and by working more hours. Asian professionals are mostly found in entry-level and mid-level technical-oriented positions. Li (1980) points out that native-and foreign-born Asian Americans have experienced, in one way or another an overqualification for occupations or an underemployment of their education. If all things are considered equal, many Asian Americans achieve less than their white counterparts.

Roos (1977) compares Japanese Americans with whites. Taking into consideration means of income, education, and income adjusted for age and school years completed, he concluded that Japanese Americans had not yet reached earnings parity with whites despite that Japanese Americans had higher average education than whites. Thus, his findings indicate that education did not close the gap between native-born Japanese Americans and white earnings.

Table 1 Original and Adjusted Individual Earnings, and Earnings Ratio of Whites, Asians, and Non-Asian Minority Groups (1980)

		Original Earnings (Dollars)	Adjusted Earnings (Dollars)	Ratio	Sample Size
Non-Asian Groups	Whites	16,822	16,822	1	54,656
	American Indians	10,449	13,255	.79	358
	Mexicans	11,009	13,967	.83	2,321
	Puerto Ricans	10,820	15,799	.94	421
	Blacks	10,586	13,484	.80	5,716
Asian Groups (Native-born)	Japanese	17,905	16,046	.95	8,668
	Chinese	16,324	15,675	.93	3,385
	Filipinos	12,566	15,401	.92	1,991
	Koreans				
	Asian Indians				
	Vietnamese				
Asian Groups (Foreign-born)	Japanese	19,939	17,857	1.06	2,515
	Chinese	14,689	12,402	.74	9,306
	Filipinos	14,988	15,056	.89	7,440
	Koreans	15,985	14,017	.83	3,488
	Asian Indians	20,112	14,283	.85	5,666
	Vietnamese	9,309	11,423	.68	2,712

Source: Hurh and Kim (1989: 522–533)

Hirschman and Wong (1981) found that with educational level considered equal, Asian Americans, especially those foreign-born Asians, receive earnings far below those of whites. Even though native-born Japanese, Chinese, and Filipino males achieved average income equivalent to or higher than white males, parity of earnings does not commensurate with education and occupation between whites and Asians. As Espiritu (1997) observes, "in 1990, highly educated Asian American men who worked full time, full year, earned about 10% less than white men—even though the former were much more likely to have a graduate degree" (p. 67). Hurh and Kim (1989) employ a theoretical approach of equity to challenge the conventional type of measurement of the Asian American success. They suggest that the reward and the cost index should be added in an empirical analysis to compare Asian ethnic groups with whites and other minority groups in terms of cost or investment and reward or achievement. They select six factors in a regression analysis of individual earnings: (1) the age of workers; (2) educational attainment; (3) prestige score for the worker's occupation; (4) mean income of the worker's state; (5) number of weeks worked; and (6) number of hours worked. The comparison is made among ethnic groups between individual original and adjusted earnings (Table 1). Adjusted earnings refer to the earnings that would be received by a member of each group, if the person has the same level of education, occupational prestige, and number of hours worked. Their findings, as measured by uneven ratio, indicate that while whites and Asians are equal in the cost of investment, Asians achieve less than whites; and although the level of achievement of some Asians may be equal to that of whites, the cost of achievement is higher for Asians than for whites. Their findings also indicate that the earnings ratio of foreign-born Asians (except Japanese whose high earning ratio is more related to Japan's export market than U.S labor market [Nee and Sanders 1985]) are no better than that of non-Asian minorities, such as black and Mexican Americans.

Related to the issue is the myth associated with statistical data showing that the annual family income is higher for Asian Americans than for whites. Again, the data is misleading because it overlooked a number of significant variables. A careful examination of the existing data points in the other direction. The 1980 U.S. Census shows that although the mean annual family income of Asians is relatively higher than that of whites, mean annual individual earnings are relatively lower for Asians than for whites. Most important, more Asian than white families live below the poverty level. In their study, Gardner et al. (1985) point out that poverty rates of Southeast Asian refugee groups are higher than those of any other minority group in America. For example, the percentage of families living below poverty level is 35.1 for Vietnamese, compared to 26.5 for blacks. Rumbaut and Ima (1988) indicate that about 90 percent of Hmong families have incomes below the poverty level. The 1994 U.S. Census further reports that while there is a higher percentage of Asians who have an annual family income of $50,000 or more than that of whites, the percentage of Asian Americans living below the poverty level is also higher than whites.

There are reasons for what seems to be contradicting figures. (1) Higher median incomes for Asian families are largely due to a greater number of workers per family, which helps to increase the higher family income. The 1980 U.S. Census shows that 63 percent of Asian Americans families had two or more paid workers and 17 percent had three or more, as compared to 55 percent and 12 percent for whites. Chun (1980) suggests that a more accurate measurement index of group comparison for household income should include the number of hours worked and the number of wage earners per household, and that Asian Americans' high income may attribute to "longer work hours or sacrificed weekends." (2) The size of the Asian family is traditionally larger than that of the white family. The average household size is 3.1 for Chinese, 2.7 for Japanese, 3.6 for Filipino, 3.4 for Korean, 2.9 for Asian Indians, and 4.4 for Vietnamese, as compared to 2.7 for whites (Gardner et al. 1985). (3) Most Asians are concentrated in metropolitan areas such as Los Angeles, San Francisco, New York, and Hawaii, where the cost of living is higher than the national average (Woodrum 1984; Takaki 1993).

Family income statistics can be misleading when applied to the foreign born and particularly for recent immigrants and refugees. There is a high percentage of Asian Americans, post-1965, who do not have higher educational attainments. The 1990 U.S Census indicates that over 22 percent of Asian Americans twenty-five years and older have less than a high school degree, and about 90 percent of these people are immigrants. The 1993 U.S. Census also indicates that there is a high percentage of Asian Americans who have difficulty speaking English. Their upward mobility is severely restricted by these disadvantages.

The median income for those with limited English ranges from $15,000 to $20,000, and the median income for those with limited English and low level of education is usually less than $10,000 for a full-time job (Ong and Hee 1994). Southeast Asian refugees, particularly those who arrived after 1978, constitute a large portion of this disadvantaged Asian population. This Asian American group suffers the most, compared to other minority groups in the United States. They have the highest percentages of low educational levels (64%) and of English deficiency (55%), and the highest rates of unemployment (33% for males, 58% for females) and of welfare dependency (Ong and Umemoto 1994). Among them, about 10 percent of Vietnamese and 16 percent of Cambodians and Laotians are extremely poor with annual incomes of only $6,307, well below the poverty level (Ong 1993). Espiritu (1997) comments that "these statistics call attention to the danger of lumping all Asian groups together because Southeast Asians—and other disadvantaged groups—do not share in the relatively favorable socioeconomic outcomes attributed to the 'average' Asian American" (p. 72).

Myth 3: "Asian Americans are successful entrepreneurs who have occupied more managerial positions."

The myth relating to the success image of Asian American entrepreneurs holding more managerial positions is misleading. Most Asian American "managers" are self-employed instead of working in larger firms. The growing number of Asian American-owned businesses in the 1970s and 1980s, primarily used to uphold the myth, only indicates Asian immigrants' own solution to social barriers created by labor market discrimination. According to a survey conducted in 1988 by Fawcett and Gardner (1994), nearly half of the Korean male entrepreneurs were college educated, but most of them are unable to find a job consistent with their education and qualifications. The problems of labor underemployment have turned many Asians toward self-employment, with Koreans being concentrated in the businesses of grocery, dry-cleaning, wholesale and retail sales, and fast-food services; Chinese in garment factories, restaurants, and gift shops; and Cambodians in the doughnut business (Espiritu 1997).

Those small businesses are heavily clustered in their ethnic communities. With limited capital, they compete in highly risky, marginally profitable businesses such as small grocery markets, garment workshops, and restaurants (Bonacich and Jung 1982). Contrary to the myth, few of those small business owners are able to gain upward social mobility. The majority of these businesses have earned low profits, and chances for bankruptcy are high. Taking Southeast Asian Americans as an example, Espiritu (1997) points out that in 1990, 18 out of 20 businesses failed during their first-year operations. Even for those that survive, they heavily depend on unpaid or minimally paid labor of family members or relatives and on staying open long hours. According to the survey of Ong and Hee (1994), about 42 percent of Asian American business owners work more than 50 hours a week and 26 percent work more than 60 hours per week. Moreover, three-quarters of Asian American businesses do not hire a single employee from outside.

Hurh and Kim (1984), in their study of Korean Americans in the Los Angeles area, found that many of those small businesses are primarily Mom and Pop stores with few or no paid employees and low profit. Gold (1994) describes those small Asian American businesses, like ones owned by Vietnamese Americans, as "exploiting themselves to maintain marginal or undercapitalized enterprises" (p. 212). Chan (1991) critically commented that a sign of success in Asian American entrepreneurship is "a disguised form of cheap labor: work long hours, and many of them could not stay afloat were it not for the unpaid labor they extract from their spouses, children, and other relatives" (pp. 169–170).

The problems that Asian entrepreneurs have encountered reflect a structural inequality of American society. Many scholars point out that the American economy is divided into a core and peripheral sectors with labor market being split into a primary and secondary market. The primary market is located in the core economic sector in which workers have higher earnings and better working conditions, while the secondary market in the peripheral sector is characterized by low-paying jobs and worse working conditions. Socioeconomic mobility is restricted by this split labor market in which workers are distributed on the basis of race, ethnicity, gender, and nativity, rather than according to education, work experience, or other kinds of human capital (Chan 1991).

Even for those few Asians who work in primary labor market and occupy managerial positions, they are facing a barrier of "glass ceiling," through which "top management positions can only be seen, but not reached" (Takaki 1989). According to Takaki, the data collected in 1988 indicate that there were only 8 percent of Asian Americans with real "managerial" jobs, compared to 12 percent for all other groups in the United States. Asians were generally absent from positions of executive leadership in American corporations, despite that they were highly educated.

Arguing against the model minority thesis, Bonacich and Jund (1982) describe Asian Americans as a "middleman minority." As assimilated "outsiders," they are constrained by structural arrangements of society, surviving by occupying certain "occupational niches" that are non- or less competitive with the dominant ethnic group. Even in those competitive occupations, Asian Americans are unable to receive the same returns on their education and reach earnings parity with the majority group. Viewed from this perspective, although a "middleman minority" is allowed for achieving relatively higher socioeconomic status than other minority groups, they are blocked from advancing into positions of authority or decision-making power. The U.S. Commission on Civil Rights (1992) admits that there exists a "glass ceiling" blocking the promotion of Asians to senior-level or top management positions in various sectors of mainstream economy.

Myth 4: "Asian American youth are 'whiz kids.'"

The evidence indicates that not all Asian American students do well in school. They vary in their experiences of academic achievement and attitude toward school work. In her field study, Lee (1996) examines the variability of Asian American students at Academic High School and found that despite some Asian students who are at the top of academic rankings, there are many low achieving Asian American students. In one of the schools she examined, during the 1988-89 school year, "fifteen Asian students were deselected from Academic due to weak academic performance and sent back to their neighborhood schools. Of the eighteen students in the class of 1989 who were deemed ineligible to graduate with their class, three (16%) were Asian" (p. 56). There was also a high proportion of Vietnamese-born youths who were neither at school nor in the labor force (Gardner et al. 1985). Trueba, Cheng, and Ima (1993) challenge the stereotypic notions of the academic success of Asian youth and discuss a large number of at-risk students from Asian backgrounds—Pacific Islander families, as well as Southeast Asian refugee families. They point out that the academic failure of those students is more associated with socioeconomic structure than culture.

Lee (1996) found that contrary to the popular belief that Asian students are culturally motivated to achieve success, some Asian students, especially recent arrivals, did not regard school as the key to success in society and resisted any behavior that motivated academic success. These students have troubles with the rules required for academic success such as regular attendance, doing homework, and so on. However, the academic problems those Asian students have encountered have been largely overlooked due to the label that Asian students have few problems with assimilation.

As one Asian American student commented:

> They [whites] will have stereotypes, like we're smart. . . . They are so wrong, not everyone is smart. They expect you to be this and that and when you're not. . . . (shook her head) And sometimes you tend to be what they expect you to be and you just lose your identity. . . . just lose being yourself. Become part of what . . . What someone else want[s] you to be. And it's really awkward too! When you get bad grades, people look at you really strangely because you are sort of distorting the way they see an Asian. It makes you feel really awkward if you don't fit the stereotype. (Lee 1996, p. 59)

Myth 5: "Asian Americans don't seem to have any problems."

Associated with the myth of model minority is the popular belief that Asian Americans do not seem to have any problems. Historically, Asian Americans are considered a "silent minority," a hidden life that is little known to American politics. As Kou (1979) points out, Asian Americans have less visibility in positions of institutional power and in political influence, as compared with other minority groups. Despite some recent efforts, there remains a slow progress in Asian American political participation. As a result, Asian Americans are generally excluded from public discourse of government policy. In the minds of most Americans, Asians are not the same as other minority groups. Minorities like African Americans, Latinos, and Native Americans are the "real" ones that need welfare assistance because they, unlike Asians, are experiencing disproportionate levels of poverty and educational underachievement.

Asian Americans do have the same problems as other minority groups. These problems are little known because "Asian Americans find themselves all lumped together and their diversity as groups is overlooked. Groups that are not doing well, such as unemployed Hmong, the Downtown Chinese, the elderly Japanese, the old Filipino farm laborers have been rendered invisible" (Takaki 1989, pp. 477–478). Chinatowns may illustrate the lives of the poor population of American Chinese and Asian American groups. The glitter of the neon signs disguises the poverty among the aged, the unemployed, and newly arrived immigrants. The people in inner-city Chinatowns suffer from deteriorating housing conditions, inadequate health care, poor working environment, and a rising crime rate—almost all the social problems that can be found in any low-income areas of American cities. For example, in the 1970s when the media was vigorously praising Asian American success, in San Francisco "inner-city Chinatown unemployment was almost double the citywide average, and two thirds of the housing stock was substandard, and tuberculosis rates were six times the national average" (Kitano and Daniels 1995, p. 52).

Low wages and exploitation are prevalent in ethnic enclaves as its economy usually operates outside the mainstream economy and labor market. Workers in garment sweatshops and restaurants often worked seventy hours a week but received much less than minimum wage and had no labor union or job security (Kwong 1987, p. 66). Kinkead (1992) calls those Asian Americans who live on the margin of American society "prisoners of Chinatown," where federal assistance is hardly available. Language barriers and unfamiliarity with the American system shut these people out of the rest of society and at the same time conceal the problems from the public. "To be out of sight is also to be without social services," Takaki observes. "Thinking Asian Americans have succeeded, government officials have sometimes denied funding for social service programs designed to help Asian Americans learn English and find employment" (Takaki 1989, p. 478).

Indeed, the image of "model minority" hurts rather than benefits Asian groups. The stereotypes of Asian Americans have caused social ignorance of the poverty, unemployment, illiteracy, and other social ills. As a result, they are denied social services they badly need to cope with those problems. For instance, many educational institutions adopt unwritten quotas to restrict the enrollment of qualified Asian American students, and some institutions even fail to consider Asian Americans as a minority who deserve the same treatment as other minorities. Additionally, the federal and state assistance to the development of small businesses often excludes Asian Americans as an eligible minority.

In addition, the stereotype has done more harm than good to interracial relationships between Asian Americans and other minorities. According to Chun (1980) and Osajima (1988), labeling Asians as a "model minority," as it emerged in the midst of civil rights movements, served a political purpose of turning public attention away from the racial tensions of American society. By praising Asian Americans, the proponents of the model minority thesis sent a political message to other minorities that they should model their behavior after Asian Americans rather than spending their time protesting inequality. If Asian Americans can make it on their own, the failure of other minority groups would be their own fault. In this sense, this model is a disservice to the community.

Asian Americans are one of the fastest growing minorities. As in the past, many people still view them as if they are all alike—coming from one society and one culture, and made it on their own in an adopted country. In a comment on this misperception, I. M. Pei, the renowned Chinese-American architect, said that "people must realize that there really isn't such a thing as an Asian-American. . . . There are Chinese, Koreans, Japanese, Vietnamese, Indians and so forth. So many different cultures. So many different experiences. We need to understand their differences and complexities, their success and failures" (*The New York Times Magazine*, November 30, 1986). While the image of Asian Americans remains more myth than reality, this reality needs to be further explored to reveal the diverse socioeconomic experiences of different Asian American groups in American society.

References

Barringer, Hebert, Robert W. Gardner, and Michael J. Levin. 1993. *Asian and Pacific Islanders in the United States.* New York: Russell Sage Foundation.

Bonacich, Edna, and Tae Hwan Jung. 1982. "A Portrait of Korean Small Business in Los Angeles, 1977," in Eui-Young YU, Earl H. Phillip, and Eun Sik Yang (eds.), *Koreans in Los Angeles: Prospects and Promises.* Los Angeles: Koryo Research Institute and Center for Korean-American and Korean Studies, California State University, pp. 75–98.

Chan, Sucheng. 1991. *Asian Americans: An Interpretive History.* Boston, MA.: Twayne Publishers.

Chun, Ki-Taek. 1980. "The Myth of Asian American Success and Its Educational Ramifications," *IRCD Bulletin* (A publication of the Institute for Urban and Minority Education, Teachers College, Columbia University), Vol. 15, No. 1, pp. 1–12.

Espiritu, Y. L. 1997. *Asian American Women and Men: Labor, Laws, and Love.* Thousand Oaks, California: Sage.

Fawcett, J. T., and R. W. Gardner (1994). "Asian Immigrant Entrepreneurs and Non-entrepreneurs: A Comparative Study of Recent Korean and Filipino Immigrants," *Population and Environment,* 15, pp. 211–238.

Gardner, R.W., B. Robey, and P. Smith. 1985. "Asian American: Growth, Change and Diversity," *Population Bulletin* 40(4), pp. 1–44.

Gold, S. 1994. "Chinese Vietnamese Entrepreneurs in California," in P. Ong, E. Bonacich, and L. Cheng (eds.), *The New Asian Immigration in Los Angeles and Global Restructuring.* Philadelphia: Temple University Press, pp. 196–266.

Hirschman, Charles, and Morrison G. Wong. 1981. "Trends in Socioeconomic Achievement among Immigrant and Native-Born Asian-Americans, 1960–1976," *The Sociological Quarterly* 22 (Autumn), pp. 495–514.

Hsia, Jayjia. 1988. *Asian Americans in Higher Education and at Work.* Hillsdale, NJ: Lawrence Erlbaum Associates.

Hurh, Won Moo, and Kwang Chung Kim. 1989. "The 'Success' Image of Asian Americans: Its Validity, and Its Practical and Theoretical Implications," *Ethnic and Racial Studies,* Vol. 12, No. 2 (October), pp. 512–538.

———. 1984. *Korean Immigrants in America: A Structural Analysis of Ethnic Confinement and Adhesive Adaptation.* Madson, NJ: Fairleigh Dickinson University Press.

Kanjanapan, W. 1995. "The Immigration of Asian Professionals to the United States: 1988–1990," *International Migration Review* 29, pp. 7–32.

Kinkead, Gwen. 1992. *Chinatown: A Portrait of a Closed Society.* New York: HarperCollins.

Kitano, Harry H. L., and Roger Daniels. 1995. *Asian Americans: Emerging Minorities.* (Second Edition). Englewood Cliffs, NJ: Prentice Hall.

Kou, Wen H. 1979. "On the Study of Asian-Americans: Its Current State and Agenda." *Sociological Quarterly* 20, pp. 279–290.

Kwong, Peter. 1987. *The New Chinatown.* New York: Hill & Wong.

Lee, Stacey J. 1996. *Unraveling the "Model Minority" Stereotype: Listening to Asian American Youth.* New York: Columbia University, Teachers College Press.

Li, Angelina H. 1980. *Labor Utilization and the Assimilation of Asian Americans.* Springfield, VA: National Technical Information Service, U.S. Department of Commerce.

Lowe, L. 1991. "Heterogeneity, Hybridity, Multiplicity: Marking Asian American Differences." *Diaspora* 1(1), pp. 24–44.

Lyman, Stanford M. 1974. *Chinese Americans.* New York: Random House.

Nee, Victor, and Jimy Sanders. 1985. "The Road to Parity: Determinants of the Socioeconomic Achievements of Asian Americans," *Ethic and Racial Studies,* Vol. 8, No. 1, pp. 75–93.

Ong, P. 1993. *Beyond Asian American Poverty: Community Economic Development Policies and Strategies.* Los Angeles, CA: LEAP, UCLA, Asian American Studies Center.

Ong, P., and S. Hee. 1994. "Economic Diversity," in P. Ong (ed.), *The State of Asian Pacific America: Economic Diversity, Issues, and Policies.* Los Angeles, CA: LEAP, UCLA, Asian American Center, pp. 165–189.

Ong, P., and K. Umemoto. 1994. "Life and Work in the Inner-City," in P. Ong (ed.), *The State of Asian Pacific America: Economic Diversity, Issues, and Policies.* Los Angeles, CA: LEAP, UCLA, Asian American Center, pp. 87–112.

Osajima, Keith. 1988. "Asian Americans as the Model Minority: An Analysis of the Popular Press Image in the 1960s and 1980s," in Okihiro et al. (eds.), *Reflections on Shattered Windows: Promises and Prospects for Asian American Studies.* Pullman: Washington State University Press, pp. 165–74.

Roos, P. A. 1977. *Questioning the Stereotypes: Differentials in Income Attainment of Japanese, Mexican-Americans, and Anglos in California.* Rockville, MD: National Institute of Mental Health (DHEW).

Rumbaut, R. G., and K. Ima. 1988. *The Adaptation of Southwest Asian Refugee Youth: A Comparative Study.* Washington, D.C.: U.S. Office of Refugee Resettlement.

Suzuki, Bob H. 1977. "Education and the Socialization of Asian Americans: A Revisionist Analysis of the 'Model Minority' Thesis." *Amerasia,* Vol. 4, No. 2, pp. 23–51.

Takaki, Ronald. 1989. *Strangers from a Different Shore: A History of Asian Americans.* Boston: Little Brown.

———. 1993. *A Different Mirror: A History of Multicultural America.* Boston: Little Brown.

Trueba, Henry T., Li Rong Lilly Cheng, and Kenji Ima. 1993. *Myth or Reality: Adaptive Strategies of Asian Americans in California.* Washington D.C.: The Falmer Press.

U.S. Commission on Civil Rights. 1992. "Civil Rights Issues Facing Asian Americans in the 1990s." Washington D.C.: U.S. Government Printing Office, February, pp. 131–136.

Woodrum, Eric. 1984. "An Assessment of Japanese American Assimilation, Pluralism, and Subordination," *American Journal of Sociology,* Vol. 87, No. 2, pp.157–169.

Article Review Form at end of book.

WiseGuide Wrap-Up

In many ways, it seems as though we have become more enlightened about the issue of race in America. With the rise of middle-class African Americans, it is easy to conclude that we no longer need to worry about racism and programs like Affirmative Action. In fact, many experts contend that we no longer need these types of programs and that, in some cases, they are counter-productive. However, the readings in this section have shown that, while we may have progressed, much more remains to be accomplished. Brian Siegel's reading is especially noteworthy, since he chronicled the history of racial categorization and showed the fluidity of the concept. Robert McNamara, Maria Tempenis, and Beth Walton discussed the issues and problems surrounding one of the most emotionally contested topics relating to race: interracial marriages. Joel Fegin and Hernon Vera offered us a glimpse of what is known as institutional racism, which was further discussed in Jieli Li's article on Asian Americans.

R.E.A.L. Sites

This list provides a print preview of typical **coursewise** R.E.A.L. sites. (There are over 100 such sites at the **courselinks**™ site.) The danger in printing URLs is that web sites can change overnight. As we went to press, these sites were functional using the URLs provided. If you come across one that isn't, please let us know via email to: webmaster@coursewise.com. Use your Passport to access the most current list of R.E.A.L. sites at the **courselinks**™ site.

Site name: Facts About Race-Color Discrimination

URL: http://www.eeoc.gov/facts/fs-race.html

Why is it R.E.A.L.? This site gives you the government's perspective on race relations by examining the main agency charged with combatting discrimination and racism: the Equal Employment Opportunity Commission. This site provides a host of additional definitions, facts, and statistics on race relations in the United States.

Key topics: discrimination, harassment, racism

Site name: Affirmative Action in America

URL: http://www.heritage.org/townhall/spotlights/10-16-95/welcome.html

Why is it R.E.A.L.? This site addresses the many controversial issues surrounding affirmative action in the United States. Included in this site are both sides of the debate, an opinion survey, as well as a chat room for those interested in discussing the issue further.

Key topics: affirmative action

Site name: Model Minority

URL: http://www.horizonmag.com/7/model.htm

Why is it R.E.A.L.? This site offers an in-depth look at what life is like for someone who is considered a model minority. This adds color to Reading 15 in that it personalizes the process by which we categorize this group.

Key topics: first-hand experience with living as a model minority

section 4

Learning Objectives

After reading these articles, you should be able to

- Describe magnet schools and their value.
- Explain the idea of tracking and its implications for students.
- Understand the questions raised about the value of standardized test scores in education.

Education

Poverty, crime, and racism are intricately related. Perhaps nowhere is this more evident than in the schools. Education, occupation, and income are also clearly related, according to sociological research. Given these two relationships, perhaps our educational institutions have the potential to solve, at least partially, many of our society's problems. Yet, the quality, quantity, and type of education one receives clearly differs according to social class. In fact, one of the best predictors of the quality of education a child receives is parents' income.

The readings in this section describe the problems found in inner-city education, as well as some of the practical consequences of being tracked or labeled in the school system. William Sakamoto White discusses the debate surrounding magnet schools, considered by many to be one of the most effective educational programs in this country. Daniel Llanes and Bridget Gorman offer insight into the environmental influences that Latino children face and the impact these influences have on school performance. Also, Vincent Roscigno and James Ainsworth-Darnell describe the realities of tracking in education. They conclude that tracking can have irreversible effects on the educational opportunities presented to some children. Finally, Thomas Smith discusses the biases built into standardized tests, which are typically used to track (and label) a student as gifted or low achieving.

Questions

Reading 16. Do you think that magnet schools efficiently address the inequality among schools? What is your reaction to the following statement: "The fundamental issue is not separation or integration but liberation. The either/or question of integration or separation does not speak to that proposition; for if our goal is liberation, it may be necessary to do both." Do you think that equality should be the goal before segregation?

Reading 17. Can Latinos maintain familism and simultaneously assimilate and improve? If familism is holding Latinos in a cycle of diminished opportunities, what can be done to break the cycle?

Reading 18. Do you think that achievement tests are an adequate measure on which to base tracking? What are some of the problems for lower track students? Do you think that diverse groups of students with varying abilities and backgrounds are the solution to unequal opportunities?

Reading 19. How can this study's findings on the effects of family life on grades be used to formulate effective reforms for promoting better educational experiences? How does this research reflect complications sociologists face when attempting to discover cause-effect relationships?

Do you think that magnet schools efficiently address the inequality among schools? What is your reaction to the following statement: "The fundamental issue is not separation or integration but liberation. The either/or question of integration or separation does not speak to that proposition; for if our goal is liberation, it may be necessary to do both." Do you think that equality should be the goal before segregation?

Do Magnet School Programs Meet the Goals of Desegregation?

William Sakamoto White

University of South Alabama

Abstract

Using existing literature and case studies, this paper evaluates whether one of the strategies employed by schools, the Magnet School program, has helped this society achieve desegregated education. This paper also evaluates the educational institution as a whole on the standards of providing equal access to quality education to all of its children and whether magnet school programs help school districts meet those paramount goals.

In 1954, the United States Supreme Court handed down the most significant civil rights case in its history—*Brown v. Board of Education.* Over forty years later, this society cannot honestly state that it has achieved the goals or met the intent of that decision. In the arena of education, children still go to segregated schools. More importantly, the quality of the schools they go to is unequal. We have returned to a situation where schools are separate and unequal.

A number of strategies and programs were devised to provide "equal access" to education. Busing clearly was a political failure. Another program, though, has become the "cornerstone" for claiming victory for "integration." The magnet school program appears to be the measure that schools and courts use to evaluate the effectiveness of "successfully" integrating schools. Does the institutionalization of magnet school programs provide "equal access" to "quality education" across the community? Does it provide "quality education" at specific sites? How can the institutionalization of magnet schools, given that there are so few of these schools in any given district, logically provide "equal access" to quality education? If magnet schools do not provide equal access to quality education, then have we met the intent of *Brown?* If we have not met the intent of Brown with magnet schools, then shouldn't we be looking for other alternatives to providing equal access to quality education across our communities, as *Brown* intended?

Does segregation of children in public schools deprive minority children equal educational opportunities? In 1954, the Supreme Court held that it does. The reality of education today is that forty years after *Brown* we have returned to a system of segregation in the schools. The segregation of schools is perpetuated by the continuing racial segregation of housing in America (Massey and Denton, 1993; Squires, 1994; and Fainstein, 1995). Schools today are not only "separate" but they are also "unequal." Given the institutionalized racism that exists as a force to retain neighborhood and school segregation, perhaps we need to revisit *Brown* and seek out the essence of that decision. Perhaps a new measure is needed when evaluating or establishing school programs. Based on *Brown,* are we providing "equal access" to "quality education"? If the white community is not willing to live with blacks in this society (Farley, 1993) and if they refuse to have their children go to school with minority children, then perhaps we should focus on providing minority children with quality education.

I will examine the emergence of the magnet school program as it relates to school desegregation and evaluate the program on two critical questions. First, do magnet schools provide equal access to educational opportunities to all of our children? Second, given the nature of schools today, does the net result of having a magnet school program in place provide all of our children an opportunity for a quality education? To place the issue into the proper context, let's first revisit the *Brown v. Board of Education* decision.

The Intent of *Brown v. Board of Education*

In Topeka, Kansas, Reverend Oliver Leon Brown, who was black, took his seven year old daughter to register at the local school (Brown-Smith, 1988). The child was turned away because the Kansas educational system was institutionally segregated. With the help of the NAACP, Reverend Brown and several other families filed federal suit against the city. The case was settled three years later under the authority of Chief Justice Warren who went against the 1898 *Plessy v. Ferguson* ruling. The Supreme Court ruled that "in the field of public education the doctrine of 'separate but equal' has no place. Separate educational facilities are inherently unequal" (*Brown v. Board of Education,* 1954). Desegregation was mandated at a national level to uphold the constitutional moral of equality and reinforced by the same plaintiffs a year later (*Brown v. Board of Education II,* 1955).

The emphasis of the Supreme Court decision was equality in the *quality* of education. Segregated education was noted to (1) "generate a feeling of inferiority as to their status in the community," (2) "(have) a detrimental effect upon the colored children," and (3) "(retard) the educational and mental development of Negro children and to deprive them of some of the benefits they would receive in a racially integrated school system" (*Brown v. Board of Education,* 1954). Brown II (1955) set up the rules for reviewing school desegregation suits. The Court ruled that the schools would have to come up with a solution to the problem. It was the role of the courts to decide whether the school's actions were implemented in "good faith."

The twenty years following the Court decision saw several policy changes that emphasized equal access to quality education for blacks and other minority groups. The Civil Rights Act of 1964 included Title IV, which refocused attention to school segregation. "Title IV expressly authorized the U.S. Attorney General to initiate and intervene in suits to enforce school desegregation through the courts" (Darden et al., 1992, p. 477). The next year, Congress passed the Elementary and Secondary Education Act, which provided money to school programs for low income families. In 1968, this Act was expanded to include bilingual education and drop out prevention programs. To facilitate desegregation, the Supreme Court institutionalized busing in 1971 with their decision on *Swann v. Charlotte-Mecklenberg Board of Education.* This decision, and the busing that followed, helped influence the further "white flight" of middle- and upper-class families from urban centers.

The reaction to the Court's decision, at times antagonistic and violent, illustrates the deep-rooted individual and institutional racism that existed, and still exists, in American society. The wholesale closure of public schools for five years in Prince Edward County, Virginia illustrates one extreme reaction (Franklin, 1967). The violence experienced in Boston over school busing illustrates another. Since the Court's decision in 1954, white families have found ways to keep public schools from desegregating. Perhaps the most significant reaction was the exodus of white families out of neighborhoods with growing numbers of black families. Many chose to remove their children from desegregated schools, believing that the quality of education had declined with busing. Magnet schools and schools of choice were a response to this white flight. Designed first with the intent of integrating schools, magnet schools and schools of choice have become mechanisms to encourage white families to live in financially strapped cities.

Magnet Schools as an Intervention

Magnet schools are often cited by supporters as one of the most effective desegregation tools available (West, 1994). They are perceived as effective desegregation tools because they can offer special curriculum capable of attracting students of different racial backgrounds. As Henig (1989) points out:

> Magnet schools traditionally have involved the assignment of extra resources, attractive programs, or special teaching approaches to schools in high minority neighborhoods in order to stimulate voluntary integration and moderate the conflict and white flight that might otherwise be generated under mandatory busing plans. (p. 244)

Magnet schools generally consist of four characteristics. First, they provide a special curricular theme or method of instruction as the foundation for their "magnet." Second, they are a program initiated by school districts as a voluntary desegregation mechanism. Third, they are schools of "choice" for students and parents. Finally, they provide access to students beyond a regular attendance zone. As originally conceived, magnet schools were designed to accomplish two goals: 1) to enhance students' academic performance through their distinctive curriculum and 2) to enhance the school's racial and social diversity (West, 1994). West further notes that magnet schools typically come into existence as a way of meeting the terms of court ordered desegregation (1994).

There are also two types of magnet school programs: full-site and partial-site. The full-site magnet program constitutes an entire school. The courses offered by the school act as the "magnet." In full-site magnets, all students transfer into the school and are mixed together in the magnet program. Full–site programs require that a school be dedicated to the magnet program and attract a racial balance through admissions, lottery, or other selection methods.

Partial-site programs offer a special magnet program within a "nonmagnet" general school, although students still transfer into the school to participate in the magnet curriculum. Partial-site magnets are often placed in schools that were predominantly minority prior to desegregation efforts, working to achieve a racial balance within the total school by attracting enough white transfer students. In both types of magnet programs, students and parents in effect make a "choice" to attend these schools.

The Social Goals of Magnet School Programs

Though originally intended to achieve more racial balance in public schools, magnet schools have also become the "poster-child" example for school choice advocates. They state that while magnet schools effectively achieve racial balance, they also increase educational quality. As the focus on magnet schools changed, so did the implied mission of magnet schools. Not only were they an intervention that led to more effective desegregation than busing, they also "satisfied" consumer demands. They could also be used to retain the middle class in urban areas and central cities (Clune, 1990).

The early "successes" of magnet schools, and particularly the magnet school program in Prince George's County, Maryland (a suburb of Washington, D.C.), received a great deal of media attention. In 1988, President Reagan used a speech at Suitland High School, a magnet school in the Prince George's County system, as the launching ground for a redefinition of magnet schools as schools of choice (Henig, 1995; Eaton and Crutcher, 1996). Magnet schools were no longer linked categorically to achieving the goals of desegregation. Rather, they were now examples of achieving educational excellence through a system of parental and student "choice" governed by "market forces." Magnet schools were to be the "miracle cure" for all educational problems, and choice would guarantee that the best students and the best parents had access to these hallways of success. Urban governments also saw magnet schools as an attraction for potential homebuyers and joined in the efforts to solidify the permanence of magnet schools in central cities (Varady and Raffel, 1995).

Research on the Effectiveness of Magnet Schools

Though still touted as the "miracle cure" for educational problems, it is ironic that an extensive evaluation of the effectiveness of magnet schools has not been conducted to date. Rossell's 1990 study found that districts with magnet schools achieved two objectives: they were more likely to reduce white flight from schools, and they did improve the interracial contact of minority students over time more than mandatory plans. Rossell concluded that, compared to busing and other mandatory desegregation plans, magnet schools were perhaps a more effective desegregation strategy. Eaton and Crutcher (1996), in their analysis of the Prince George's County magnet schools, point out that the claims of improved achievement from magnet schools were probably based on outdated and invalid measures. The appearance of "success" may have been the result of politics and public relations efforts rather than any real educational improvements.

There is much disagreement on the value of magnet school programs. The biggest skeptics exist within public schools themselves, namely professional educators and local school administrators. According to Finn (1990), their opposition is based on that "choice is disruptive, costly, and logistically cumbersome; that choice ill serves poor, disadvantaged, and minority students."

Magnet schools take the "better students" away from their neighborhood schools, leaving the problem of educationally at-risk students behind in these schools (Finn, 1990; Rossell, 1990). Indeed, magnet schools are not generally instituted as a major solution for the problems of at-risk students (Blank, 1990). Providing spaces for middle-class students at magnet schools is viewed by many as denying others, especially poor minority students, equal access. As Moore and Davenport (1990) point out, magnet schools become new forms of educational segregation.

Running Away from the Social Intent of *Brown*

The major thrust of *Brown v. Board of Education* was to provide minority children with equal access to quality education. Indeed, the issue of equal access is the foundation for desegregation arguments. Forty years after Brown, this intent has been lost in the variety of policy initiatives intended to remedy segregated education.

As previously noted, magnet schools have increasingly become a center point in the "school-choice" agenda. In this process, their utility as a means toward desegregating school systems has been diminished. As critics of magnet schools point out, they may be serving the needs of powerful middle-class interests rather than meeting the needs of lower-class minority at-risk students (Metz, 1990). A number of key points need to be addressed in any reassessment of the magnet school/school choice/desegregation debate.

First, it must be recognized that magnets do siphon off the better students from a school district, leaving the problem of educationally at-risk students in the nonmagnet neighborhood school. Second, magnets may be aimed at already well-served middle-class families. Third, removing students from a given school district removes resources from students most in need of this interaction (Metz, 1990). Fourth, magnets are not generally instituted as a major solution for the problems of at-risk students, the students most in need of any school reform initiatives (Blank, 1990). Fifth, even in partial-site situations, segregation continues within the walls of the school, especially in the classrooms (West, 1994).

One tragic outcome many times forgotten in the magnet school debate is that providing seats for middle-class children in magnet schools denies at-risk students equal access to those seats. Moore and Davenport (1990) found that the magnet school selection process is inequitable. In their study of magnet schools in New York City, they found that blacks, the poor, and low attendees are more likely to wind up in nonselective neighborhood high schools. Junior high school counselors, for example, work more with students "likely" to succeed in magnet programs. Middle-income parents are also a political force, insisting on programs and policies that benefit their children over at-risk youth. Though "lottery selection procedures" are a mechanism to check against any unfair influence in the selection processes by middle-class parents, Metz (1990) points out that lotteries "undercut the sense of parental control over children's fate that is a very significant benefit of choice" (p. 132). According to Metz's reasoning, magnet schools are a better alternative than no magnet schools because they do benefit "some" at-risk youth. Magnet schools begin to move toward a "tug-of-war" atmosphere where school boards must attempt to balance the needs of powerful middle-class parents with the real needs of at-risk children.

To be sure, it is not the sole responsibility of the schools themselves to remedy the situation of inequality in education. Perhaps this is where *Brown* made a significant error in demanding that only the schools were responsible for desegregating themselves. The institutionalized racism that exists in the housing market, perhaps the real foundation for educational inequality, must be addressed first.

What Are We to Do?

Desegregation efforts, mandatory and choice oriented, have failed to provide an integrated, let alone an "equal," education opportunity for our nation's children. We can theorize all we want about the potential for integrating our schools and neighborhoods, and we can encourage policies that aid in the reintegration efforts. Indeed, studies continue to show that integration provides significant economic and cultural benefits when implemented (Massey and Denton, 1993). Logic, reason, and a national self-interest should lead us as a society toward working to integrate our schools. Self-interest, prejudice, and institutional racism, though, all play a major role in continuing to perpetuate a system of unequal and separate educational systems for whites and minority students. The *Brown* decision was significant because it opened the door toward creating an integrated society, but we have seen the process of integration failing in most every attempt. Though integration is a noble goal, and one which should be pursued from a variety of policy initiatives (Darden et al., 1992), what are we to do *in the short run* with communities and schools that remain segregated? If we do nothing beyond magnet schools, aren't we relegating whole communities and children to a life of hopelessness?

First, we must recognize that there is a tremendous problem in our public educational system, one largely created by our social neglect in squarely addressing the needs of at-risk children and their families. There is a growing number of children living in poverty, for example, and this significantly contributes to their life chances. As Raffel et al. (1992) state rather clearly:

> One could argue that America's urban educational casualties are high, the war is being lost, the future looks bleaker, we are not properly organized to achieve victory, and we are losing this war in large part because we never made a commitment of resources (as opposed to rhetoric) to win. (p. 264)

Indeed, it can be said that magnet schools added to this rhetoric (Eaton and Crutcher, 1996). Promoted as schools of choice, magnet schools were not effectively measured for their academic performance nor for their lack of integrating school systems. Even without any strong evidence, magnet schools continue to be seen by many as a major strategy in efforts to increase educational quality. These hopes may be, at best, farfetched.

We cannot neglect the findings from numerous studies that student background and attitudes influence school performance (Coleman et al., 1966; Ogbu, 1986; Lareau, 1989; Farkas, 1996). Any sort of policy in educational reform must begin from these findings. Given these facts, and that little has been done to manage the gap between student background and school success, some researchers are skeptical of the future, speculating that the problems in education will only get worse (Raffel et al., 1992). Poor and minority students (especially poor minority students) are affected by sets of liabilities that will influence their potential performance before they ever set foot in the schools (Jencks et al., 1972; Bowles and Gintis, 1976; Ogbu, 1986; Farkas, 1996). Taken from an integrationist perspective, the interaction between high achieving and low achieving students creates the potential for the development of the positive attitudes necessary for school success. However, as W.E.B. DuBois clearly observed in 1935,

> The Negro needs neither segregated schools nor mixed schools. What he needs is *education.* What he must remember is that there is no magic, either in mixed schools or in segregated schools. A mixed school with poor and unsympathetic teachers, with hostile public opinion, and no teaching of truth concerning black folk, is bad. A segregated school with ignorant placeholders, inadequate equipment, poor salaries, and wretched housing, is equally bad. Other things being equal, the mixed school is the broader, more natural basis for the education of all youth. It gives wider contacts, it inspires greater self-confidence; and suppresses the inferiority complex. But other things seldom are equal, and in that case, *sympathy, knowledge, and truth,* outweigh all that the mixed school can offer. (emphasis added)

If high self-esteem of minority students will help them succeed in school, and they are not getting it from either the magnet school or segregated school experience, then it is incumbent on society to help predominantly black schools raise it. A return to a segregated, minority-centered curriculum may be a viable alternative for school success. The curriculum must integrate neighborhood, parents, and schools to help change the attitudes of the students so that they could develop a positive self-image and believe that they can control their environment. Any discussion about returning to "segregated" education, though, must be tempered with the provision that it is a short–run strategy to develop quality education for students currently being left behind in society. As Lerone Bennett pointed out in 1970, a return to segregated education must not mean a return to inferiority and subordination.

> The fundamental issue is not separation or integration but liberation. The either/or question of integration or separation does not speak to that proposition; for if our goal is liberation it may be necessary to do both.

We, as a society, have not lived up to the promise of an equal opportunity to a quality education as demanded in the *Brown* decision. Magnet schools do achieve some racial integration, and this is positive. However, it is not the "cure-all" for integrating our schools. The focus on magnet schools as a mechanism for integrating schools probably ended in the late 1980s. As we continue to move away from the intent of *Brown*, more children are being left behind. As a society, can we continue to wait for whites to integrate schools or neighborhoods? Can minority parents afford to wait for programs to reach them? Do we need to engage in demanding quality education across the board to all students in a given community? Look into the eyes of an at-risk student in kindergarten, and see his or her eagerness to learn, to achieve, to be successful in school. The answer to our dilemma is there, if we only move to give him or her the opportunity to achieve the skills necessary to succeed.

References

Bennett, Lerone. 1970. "Liberation." *Ebony* 25 (August): 36–43.

Blank, Rolf K. 1990. "Educational Effects of Magnet Schools." In *Choice and Control in American Education, Volume 2.* William H. Clune and John F. Witte, eds. London: Falmer Press, 77–109.

Bowles, Samuel, and Herbert Gintis. 1976. *Schooling in Capitalist America.* New York: Basic Books.

Clune, William H. 1990. "Educational Governance and Student Achievement." In *Choice and Control in American Education, Volume 2.* William H. Clune and John F. Witte, eds. London: Falmer Press, 391–423.

Coleman, James S., Ernest Q. Campbell, Carol J. Hobson, James McPartland, Alexander Mood, Frederick D. Weinfield, and Robert York. 1966. *Equality of Educational Opportunity.* Washington, D.C.: U.S. Government Printing Office.

Darden, Joe T., Harriet Orcutt Duleep, and George C. Galster. 1992. "Civil Rights in Metropolitan America." *Journal of Urban Affairs* 14 (3/4): 469–496.

DuBois, W.E.B. 1935. "Does the Negro Need Separate Schools?" *Journal of Negro Education* 4: 328–335.

Eaton, Susan E., and Elizabeth Crutcher. 1996. "Magnets, Media, and Mirages: Prince George's County's 'Miracle' Cure." In *Dismantling Desegregation: The Quiet Reversal of Brown v. Board of Education.* Gary Orfield and Susan E. Eaton, eds. New York: The New Press, 265–289.

Fainstein, Norman. 1995. "Black Ghettoization and Social Mobility." In *The Bubbling Cauldron: Race, Ethnicity and the Urban Crisis.* Michael Peter Smith and Joe R. Feagin, eds. Minneapolis, MN: University of Minnesota Press, 123–141.

Farkas, George. 1996. *Human Capital or Cultural Capital? Ethnicity and Poverty Groups in an Urban School District.* New York: Aldine de Gruyter.

Farley, Reynolds. 1993. "Neighborhood Preferences and Aspirations among Blacks and Whites." In *Housing Markets and Residential Mobility.* G. Thomas Kingsley and Margery Austin Turner, eds. Washington, D.C.: Urban Institute Press.

Finn, 1990. "Why We Need Choice." In *Choice in Education: Potential and Problems.* William L. Boyd and Herbert J. Walberg, eds. Berkeley: McCutchan.

Franklin, John Hope. 1967. *From Slavery to Freedom.* Third Edition. New York: Knopf.

Henig, Jeffrey R. 1989. "Choice, Race and Public Schools: The Adoption and Implementation of a Magnet Program." *Journal of Urban Affairs* 11(3): 243–259.

—. 1995. "Race and Choice in Montgomery County, Maryland, Magnet Schools." *Teachers College Record* 96(4): 729–734.

Jencks, Christopher, Marshal Smith, Henry Acland, Mary Jo Bane, David Cohen, Herbert Gintis, Barbara Heyns, and Stephen Michelson. 1972. *Inequality: A Reassessment of the Effect of Family and Schooling in America.* New York: Basic Books.

Lareau, Annette. 1989. *Home Advantage: Social Class and Parental Intervention in Elementary Education.* London: Falmer Press.

Massey, Douglas S., and Nancy A. Denton. 1993. *American Apartheid: Segregation and the Making of the Underclass.* Cambridge, MA: Harvard University Press.

Metz, Mary H. 1990. "Potentialities and Problems of Choice in Desegregation Plans." In *Choice and Control in American Education, Volume 2.* William H. Clune and John F. Witte, eds. London: Falmer Press, 111–117.

Moore, Donald R., and Suzanne Davenport. 1990. "School Choice: The New Improved Sorting Machine." In *Choice in Education: Potential and Problems.* William L. Boyd and Herbert J. Walberg, eds. Berkeley: McCutchan.

Ogbu, John. 1986. "Consequences of the American Caste System." In *The School Achievement of Minority Children.* Ulric Neisser, ed. Hillsdale, NJ: Lawrence Erlbaum, 19–56.

Raffel, Jeffrey A., William Lowe Boyd, Vernon M. Briggs, Jr., Eugene E. Eubanks, and Roberto Fernandez. 1992. "Policy Dilemmas in Urban Education: Addressing the Needs of Poor, At-risk Children." *Journal of Urban Affairs* 14(3/4): 263–289.

Rossell, Christine H. 1990. *The Carrot or the Stick for School Desegregation Policy: Magnet Schools or Forced Busing.* Philadelphia: Temple University Press.

Smith, Linda Brown. 1988. "Forward." In *Eliminating Racism: Profiles in Controversy.* Phyllis A. Katz and Dalmas A. Taylor, eds. New York: Plenum Press, xi–xiii.

Squires, Gregory D. 1994. *Capital and Communities in Black and White: The Intersections of Race, Class and Uneven Development.* Albany, NY: State University of New York Press.

Varady, David P., and Jeffrey A. Raffel. 1995. *Selling Cities: Attracting Homebuyers Through Schools and Housing Programs.* Albany, NY: State University of New York Press.

West, Kimberly C. 1994. "A Desegregation Tool that Backfired: Magnet Schools and Classroom Segregation." *Yale Law Journal* 103: 2567–2592.

Article Review Form at end of book.

Can Latinos maintain familism and simultaneously assimilate and improve? If familism is holding Latinos in a cycle of diminished opportunities, what can be done to break the cycle?

Childhood Environment and Educational Attainment Among Latinos

Daniel Llanes and Bridget K. Gorman

The Pennsylvania State University

Abstract

Using the Latino Panel Study of Income of Dynamics (LPSID) for 1990, we attempt to assess the impact of childhood environment on Latino educational outcomes in adulthood. Parental characteristics, which directly shape a child's environment, have a significant impact on future educational outcomes. Specifically, we find that Latinos raised in poor households are less likely to complete both high school and college. In addition, Latinos who live in households where parents were married and well-educated significantly increased the odds of college and high school completion in adulthood. Latinos raised in rural areas were less likely to finish both high school and college, reflecting the importance of environmental factors in producing future educational outcomes.

Direct any correspondence to Daniel Llanes, Population Research Institute, The Pennsylvania State University, 601 Oswald Tower, University Park, PA 16802, e-mail: llanes@pop.psu.edu.

Introduction

Throughout the past few decades the Latino population in the United States has undergone significant transformations. Demographically, the Latino population has grown by leaps and bounds, rapidly becoming the second largest minority group in the United States (Moore and Pinderhughes, 1993). However, Latinos are facing great obstacles on several fronts. Most importantly, Latinos as a group have educational levels that are much lower than that of any other minority group (Bean and Tienda, 1987; Brown, Rosen, Hill, and Olivas, 1980), and Latinos are also more likely than any other ethnic minority to drop out of high school (DeFreitas, 1991). These alarming trends point to an emergent social problem for the fastest growing minority population in the United States.

Our focus in this analysis is to assess the impact of childhood environment on future educational outcomes among Latinos of Mexican, Puerto Rican, and Cuban ancestry. Among the array of factors that shape a child's environment, the family is the most important component of a child's social structure. Its importance and influence are crucial for a person's successful development and transition to adulthood. However, the Latino family has been at the center of much controversy (Keefe, 1984; Miller, 1978; Rumbaut, 1995; Tienda, 1980). The debate centers around (1) Do Latino families promote and instill attitudes and beliefs among their young that help maximize individual talents and strengths through schooling?

(2) Has familism, defined as the belief that family's collective interest outweighs individual gain, become normative among Latino families? Under the familism framework, Latino children might be more likely to succumb to family pressures that emphasize work over schooling. A sizable portion of Latino families live in poverty; therefore they are more likely to employ multiple earner strategies to maintain a minimum subsistence level. Multiple earner households encourage family members to make economic contributions, potentially sacrificing educational goals among the young.

This analysis differs from most in that it attempts to analyze the role of family life from a retrospective vantage point. Thus, we assess the impact of Latinos' childhood environments through *specific* measures of parental and environmental characteristics. This perspective offers us an opportunity to analyze how the family might promote or hinder educational achievement among Latinos.

Familism and Attainment

The family is an important element in all our lives. Among Latino children, the family can serve as an available pool of social and economic resources that facilitate adaptation and social integration (Portes and Sensenbrenner, 1993). Past studies have found a positive relationship between strong family bonds and socioeconomic attainment (Hirschman and Wong, 1981; Silverman, 1989). Specifically, strong family ties can promote more stable environments that ease the pressures associated with adapting to a new society among immigrant children. Given the large proportion of foreign born Latinos living in the United States, we must look closely at this relationship.

Studies have also found a positive relationship between stable family environments and educational achievement among Mexican adolescents, as long as parents have a minimum of twelve years of schooling. They conclude that strong family ties are a specific type of social capital that promotes educational success. In this application, social capital captures the quality of interaction between parents and their children. Thus, parental education is an influential factor for future schooling success among children. Essentially, parents with higher levels of schooling promote attitudes and norms that value education and schooling success among their children (Sewell, Hauser, and Wolf, 1980).

However, there are studies that find that strong family bonds limit and hinder the development of individualism, making Latino children less competitive in U.S. society because they are more likely to sacrifice personal gain to improve their families general well-being (Horowitz, 1981). Scholars arguing this perspective make a case that families limit options associated with job mobility and higher educational attainment by encouraging more immediate monetary returns (Kuvelesky and Patella, 1971). For example, familial obligations could have potentially damaging implications if work expectations are greater than those to continue schooling. Families living in poverty might place a greater emphasis on children obtaining jobs versus attending school (Ballesteros, 1986). In addition, children living in first generation families face expectations that resemble life in the country of origin. Among Mexican children, this is significant because compulsory education ends in the sixth grade. Thus, families could view children as potential economic contributors at an early age and devalue the worth and importance of education.

In sum, what exact role the family plays in the lives of young Latinos remains a controversy. Studies have found a positive and significant relationship between living in a stable family environment and general well-being. The question remains, what specific role does the family play in the educational attainment of Latinos? To better understand this relationship, we begin by treating the family as an instrumental source of social and physical capital.

Social and Physical Capital

In the immigrant literature, we find the term capital used to describe several social processes. Of these, social and physical capital have been of particular interest to scholars. Individuals do not act in a vacuum, nor should their environment be treated as an insignificant factor in their lives. Broadly, the concepts of social and physical capital help explain social interaction and the structure and nature of those interactions. Of significance, the quality of the social environment in which individuals obtain information and meaning is shaped by resources manifested in social and material forms. Social capital allows researchers to examine the impact of environmental settings and the quality of contact between individuals in these settings. Physical capital, on the other hand, is a direct and tangible resource that can be tapped by examining the specific material characteristics of families.

Social Capital

For our purposes, the family serves as a primary source of social capital, becoming the nucleus of a child's development and potential success. Conceptually, the family functions as an integrated web of social relations, transferring its influence, knowledge, values, norms, and priorities to its young (Keefe, Patella, and Carlos, 1979). Family membership becomes the ultimate "credential" through which access to social and material resources are mitigated. Coleman (1988) suggests that social capital is a process by which supportive relationships (in this case between parents and their children) enable and promote norm sharing behavior, which aids individual adaptation. Hence, educated parents are more likely to pass on values and share norms that emphasize the importance of school and professional training. Also, an intact nuclear family where both parents are present in the household becomes relevant, as married couples can pool their resources more efficiently, thereby improving the general well-being of children and increasing their odds of school success (Ortiz, 1995).

Physical Capital

Physical capital can be defined as the material assets of a family. The financial resources of a family can be used to improve the social and economic standing of children. Greater amounts of resources available to families directly benefits children through several contextual outcomes (Lareau, 1989). Families who are well-off are more likely to live in better neighborhoods and send their children to better schools. They are also more likely to provide their children with instructional resources that disadvantaged families might not enjoy. Affluent parents are also more likely to be well-educated and pass on values and norms that promote school achievement. In addition, well-educated parents place greater emphasis on school success and are more likely to participate in school events and other related activities, such as helping children with homework assignments (Ringawa, 1980).

By assessing specific measures of social and physical capital, the complex process of predicting educational attainment becomes more manageable. Examining the context in which children are raised can help answer the critical question: What is the family's role in promoting educational achievement among Latinos?

Characteristics of Latinos

As shown in Figure 1, in our sample of 5,430 Latinos from the Latino Panel Study of Income Dynamics for 1990, only 32 percent of Mexicans completed high school, compared to 36 percent and 63 percent of Puerto Ricans and Cubans. Cubans have the highest percentage of college educated individuals (15%), versus Mexicans (5%) and Puerto Ricans (7%). These trends reflect the large variation found among groups under the umbrella "Latino" or "Hispanic" label. The usefulness of these broad ethnic labels is an interesting question, but beyond the scope of this analysis. With such distinct differences between these three groups, we must attempt to understand and analyze the environmental differences that might produce these sharp disparities.

For example, Mexican children are more likely to be attached to school districts temporarily, as their parents harvest employment shifts from one area to another. The Mexican population is highly mobile; therefore Mexican children probably have a harder time adjusting to new schools and new teachers who are not in tune with their specific needs as students. Hence, this process of continual uprooting can severely hinder their prospects for future academic success. Cuban children, on the other hand, are raised in areas where ethnic concentrations are high, meaning they are more likely to be exposed to ESL (English as a Second Language) programs and other basic skill attainment courses sensitive to their English deficiencies.

As stated previously, household resources are important predictors of future schooling achievement. The socioeconomic status of the family is used as a measure for the material resources available to children. This measure has three levels: poor, average, and well-off. Seventy percent of Mexicans and 68 percent of Puerto Ricans reported growing up in a poor family, compared to only 44 percent of Cubans (Figure 2).

Most striking though is that 17 percent of Cubans reported living in a well-off family as children, versus only 8 percent and 7 percent of Mexicans and Puerto Ricans respectively. This trend is indicative of the nature of Cuban migration to the United States because most professionals left Cuba early on in search of more stable and profitable returns on their skills and knowledge. Hence, Cuban children are more likely to be living in households that have abundant resources and, in turn, more stable family environments. The ramifications of this trend are important because poor families have greater difficulties providing their children with resources necessary for scholastic achievement.

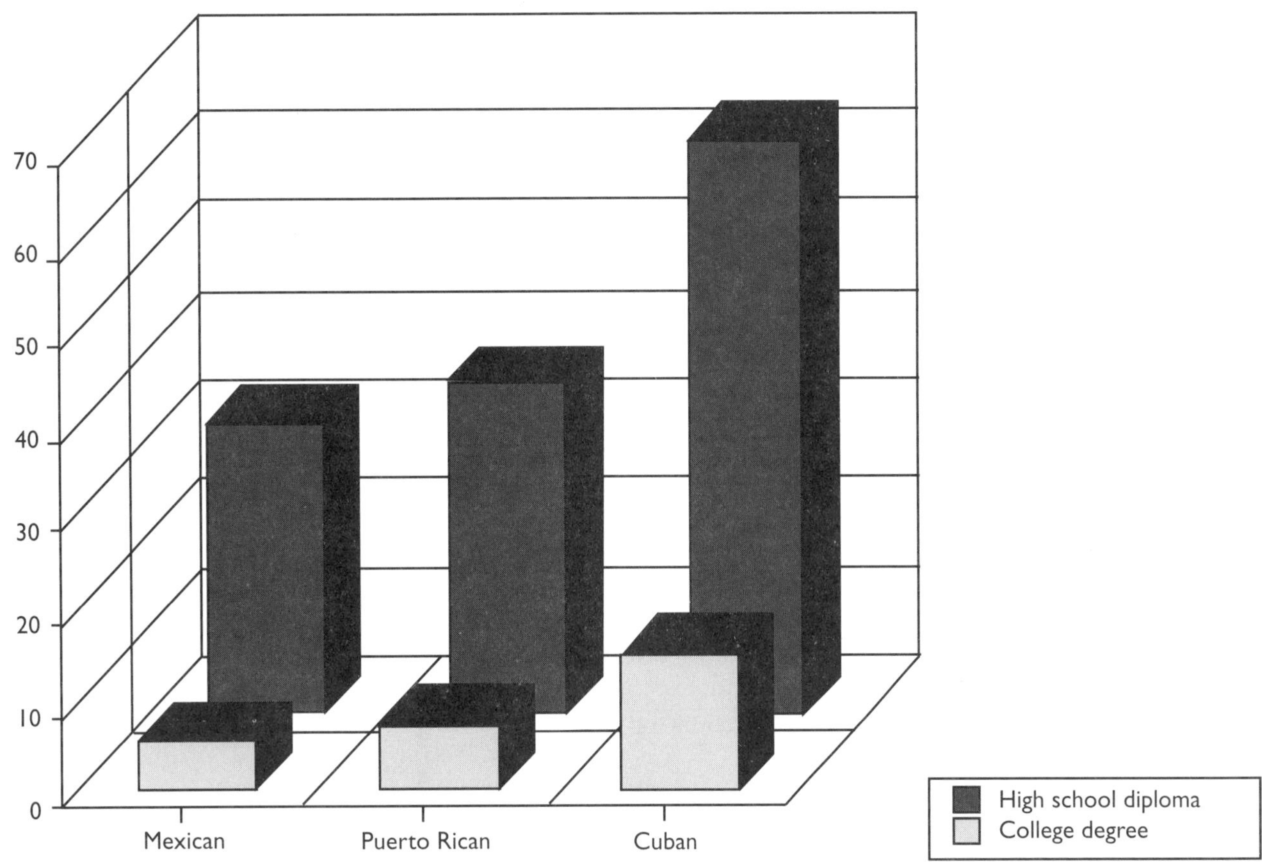

Figure 1. Education level by Latino ethnicity.

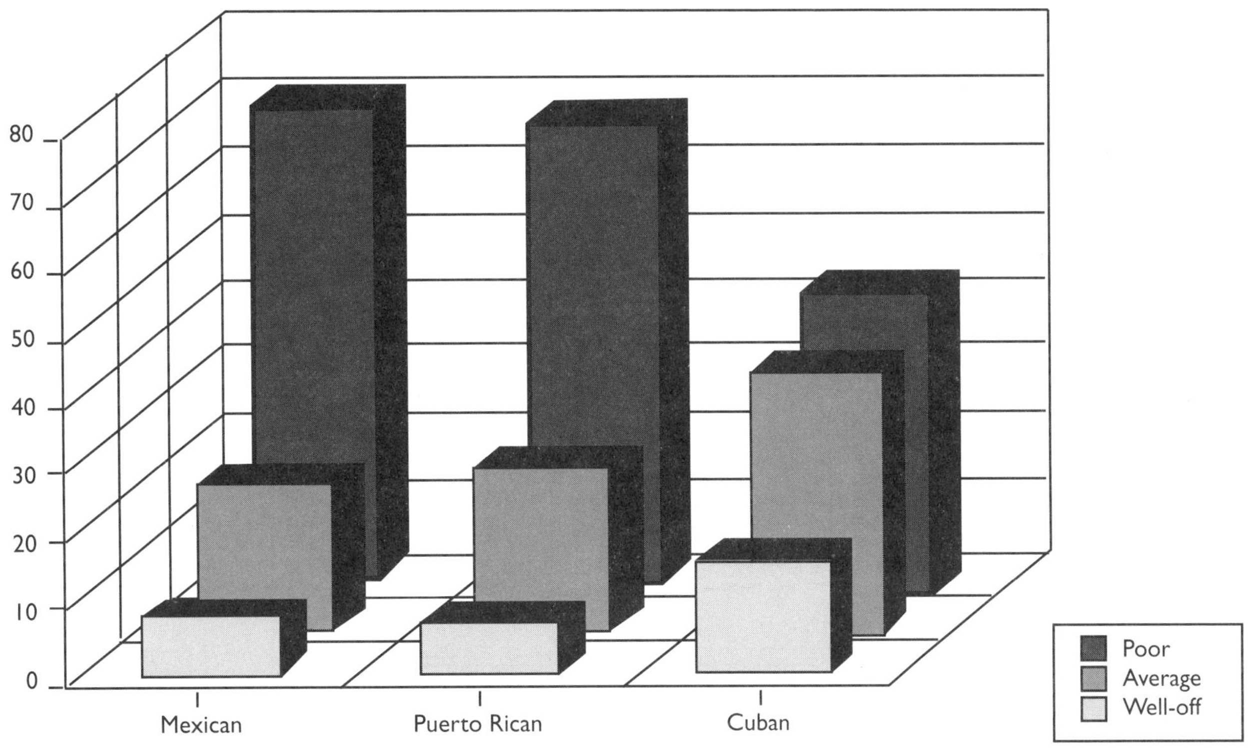

Figure 2. Socioeconomic status of parents during respondent's childhood.

As mentioned, children in well-off families are also more likely to have well-educated parents who promote school success. We include measures of parental education in the form of father and mother's completion of high school or more (Figure 3). Only 6 percent of Mexicans had fathers with at least a high school diploma, compared to Puerto Ricans (12%) and Cubans (29%). Mother's education is slightly lower than that of father's, where 7 percent of Mexicans had mothers with at least a high school diploma, in comparison to 12 percent of Puerto Ricans and 22 percent of Cubans. This striking gap in parental education is significant, indicating that Cubans and Puerto Ricans are more likely to finish high school and go on to college if the social and physical capital framework applies. Again we must look at the distinct migration experience of Cubans to the United States to fully understand the vast gap between these groups. Early Cuban migrants were well-educated and many were professionally trained. This directly translates into more resources (specifically, money) being made available to Cuban children. Not only can well-educated parents offer more resources to their children, they are also more likely to enforce and promote norms that favor schooling over other alternative activities such as work.

Living in a household where parents are married and present is important. Married households can pool the resources of both partners, increasing the amount of resources available to children. Cubans (82%) and Mexicans (80%) are more likely to grow up in a married couple household compared to Puerto Ricans (69%). Again, migration histories play an important role in explaining the variability between Mexicans and Cubans compared to Puerto Ricans. Cubans typically arrived in the United States with intact nuclear families, making it much more likely for Cuban children to grow up in two parent families. Puerto Ricans, though, come from more disadvantaged and unstable family backgrounds. Scholars have attributed this difference to the increased discrimination faced by Puerto Ricans in the mainland United States due to their darker skin color. Discrimination makes it harder for Puerto Ricans to obtain good paying jobs, making it difficult for Puerto Rican men to support their families. In addition, the markedly lower socioeconomic status of Puerto Ricans contributes to higher levels of divorce

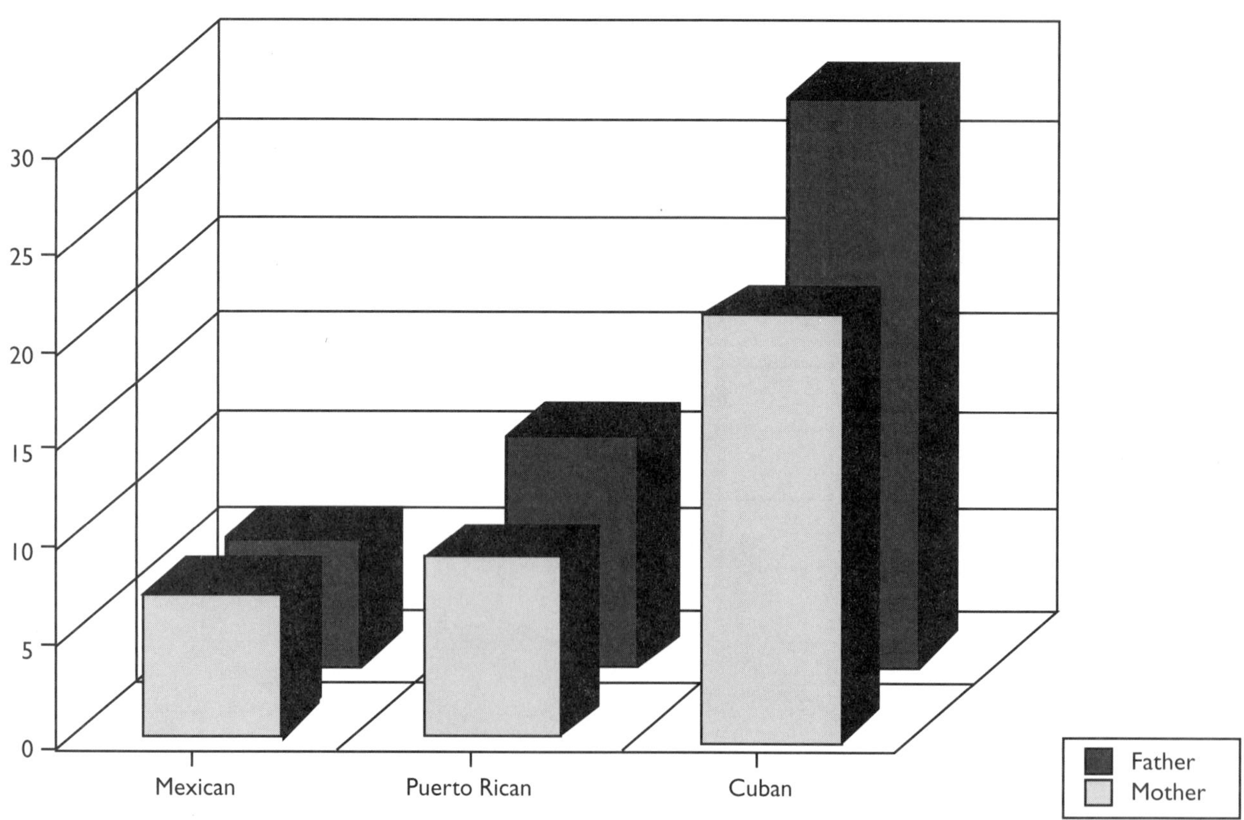

Figure 3. Percent of respondent's parents with at least a high school diploma.

and female family headship than that experienced among Cuban Americans. At the same time, unwed Puerto Rican mothers may experience less incentive to marry when the father of their children can offer little or no economic support to the family.

Latino High School Completion Rates

To assess the impact of childhood environment on Latinos future educational outcomes, we present models that control for current (adulthood) characteristics. These models are reported in Figures 4 and 5 as the effect of ethnicity—that is being Cuban, Puerto Rican, or Mexican—on the odds of completing high school (Figure 4) and/or a college degree (Figure 5). As shown in Figure 4, Cubans and Puerto Ricans are significantly more likely to complete high school versus Mexican Americans. Cubans are almost five times more likely to finish high school than are Mexicans. Puerto Ricans are about 50 percent more likely to finish high school when compared to Mexicans. Despite Puerto Ricans' disadvantaged position in the U.S. labor market, their attachment to U.S. schools at an early age probably improves their chances of finishing high school. Cubans, who come from generally more affluent backgrounds, stand far apart from Mexicans and Puerto Ricans. This gap is expected, due to the markedly different environments in which Cuban children are raised.

Indicators of childhood environment are significant predictors of future schooling success throughout our models. Respondents who grew up in a poor family are 56 percent less likely to complete high school compared to those raised in average and well-off families. Respondents who grew up in a rural area are 58 percent less likely to finish high school or obtain a GED, versus those raised in a large city. Respondents with high school educated fathers were almost twice as likely to complete high school, while mother's education had no significant effect. Clearly, parental (especially father's) education contributes to the future academic success of children.

College Completion

Figure 5 shows the odds of Mexicans, Puerto Ricans, and Cubans obtaining a college degree. Again, Cubans and Puerto Ricans are more likely to receive a college

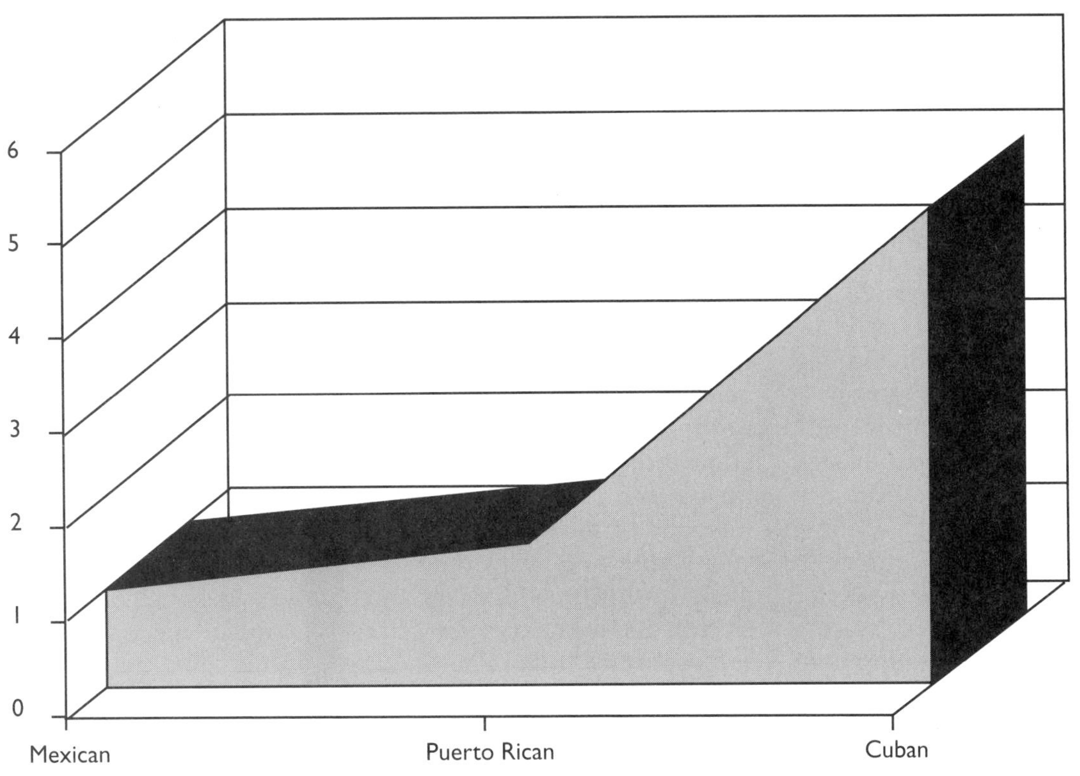

Figure 4. Odds of high school completion.

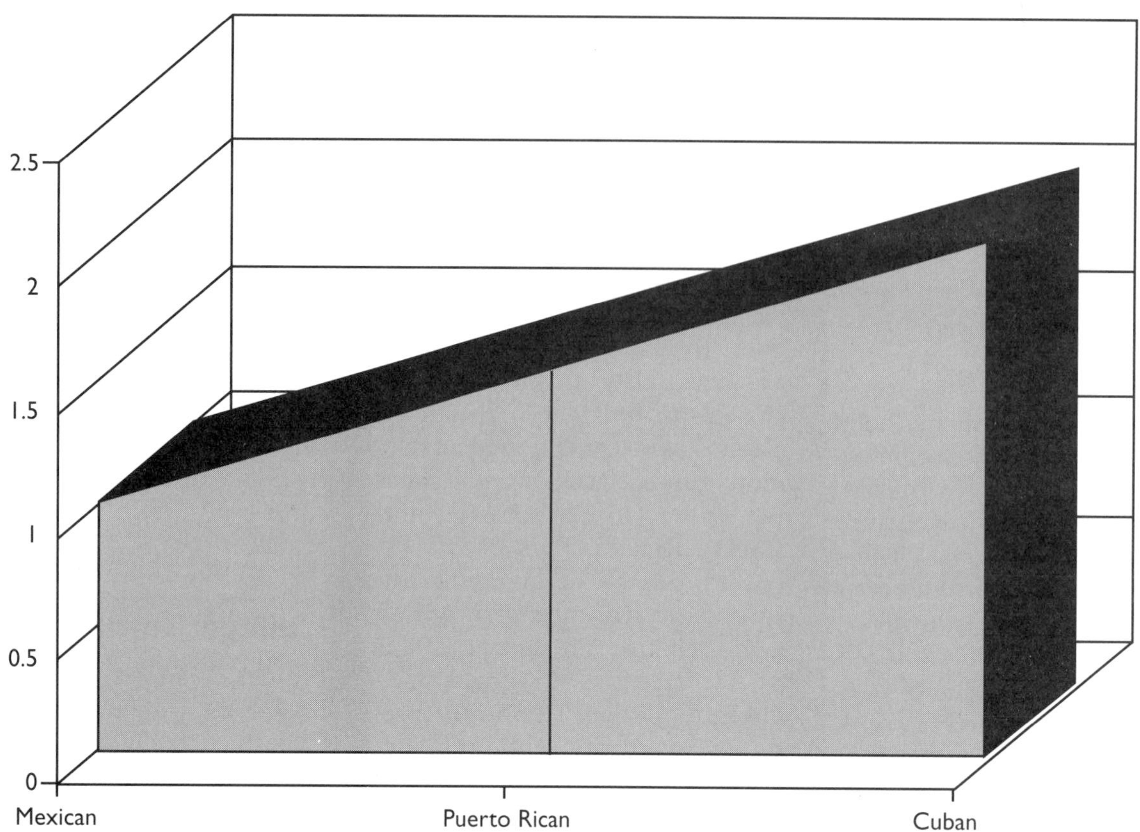

Figure 5. Odds of college completion.

degree compared to Mexican Americans. Using Mexicans as a reference group, we find that Cubans are almost twice as likely as Mexicans to receive a college degree. Puerto Ricans are 50 percent more likely to obtain a college degree in reference to Mexican Americans.

The effects of childhood environment are also important predictors of college completion. Having lived in a poor family significantly reduces the odds of having a college degree among Latinos by 53 percent, compared to those who lived in a well-off family setting. In the case of college completion, both father and mother's educational attainment are significantly associated with more favorable odds of having obtained a college degree. Individuals with at least high school educated fathers are 1.3 times more likely to have finished college. Those with high school educated mothers are 50 percent more likely to have obtained a college degree.

Being raised in a household where one's parents were married does have a significant effect on college completion risks: respondents from married couple households are twice as likely to complete college from those raised in a single parent home. Respondents who grew up in a rural area are 65 percent less likely to finish college compared to those raised in large cities. Interestingly, individuals who grew up in a small town are 43 percent more likely to earn a college degree versus those from a large city setting.

Conclusion

Childhood environmental factors play a significant role in promoting educational outcomes. We have shown that parental characteristics, which directly shape a child's environmental setting, have significant repercussions on future educational outcomes among Latinos. Specifically, Latino children raised in poor households are significantly less likely to finish both high school and college. Similarly, Latino children raised in rural areas are also less likely to complete high school and college. Father's educational levels during the respondent's childhood significantly improves educational attainment among Latinos in adulthood. Parental marital status also drastically increased the odds of scholastic achievement for both high school and college completion models.

Education is an important determinant of an individual's life chances. This analysis has demonstrated the significant impact of childhood environment on future educational outcomes among Latinos. To diminish the education gap between Latinos and non-Hispanic whites, it is clear that we must begin by addressing issues relating to poverty. Latinos raised in stable, well-off families, where parents had some formal schooling, are much more likely to complete both high school and college. Expanding opportunities for Latino children in schools is an important policy step. To truly attack this problem, poverty must be included as perhaps the most important determinant of a child's future success. Despite the growing opportunities for Latinos in America's institutions of higher learning, there remains a gap between those who are given the opportunity to take advantage of these benefits (such as scholarships) and those who fail to advance far enough to know they are available. Poverty cuts off young Latinos before they are able to realize their full potential.

Continued research is needed to further address the impact of environmental factors in promoting and/or hindering social and economic outcomes. Future studies should consider more specific measures of environmental effects, as well as more microlevel processes such as network functions among children and adolescents. Educational outcomes are central to the many theories of assimilation and adaptation (Kao and Tienda, 1995; Portes and Bach, 1985). There is a need for further in-depth analyses of the processes associated with educational success and failure. The children of the second largest minority population in the United States will play a major role in societal affairs. Attempts should be made to further develop the human capital stock of the next generation, making current analyses of educational achievement a key component of this endeavor.

References

Ballesteros, Ernesto. 1986. "Do Hispanics Receive an Equal Educational Opportunity? The Relationship of School Outcomes, Family Background, and High School Curriculum." In *Latino College Students*, ed. M.A. Olivas, pp. 47–70. Teachers College Press.

Bean, Frank D., and Marta Tienda. 1987. *The Hispanic Population of the United States.* New York: Russell Sage Foundation.

Brown, G., N. Rosen, S. Hill, and M. Olivas. 1980. "The Condition of Education for Hispanic Americans." Washington, D.C.: National Center for Educational Statistics, U.S. Government Printing Office.

Coleman, James S. 1988. "Social Capital in the Creation of Human Capital." *American Journal of Sociology.* 94: 95–120.

DeFreitas, Gregory. 1991. *Inequality at Work, Hispanics in the U.S. Labor Force.* New York: Oxford University Press.

Hirschman, Charles, and Morrison G. Wong. 1981. "Trends in Socioeconomic Achievement among Immigrant and Native-Born Asian-Americans, 1960-1976." *Sociological Quarterly.* 22:495–514.

Horowitz, Ruth. 1981. "Passion, Submission and Motherhood: The Negotiation of Identity by Unmarried Innercity Chicanas." *Sociological Quarterly.* 22:241–52.

Kao, Grace, and Marta Tienda. 1995. Optimism and Achievement: The Educational Performance of Immigrant Youth." *Social Science Quarterly.* 76, 1:1–19.

Keefe, Susan E. 1984. "Real and Ideal Extended Familism among Mexican Americans and Anglo Americans: On the Meaning of Close Family Ties." *Human Organization.* 43:65–69.

Keefe, Susan E., Amado M. Patella, and Manuel L. Carlos. 1979. "The Mexican-American Extended Family as an Emotional Support System." *Human Organization.* 38:144–52.

Kuvelesky, William P., and Victoria M. Patella. 1971. "Degree of Ethnicity and Aspirations for Upward Social Mobility among Mexican American Youth." *Journal of Vocational Behavior.* 1:231–44.

Lareau, Annette. 1989. *Home Advantage: Social Class and Parental Intervention in Elementary Education.* New York: Falmer.

Miller, Michael V. 1978. "Variations in Mexican American Family Life: A Review Synthesis of Empirical Research." *Aztlan.* 9:209–31.

Ortiz, Vilma. 1995. "Generational Status, Family Background, and Educational Attainment Among Hispanic Youth and Non-Hispanic White Youth." In *Latino Language and Education: Communication and the Dream Deferred*, ed. A.S. Lopez, pp. 95–112. Garland Publishing, Inc.

Portes, Alejandro, and Julia Sensenbrenner. 1993. "Embeddedness and Immigration: Notes on the Social Determinants of Economic Action." *American Journal of Sociology.* 98:1320–50.

Portes, Alejandro, and Robert L. Bach. 1985. *Latin Journey: Cuban and Mexican Immigrants in the United States.* University of California Press.

Ringawa, Marcel. 1980. "Cultural Pedagogy: The Effects of Teacher Attitudes and Needs in Selected Bilingual Bicultural Education Environments." In *Ethno-Perspectives in Bilingual Education Research: Theory in Bilingual Education*, ed. Raymond V. Padilla. Ypsilanti, MI: Bilingual Bicultural Education Programs, Eastern Michigan University.

Rumbaut, Ruben G. 1995. "Ties that Bind: Immigration and Immigrant Families in the United States." Presented at The National Symposium on International Migration and Family Change, The Pennsylvania State University.

Sewell, W., R. Hauser, and W. Wolf. 1980. Sex, Schooling, and Occupational Status. *American Journal of Sociology.* 86:551–83.

Silverman, Myrna. 1989. *Strategies for Social Mobility: Family, Kinship and Ethnicity within Jewish Families in Pittsburgh.* New York: AMS Press.

Tienda, Marta. 1980. "Familism and Structural Assimilation of Mexican Immigrants in the United States." *International Migration Review.* 14, 3:383–408.

Article Review Form at end of book.

Do you think that achievement tests are an adequate measure on which to base tracking? What are some of the problems for lower track students? Do you think that diverse groups of students with varying abilities and backgrounds are the solution to unequal opportunities?

Tracking Matters

Vincent J. Roscigno and James W. Ainsworth-Darnell
The Ohio State University

Academic tracking is a common practice in most classrooms and schools in the United States. Beginning at early elementary levels, children are placed in unique reading groups based on what is seen as their intellectual ability or potential. Often schools set up distinct "gifted and talented" classrooms by later elementary grades for those who have performed well the first few years or who are viewed as academically advanced relative to their same grade counterparts. This process only intensifies—students typically end up on a distinct academic track by high school and are, more often than not, well aware of their track position and that of others. These tracks are typically deemed "academic/advanced," "general," "vocational," or one of a variety of educationally impaired tracks, most often having to do with a learning disability, emotional impairment, or mental retardation.

The reasoning behind tracking, and its rationale, are relatively straightforward. Advanced students, when grouped together, spur one another along, will not become bored or have to wait for lower achieving students to catch up, and therefore will achieve at a higher level. Lower track students, in comparison, can work at a pace commensurate with their comfort and ability level and will not become overwhelmed by the brisk pace of high achievers in their classroom or at their grade level.

At face value the logic behind tracking is one in which all students benefit. Students work at their potential. They are not held back by slower learners, nor are they overwhelmed by material that is beyond their ability. These goals, however, as well-intentioned as they may be, mask some underlying and incorrect assumptions about the neutrality of the tracking process. One such supposition is that students are tracked solely on the basis of intellectual ability or innate potential. Another questionable assumption has to do with whether the quality of education received is equitable across tracks. Sociological and educational research has explored each of these questions, revealing relatively clear patterns of race and class inequality in tracking in U.S. schools.[1] There is also clear variation in the quality of education received across tracks.

Who Gets Tracked Where, and Why?

The institution of education in this country has historically been viewed as the "great equalizer," whereby individuals and groups can remedy disadvantages faced by previous generations. Inequalities associated with tracking, however, represent one way in which broader societal inequalities tend to be reproduced during the schooling process. Rather than a direct form of discrimination against poor or nonwhite children, the stratification dynamics associated with tracking, discussed later, represent *institutionalized discrimination;* discrimination that occurs without conscious intent, that is largely a function of institutional practices and rules, but that nevertheless works against and perpetuates inequalities for certain segments of our society.

Empirical evidence has been relatively clear regarding the social class and race character of tracking. Poor and nonwhite students are more likely than their well-to-do and middle class white counterparts to be low tracked through their elementary and high school years. Figures 1 and 2, derived from a national sample of U.S. high school students, offer clear evidence of these patterns.

White students are more likely than their Asian, Black, Native-American, and Hispanic counterparts to be on high, college-bound tracks in math/science and English/history. Racial inequalities in placement are most profound for African-American, Native-American, and Hispanic students. As a result, these students are more likely than white students to be placed in lower track classes in high school; classes that are usually general or vocational.

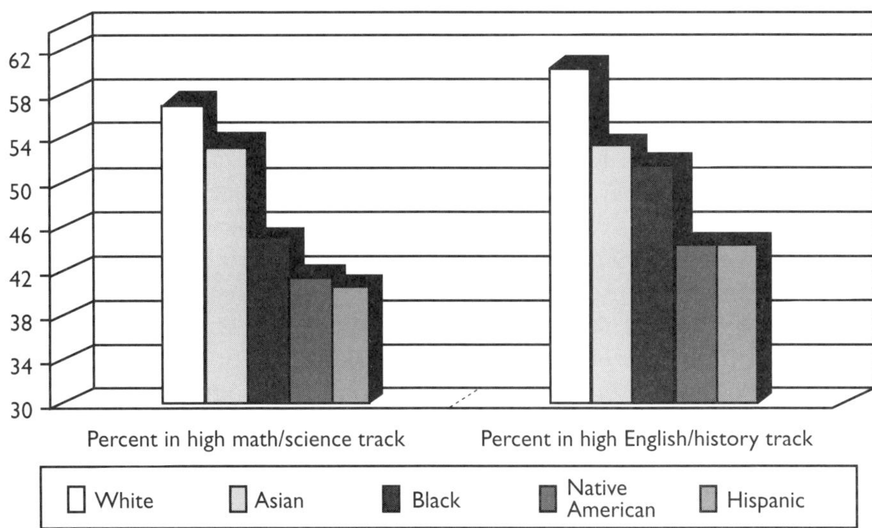

Figure 1. Student placement on high academic track in math/science and English/history, by racial and ethnic group, 1990. (Source: National Educational Longitudinal Survey, first follow-up.)

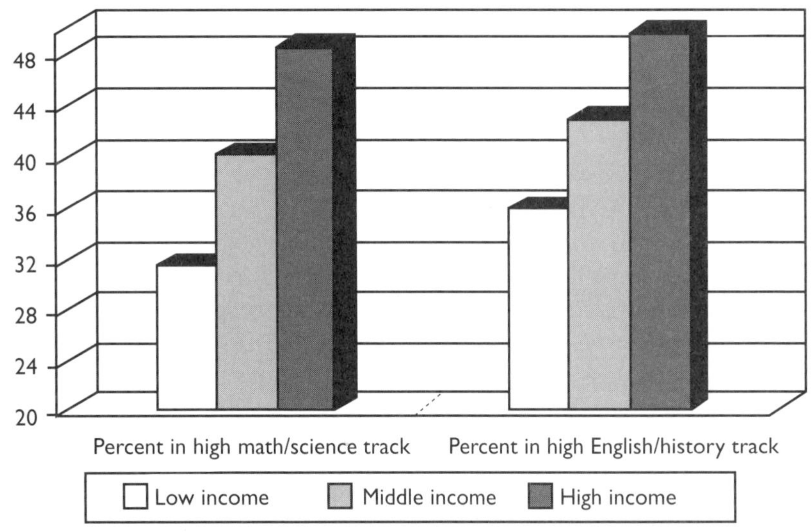

Figure 2. Student placement on high academic track in math/science and English/history, by family income, 1990. (Source: National Educational Longitudinal Survey, first follow-

Track placement is influenced not only by race, but also by social class background. Students from poorer families are less likely to be placed high relative to their more well-to-do counterparts (see Figure 2). Middle-class students fall somewhere between. These race and class patterns do not suggest that all poor and nonwhite kids are tracked low or that all well-to-do white children are placed high. What they do suggest, however, are general patterns and inequalities in where one is likely to end up, depending on race and socioeconomic background. Such evidence of race and class stratification in tracking is troubling not only because it represents a form of inequality perpetuated in the schooling process, but also because it has very real implications for the likelihood of dropping out and what students do after high school (i.e., go to college, obtain a blue-collar job, etc.).

Traditional social scientific reasoning associated with what has been called *Social Darwinism* would explain the trends presented previously in biological terms, suggesting that low SES and nonwhite groups are disproportionately in low tracks due to inherent intellectual differences.[2] Historically, such pseudoscientific views were used to first justify slavery then maintain racially segregated schools in the South. It also led to the placement of many Latino children in classrooms for the mentally retarded in the Southwest and, at the broadest level, led to the adoption of the Immigration Act of 1924. This piece of legislation severely limited the further immigration of certain southern and eastern European white ethnic groups (e.g., Italians, Polish, etc.), believed to be less intelligent and therefore more inclined toward criminal activity, into the United States.[3]

Although most contemporary research has moved away from sociobiological explanations of class and racial inequalities, such views continue to garner attention. A clear example is the publication and publicity surrounding Hernnstein and Murray's *The Bell Curve*, in which the authors suggest that biology has more to do with achievement than do social factors.[4] Contemporary sociological and educational researchers rightly dismiss such overly simplistic viewpoints, especially when they are used to exclude one group to the benefit of another. Instead, research over the past thirty years has focussed on how kids are placed on tracks in the first place. It is from this research that two clear biases in track placement have been uncovered.

First, children tend to be tracked on the basis of their performance on a standardized test. It is usually assumed that such tests measure innate potential or intellectual ability. Research, however, suggests that these tests measure much more. They tap into a child's experiences in life thus far and are biased in their construction, measuring more so the white middle-class normative standard than they do the day-to-day experiences of poor children and racial/ethnic minorities.[5] On comprehension portions of standardized tests, for instance, scenarios often depict that which is commonplace to middle-upper class white students, but foreign to a black child living in an urban ghetto, a Latino child living in a poor barrio, a Native-American child living on a reservation, or a white child living in a rural and poor agricultural area of the United States.

Likewise, such tests capture one's educational experiences thus far, rather than merely potential. It is for this reason that children from higher socioeconomic backgrounds, who have had greater educational resources and opportunities in their homes from early on, tend to outperform poorer students. One's parents' education is consistently one of the best predictors of how low or high one performs in school and on achievement tests.[6] The relation between socioeconomic status and achievement is typically true not only for young children, but rather is consistent throughout the educational process, including performance on tests such as the SAT or GRE. It is no surprise then that when testing is used as a gatekeeping tool to see who is placed low and who is placed high, that broader patterns of societal inequality tend to be reproduced.

An important second mechanism that often comes into play during track placement is teacher expectations of a given student. Although we would like to believe that educators are capable of employing objective evaluation of student effort, intelligence, and potential, research has demonstrated that there is a subjective element that comes into play and that, like testing, places poor and nonwhite children at a unique disadvantage.

Rist, for instance, in his observations of reading group placement at the earliest educational levels in the early 1970s, found that teachers typically employ subjective judgments about potential.[7] Beyond student academic performance in front of the teacher, he found that teachers' judgments and conclusions about potential were also based on the student's ability to speak proper, middle-class English and on the way in which the student dressed. Indeed, he found that by the eighth day of kindergarten, seating arrangements had been made along these lines, that those at the "fast learner" table received greater attention and privileges, and that students began to adopt their roles as "fast learner" or "slow learner" accordingly.

Alexander, Entwisle, and Thompson, undertaking more recent analyses with a similar concern in mind, uncovered similar results.[8] They found that class and racial biases in teacher evaluation, and consequently expectations, exist even at the earliest educational levels. Such biases seem even more pronounced when the teacher and the student are from distinct social origins. These biases, they note, are not only important for a student's experiences and performance in a given classroom. Rather, teacher expectations are crucial at early elementary levels due to their effects on a student's long term educational trajectory, part of which is perpetuated through track placement. They conclude,

> The evidence indicates that high status teachers, both black and white, experience special difficulties relating to minority youngsters. They perceive such youngsters as relatively lacking in the qualities of personal maturity that make for a 'good student,' hold lower performance expectations of them, and evaluate the school climate much less favorably when working with such students. As a result, blacks who begin first grade with test scores very similar to their white age-mates have fallen noticeably behind by year's end.[9]

Thus, testing and teacher expectations represent two mechanisms through which race and class biases in the track placement process are played out. Nonwhite and poorer students tend to perform less well on such tests, due largely to cultural and class biases in the construction of the tests themselves, and because such tests measure one's background experiences and family educational resources as much as they capture intelligence. These students receive less in the way of expectations as well, often determined by subjective criteria rather than true academic potential. What occurs once student track placement is determined? Is the educational experience similar across tracks?

Educational Opportunity and Why Tracking Matters

It is clear that children in higher track classes perform academically at a higher level than do their lower track counterparts. Not all of this difference, however, is associated with greater intelligence or academic potential among higher track kids. Rather, analyses of high and low track classrooms suggest that the quality of education received varies markedly by track level.

There are relatively clear differences across tracks in terms of the availability of educational resources, teacher quality, and expectations. As a consequence, classroom climate also differs as does peer encouragement of educational success. Figure 3 displays such differences across high and low tracks for our nationally representative sample of U.S. high school students.

Low track classes are less likely to have the types and quality of educational resources as do high track classes. Take, for instance, access to and use of computers as one indicator of educational resources. The percentages reported in Figure 3 reveal that high track students are almost four times as likely as low track kids to use and/or have such a resource at their disposal. Similar, if not more profound, is the association between track and teacher training. Fewer than 2 percent of low tracked students are taught by a teacher with greater educational training and experience. This is in contrast to high track kids, 30 percent of whom are being taught by teachers holding at least a master's degree.[10]

Typically, the newest and youngest teachers in a given school are asked to teach the low track classes. Those with the greatest credentials and seniority, in contrast, tend to avoid lower track classes. Research has suggested that teachers prefer to teach children who they believe to be more intelligent. One consequence is that those who teach lower track children tend to prepare less in the way of daily lesson plans and classroom activities and hold lower expectations of their students. The reader will note this dramatic difference in expectations, displayed in Figure 3. Rather than seeing it as an opportunity to help "all grow to their potential," teachers given low track classes often see their job as one of "weeders, getting rid of the kids who can't make it."[11]

The tendency to avoid low track classes and to hold lower expectations of students in such classes is unfortunate, not to mention unfair. Indeed, some research has demonstrated that these patterns lend themselves to a

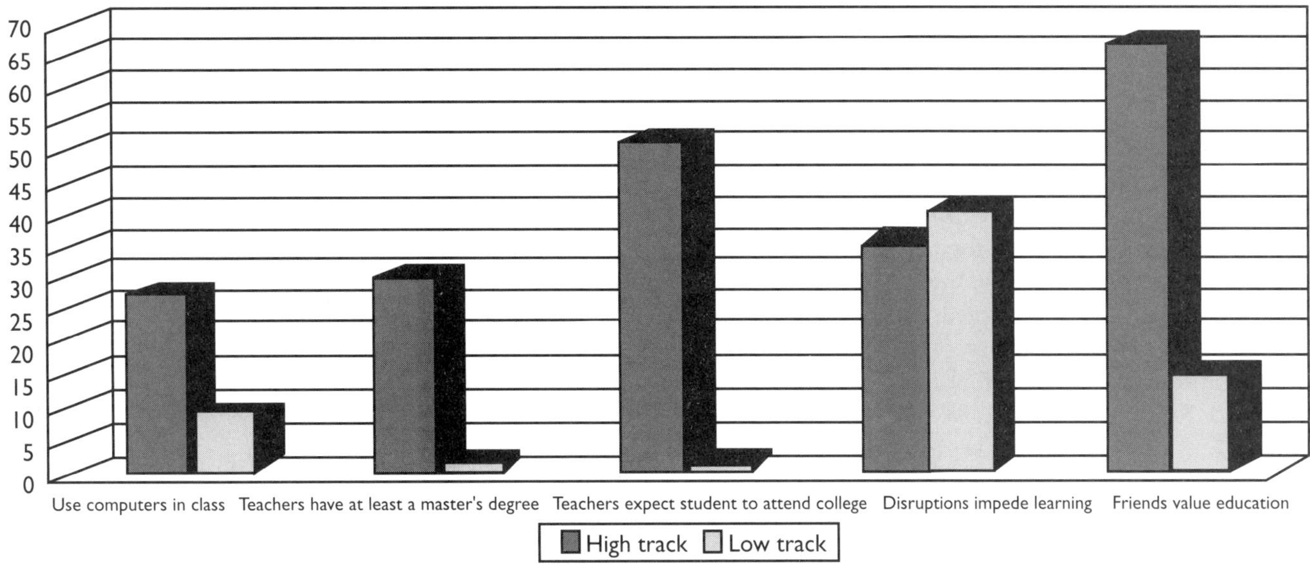

Figure 3. Percentage track differences in educational resources, teacher expectations, and general classroom climate, 1990. (Source: National Educational Longitudinal Survey, first follow-up.)

self-fulfilling prophecy; a situation in which people, in this case children, alter their behavior to conform to what is expected of them, thereby creating the reality others thought was true in the first place. Such an unfortunate causal loop of expectations and performance then serves to justify, in the eyes of policymakers and school administrators, greater classroom resources and teacher energy for high track kids.

A clear example of the processes we are discussing is reflected in the now classic "pygmalion in the classroom" experiment undertaken in the 1960s by Rosenthal and Jacobsen.[12] In this study, the researchers *randomly* selected five students from each classroom in a given elementary school and told the teachers these students were identified by a test as "potential academic spurters." By year's end, these students for whom the teacher expected great intellectual gains not only showed greater academic achievement than their nonidentified counterparts, but were viewed by the teacher, as well as their classmates, as smarter, happier, and more likely to succeed. This example demonstrates that a self-fulfilling prophecy can work in a positive direction and underscores the critical importance of teacher expectations for student performance.

Another problematic feature of the low track class, given lower expectations, less resources, and the self-fulfilling prophecy described, is the resultant classroom climate. Students typically realize the tracks they are on, are *labeled* by teachers and other students, and often buy into this labeling themselves. Children understand where they fall on this continuum as early as second grade, and are affected not only in terms of their own expectations, but their self-esteem as well.[13] An unfortunate yet understandable consequence, some have noted, is the formation of a student subculture in low tracked classrooms; one that is antagonistic toward education and that has its own system of rewards, often valuing classroom rebellion and doing opposite of what the teacher desires.[14] As indicated in Figure 3, this obviously leads to a climate where disruption is more likely to impede on the learning process and a scenario in which one's peers lose respect for, and no longer value, the educational process and educational effort.

Achievement and Attainment Across Tracks

So what are the consequences of the patterns of track placement and inequalities in classroom resources, noted previously, for student achievement over the long run? Does tracking shape one's likelihood of completing high school? How, if at all, does the tracking process that begins early on in each of our educational histories effect our long term educational and occupational attainment once we exit the high school doors?

Figures 4 and 5 address the first of these questions by focusing on achievement levels throughout high school. As one can see, the initial gap in academic achievement across tracks in eighth grade intensifies and widens by tenth grade, and then again by twelfth grade.[15] Similar patterns are found for math and reading. The widening gap between high and low track students, and depressed general achievement for those in low tracks in these subject areas, have clear implications for performance on SAT and ACT examinations and, therefore, one's likely admittance and/or success at the collegiate level.

With regard to long term educational attainment and even occupational opportunity, being low tracked in high school is clearly consequential. Interestingly, although not too surprising, is that

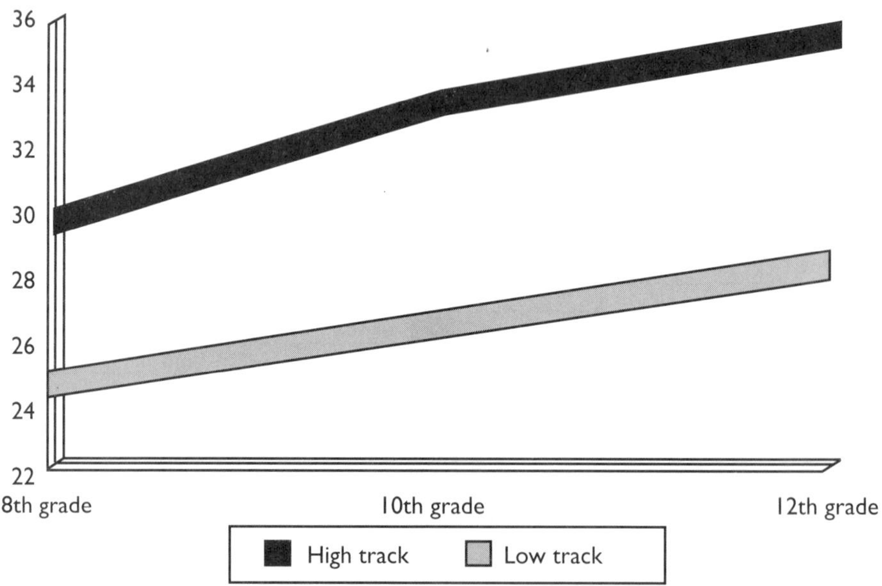

Figure 4. Reading achievement and the gap between high and low tracked students between 8th and 12th grade. (Source: 1990 National Educational Longitudinal Survey, base year, first, and second follow-up.)

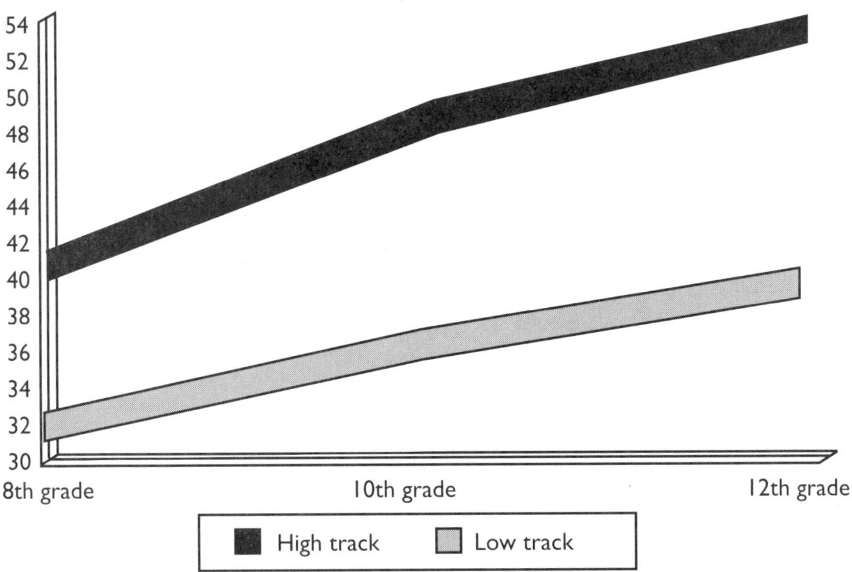

Figure 5. Math achievement and the gap between high and low tracked students between 8th and 12th grade. (Source: 1990 National Educational Longitudinal Survey, base year, first, and second follow-up.)

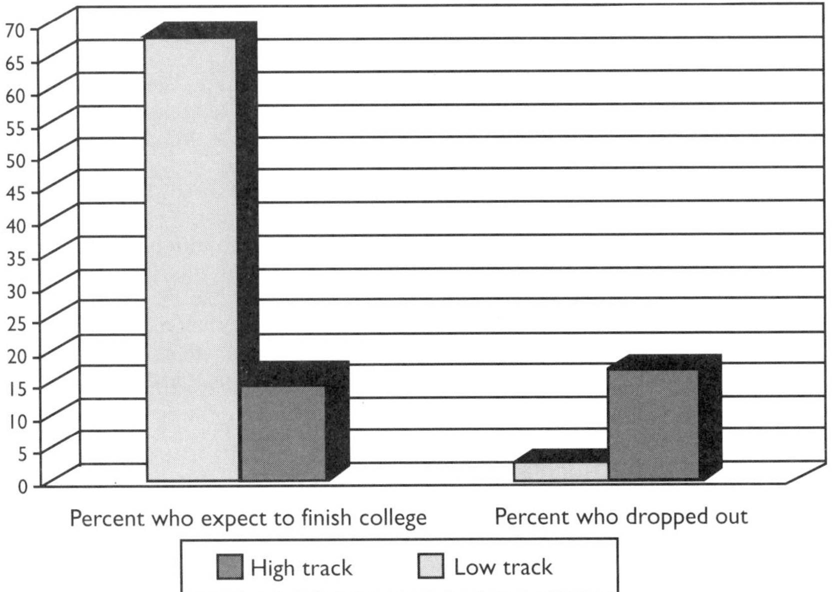

Figure 6. Educational expectations/aspirations and dropout rates for high and low tracked students, 1992. (Source: National Educational Longitudinal Survey, first and second follow-up.)

students are relatively aware of where they stand. Expectations for low track students are depressed considerably by the twelfth grade, and this translates into a wide disparity among students in whether they expect to finish college. Figure 6 reveals this profound difference in expectations, with 67 percent of high track students believing they will complete college in contrast to only 15 percent of low track students.

Perhaps even more disconcerting are dropout rates, also reported in Figure 6. Only 2 percent of high track students drop out of high school by the twelfth grade. This is in stark contrast to students who are low tracked throughout high school, who are nine times more likely to drop out by the twelfth grade. Given the patterns and disparities in achievement, college expectations, and dropping out of high school, the practice of tracking should not be seen as merely something that happens in schools. It begins in school, but ultimately shapes one's life chances over the long term. It has consequences for the preparedness of our labor force in general, and the ability to eventually provide one's children with adequate health care, food, and shelter. Given the consequences of tracking for the likelihood of dropping out, it also has real implications for a number of other social problems including poverty and crime. Through tracking in education, inequalities by race and social class are partially reproduced and, indeed, passed from one generation to the next.

Why Track in the First Place?

Traditional functionalist theory in sociology has viewed the institution of education as critically important, not only because it socializes the younger generation and new immigrants into appropriate norms of conduct, but also because it represents a *meritocratic* sorting process; one based on ability, one that insures the "best and brightest" move on to the next level, and one that ultimately helps to decide who ends up in the most important societal positions.[16] Tracking clearly represents one aspect of this "sifting and sorting" function. Similar to assumptions made about tracking, however, this view of education and its functions put forth by social theorists rests on the assumption that the sorting that occurs is neutral, based solely on ability, intellect, and potential. Evidence presented here, along with countless other studies of stratification and the schooling process, present a serious challenge to this claim.

First, one's track placement (or the sifting and sorting that occurs, if you prefer) is shaped by more than ability or potential. *Ascribed characteristics* one is born with or into, such as one's social class or race, come into play during this process. Although they have no relation to intelligence or potential, they affect the likelihood of being tracked high or being tracked low and, therefore, one's educational and occupational trajectory and future success. Race and class biases in track placement, and the gatekeeping effects they have at initial stages, challenge the key assumption made by advocates of tracking and social theorists who suggest that the sorting that occurs is meritocratic in nature.

Second, it is typically assumed that the educational process is relatively neutral and equitable once track placement has been made. Low track classes, as we and others have shown, receive less in the way of important educational resources, are usually staffed by new, less experienced teachers, and students in these classes are expected to do less than their higher track counterparts. It is no surprise that, under such circumstances, classroom climate less conducive to achievement and antagonism toward the educational process develop. Not only is the starting line different for poor and nonwhite students, but the race they run is on the outside lane of the track, and with a variety of hurdles that they must attempt to overcome.

Finally, the logic behind tracking itself, that high achievers will work harder and low achievers can work at a pace commensurate with their ability, is questionable at best. Evidence suggests that high achievers do as well in heterogenous settings as they do when tracked with similar students. It also appears to be the case that those who are academically behind do better, and are spurred on to try harder, when grouped with high achievers.[17] So why track then, especially given the stigma and labeling of lower students? Who gains? These are perhaps the most fundamental questions. If there is little, if any, tangible achievement benefit for already high achieving students, but a real, unjust cost for those at the lower end who are disproportionately poor and nonwhite, tracking in schools makes little sense.

What seems more practical, not to mention sensible, would be diverse groupings of students of varying abilities and backgrounds. Not only will achievement of otherwise low tracked students be raised in such a situation, but high achievers might also learn valuable leadership, creative, and communication skills that they might otherwise not. For education is not (or should not be) about grasping knowledge of English, math, science, and history. It should also be concerned with teaching students how to live and apply their knowledge and skills in a diverse world; one that is comprised of people and future coworkers of varying abilities, perspectives, and life experiences.

Notes

1. Class and race disparities in tracking placement are more apparent throughout the educational process, whereas gender disparities in tracking are more apparent in later high school grades, especially in math and science. See also Susan L. Dauber, Karl L. Alexander, and Doris R. Entwisle, "Tracking and Transitions Through the Middle Grades: Channeling Educational Trajectories," *Sociology of Education* (1996) 69:290; Adam Gamoran and Mark Berends, "The Effects of Stratification in Secondary Schools: Synthesis of Survey and Ethnographic Research," *Review of Educational Research* (1987) 57:415–435; Caroline Hodges Persell, *Education and Inequality* (New York: The Free Press, 1977); Terry Kershaw, "The Effects of Educational Tracking on the Social Mobility of African Americans," *Journal of Black Studies* (1992) 23:152–169; Jeannie Oakes, *Keeping Track: How Schools Structure Inequality* (New Haven: Yale University Press, 1985); Beth E. Vanfossen, J. D. Jones, and Joan Z. Spade, "Curriculum Tracking and Status Maintenance," *Sociology of Education* (1987) 60:104–122.
2. Similar arguments have been made with regard to differential gender effects in math or science, citing "proclivities" or "biological" tendencies, which makes males and females each better suited for particular educational training and occupations.
3. Chinese and Japanese immigration was practically halted even earlier by the Federal Government via the Chinese Exclusion Act and the Gentleman's Agreement, respectively. For elaboration on white ethnic immigration, related legislation, and its justifications, see Stanley Lieberson, *A Piece of the Pie: Black and White Immigrants Since 1880* (Berkeley: University of California Press, 1980).
4. Richard J. Hernnstein and Charles Murray, *The Bell Curve: Intelligence and Class Structure in American Life* (New York: The Free Press, 1994); for a response to the biological position, see Claude S. Fischer et al., *Inequality by Design: Cracking the Bell Curve Myth* (Princeton: Princeton University Press, 1996).

5. Jerome Kagan, "What is Intelligence?" *Social Policy* (1973) 4:88–94.
6. For instance, see Annette Lareau, *Home Advantage: Social Class and Parental Intervention in Elementary Education* (New York: Falmer Press, 1989); Vincent J. Roscigno, "Race, Institutional Linkages, and the Reproduction of Educational Disadvantage," *Social Forces* (1998).
7. Ray C. Rist, "Student Social Class and Teacher Expectations: The Self-Fulfilling Prophecy in Ghetto Education," *Harvard Education Review* (1970) 40:411–451.
8. Karl L. Alexander, Doris R. Entwisle, and Maxine S. Thompson, "School Performance, Status Relations, and the Structure of Sentiment: Bringing the Teacher Back In," *American Sociological Review* (1987) 52:665–682.
9. Alexander, Entwisle, and Thompson, 1987, p. 679.
10. The National Educational Longitudinal Survey, from which we draw the data used to generate these comparisons, surveyed two of the student's teachers. Teacher responses were combined in determing credentials and expectations for the student. Where both teachers have at least a master's degree or both have college expectations for the student, the student was placed into the high category.
11. Jill Rachlin, "The Label that Sticks," *U.S. News & World Report* (July 3, 1989), p. 52.
12. Robert Rosenthal and Lenore Jacobsen, *Pygmalion in the Classroom* (New York: Holt, Rinehart & Winston, 1968).
13. Sheila Tobias, "Tracked to Fail," *Psychology Today* (1989) 23:54-60.
14. David H. Hargreaves, *Social Relations in a Secondary School* (London: Tinling, 1967); Paul Willis, *Learning to Labor: How Working Class Kids Get Working Class Jobs* (New York: Columbia University Press, 1981).
15. These figures underestimate the gap by twelfth grade, given the loss of dropouts in the sample, who tend to be disproportionately represented among low academic tracks.
16. For the classical functionalist position, see especially Kingsley Davis and Wilbert E. Moore, "Some Principles of Stratification," *American Sociological Review* (1942) 10:242–249.
17. John M. Peterson, "Tracking Students by Their Supposed Abilities Can Derail Learning," *American School Board Journal* (1989) 176:38; Jill Rachlin, "The Label that Sticks," *U.S. News & World Report* (July 3, 1989), p.52.

Article Review Form at end of book.

How can this study's findings on the effects of family life on grades be used to formulate effective reforms for promoting better educational experiences? How does this research reflect complications sociologists face when attempting to discover cause-effect relationships?

School Grades Versus Academic Achievement Scores in Assessing Contemporaneous Influences on Academic Success

A research note

Thomas Ewin Smith

University of South Carolina

Abstract

It is argued that relationships between school grades and variables reflecting concurrent and recent behavior and environment are less apt to be artifactual than are relationships of such variables to academic achievement scores, mainly determined by long-term factors (intellectual ability and cumulative learning). Further, it is assumed that controlling academic achievement scores will tend to remove confounding effects of preexisting factors on relationships between grades and other variables. A replication and extension of a recent study that found several effects on academic achievement reveals that most of the effects disappear, diminish, or change in direction when the dependent variable is school grades, especially when achievement scores are controlled.

The research was supported by Grant Number SES-8507004 from the Sociology Program of the National Science Foundation and by The University of South Carolina.

Direct correspondence to Dr. Thomas Ewin Smith, Department of Sociology, University of South Carolina, Columbia, SC 29208.

The possibility of spurious relationships caused by confounding factors is a perpetual thorn in the methodological flesh of social science. Statistical associations, which may be mere artifacts of unexamined factors, can easily be interpreted as theoretically meaningful causal relationships. One area in which the danger of spurious relationships would appear to be large is the study of academic success, as indicated by standardized academic achievement scores.

Academic achievement test batteries are not intended primarily to measure a student's academic performance in recent days, weeks, or months. They are designed to measure the extent to which a student has learned the information and concepts taught over the years he/she has been in school. Therefore, achievement scores may not be the appropriate indicators of academic performance if one is trying to assess the effect on performance from a contemporaneous variable or recent event, such as a parental divorce.

This would amount to reversing the usual temporal order of independent and dependent variables. One would not, of course, expect a child's academic achievement to affect parental divorce, but a spurious correlation might exist if a variable that affected cumulative achievement over the years also affected the probability of divorce (e.g., parental marital conflict, alcoholism, or mental illness of a parent). Furthermore, one variable that influences many behaviors of children and adolescents—basic intellectual ability—is known to influence academic achievement to a considerable degree.

The long-term cumulative learning measured by achievement tests is strongly related to intellectual ability. Strong correlations between tests of intellectual ability and tests of academic achievement (generally with correlation coefficients of .6 and above) have been found repeatedly, according to a review of the research by Sattler (1982:150).

An obvious reason for the strong association between achievement and ability is that the level of learning a student achieves in school is largely, although not entirely, determined by the student's basic ability. If, therefore, a researcher finds that academic achievement scores are related to variables that have substantial relationships with intellectual ability, such as variables related to socioeconomic status, which has a strong positive association with ability (Sattler, 1982:56), the found relationships may be partly or entirely artifacts of ability effects. This follows that intellectual ability is established prior to academic achievement and various ability-related variables often used to account for achievement. After all, basic intellectual ability is mainly determined by factors of heredity and early childhood environment (e.g., Chipuer, Rovin, and Plomin, 1990; Rodgers and Rowe, 1987; Storfer, 1990) and to some degree by prenatal environment (e.g., Streissguth, Barr, Samson, and Darby, 1989).

When the possibility of confounding effects from ability exists, taking ability into account by controlling IQ is advisable (Kerckhoff, 1972). Unfortunately, an adequate measure of ability is often unavailable in the data, and many studies have used academic achievement as a dependent variable without taking intellectual ability into account (e.g., Astone and McLanahan, 1991; Gamoran, 1992; Keith, Reimers, Fehrmann, Pottebaum, and Aubey, 1986; Milne, Myers, Rosenthal, and Ginsburg, 1986; Smith, 1990). However, a possible alternative is to use a different indicator of academic success—one that appears to be less subject to the effects of intellectual ability and other long-term antecedents and more sensitive to contemporaneous conditions.

Achievement Scores and School Grades as Indicators of Academic Success

When school grades and academic achievement scores are available, a researcher has sound reasons for preferring the achievement scores as an indicator of academic success. The achievement tests have been rigorously standardized and examined for validity and reliability in large, meticulously designed samples of students. In comparison, the teachers' evaluations on which grades are based appear grossly unscientific. A student's grades depend, in part, on what teachers the student happens to have, on the current grading policies advocated by the school principal, and perhaps on the emotional moods and states of mental alertness of teachers when they evaluate the student's work. With all their obvious defects, school grades may be superior, in one respect, to academic achievement scores.

Empirical tests have indicated that school grades are influenced more by effort and less by ability than are academic achievement scores (Keith, 1982; Natriello and McDill, 1986). Furthermore, other research evidence indicates that contemporaneous and recent social environment influences grades more than academic achievement. The evidence comes out of a pair of studies concerned with school success. Analyzing data from the "High School and Beyond" sample, Keith et al. (1986) failed to find a significant parental-involvement effect on academic achievement test scores; but Fehrmann, Keith, and Reimers (1987) found that parental involvement had a substantial effect on school grades in the same sample of high school seniors. Fehrmann, Keith, and Reimers explained the divergent results in terms of the fact (mentioned earlier) that grades are more sensitive to student effort and less affected by basic ability than are achievement test scores. It stands to reason that parental involvement with the adolescent and other aspects of recent social environment would affect students' academic effort but not their basic intellectual ability, which, as was pointed out earlier, is determined mainly by heredity and early-childhood environment. Effort affects grades more than achievement scores, so we can expect such recent environmental factors to affect adolescents' school grades more than their standardized achievement scores. It also stands to reason that statistical associations between contemporaneous environmental factors and school grades are less apt to be artifacts of differences in individual ability or other long-term antecedents of cumulative learning than are associations between contemporaneous environmental factors and achievement scores, designed to measure long-term cumulative learning, rather than current academic behavior.

The primary objective of the present research was to compare the effects of a variety of pertinent variables on academic achievement with the effects of the same variables on self-reported school grades, using a measure of grades proven to be a reasonably valid indicator of official grades. The independent variables represented racial and gender identities; parental SES; family structure; and time uses relevant to family, school, peers, and various mass media. Smith (1990) reported that academic achievement scores were related to most of these variables. In the same data set, I compared the effects of the independent variables on grades to their effects on overall academic achievement and compared their effects on grades when overall achievement was controlled to their effects on grades when achievement was not taken into account.

In accord with the research findings discussed earlier, I assumed that a marked decline in the strength of an independent variable's effects from its effect on achievement to its effect on grades without a control on achievement to its effect on grades with achievement controlled indicated that the effect on achievement was largely an artifact of variables that influenced long-term cumulative learning and the relevant adolescent behavior. A marked increase, rather than decrease, in an effect in the same comparisons was assumed to indicate an effect on academic success masked, or partially masked, by the effects of variables that affected long-term cumulative learning when achievement was used as the indicator of academic success.

Method and Procedures

The Respondents

The data were supplied by 1,596 seventh and ninth grade students in 14 selected public schools in the county that contains the bulk of the population of a racially mixed and economically diverse medium-sized Southeastern metropolitan area. Questionnaires were administered in classrooms selected to supply a full range of the non-educationally handicapped seventh and ninth graders in the county's public schools.

Tests of the representativeness of the sample (Smith, 1990) found that the respondents were essentially the same in racial composition as students in the fourteen schools from which they were drawn and were similar to county residents of their age level in racial composition and family type, but that they were above the average for the fourteen schools in academic achievement. The primary explanation for this difference is that the educationally handicapped students in the schools were not included in the sample. Also high achievers probably have fewer absences than others and a stronger motivation to attend to informed consent forms given to them in school necessary for obtaining achievement test results.

Questionnaire data and achievement test results were obtained for 2,236 students, but deletion of Asians and Hispanics, too few for analysis (74), reduced the number to 2,162. Listwise deletion of those with missing data on at least one of the variables used in the analysis (566) reduced the actual N to 1,596 (73.8 percent of the black and white respondents). The only major change in the demographic composition of the respondents produced by the listwise deletion was a reduction of black students from 48.2 to 41.1 percent. The above average attrition among the black respondents will be included later in a possible explanation to the effect of black identity on school grades when academic achievement is controlled.

Measurement and Analysis

The Dependent Variables

Academic achievement was measured by the "Total Battery" scale (an equal-interval scale of overall academic achievement) from the Comprehensive Tests of Basic Skills (CTBS) form U, levels H and J, administered by the schools less than a month after the collection of the questionnaire data. The CTBS, for which norms were developed in a nationally representative sample of 250,000 students, is a set of tests administered in 313 minutes, spread over four sessions (CTB/McGraw-Hill 1982). The Total Battery Scale is based on tests of Vocabulary, Reading Comprehension, Language Mechanics, Language Expression, Mathematics Computation, and Mathematics Concepts and Applications. The equal-interval scale was developed, by means of an overlapping pooled-analysis procedure, to be comparable across grade levels, in the sense of indicating degrees of increase in knowledge and skills from one grade level to another.

Self-reported school grades were measured by the following question: "In the past year, what have most of your grades been? 1 A's 2 A's and B's 3 B's 4 B's and C's 5 C's 6 C's and D's 7 D's 8 D's and F's 9 F's." The lowest and next-lowest categories were collapsed, as few students reported that most of their grades had been F's. Then the metric was reversed, so that the scale went from 1 "D's and F's or F's" through 8 "A's." This measure, therefore, had precisely the same categories that were used for the self-report measure of grades in the "High School and Beyond" study—a scale that correlated strongly (r=.77) with grade point averages on official transcripts (National Center for Educational Statistics, 1984). That finding supports the idea that the self-report measure is a reasonably valid, although not perfect, indicator of actual grades.

The Independent Variables

Six demographic factors were included among the independent variables: (a) black identity (coded 0 for whites and 1 for blacks), (b) female identity (coded 0 for males and 1 for females), (c) year in school (0 for seventh and 1 for ninth), (d) family type (decomposed into two dummy variables), (e) parental occupation, and (f) parental education. One of the dummy variables representing family type, "single parent," was coded 1 if the biological parents were separated and the parent with whom the child was living had not remarried; the other, "remarriage," was coded 1 if the biological parents were separated and the parent with whom the child was living had remarried. Occupations were measured initially by an updated version of the Hollingshead (1957) scale, ranging from 1 (unskilled workers) through 7 (major professionals, higher executives, and owners of large businesses). Parental occupation was represented by the mean occupational level of the mother and father, if information on both was available. Otherwise, the occupational level of the one available parent was used. Education was measured in terms of four levels: 1, high school graduation or less; 2, a year or more of formal education beyond high school; 3, a four-year college degree; 4, a postgraduate degree. Parental education was the mean formal education of the mother and father, if information on both was available. Otherwise, one parent was used.

The other independent variables represented amounts of time devoted to various persons and activities relevant to the family, the school, the peer group, and the mass media. The seven time variables were time devoted to (a) the parent, (b) household chores, (c) friends, (d) television, (e) radio and recordings, (f) leisure reading (reading not assigned in school), and (g) homework. All of the variables reflecting use of time were measured in the number of hours per week devoted to the particular activity or persons. In each case, the measure constituted the sum of responses to a questionnaire item that elicited number of hours on an average weekend and an item that elicited number of hours after school on an average weekday. The latter item was given a weight of four, rather than five, on the assumption that time after school on Fridays is regarded as a part of the weekend.

The only one of the seven time variables that requires further explanation is "time spent with the parent." It would have been possible to use a variable based on the sum of the amounts of time spent with the mother and the father, but the use of such a measure presented two problems. Almost one-fourth of the respondents were living in single-parent households, and, for those in two-parent families, time spent with the mother and father often overlaps. To circumvent these problems, a variable was created that reflected the number of hours per week spent with the parent (either mother or father) with whom the respondent reported spending the greater amount of time.

The Statistical Analysis

The data were analyzed in multiple regression analyses, using SPSSx "Regression" (SPSS, 1986). The .05 level was established as the criterion of statistical significance.

Results and Interpretations

Table 1 shows the means and standard deviations of the research variables and the complete correlation matrix; Table 2 shows the results of three multiple regression equations. In the first of these, the dependent variable is overall academic achievement. In the second, self-reported school grades is the dependent variable, and the independent variables are the same as those in the first equation. The third regression analysis is the same as the second, except that overall achievement is included in the equation as one of the independent variables.

In accord with the ideas presented in the introduction, I assumed that academic achievement

Table 1 Descriptive Statistics and Correlation Matrix

Variable	Descrip Stats Mean	s.d.	Product Moment Correlation Matrix 1	2	3	4	5	6	7	8
1 Black identity	0.41	0.49	1.00	−.20	−.37	.19	−.04	.02	−.14	.13
2 Parental education	1.89	0.96		1.00	.59	−.08	.01	−.03	.11	−.13
3 Parental occupation	4.03	1.75			1.00	−.19	−.01	−.05	.20	−.13
4 Single-parent	0.24	0.43				1.00	−.22	−.01	−.02	.02
5 Step-parent	0.13	0.34					1.00	−.01	.03	−.02
6 Female identity	0.58	0.49						1.00	−.02	.15
7 Year in school	0.53	0.50							1.00	−.12
8 Time with parent	17.03	9.13								1.00
9 Time on chores	9.15	7.12								
10 Time with friends	16.66	8.56								
11 Television time	17.65	8.29								
12 Radio and recordings	12.80	8.95								
13 Leisure reading	6.83	6.92								
14 Homework time	9.21	5.34								
15 Academic ach.	744.32	37.30								
16 Self-rep. grades	5.42	1.69								

N=1596

Table 2 Regressions upon the Independent Variables of Academic Achievement, Self-Reported Grades without a Control for Achievement, and Self-Reported Grades with Achievement Controlled

	Regression Analysis								
	Academic Achievement			Self-Reported Grades			Self–Reported Grades (with Ach. Controlled)		
Indep. Variable	B	S.E.	Beta	B	S.E.	Beta	B	S.E.	Beta
Academic ach.							0.027***	0.001	.59
Black Id.	−17.640***	1.660	−.23	0.222*	0.089	−.06	0.246***	0.080	.07
Parental ed.	4.723***	0.923	.12	0.216***	0.050	.12	0.090*	0.044	.05
Parental occu.	4.957***	0.542	.23	0.158***	0.029	.16	0.027	0.026	.03
Single parent	−3.827*	1.760	−.04	−0.284**	0.095	−.07	−0.183*	0.082	−.05
Step-family	−4.596*	2.161	−.04	−0.436***	0.116	−.09	−0.314**	0.101	−.06
Female Id.	8.125***	1.494	.11	0.461***	0.080	.13	0.245***	0.071	.07
Year in school	18.919***	1.488	.25	−0.490***	0.080	−.14	−0.992***	0.073	−.29
Parent time	−0.118	0.085	−.03	0.003	0.005	.02	0.006	0.004	.04
Chores time	−0.694***	0.119	−.13	−0.029***	0.006	−.12	−0.010	0.006	−.04
Friends time	−0.455***	0.089	−.10	−0.019***	0.005	−.10	−0.007	0.004	−.03
Television time	0.161	0.096	.04	0.005	0.005	−.02	0.001	0.005	.00
Radio and records	−0.347***	0.090	−.08	−0.013**	0.005	−.07	−0.004	0.004	−.02
Leisure reading	0.206	0.115	.04	−0.001	0.006	−.01	−0.007	0.005	−.03
Homework time	0.031	0.144	.00	0.044***	0.008	.14	0.043***	0.007	.14
Constant	725.413***	3.651		4.789***	0.196		−14.466***	0.870	
R Squared	.426***			.195***			.391***		
Adj. R Squared		.421			.188			.386	
Number of Cases		1596			1596			1596	

* p<.05. ** p<.01. ***p<.001.

Product Moment Correlation Matrix (continued)

9	10	11	12	13	14	15	16
.28	.05	.28	.15	.16	.17	–.42	–.16
–.17	–.05	–.16	–.10	–.05	.01	.36	.24
–.23	–.08	–.18	–.13	–.07	–.03	.49	.27
.05	.07	.10	.10	.03	–.04	–.16	–.13
.00	.02	–.05	.06	.03	–.03	–.03	–.09
.05	–.02	–.04	.15	.11	.11	.07	.13
–.09	.03	–.13	.10	–.05	–.06	.34	–.11
.30	.15	.23	.09	.18	.18	–.17	–.02
1.00	.20	.21	.29	.35	.28	–.32	–.17
	1.00	.15	.28	.16	–.01	–.18	–.17
		1.00	.20	.22	–.00	–.19	–.08
			1.00	.29	.11	–.18	–.16
				1.00	.22	–.11	–.05
					1.00	–.09	.12
						1.00	.51
							1.00

and grades were determined by long-term antecedent factors and contemporaneous factors, but that long-term antecedents were less important and contemporaneous factors were more important in the determination of grades than in the determination of achievement. If, therefore, an independent variable had a stronger effect on grades than on academic achievement, I assumed that the variable's effect on academic success was mediated more by contemporaneous variables than by long-term antecedents of cumulative learning, especially if the effect on grades held up or increased when achievement was taken into account.

Divergent Effects of Black Identity on Achievement and Grades

Table 2 shows that black identity had a moderately strong negative effect on achievement, a weak negative effect on grades when achievement was not controlled, but a weak positive effect on grades when achievement was taken into account. The respective standardized partial regression coefficients (Betas) were –.233 ($p< .001$), –.064 ($p< .05$), and .072 ($p< .01$). African-American students had substantially lower achievement and slightly lower grades than whites, but their grades were slightly higher than those of the white students when achievement scores were controlled. In relation to the assumptions stated earlier, this pattern would suggest that black identity affected school success negatively through long-term antecedent factors but affected school success positively through contemporaneous factors. There are, however, three reasons to doubt this interpretation of the effects of black identity.

First, some theory and research has suggested that academic achievement tests underestimate the cumulative learning of black students and are, therefore, less valid for blacks than for whites (e.g., Osborne, 1995; Steele and Aronson, 1995). As much as that is the case, we must doubt the negative effect of black identity on academic achievement and the positive effect of black identity on school grades when achievement is controlled.

Second, some research has indicated that black students tend to exaggerate their grades in self-reports of school grades (Kaufman and Rasinski, 1991; National Center for Educational Statistics, 1984). If that is the case, we must doubt the positive effect of black identity on grades when academic achievement is controlled.

Finally, as I mentioned, listwise deletion of missing data resulted in higher attrition among black than among white respondents, reducing blacks from 48.2 percent of the sample to 41.1 percent of those included in the statistical analyses. If students who failed to respond to some items in the questionnaire were less conscientious than those who left no blanks, then we can assume that the blacks included in the analyses tended to be more conscientious than black students in their schools and that this difference was greater than the equivalent difference among the whites. Furthermore, there is reason to assume that conscientious attitudes will affect students' grades, because extensive research evidence has shown that grades are strongly related to teacher perceptions of such variables as student work habits and disruptiveness (Farkas, Grobe, Sheehan, and Shuan, 1990; Farkas, Sheehan, and Grobe, 1990). According to the findings of Farkas and associates, teachers would give higher grades, relative to coursework mastery, to black students whom they perceived as more conscientious than their other black students. Therefore, the pattern of attrition might account for the fact that controlling academic achievement changed the effect of black identity on grades from negative to positive. Previous research has also suggested that this shift could have been influenced by measurement error in either achievement test results or self-reported grades for black students; therefore the effects of black identity in the current analyses cannot be interpreted as the other results will be interpreted, in terms of contemporaneous variables and long-term factors affecting cumulative learning.

Socioeconomic Variables

Parental formal education and occupation had positive effects in all three of the analyses, but the effects varied considerably in strength. Education had equivalent moderate effects on achievement and on grades when achievement was not controlled. The respective Betas were .121 and .122 ($p < .001$). However, the effect on grades was weakened when achievement was taken into account (Beta = .051, $p < .05$), suggesting that the effect of parental education on academic success partly involved long-term antecedents but also was partly mediated by contemporaneous variables, such as effort.

Parental occupation had a moderately strong effect on academic achievement (Beta = .233, $p < .001$), a moderate effect on grades when achievement was not controlled (Beta = .164, $p < .001$), and essentially no effect on grades with achievement taken into account (Beta = .028, nonsignificant). This pattern suggests that the association between parental occupational status and adolescent academic success is primarily a result of the relationship between parental occupation and long-term antecedents of cumulative learning, such as intellectual ability and aspects of childhood environment. Contemporaneous variables, such as the student's academic effort during adolescence, appear to play little or no role in the association.

Family Structure

The two dummy variables representing different conditions of parental separation had weak negative effects across the board. Living in a single-parent family had negative effects on academic achievement (Beta = –.044, $p < .05$), on school grades (Beta = –.072, $p < .01$), and on grades when achievement was taken into account (Beta = –.046, $p < .05$). Similarly, living with one biological parent and a step-parent had negative effects on achievement (Beta = –.042, $p < .05$), on grades (Beta = –.088, $p < .001$), and on grades with achievement controlled (Beta = –.063, $p < .01$). Therefore, the weak negative effects of parental separation were somewhat stronger, if still weak, in the case of grades than in the case of achievement scores, and the effects on grades were reduced only slightly when achievement was controlled. The pattern suggests that separation of the biological parents has a small negative effect on academic success, which results partly from long-term antecedents of cumulative learning prior to adolescence and partly from differences in effort made during adolescence and other contemporaneous variables, with, perhaps, somewhat more of the effect related to contemporaneous than to long-term factors.

Age and Gender

Year in School

The ninth graders had higher achievement scores but lower grades than the seventh-grade students. The respective Betas were .253 and –.144 ($p < .001$). (The much stronger negative effect on grades with achievement controlled—Beta = –.293—is theoretically meaningless, as the naturally higher achievement scores of the ninth graders, resulting from two additional years of maturation and learning, further depressed their grades, relative to those of the seventh graders, when achievement was controlled.) It appears that ninth graders have higher levels of academic achievement than seventh graders: that is to say that they know somewhat more of what is taught in school. However, the older students report lower grades than the younger ones, suggesting that they may put in less effort, relative to what teachers expect of them.

Gender

Female identity had a positive effect on academic achievement (Beta = .108, $p < .001$) and a slightly stronger positive effect on grades (Beta = .134, $p < .001$). Controlling achievement reduced the effect on grades considerably (Beta = .071, $p < .001$). This pattern suggests that female identity affects academic success through long-term antecedents and through contemporaneous variables operating during adolescence. The research of Farkas and associates (Farkas, Grobe, Sheehan, and Shaun, 1990; Farkas, Sheehan, and Grobe, 1990) indicates that the positive effect of female identity on grades results from behavior in school that is more pleasing to teachers than the behavior of males.

Time Use

Three time-use variables—time spent with the parent, watching TV, and in leisure reading—will not be discussed, as they did not have statistically significant effects on either achievement scores or grades.

Three of the time-use variables—time spent on household chores, with friends, and listening to radio and recordings—had statistically significant negative effects on academic achievement. The Betas ranged from .083 to .133 ($p < .001$). These variables also had slightly weaker but statistically significant negative effects on grades, when achievement was not controlled. The Betas ranged from .071 to .121 (p's were less than .001 or .01). When achievement was taken into account, however, these negative effects on grades became nonsignificant (Betas ranged from –.022 to –.044). This pattern suggests that the effects on academic success from time spent on chores, with friends, and listening to radio and recordings are connected with long-term antecedents of cumulative learning, rather than being direct effects of time use during adolescence. Based on the present data, it is not possible to determine what long-term antecedents are operative. For example, these relationships may be spurious results of intellectual ability or they may be related to long-term patterns of time use established in childhood.

One of the time-use variables —time spent on homework—had no effect on academic achievement (Beta = .004, nonsignificant) but a moderate positive effect on grades (Beta = .139, $p < .001$). The effect on grades remained essentially the same when achievement was taken into account (Beta = .137, $p < .001$). It appears that the effect of homework time on grades is not a spurious result of long-term antecedents. Rather, the pattern of the findings suggests that time devoted to homework during adolescence influences contemporaneous school grades, perhaps through increased learning in current courses, increased grade credit for the homework, and more favorable teacher attitudes toward the student.

Discussion

The findings show that some of the results of research on academic success depend on whether the indicator of academic success is academic achievement scores or school grades. The positive effect of parental occupational status was somewhat weaker, and the negative effect of black identity was much weaker when grades were used, rather than achievement scores. By contrast, the negative effect of living with a step-parent was somewhat stronger on grades than on achievement; and time spent on homework had a substantial positive effect on grades, even though it had no effect on achievement scores. Furthermore, controlling academic achievement markedly changed the effects of several independent variables on grades. The effect of black identity changed from negative to positive. Positive effects of female gender and parental education became considerably weaker. The statistically significant positive effect of parental occupation and negative effects of time spent on household chores, with friends, and listening to radio and recordings became nonsignificant.

The pattern of effects of black identity could not be interpreted with any assurance because of the possibilities of greater error in the measurements of academic achievement and self-reported grades and the possibility of greater selectivity for "conscientiousness" among black than among white students included in the analyses.

In the other results, the differences in effects on achievement scores and grades and the results of controlling achievement when examining effects on grades have been tentatively interpreted in relation to effects on academic success from long-term antecedent factors affecting cumulative learning, such as intellectual ability, which influence achievement scores more than grades, and contemporaneous variables, such as academic effort during adolescence, which influence recent grades more than achievement scores. According to this interpretation, a stronger effect from an independent variable on grades than on achievement scores indicates that the relationship between the independent variable and academic success primarily involves recent or contemporaneous effects. If the independent variable has a substantially stronger effect on achievement scores than on grades or if the effect on grades disappears when achievement is controlled, the interpretation assumes that the relationship between the independent variable and academic success primarily involves long-term effects on cumulative learning. If the effects on achievement scores and grades are similar and the effect on grades holds up when achievement is controlled, the interpretation assumes that long-term and contemporaneous effects are important. These interpretations, of course, must remain tentative until they are tested in further research. However, the results of the present study demonstrate that standardized achievement scores and school grades may yield markedly different results as indicators of academic success.

The choice of an indicator ought to be determined by the aspect of academic success one is trying to measure, and the appropriate aspect to measure ought to be selected with one's independent variables in mind. Standardized achievement scores indicate long-term cumulative learning. Therefore, we cannot expect contemporaneous behaviors and events to affect them. For that reason, for example, the negative relationship between achievement scores and time spent currently listening to radio and recordings had to be confounded by antecedent variables, such as intellectual ability or long-term patterns of time use. Recent grades indicate current success in courses, partly determined by long-term cumulative learning but also partly determined by more contemporaneous variables. For example, controlling academic achievement when examining the effect of parental occupation on school grades indicated that the effect of occupation operated through its effect on long-term cumulative learning, not through effects on contemporaneous behaviors.

Further research is needed to examine the interpretations of the statistical effects in the present study. It is important that sociologists sort out the mechanisms by which social structural and social behavioral factors affect variables of sociological interest, such as academic success. Without an understanding of the mechanisms involved, we will inevitably at times attribute causality to spurious relationships and devise fallacious interpretations of actual causal relationships.

References

Astone, Nan Marie, and Sarah S. McLanahan. 1991. "Family Structure, Parental Practices and High School Completion." *American Sociological Review* 56: 309–320.

Chipuer, Heather M., Michael J. Rovin, and Robert Plomin. 1990. "LISREL Modeling: Genetic and Environmental Influences on IQ Revisited." *Intelligence* 14: 11–29.

CTB/McGraw-Hill. 1982. *Comprehensive Tests of Basic Skills Technical Report.* Monterey, California: McGraw-Hill.

Farkas, George, Robert P. Grobe, Daniel Sheehan, and Yuan Shuan. 1990. "Cultural Resources and School Success: Gender, Ethnicity and Poverty Groups within an Urban School District." *American Sociological Review* 55: 127–142.

Farkas, George, Daniel Sheehan, and Robert P. Grobe. 1990. "Coursework Mastery and School Success: Gender, Ethnicity and Poverty Groups within an Urban School District." *American Educational Research Journal* 27: 807–827.

Fehrmann, Paul G., Timothy Z. Keith, and Thomas M. Reimers. 1987. "Home Influence on School Learning: Direct and Indirect Effects of Parental Involvement on High School Grades." *Journal of Educational Research* 80: 330–337.

Gamoran, Adam. 1992. "The Variable Effects of High School Tracking." *American Sociological Review* 57: 812–828.

Hollingshead, August B. 1957. *Two-factor Index of Social Position.* New Haven: Author.

Kaufman, Philip, and Kenneth A. Rasinski. 1991. *National Education Longitudinal Study of 1988: Quality of the Responses of Students.* Washington, D.C.: U.S. Department of Education, National Center for Education Statistics.

Keith, Timothy Z. 1982. "Time Spent on Homework and High School Grades: A Large-sample Path Analysis." *Journal of Educational Psychology* 74: 248–253.

Keith, Timothy Z., Thomas M. Reimers, Paul G. Fehrmann, Sheila M. Pottebaum, and Linda W. Aubey. 1986. "Parental Involvement, Homework and TV Time: Direct and Indirect Effects on High School Achievement." *Journal of Educational Psychology* 78: 373–380.

Kerckhoff, Alan C. 1972. *Socialization and Social Class.* Englewood Cliffs, New Jersey: Prentice Hall, Inc.

Milne, Ann M., David E. Myers, Alvin S. Rosenthal, and Alan Ginsburg. 1986. "Single Parents, Working Mothers and the Educational Achievement of School Children." *Sociology of Education* 59: 125–139.

National Center for Educational Statistics. 1984. *Quality of Responses of High School Students to Questionnaire Items.* Washington, D.C.: U.S. Government Printing Office.

Natriello, G., and E. L. McDill. 1986. "Performance Standards, Student Effort on Homework and Academic Achievement." *Sociology of Education* 59: 18–31.

Rodgers, Joseph L., and David C. Rowe. 1987. "IQ Similarity in Twins, Siblings, Half Siblings, Cousins, and Random Pairs." *Intelligence* 11: 199–206.

Sattler, Gerome M. 1982. *Assessment of Children's Intelligence and Special Abilities* 2nd ed. Boston: Allyn and Bacon.

Smith, Thomas Ewin, 1990. "Time and Academic Achievement." *Journal of Youth and Adolescence* 19: 539–558.

SPSS. 1986. *SPSSx User's Guide.* New York: McGraw-Hill.

Storfer, Miles D. 1990. *Intelligence and Giftedness: the Contributions of Heredity and Early Environment.* San Francisco: Jossey-Bass.

Streissguth, Ann P., Helen M. Barr, Paul D. Samson, and Betty L. Darby. 1989. "IQ at Age Four in Relation to Maternal Alcohol Use and Smoking During Pregnancy." *Journal of Developmental Psychology* 25: 3–11.

Article Review Form at end of book.

WiseGuide Wrap-Up

Of all the possible solutions to many of our nation's social problems, education is heralded as the most promising. Without a solid educational foundation, many people suffering from the effects of poverty, racism, and crime are hard-pressed to discover any level of success in society. However, as the readings in this section have shown, even obtaining a quality education presents problems for some people since it, too, is unequally distributed. The biases built into the effects of being tracked into nonacademic categories can result in inadequate educational opportunities for many children.

R.E.A.L. Sites

This list provides a print preview of typical **coursewise** R.E.A.L. sites. (There are over 100 such sites at the **courselinks**™ site.) The danger in printing URLs is that web sites can change overnight. As we went to press, these sites were functional using the URLs provided. If you come across one that isn't, please let us know via email to: webmaster@coursewise.com. Use your Passport to access the most current list of R.E.A.L. sites at the **courselinks**™ site.

Site name: Magnet Schools of America
URL: http://www.magnet.edu/index.html
Why is it R.E.A.L.? This site provides information about magnet schools, their mission, as well as conferences and opportunities for children who attend them.
Key topics: membership, conferences, background information

Site name: The LSS Urban Education Enhancement Program
URL: http://www.temple.edu/LSS/ue.html
Why is it R.E.A.L.? This site offers a ray of hope for the problems facing inner-city schools. It combines in-depth research with practical community programs designed to improve the quality of education in American cities.
Key topics: community building, role models, empowerment

section 5

Learning Objectives

After reading these articles, you should be able to

- Understand why women find it so difficult to leave violent relationships.
- Define stalking and the different types of stalking behavior.
- Describe the problems women have encountered in the military.

Gender Inequalities

In many ways, our society has become more sensitive to issues surrounding the concepts of race. We have also become cognizant, to some degree, of the ways in which the poor struggle to achieve the American dream. However, we still have difficulty understanding issues relating to gender. In many ways, we remain unenlightened to women experiencing similar, if not worse, discrimination than racial minorities. A good example is the Shannon Faulkner case in South Carolina. The Citadel is a state-funded military school that was exclusively male until Faulkner applied. Of the people who have an opinion about this case, none would argue that an African American should not be allowed to apply for admission to the school. Yet, because Faulkner was a woman, somehow that type of discrimination was acceptable. Thus, our lack of understanding of women in society and stereotypical images of women prevail and cloud our thinking about fairness and opportunities for everyone.

The readings in this section describe some of the practical problems women face in American society. In the first reading, Denise Donnelly describes how and in what ways women leave violent relationships. She also looks at their experiences living in battered women's shelters. To show the subtlety with which we stereotype women, Livia Pohlman then uses a series of advertising campaigns to demonstrate how we continue to perceive women as sexual objects. Next, N. Jane McCandless examines an extreme version of the objectification of women: stalking. In her discussion, she offers us insights into the different types of stalkers, as well as their motivations for engaging in this type of behavior. Finally, Gina Carreño uses feminist standpoint theory, as well as a theory of masculinities, to address one of the most controversial issues in recent times: women in the military.

Questions

Reading 20. Why do you think society is quick to judge battered women and question their lack of ability to leave an abusive relationship? Why are battered women least satisfied with social services and follow-up care? What can be done to change this?

Reading 21. Do you believe that current advertisements of powerful women continue to portray inferiority? Are the differences between advertisements featuring women and advertisements featuring men crucial? What impact does this have on society?

Reading 22. Stalking is one of the most frightening crimes in our society. However, it is not a new phenomenon. What do you think causes stalking? Is it simply that the people who engage in this activity are psychologically unbalanced or are there sociological explanations for it? How does society prevent stalking? Is there some way we can dissuade individuals from engaging in it? Would additional laws and penalties deter people or must we simply accept stalking as a consequence of living in an industrialized society?

Reading 23. Do you think that gender equality should entail equality among the sexes, or equal respect and opportunities between the sexes? Do you agree with Smith's assessment that women are still trying to escape their exclusion from the male creation of American culture? How do women's struggles in the military reflect this assessment?

Why do you think society is quick to judge battered women and question their lack of ability to leave an abusive relationship? Why are battered women least satisfied with social services and follow-up care? What can be done to change this?

Battered Women's Experiences with Leaving Violent Relationships

Denise Donnelly
Georgia State University

My early home life wasn't so good—my dad was an alcoholic, and he'd always get drunk and yell at my mom and me. I don't think he ever hit my mom, but he'd break things and stomp around and yell. My mom, she was scared of him, and tried to stay out of his way. When I was 16, I got this job working at McDonald's so I wouldn't have to be home much and because I needed the money. That's where I met Bart. He was older, around 20, and he'd come in all the time on his breaks [from working construction]. We got to talking, and he asked me out. He was really the only boyfriend I had, and we got married right after I finished high school. Our little girl Jessie was born a year later, and Johnny . . . 14 months after that. Jessie's almost two now, and Johnny is 9 months old. Bart really didn't get violent until after we were married, but he was jealous of me from the first . . . even when we were dating. You know, always thought I was looking at other guys, trying to attract them . . . wanted to know where I'd been, and always calling me. If he couldn't find me, he'd get mad, and accuse me of seeing someone else. I just thought it was cute, and that he did it because he loved me. I'd never had someone love me like that—he was my first real boyfriend and all. The first time he hit me was the day I found out I was pregnant with Jessie. I forgot to take my birth control pills, and when I came home from the doctor and told him I was expecting, he was furious. He called me retarded and said that any stupid idiot could remember to take a pill every day. He didn't want the baby, and I started crying because I wanted to be a mother, I wanted to have his child. My crying made him mad. The madder he got, the more I cried. Finally, he said, "Why don't you shut the hell up?" and he slapped me across the face. I fell into an end table and cut my back, and he left. When he came back three days later, he smelled like . . . ummm . . . that he'd been with another woman. But, he apologized, and I thought he meant it. He went right out and bought a bunch of baby stuff, like a crib and furniture, to show me how sorry he was. For a while, things were really good between us, but then he started pushing and slapping me maybe once or twice a month . . . just about whenever we'd fight, he'd shake me, or slap me, or pull my hair. When he'd get mad, he'd always bring up how he didn't want kids and how I was a cow who kept making babies. He'd tell me how stupid I was, and how no man would ever want me. About three months ago, he decided that he didn't want to be married anymore, and that he wanted to see other people. He said he felt trapped, and that he was too young (he's 24) to be saddled down with a wife and kids. I mean two kids later, and he doesn't want to be married? What am I supposed to do? He started seeing this other woman, and he moved in with her for a while. When he came home to get his stuff, I begged him to stay. So he stayed the night, and things went really well . . . he said he missed me, and we made love and all. I thought we'd be okay, but then he didn't come home from work the next Friday night. I had my friend Sheila take me to where this girl he's seeing lives. I went in to talk to him, and he got really, really mad because he hadn't told her he was married. He pulled me by my hair all the way to the car and drove back to our apartment. He was driving really fast, and I was scared we'd have a wreck. He kicked me in the butt all the way from the car to the apartment, and was screaming about how I'd embarrassed him, and he was tired of me and these babies and he never wanted them in the first place. When we got in the apartment, he . . . hit me several times, knocked me on the floor and kicked me in the ribs. It hurt so bad I couldn't get up, so I lay there for a long time. It got real quiet, and I thought he'd left. I finally was able to crawl to the bathroom, and I was washing my face. Well, he'd been in the bedroom upstairs, and when he heard the water running, he came back downstairs, and when he saw me, he ran down the hall and tackled me like a football player or something. I hit my head on the top of the vanity (it was marble) really hard and blacked out for a second. My friend came in with the kids a little later and found me, and took me to the emergency room. I had a concussion, and a couple of cracked ribs. One of my teeth was chipped, and both my eyes were black. I had to have over 30 stitches where my head split open. . . . I spent the night in the hospital, and then they brought me and the kids here to the battered women's shelter. All I want . . . all I've ever wanted . . . is to be Bart's wife and to be the mother of his children. I'm a religious person—I truly believe that marriage is forever, and I want to make this work. I mean, I don't understand, he never wanted me to even look at another man, and now he's gone and found another woman. It just doesn't make sense . . . you know? I don't know what I'm going to do now. . . . I know he's wrong to hit me, but I really wish we could make it work.

—Jenny, age 20, mother of two, married three years, clerical worker

Women's Experiences with Violence

Stories such as this are repeated every day in every city around the country. Although public awareness and disapproval of woman battering have grown tremendously, researchers estimate that one in ten American women are beaten by their husbands and partners each year (Straus and Gelles, 1986). The American Medical Association predicts that as many as one-quarter of women will be physically abused by a partner during their lifetimes (Flitcraft, 1992). For many women, violence is not a one time occurrence; it is a fact of everyday life, occurring with frightening regularity (Langan and Innes, 1986). Woman battering is a social problem of enormous magnitude.

Not all battered women are as young as Jenny, and not all are working class. While woman battering is more common among the young and those at the lower end of the socioeconomic scale, it occurs across all age, race, and income groups (Straus, Gelles, and Steinmetz, 1980). Contrary to popular beliefs, alcohol or drugs are not always factors in woman battering (Kaufman-Kantor and Straus, 1990). Nor are heterosexual women the only victims of battering—lesbian women; gay men, and even straight men—can also be the targets of intimate violence (Renzetti, 1992; Donnelly and Kenyon, 1996). Heterosexual women make up the overwhelming majority of battered women; therefore, this chapter focuses on their experiences.

Often, when stories such as Jenny's appear in the news, people ask "Why did she stay with someone who beat her?" They assume that because the woman is an adult, she can leave any time she wants. In many ways, this view blames the victim and doesn't take into account the numerous complicated reasons that prevent women from leaving men who beat them. Rather than focusing on why the man felt that he had the right to hit his wife or partner, on how he continued to get away with battering (many times over months or years), or on whether she tried to get and received help, we focus instead on why she stayed.

In my research, I examined women's experiences with intimate violence, their decisions to leave (even temporarily) abusive relationships, and their help-seeking behaviors. My aim was not to blame battered women for their problems, nor was it to relieve the batterer of responsibility. Rather, the research focused on giving women a chance to tell their stories, in their words, in an attempt to better understand the barriers and decisions that women face when they leave their abusers.

The stories told in this chapter come from in-depth interviews conducted with battered women in one rural Southeastern county. I began this research after three years of volunteer work (as hotline counselor and shelter worker) that brought me into contact with a variety of battered women and children in a number of situations. I talked with thirty-two women over a six-month period. Each gave permission for her interview to be used in research publications. While names were changed and minor details altered slightly or omitted to insure safety and preserve privacy, the stories presented are as the women told them.

Twelve women were residing in a battered women's shelter at the time of the interview, and twenty were living alone or with their children, friends, or family members. Most of the nonsheltered women were approached as they waited for their requests for temporary protective orders to be heard by the judge or while waiting for other social services. I asked the women a series of questions about their lives, previous experiences with violence, decisions to leave, and their help-seeking behaviors. If they agreed, the interview was tape recorded and transcribed later. If not, I took detailed notes and reconstructed the interview immediately upon returning to my office.

The majority of women who participated in this study were white, reflecting the racial/ethnic distribution of the county where the interviews were conducted. Of the thirty-two women I talked with, only three were women of color (one African American, one Latina, and one Pacific Islander). Most were young, and all but one had children (though three were not living with their children at the time of the interview). Only four women were over thirty-five, and none were over forty-five. Most came from the working or lower middle-class, and most had been homemakers or were working at low-paying jobs when the violence took place. All the women in my sample were living apart from their partners at the time of the interview.

The types of violence perpetrated on the women in my study ran the gamut from fairly minor physical violence such as pushing or hair pulling, to moderate violence such as slapping, hitting and kicking, to severe violence such as being threatened with a weapon, hit with a fist, pushed out of a moving vehicle, pushed down stairs, or dropped from a window. Thirteen percent had experienced only minor violence, 68 percent at least moderate violence, and 19 percent severe violence. Every woman that I interviewed had been emotionally abused (name calling, ridicule, or humiliation in front of others), and sexual abuse (ranging from unwanted sex to bondage, torture, and rape) occurred in all but two cases. Economic abuse (such as destroying property or withholding money) was reported by 81 percent of the women.

Sarah, who was living with Bennie when he became abusive, is an example of a woman who experienced fairly mild violence, yet decided to seek help because of past experience. I met her while she was waiting for her court case to be called.

> Bennie wasn't that violent before [the incident that lead to his arrest], but he's always threatening me and calling me names. Sometimes he'd shake me or say he was gonna hit me, but he never did. He's not working right now, and we completely ran out of money a couple weeks ago. He wanted me to borrow money from my mom, but I was too embarrassed. We started fighting, and I told him that if he wasn't too lazy to hold a job, we might have some money. So, he got really mad, and turned over the [dining room] table and then he started punching his fist through the wall. I got scared and asked him to stop because we'll lose our deposit [on the trailer], and he came and stood over me and grabbed my shoulders and started shaking me. Then, he lifted me up and shoved me back in the chair really hard. He went in the kitchen and got a beer, and walked out. I put the baby in the stroller and walked to my mom's. I went down and took out a temporary protective order the next day. I was married to an abuser before, and I don't intend to take this from Bennie.
>
> —Sarah, age 27, stay-at-home mother of a six-month-old daughter.

Stories like Sarah's are fairly rare, because most women don't leave the first time physical abuse occurs, and if they do, they tend to return to their abusers (Gondolf, 1988). Sarah, because of past experience, recognized the potential for violence to escalate, and left before the situation worsened. Sarah's two older children (from her first marriage) were living with her mother because their father (Sarah's ex-husband) had abused them, and child protective services had removed them from the home. Sarah was working toward being reunited with her children, so she was especially motivated to leave Bennie at the first sign of violence. When I talked with her six months after the original interview, she was working at a fast food restaurant (having been promoted to assistant manager) and living with her mother and three children.

Other women, like Melanie in the following case, experience violence over a longer period. Typically, the violence escalates until it becomes so bad that they leave, the abuser is arrested, or too frequently, the woman is murdered (Browne, 1987). Often, women only leave their batterers (as Jenny did) when they are seriously injured, they believe they will be killed, or when a child is hurt (Snyder and Fruchtman, 1981). In Melanie's case, the abuse had gone on over a long period and continued to worsen as time passed. She left her situation only after her husband was violent toward her son. An articulate and middle-class woman in her early thirties, Melanie commented:

> I am in my second marriage. The first one was abusive too. I have an 11-year-old son from my first marriage and a 4-year-old daughter from my second. My second husband, Tony, was so nice when we were dating. So gentle, and so different from my first husband. But then it started. A couple of months after we were married he started grabbing me. When he'd get mad, he'd grab me and hold me and make me listen to him. I was a little scared, but figured that he wasn't really hitting me, so I never thought about leaving. But it didn't stop, and

it got worse. By the time our daughter was born, he was slapping me and shoving me. And he started kicking me on my legs, or he'd grab my arm and not let go, and I'd have fingerprints. Or, he'd hold me down and pin my arms down and slap me. He'd always apologize after it was over, but things kept getting worse. The last time, before I left him, I don't even remember what we were arguing about. He got me on the couch, and he laid down on top of me so I couldn't get up and he yelled right in my face. Then he straddled my waist with his legs and started slapping me in the face. The children saw, and they were begging him to stop. He picked my son up and tossed him across the room. The baby was crying so hard she was losing her breath, and my son was so startled and stunned (he wasn't hurt) that he just sat there. I knew then that I had to leave, so I waited until Tony left for work the next day, and I took the car and came to the shelter.

—Melanie, age 33, twice married mother of two, working as a dental hygienist

The abuse that Melanie experienced was fairly typical of the experiences of women in the sample, but 1 in 5 (19 percent) had experienced even more severe attacks. Sandra's story is an example of a woman who was almost killed because of her partner's violence. Sandra is a 22-year-old woman living with her boyfriend at the time of the violent incident that led to his arrest. After she was released from the hospital, she came to the shelter. Her story illustrates the impact of a lifetime of abuse:

As far back as I can remember, men have been violent with me. First my daddy, then my step-father, even my boyfriends. My step-father raped me when I was 11 or 12, and I started using drugs to deal with that. Two years ago, I was back at the hospital to get dried out, and I met Mike. He was working maintenance at the hospital, and we used to talk when I'd go out for a smoke. When I got out of the hospital, I moved in with him. He wasn't violent at first, but he destroyed some of my clothes because they were too sexy, and some of my country music tapes because he thought they were trashy sounding. Then I started using drugs again, and he hated that, and that's when he started hitting me. Said I was a whore, and an addict, and worthless bag of bones. I got pregnant, and quit using, and he stopped [hitting] for a while. But after our daughter was born, he got bad again. He wouldn't let me work, and had the phone taken out so I couldn't use it. He wouldn't let me see my friends. I wasn't supposed to leave the apartment—he even went grocery shopping with me. The day I had to go to the hospital [because of injuries from abuse], he came home from work, and accused me of taking some of his pain pills [for a back injury]. He said he was missing a bunch of pills, and accused me of taking them. He beat me up really bad, and would dunk me in the bathtub [filled with cold water] to wake me up when I passed out. He did this several times, and finally he calmed down and apologized. He told me that he was sorry for hurting me, but that it was my fault. Then he wanted to have sex to make up and all. I couldn't, just couldn't, because I hurt all over. So, he got mad again, and said that I must be sleeping with someone else. When I told him I was hurt too bad, he got even madder and held me out the window of our apartment by one arm, and dropped me in the bushes under our window. We live on the second story, so I was all scratched up and bleeding, and I crawled under the shrubs to rest. He came down after a while, and said he'd take me to the hospital. After we were in the car, he got mad again, and said that I was a no good whore, taking his pills and sleeping around. I wouldn't answer him or look at him, so he slowed down and opened the car door while we were going down the highway and pushed me out. I rolled into a ditch, and the people behind us stopped and carried me to the hospital. The police arrested Mike the next day. He's still in jail right now.

—Sandra, age 22, never married, recovering addict, mother of one, unemployed

Sandra's story was one of the most heartbreaking I heard. She also told of Mike destroying her property (once, when he thought she was dressing too provocatively, he threw all her clothes in the bathtub and dumped a bottle of bleach on them). Sexual abuse and torture were also common. He often forced Sandra to have sex with his friends while he videotaped. She told of waking at night with his hand over her mouth as he forcibly anally raped her. Sandra was afraid to leave because Mike had threatened to kill her and their daughter if she tried. Given his past behavior, she had every reason to believe that he would.

Common Themes in the Stories of Abused Women

While I soon learned that there is no such thing as a "typical" case of intimate assault, the stories presented here share common elements and help to illustrate what family violence researchers know about abusive relationships. For example, many victims of violence have histories of growing up in violent households and of experiencing violent relationships as adults (Doumas, Margolin, and John, 1994). All four of the women discussed previously had experienced violence in past relationships. Sarah and Melanie had been in battering relationships previous to their current relationships, and

Jenny and Sandra had grown up in violent households. Of the thirty-two women I interviewed, only two (6 percent) said that their current relationship was the first in which any sort of violence had taken place. Family violence researchers speculate that growing up in a violent household may lead one to see violence as a normal and expected part of adulthood (Doumas et al., 1994; Hotaling and Sugarman, 1986), and women who have experienced intimate violence as adults may become desensitized to warning signs in future relationships (Holiman and Schilit, 1991).

Another common theme in the interviews was that violence started early in the relationship. For many women, like Sandra, violence occurs almost from the time they meet their future partners (Roscoe and Benaske, 1985). For others, like Sarah, Jenny, and Melanie, violence begins in the first year of marriage or cohabitation. All the women I talked with noted that violence did not suddenly start after five, ten, or fifteen years—it was there from almost the beginning.

For most of the women in my sample, violence escalated over time. What started out as psychological abuse, or mild physical violence, later became severe abuse that caused (or had the potential to cause) permanent physical or mental impairment. For Jenny, Bart's violent behavior began as jealousy and control, but escalated into physical abuse early in the relationship. Likewise, Sandra's abuse began with her property being destroyed, then almost immediately progressed to physical violence, and from there to sexual abuse and torture. Melanie's abuser began with grabbing (which she didn't define as "real" violence), and subtly moved on to more severe forms of violence, such as pinching and slapping. In every case, physical abuse was accompanied by at least one other type of abuse. Psychological abuse was most common, with batterers literally wearing down their victims through intimidation, control, and humiliation.

Though researchers have found no causal relationships between drug and alcohol use and violence, these substances are often used (by the batterer and the victim) in violent relationships. While substance use doesn't cause violence, it may be used by the abuser as an excuse to batter (Collins and Schlenger, 1988) or to relieve the guilt of battering (Kaufman-Kantor and Straus, 1990). Victims often use alcohol or drugs as a way of mitigating the physical and emotional pain of abuse (Hotaling and Sugarman, 1990). In my sample, alcohol or drugs were present in over half the battering incidents described.

Another element associated with battering is stress. Finn (1985) found that financial problems, unemployment, alcoholism, unplanned pregnancies, and other family problems were more common in families where abuse was taking place. My sample was no exception. In Jenny's case, as with many battered women (Helton, 1987), an unplanned pregnancy preceded physical violence. For Sarah, financial problems and unemployment seemed to contribute, while in Sandra's situation it was drug abuse. Although stress may have contributed to the violence, we should not forget that the male partner in each of these situations made a conscious decision to use violence, as opposed to another way of dealing with stress. One woman that I talked with noted that her husband explained hitting her as "his way of calming down." It is also possible that stress is used as an excuse for battering, as a way of relieving the batterer of responsibility for his actions after a violent incident has taken place.

As the previous stories illustrate, battering is about power and control (Paymar, 1993). Husbands and boyfriends believe that they have the right to control every aspect of the woman's life. They disregard boundaries and fail to respect their partner's body, her possessions, or her mental well-being. Jealousy is common among batterers, and because of this, they may try to isolate their partners from friends, coworkers, and families, or they may try to keep tabs on her every movement, as Sandra's story illustrates.

A final commonality in the stories that I heard was that after the battering, the abuser was sorry for what he'd done and often very apologetic. Lenore Walker (1979) noted that violence may occur in cycles consisting of a buildup phase (where tension mounts), a blowup phase (where battering occurs), and a makeup phase (where the batterer is apologetic and romantic after the battering event). According to the women I interviewed, batterers often used charm and manipulation to get them to stay. In Jenny's case (at least initially), it was new furniture for the baby. Sarah's partner continued to call and beg her to come back for several months after she left, and Melanie's husband always apologized and seemed sorry for what he'd done. Sandra's boyfriend also apologized for hurting her, but then would hurt her again, often almost as soon as he'd apologized. Each of these men was using kindness and apologies as ways to manipulate the women in their lives into continuing the relationship. Sadly, when they agreed, they were likely to be battered again.

Reasons for Staying in a Battering Relationship

For most battered women, the decision to end an abusive relationship is difficult. Women stay with their abusers for a variety of complicated reasons. Many stay because of a lack of money. Women with fewer financial resources and limited educations are more likely to stay and more likely to return after leaving, because they can't afford to live as single parents (Johnson, 1992; Strube, 1988). Even women with relatively high family incomes may hesitate to leave, because they know that their standards of living will drop substantially. Women who have never worked, have small children or have low levels of education, often find the costs of housing, food, transportation, and child care beyond their reach. Melanie, for example, was able to leave her batterer only because she moved in with her mother, who provided housing, transportation, and child care.

Some women stay in abusive relationships because of the psychological consequences of prolonged battering and emotional abuse. These injuries may hinder their ability to be employed productively, to make daily decisions regarding their own or their children's well-being or safety, and to sustain family and social relationships (de las Fuentes and Wright, 1991). For some women, such as Sandra, the abuse is so severe that it results in Battered Woman Syndrome (Walker, 1989), recognized as a sub-category of Post-Traumatic Stress Disorder (PTSD). Women with Battered Woman Syndrome frequently experience recurring nightmares, diminished responsiveness, loss of interest in activities, detachment from others, disturbed sleep, memory loss, difficulty concentrating, and avoidance of activities.

Victims of domestic violence, because of past experience, may feel that they can do nothing to change their situations, and may give up trying. They may have tried to leave, without success, or their batterer may have convinced them (through psychological manipulation) that they would be unable to survive if they left (Johnson, 1992). For some, like Jenny in the opening story, the predictability of staying in an abusive situation is more comfortable than the unpredictability of leaving.

Other women stay because they love their batterer or feel that they have invested too much in the relationship to end it (Strube, 1988). They may feel responsible for their partner and guilty over leaving because they believe that the partner cannot make it without them (Ferraro, 1979).

Still others hesitate to leave because they are embarrassed for others to find out about the battering or because they believe that marriage is a lifetime commitment (Vaughn, 1987). They may be pressured by friends, family, and clergy into trying to preserve the relationship. Some stay because they believe it is better for the children to be with their father (even one who is violent) than to be raised by a single parent. Others believe the batterer when he says that he will stop the abuse and stay with him in hopes that the physical violence will end (Aquirre, 1985).

Jenny loved her husband and didn't want to leave him. Even when he began seeing other women and asked for a divorce, she hoped to make it work. As a deeply religious woman, she believed in "the sanctity of marriage" and felt that her commitment was "till death do us part." Ending the marriage was not an option for her.

Another reason that women stay with their batterers is fear. Abusive men often threaten to harm the woman, her children, family members, or pets if she attempts to leave. Research shows that these fears are not ungrounded. Battered women are most at risk for serious harm or death from their abusers when they make life changes, threaten to leave, or actually leave (Snyder and Fruchtman, 1981).

Finally, many women stay because they have nowhere to go. Most people assume that everyone is aware of hotlines and shelters for battered women and that we have sufficient resources to assist women and children in need. As the findings discussed later in this chapter show, however, battered women are often unaware of available services, and even if they are familiar with agencies that can assist them, they may not be able to get the help they need.

The Decision to Leave

When asked why they decided to leave, the women in my sample gave a variety of answers. The most common reason for leaving was concern for their children. Like Melanie in the previous case, Wanda left her husband when she felt his behavior was beginning to endanger her children. Jeff, aged 9, is her son by a previous marriage. Hannah, aged 2, is her daughter by her current husband.

I left because of my kids—I didn't want them in danger. My son, especially. His step-father was spanking him way too hard—beating him really, and expecting too much of him. And Jeff was becoming just like his step-father. He was getting aggressive, he'd lost compassion, and he behaved to his sister like his step-father behaved to him. He started trying to control Hannah . . . stuff like where to sit and what she was doing. If she wouldn't cooperate, he'd slam doors or blow up and yell. He even backhanded her across the face once, and she's just a little kid. He'd get this 'I hate you' look in his eyes. He used to be such a sweet kid. Now, I dunno. . . . I hope it's not too late. I left his father on account of violence, and then married another violent man. I feel like this is my fault.

—Wanda age 28, mother of two, retail sales clerk, married for the second time

Wanda was seeing firsthand the effects of raising her children in a violent household. While concern for her own safety wasn't enough to motivate her to leave, her hopes for a better life for her children were. Like many battered women, she blames herself (rather than her violent husband) for the damage her children have suffered.

Connie was also concerned about her children, but left her husband because of a different type of danger. She suspected him of sexually abusing their six-year-old daughter.

Butch was abusive throughout our marriage, but I never really thought of leaving him until he started in with Christy. He'd hit the boys, but he always treated her like she was a doll . . . very special. . . . Daddy's little girl. Over the last few months, he got to where he wanted to spend a lot of time with her alone. I didn't really think much about it, until she started complaining that her 'pee-pee' hurt. When I asked her what made it hurt, she said that Daddy hurt it when he rubbed her down there. I started asking her questions, and I think he's been fondling her. It just made me sick . . . physically sick . . . and I knew I had to leave him. I mean, hitting me is one thing, but to do sexual things to his own daughter? That's disgusting.

—Connie, age 31, mother of two teenaged boys and a 6-year-old girl, married to Butch for 14 years

Like Wanda, Connie never contemplated ending the relationship until it began to explicitly endanger her youngest child. Only when she suspected Butch of abusing their daughter did she decide to end the relationship and report him to Child Protective Services. Six months later, he was still denying these charges and had sued for joint custody.

Another common reason for deciding to leave an abusive relationship was serious injury or hospitalization, as was the case with Jenny and Sandra, whose stories were presented earlier. Several of the women in my sample mentioned leaving because they feared that next time their husbands or partners might kill them. Barbara was one of these women. She left her husband after he held a gun to her head.

What finally made me leave was when he took a gun and threatened to shoot me. He'd hurt me bad before, and threatened to kill me, but I never believed him 'til then. I'd threatened to leave, and he'd promised me that he'd stop drinking. He came in drunk, and I got mad because it was the same old story, and I'd believed it. I told him that I was leaving. That made him angry, and he shoved me into the kitchen sink. The door was open and I fell under it. He kicked me a few times and went out to his truck. I looked out the window and saw him getting his gun. I picked up the phone to dial 911, and when he walked in and caught me, he pulled the phone out of the wall. I started out the back door, and he yelled that he'd shoot me if I didn't stop. So, I did, and he held the gun to my head for [what seemed like] hours, and said that if he couldn't have me, nobody else would either . . . he wasn't having his kids raised by another man [Charles wrongly suspected Barbara of having an affair with a neighbor who had intervened in an earlier violent incident]. All this time, he was crying and ranting, but not hitting me. But he wouldn't let me go. I finally told him to just go ahead and do it. After a minute he let me go and went in the bedroom, and passed out. You know, I think if he hadn't been so drunk, he'd of done it. I found the truck keys, picked the kids up from school, and went to a gas station and called the police. Then I called the hotline and came to the shelter. I'm leaving to go back to Colorado, where my parents live, next week. I'm afraid he'll kill me if I stay.

—Barbara, age 33, mother of 2 girls, married to Charles for 10 years

Women sometimes used the arrest of their husband or partner as a window of safety in which to leave. Lisa's husband of five years had battered her since before they married. Each time she'd make plans to leave, he'd take the children and go to his brother's house in another state, wouldn't let her take the children, or would threaten to come back and hurt Lisa and her two toddlers.

Greg had been hitting me for years, and at times it would get so bad that I'd threaten to leave. Whenever I'd do that, he'd take the kids and go to his brother's house in [another state] and tell me to go ahead and leave. I'd worry about the kids—let me tell you, he is not a responsible father—and I'd call and apologize and beg him to bring them back. Or, anytime I'd try to go somewhere, he'd keep one of the kids at home and not let me take both with me, like he knew I was about to leave. For the last year, I don't think I ever even left the house with both kids. He'd either come with us, or he'd keep one of them at home. I was finally able to leave because one of our neighbors happened to drive up while Greg was beating me, and called 911 on his car phone. When the police got there, Greg had our daughter in his arms, and was telling our little girl, "Mommy is being bad, she's making me hit her, she wants to take you away from me, and I won't let her." They took one look at me, and arrested him. Since I was afraid he'd get out on bond, they brought the kids and I right to the shelter. We're leaving day after tomorrow to move to another state. I'd probably still be there if that neighbor hadn't driven up when he did.

—Lisa, age 26, stay-at-home mother of two children under age 4

Sadly, it is the woman and her children who often have to leave their homes and rearrange their lives to escape battering. Even when the court awards the family home and financial support to the battered woman, many times she is afraid to stay because the batterer can find her so easily. Although protective orders offer some protection (the batterer can be arrested for coming near his victim), many batterers disregard the order. After all, these are men who violate the law when they batter their wives. Why should a piece of paper suddenly turn them into law abiding citizens?

One of the women that I interviewed briefly while waiting for a hearing on her husband's violation of a protective order told me that even though she was awarded the house and furniture, her ex-husband kept a garage door opener and would routinely let himself in. He damaged furniture and electronic equipment (he once poured crazy glue into her VCR), smoked and left his cigarette butts in evidence, masturbated on her pillow, and even fixed himself meals and left dirty dishes in the sink. Although he never came into the house while she was there, she felt violated and lived in fear of what he might do. Even though her finances were stretched to the limit, she didn't feel safe until she bought a new garage door opener and had an alarm system installed.

Asking for Help

Even when women made the decision to end an abusive relationship, they often ran into difficulties when they tried to leave. Some were too ashamed to ask for help, but most eventually did. Many sought informal assistance from friends, neighbors, and relatives, while others sought help through more formal channels such as the clergy, hotlines and shelters, the legal system, and social services.

Brenda was a stay-at-home mom who left with only the clothes on her back. Friends let her live in their basement until she found a job and apartment. Angela found the courage to leave her abusive husband when her friend Nancy (also a battered woman) decided to leave her husband. They came to the shelter together and later shared a rented apartment with their children. Several other women that I interviewed told similar stories of support from friends.

Some women, like Monica, sought and received help from their families. I met Monica and her mother, Mrs. Johnson, outside the courtroom while they waited for her temporary restraining order (TRO) hearing. They were close, with Mrs. Johnson talking Monica through her fears of seeing Danny (her husband) at the hearing. Monica acknowledged how fortunate she was.

I don't know what I'd have done if it hadn't been for my mom and sisters. When they saw how bad the abuse was getting, they kept telling me that I needed to leave. The last time he beat me, my brother-in-law invited Danny hunting for the weekend, and my sisters and mother came over with a U-Haul and helped me move out. My mom put a deposit down on an apartment, and we took all my furniture and moved it in. When Danny got back, we were gone.

—Monica, age 28, mother of two school-aged children

Other women got no support from families and friends. Often, family and friends had tried in the beginning, but became less supportive. Many of the women in my sample told of how their husbands or partners had antagonized friends and family with their behavior, cutting the women off from valuable social supports. Often, batterers would deliberately isolate their victims to keep friends and family from seeing signs of abuse and to keep their victims from leaving.

Some of the women I talked with left abusive situations in spite of their families. Sasha, aged 20, was in her third battering relationship. Her parents were divorced, and she described her parents as alcoholics. After sending her money to leave the first battering relationship, they refused to assist her any further. She came to the shelter pregnant and penniless, and later returned to her abuser. Jenny, whose story appeared at the beginning of this chapter, was estranged from her parents, and had not seem them in several years. Asking them for help was not a viable option. Angela was told by her mother, "You made your bed, now lie in it."

Some families and friends even encouraged battered women to stay with their husbands and partners and to work on the relationship. In several cases, the batterer put on such a good "front" that the woman was accused of making up stories. As Carol, a middle-class mother of two shared with me,

> No one believed that Mark was beating me. He never hit me where it showed, and he was always so charming and caring around my family. He turned into a different person when we were alone. He'd hit me on my head or punch me in the stomach, since no one would see what he had done. I knew about the women's shelter and all, but didn't want to ask for help. I mean, our families are well known and respected in this community. Mark is a teacher. It would be too embarrassing.
>
> —Carol, age 36, real estate agent and mother of two school-aged children

Carol finally got help when her family physician confronted her about her injuries during a routine visit. Only when she had "evidence" to back her statements did her family believe her. I talked with her briefly by phone after her case came before the judge. While the court believed her and gave her possession of the family home and children, some relatives still accused her of trying to "ruin a good man's name."

Although most women sought help from friends and family members first, it was often not until professionals were involved that they were able to leave battering relationships. In many instances, battered women sought help from the clergy before turning to other professionals. Eight of the women in my sample called their pastors first before deciding to leave abusive relationships. Although other researchers (Alsdurf, 1985; Bowker and Mauer, 1986) found that the clergy tend to encourage the woman to stay with a batterer, to do her "duty," or to honor her marriage vows and "submit" to her husband, I found quite the opposite. In only two cases did the clergy recommend that the woman stay and try to work things out. One of these was quite disturbing, however, because the pastor put a battered woman in serious danger. After coming to the shelter, Doris's pastor (who was a close friend of her husband) tried several times to get in touch with her, calling friends and family, and even leaving messages with the shelter office. When she eventually returned his call, he asked her to come to his office to "talk about all this." When Doris arrived at the church, her husband's truck was parked in the lot, and she drove by without stopping. Apparently, the pastor had planned to use the session to try and get the couple to reconcile.

In all other cases where women contacted their pastors, they were advised to call the domestic violence hotline or shelter or were given material on battered women's programs. Two of the women noted that their churches had given them assistance with finances, transportation, or housing. One pastor even helped a battered woman find a job that enabled her not to return to her abuser. Keep in mind, however, that the women in my study were all living apart from their batterers when I interviewed them. It is possible that those women whose clergy advised them to stay, did stay and were not included in my sample.

The police also received high marks from the women I talked with. For many, the police were the first outside persons to intervene in their violent relationships. Often, the women or their children called 911, and in several cases, a neighbor or family member had called police. For the most part, the police acted appropriately, arresting the batterer; advising the woman of her rights; and arranging to transport her to a safe place, hospital, or shelter, if needed.

When problems did occur, it was after the initial incident. Eight of the twenty-four women who had contacted the police had problems with paperwork. Police reports were sometimes not filled out correctly, not noted as domestic violence cases, or had portions missing, resulting in problems when hearings were held.

In four cases, the woman was taken to the hospital because of her injuries. Each noted that the hospital assisted her in locating a safe place when she was released. Two women came directly to the battered women's shelter, one went to a shelter in another county and another was released to her mother.

The women I talked with were also pleased with the hotline and shelter. Twenty had contacted the hotline, and twelve had actually used the shelter. Many were not aware of the services offered to battered women until told of them by their clergy, the police, or the hospital. Hotline callers felt that they were given good information, and that counselors were supportive and knowledgeable. Shelter residents were pleasantly surprised with the shelter (a four-bedroom, two-bath house), noting that they expected "a gym filled with rows and rows of bed and lockers." Most said that their shelter stays had given them a safe environment in which to "get their heads together and make plans."

The safety net for battered women broke down, however, when the legal system and social services stepped in. Women often felt the courts were unresponsive, asking them to share blame or putting them or their children in danger. One woman noted that

> I'd just gotten out of the hospital and went to my TPO hearing. This guy [her husband] had beaten me within an inch of my life. The judge decided to order visitation for my husband, and wanted me to meet him at Burger King every other weekend to drop the children off. I mean, this man almost killed me, and now I'm supposed to entrust my children to him and have to see him every two weeks? It seems like I'm the one being punished here.
>
> —Robin, age 26, mother of two toddlers

Other women felt that going to court was a frightening experience, because in the state where this research took place, the batterer was told of the TPO hearing date and had the right to present his side of the story in court. Often, batterers threatened women while waiting cases to be heard, tried to intimidate them with stares or gestures, or tried to convince them to return. I observed one ex-partner smile at his victim in the hallway before court and slowly run his finger around his neck in a throat slitting gesture. Another brought a dozen red roses to court in an attempt to reconcile with his wife.

The greatest amount of dissatisfaction was with social services and follow-up care. The shelter had room for only four families; therefore stays were limited to thirty days, and decisions and arrangements had to be made quickly. Other than a support group, the shelter offered no follow up or after-care (because of a lack of funding). Social services (such as welfare, food stamps, housing, and job services) were not located in central locations, nor were they convenient to the shelter. Women often had to go to as many as five different offices to arrange for services. Often, they lacked the transportation, funds, or child care to do this. Bureaucratic regulations were difficult to understand, and the paperwork they needed to qualify for assistance was many times left behind when they fled the abusive relationship.

Sadly, it was at this point that many of the women in my sample returned to their batterers. Feeling overwhelmed and lacking necessary supports, it was sometimes easier to return to the batterer than to continue to seek assistance and to locate housing, jobs, and child care. I was able to keep in touch with only ten of the women in my sample after the interview. Of those, seven had returned to their batterers within six months of the interview. This is consistent with Gondolf's (1988) findings that women return to their batterers an average of six times before they leave for good.

Conclusion

As the stories presented here illustrate, battered women face a daunting array of barriers in leaving their abusers. Several social actions are needed to combat this problem. First, even though the public is becoming better informed regarding domestic violence, additional education is necessary to continue to raise awareness of the problem, help people to understand the dynamics of woman battering, and to make sure that all women are aware of the services available in their communities. Second, improved follow-up services for battered women are of vital importance in helping them to stay free of their batterers. With cuts to social service budgets following recent welfare reforms, services for battered women are likely to become even harder to obtain. Our society must work together to insure that no woman becomes trapped with an abuser because she lacks the funds to leave. Finally, after almost thirty years of attention to this problem, it is time that we begin to shift the focus of our efforts from treating victims of battering to preventing violence from occurring in the first place.

References

Alsdurf, J. (1985). Wife abuse and the church: The response of pastors. *Response* 8(1): 9–11.

Aquirre, B. (1985). Why do they return? Abused wives in shelters. *Social Work* 30: 350–354.

Bowker, L., and Mauer, L. (1986). The effectiveness of counseling services utilized by battered women. *Women and Therapy* 5: 65–82.

Collins, J., and Schlenger, W. (1988). Acute and chronic effects of alcohol use on violence. *Journal of Studies on Alcohol* 49: 516–521.

de las Fuentes, C., and Wright, D. (1991). *Surviving Rape: A Structured Group Manual.* Austin, TX: Counseling and Mental Health Center, University of Texas at Austin.

Donnelly, D., and Kenyon, S. (1996). "Honey, we don't do men": Gender stereotypes and the provision of services to sexually assaulted males. *Journal of Interpersonal Violence* 11(3): 441–448.

Doumas, D., Margolin, G., and John, R. (1994). The intergenerational transmission of violence across three generations. *Journal of Family Violence* 9: 157–175.

Ferraro, K. (1979). Hard love: Letting go of an abusive husband. *Frontiers* 4: 16–18.

Finn, J. (1985). The stresses and coping behavior of battered women. *Social Casework* (June): 341–349.

Flitcraft, A. (1992). *Diagnostic and Treatment Guidelines on Domestic Violence.* Chicago, Il: American Medical Association.

Gondolf, E. (1988). The effect of batterer counseling on shelter outcomes. *Journal of Interpersonal Violence* 3: 275–289.

Helton, A. (1987). Battered and pregnant: A prevalence study. *American Journal of Public Health* 77: 1337–1339.

Holiman, M., and Schilit, R. (1991). Aftercare for battered women: How to encourage the maintenance of change. *Psychotherapy* 28: 345–353.

Hotaling, G., and Sugarman, D. (1986). An analysis of risk markers in husband to wife violence: The current state of knowledge. *Violence and Victim* 1: 101–124.

Hotaling, G., and Sugarman, D. (1990). A risk marker analysis of assaulted wives. *Journal of Family Violence* 5: 1–13.

Johnson, I. (1992). Economic, situational, and psychological correlates of the decision-making process of battered women: Decisions to return home after shelter termination. *Families in Society* 73: 168–76.

Kaufman-Kantor, G., and Straus, M. (1990). The "drunken bum" theory of wife beating. In M. Straus and R. Gelles (Eds.), *Physical Violence in American Families* (pp. 203–224). New Brunswick, NJ: Transaction.

Langan, P., and Innes, C. (1986). *Preventing Domestic Violence Against Women* (Bureau of Justice Statistics special report). Washington, D.C.: U.S. Dept of Justice (NCJ No. 102037).

Paymar, M. (1993). *Violent No More: Helping Men End Domestic Abuse* Alameda, CA: Hunter House.

Renzetti, C. (1992). *Violent Betrayal: Partner Abuse in Lesbian Relationships.* Newbury Park, CA: Sage.

Roscoe, B., and Benaske, N. (1985). Courtship violence experiences by abused wives: Similarities in pattern of abuse. *Family Relations* 34: 419–24.

Snyder, D., and Fruchtman, L. (1981). Differential patterns of wife abuse: A data-based typology. *Journal of Consulting and Clinical Psychology* 49: 878–885.

Straus, M., and Gelles, R. (1986). Societal change and change in family violence from 1975 to 1985 as revealed by two national surveys. *Journal of Marriage and the Family* 48: 465–79.

Straus, M., Gelles, R., and Steinmetz, S. (1980). *Behind Closed Doors: Violence in the American Family.* Garden City: Doubleday.

Strube, M. (1988). The decision to leave an abusive relationship: Empirical evidence and theoretical issues. *Psychological Bulletin* 104: 236–250.

Vaughn, D. (1987). The long goodbye. *Psychology Today* (July): 37–38, 42.

Walker, L. (1979). *The Battered Woman.* New York: Harper and Row.

Walker, L. (1989). *Terrifying Love: Why Battered Women Kill and How Society Responds.* New York: Harper and Row.

Article Review Form at end of book.

Do you believe that current advertisements of powerful women continue to portray inferiority? Are the differences between advertisements featuring women and advertisements featuring men crucial? What impact does this have on society?

Gender and Advertising

Are powerful women in ads challenging feminine stereotypes?

Livia Pohlman

Georgia Southern University

At first glance, advertisements represent a fantasy world, a world that is not real or accurate in any sociological sense. That element of fantasy and unreality is exactly the allure, the intent, and the source of power of advertisements. Ads represent an imaginary and depoliticized utopia, an unreal world in which social problems and inequities are airbrushed away (Manca & Manca, 1994). Through advertisements, we dream of who we might become. Through advertisements, we hope. Through advertisements we gather our images of what is and isn't possible. This social construction of the possible is particularly important for groups who are trying to gain power and equality in a real, social world that has not allowed those possibilities to exist.

Advertisements have fueled the growth of mass media. Behind the widespread profusion of radio and television stations, daily newspapers, and glossy magazines are advertisers. They are hungry to capitalize on the material longings of millions of listeners, readers, and viewers and are therefore willing to foot the bill of many media. For example, advertisers pay the full cost of running radio and television stations. Aside from investing in the equipment, we the listeners and viewers pay nothing (as long as we resist the temptation to subscribe to cable). Advertisers subsidize most of the costs of daily newspapers; we the readers pay a mere 50 cents per day. Advertisers subsidize glossy magazines; we the subscribers pay a discounted 75 cents per issue.

Over the years, advertisers have become more sophisticated and sensitive. Knowing that the public reads less than ever before, advertisers rely more on images and less on text. Knowing that many minority groups are gaining power and wealth, advertisers no longer cater exclusively to a white middle-class audience but instead develop specific ads for African-Americans, Hispanics, Asians, the elderly, and the disabled. Advertisers do respond to community outrage over particularly racist or sexist ads. For example in the 1970s the infamous Frito-Bandito advertisements portrayed a cartoon Mexican bandit who repeatedly stole Fritos corn chips because they were so delicious. Though this campaign was successful as a marketing tool, these ads were withdrawn due to protests from the Latin American community, outraged at being stereotyped as untrustworthy criminals. In the 1990s, the same company, Frito-Lay, offered new advertisements for Tostito corn chips in which a debonair Latin man explained the sophisticated uses for these chips as well as the proper pronunciation of this "exotic" new food. Similarly, Kodak was forced to withdraw its sexist "Shoot your Mother-In-Law" campaign in which easy-to-use throw-away cameras were being advertised to hapless new husbands. Now, rather than waiting for community outrage to erupt, advertisers spend millions of dollars researching what the public likes and wants to see and which images convey a sense of respect, allure, and excitement that will attract new buyers to their products.

One increasingly large and powerful group of new buyers are working women, particularly professional women and single women with discretionary income to spend. Women streamed into the workforce during the first three decades of the twentieth century. Over 90 percent of women work in the paid labor force at some point during their adult lives, including 85 percent of all women with children. Women are entering professional careers, fighting to close the wage gap, attempting to break the glass ceiling, and working to end sexual harassment. Women are demanding respect and power. In turn, advertisers are increasingly directing themselves toward these powerful women.

This study examines recent magazine advertisements of these powerful women and explores whether "we've come a long way, baby" (to borrow the slogan of the very successful Virginia Slims campaign).

Previous Sociological Research on Gender and Ads

Gendered images in advertising have been explored by many researchers since Erving Goffman's classic 1976 study, *Gender Advertisements*. Goffman first noticed that women in printed advertisements tend to be portrayed as the object rather than the subject. Women were the one-gazed-at rather than the one-who-gazed. Women were the recipients of the activity in ads rather than the actors. Goffman also noted that women were more likely than men to be posed in unstable or vulnerable positions, such as balancing on one foot, leaning on an elbow, or about to fall over. These positions conveyed precariousness and weakness, and existed in contrast to the common portrayal of men as confident and strong with their feet firmly planted on the ground or their bodies aggressively posed to take charge. Furthermore, Goffman noted that women were more likely than men to be posed in subordinate or provocative positions, such as women on their knees, women bowing, women lying down, and even women falling down stairs or being stepped on by men.

Since then, many other researchers have expanded on these ideas, most notably Jean Kilbourne in her classic presentation *Killing Us Softly*, updated in 1987 and renamed *Still Killing Us Softly*. Kilbourne concurs with Goffman that women in advertisements are often portrayed as objects rather than subjects, and more specifically that women are seen as the objects of men's sexual desire. She points out images of impending "ravagement," which the advertisers claim are supposed to be romantic and exciting to women. Some of these images of women being "seduced" imply impending assault, show a violent struggle between a woman and a man or even suggest that the woman has been raped and/or murdered. Kilbourne shows the objectification of women in its extreme, noting an alarming growth of images of dismemberment. She examines the images of "unattainable female perfection" in which beauty is defined as extreme thinness as well as extreme youth. When advertisements do show women in professional settings or powerful roles, Kilbourne asserts that these portrayals trivialize and minimize women's accomplishments. For example, one ad portrays a female executive at a board meeting reading her presentation to an all-male audience. The men appear preoccupied rather than attentive because they are busy looking down her open blouse.

Since Kilbourne's study, research into advertising has branched off into examinations of music videos, children's cartoons, trade publications, and other areas. However, there have been few updates regarding magazine images of women. This is particularly surprising given the great strides that women and other minority groups have made in the past decade. The current study revisits the magazine advertising world since Goffman's 1976 study and Kilbourne's 1987 research to find out if, after a decade or two of progress, advertisers have begun to show women in their powerful, professional, serious, strong, and productive roles.

Methods

This study examines magazine advertisements from recent issues of mainstream publications with a circulation over 100,000 such as *Glamour, Cosmopolitan, Men's Health, Field and Stream, Newsweek, U.S. News and World Report, Ebony,* and *Esquire*. These magazines were selected because of their large general readership and their tendency to publish advertisements for popular items produced by the nation's largest corporations.

In keeping with the methods of Goffman and Kilbourne, this study is based on a purposive sample of ads to illustrate emerging themes regarding images of powerful women. The sample was generated by systematically examining each ad to identify those that appeared to portray women in powerful, nontraditional, or nonstereotypical roles. The next phase involved searching through the same magazines to find ads for similar products that used male models rather than female models. This two-phase approach, developed by Robert Jensen of the University of Texas at Austin (1996), provides a basis of comparison for exploring the meaning of gender in popular culture. It is important not only to examine women in their own right but also to examine how women are viewed in comparison to men because our culture understands gender as a duality.

This study is not based on a random sample of ads because the likelihood of missing the few ads of powerful women would have been too great. Furthermore, although it would be very interesting to explore possible relationships between the images in ads and the types of magazines, readers, and editorial staffs involved in their publication, this study focuses instead on a cultural analysis of the hidden meanings in magazine imagery of nontraditional women.

In the analysis that follows, these images of powerful women are examined from two points of view. First, we will look at these ads as advertising executives might explain the meanings and intended messages to their clients. Then we will go back over the ads, comparing them with similar ads using male models, to explore some of the sociological meanings that emerge upon deeper analysis.

Powerful Women at First Glance

True to the claims of advertisers, there are indeed advertising images that portray women as strong, athletic, independent, smart, and active—at least at first glance. Let us first look at the ads of women alone, and then we will return to compare them with similar ads of men.

First Glance 1: Women Climbing to New Heights

In recent years, women seem to have sprung from their housewife roles and taken to the outdoors. More than ever, we find women riding mountain bikes, racing down ski slopes, and hiking across uncharted terrain. This ad for backpacks by Dana Design shows a woman climbing to the top of a sun-kissed, golden rock outcrop. She is climbing without ropes, pulling herself to the top with her hands. The wind blows through her hair, adding to the sensation of movement, progress, and effort. In the sky, a fading moon highlights the word "great."

The text in bold letters reads "At Dana Design we do more than build great packs." It goes on to explain that "we build great packs for everyone," chiding other backpack manufacturers for being so late in their entry to the field of women's backpacks "as if women had only recently discovered the outdoors." Dana, after all, has been making women's outdoor packs for ten years.

This image conveys a sense of bold adventure. The woman climbs alone, without assistance from men, guides, or ropes. She is conquering a peak. If she is the first climber to conquer this peak, she would be entitled to name the mountain. Furthermore, the moon appears to be within her grasp, as if the image is saying "reach for the stars and the moon."

First Glance 2: Built for Any Path You Take

This ad for Merrell hiking boots follows a similar theme: a woman in the great outdoors, hiking over a ridge. She is alone, except for an unleashed male dog to whom she seems to be speaking. It appears that she is fearlessly making friends with this animal. The text appeals to the free, liberated woman by asserting that Merrell Hiking Boots are "built for any path you take." In smaller print beneath the Merrell insignia is a similar message, "Takes you where you want to go."

This image is in black and white, and therefore less powerful and eye-catching than the first. Nevertheless, the text is encouraging and the photograph is captivating. The woman appears to have climbed near the top of a ridge. She must be at a rather high altitude because the tree line disappears on the ridge behind her, and she is wearing a turtleneck and vest. The model is relatively androgynous: a blunt haircut, no discernable makeup, a strong nose, her hand in a relaxed fist. This image conveys an almost masculine impression of power and conquest over nature.

First Glance 3: Female Body Building

Antiperspirant ads are notoriously sexist, as are most images that pertain to apparently embarrassing hygiene products such as mouthwash, toothpaste, and dandruff shampoo. This ad for Secret, however, seems to break the mold. A strong female model stands in her workout leotard with two weights in her hands. Her back is to the audience, and light shines on her sweating shoulder blades. The text reads "pH balanced for a woman." Unlike her squeamish and embarrassed predecessors in earlier antiperspirant ads, this body builder is not stopped by woeful perspiration. Instead she appears to be enabled by Secret to continue developing her muscles, her strength, and her power without losing her "balance" as a feminine woman.

First Glance 4: Gaining an Edge

Switching from products for the body (backpacks, boots, antiperspirants) to products for the mind, this advertisement for a Macintosh Proforma computer shows a young Asian American girl wearing school clothes, leaning over a stack of books. Her elbow rests on the books, and her smiling face with raised eyebrows rests on her hand. She seems to be a pleasant, eager, 10-year-old student. Above her the text shouts in large font, "WILL a personal computer give your kids an edge?" In the upper corner of the ad, a cartoon kitten plays with a printout of a lizard that is apparently so realistic that the kitten mistakes it for the real thing.

This image is particularly interesting given that computer programmers, computer engineers, and even computer users are primarily men. Encouraging young girls to use computers could certainly give them an edge later in life, and this ad is aimed to encourage computer use among girls.

First Glance 5: Monitors for Women, Too

Fortunately, it's not too late for grown women to become computer literate. This ad for Nokia monitors shows a sophisticated woman in a black dress looking avidly into her screen. The text reads "European art comes to the screen without those annoying subtitles." She appears to be doing art history research or engaging in aesthetic appreciation of masterpieces. Based on the woman's elegant manner, we might assume that she is sophisticated and intelligent. Like the Macintosh ad, this Nokia ad takes computer literacy out of the hands of men and gives women an invitation to participate in a male-dominated realm.

First Glance 6: Doing Better Than Our Fathers and Grandfathers

As women have moved into the paid workforce, more women are attaining high-paid positions than ever before. With such economic success comes the responsibility to invest wisely and plan ahead for retirement. This ad for TIAA/CREF's retirement planning services features a woman sitting on her front porch, dressed in casual, androgynous clothes: a golf shirt, a sweatshirt wrapped around her shoulders, jeans, and loafers. At her feet is a large and attentive dog, an animal we usually associate with being "a man's best friend." She is apparently pondering the financial choices ahead of her as she plans for retirement. The text reads "Your grandfather did better than his father. Your father did better than his father. Are you prepared to carry on the tradition?" This text implies that women are now reaching farther than the men before them have, and it proposes a challenge to "carry on the tradition" of success. This ad appeals to women not following the traditional role of being dependent housewives but instead are forging ahead as independent career women.

First Glance 7: Confidence, Pride, and Power

For decades, ads have been dominated by white models. This conveyed a message of obliteration to members of minority groups. Only as the African American middle class has grown, have advertisers begun to use black models and spin their ad campaigns to attract consumers from a variety of ethnic groups.

This ad features an African American woman looking boldly into the camera with her arms crossed. She wears a white shirt and what appears to be an untied man's tie. She is neither smiling nor glaring, but assessing the viewer in a straightforward way. The text reads "African Pride. Confidence. Pride. Power." These are bold words to associate with women, appealing to strength rather than to beauty. The text goes on to claim that "nothing can help you get that feeling like African Pride relaxers," a common ploy of advertisers. The solution to institutionalized racism in this country is not hair relaxers; but, as an image of a powerful woman, this stands out for its straightforward expression, its lack of guile, and its powerful text.

First Glance 8: Winning the Race

This famous series of advertisements for milk, shot by world-class photographer Annie Leibowitz, feature some of the biggest stars of popular culture.

Many athletes, movie stars, and public figures have been included in the ongoing series that features each important luminary with a child's silly "milk moustache." Even President Clinton and Senator Bob Dole, in the week before the 1996 presidential election, were featured together with milk moustaches in a *Newsweek* ad. Milk appears to be the great equalizer.

This particular milk ad features Jackie Joyner-Kersee, an Olympic gold medalist. Her muscular body is posed in a running position, and she wears her flamboyant red running suit with one leg bare and the other covered. After winning her gold medals, Ms. Joyner-Kersee became an entrepreneur and marketed this line of daring and creative clothes. Her hand is raised in what could be a fist, and the wind is blowing her hair back. Like the woman in the African Pride ad, she looks directly into the camera, without guile, without cuteness, without malice, but with confidence.

The text reinforces this confidence. It reads "How fast am I? Well, I caught a jackrabbit when I was 6, and in 1988, I clocked in at 23.5 mph in the 100-meter. Sure, some of that's nature, but I do train hard and drink milk." The text emphasizes speed, power, athletic ability, hard work, and success, different messages than the usual ads aimed at women's beauty.

From First Glance to Double Take

At first glance, these eight images appear to portray women in new and powerful ways. Women are climbing mountains and taking new paths to high altitudes. Women are building their bodies with weights and building their minds with computers. Women are taking over the traditions that their fathers and grandfathers bore, possibly surpassing them, certainly worrying alongside them. Women are confident, proud, and powerful. Women might even be "winning the race," as Jackie Joyner-Kersee's ad implies.

However, conceptions of gender are not formulated in a vacuum. Conceptions of gender rest fundamentally on difference and comparison (Gilligan, 1982). In our gendered culture, to be feminine means to be not masculine; to be masculine means to be not feminine. It becomes impossible for the mind to conceive of one gender without conceiving of its opposite. For that reason, it is important to compare these ads of powerful women to ads that feature men. To compare apples with apples, rather than apples with oranges, the following section pairs each of the previous seven ads with an advertisement of a man using similar products. When we compare these female ads to male ads for similar products, we find striking patterns of inequality and subtle new forms of sexism.

A final note on interpreting these ads with a sociological imagination: advertisers do not expect viewers to pay close attention to details. Instead they expect that viewers will page through ads quickly, absorbing at a conscious level only the initial messages that we have just explored. At a subconscious level, however, the mind registers thousands of subtle cues, encoded symbols, and shades of meaning. These are the cues, symbols, and meanings that are explored next. These cues, symbols, and meanings convey surprisingly traditional and stereotypical gender messages that undo the progress that advertisers claim to be making with their images of powerful women. When we do a "double take" on these ads, examining them carefully for hidden messages about power, a troubling set of meanings emerge.

Double Take 1: Women Clinging Precariously to New Heights

Reviewing this slide of our peak-conquering backpacker, we discover that she is actually clinging somewhat precariously to this peak. Her muscles strain as her thin body struggles to make it to the top. She must even lean on all fours to pull her weight up, signifying a position of deference and weakness. The wind beats through her hair, obscuring her face and invoking anxiety in the viewer; we fear she is about to fall. In addition, the peak she is about to conquer is not the highest one. Just ahead, the thin edge of another peak looms beyond a chasm. She is not quite as powerful as we first imagined. Under the bold headlines, the small text says, "Get a pack. Take a hike." This could be interpreted as a derogatory statement. It signifies pack animals, and it implies that women who try to attain these heights should "take a hike" or "get lost."

In comparison, an advertisement for MountainSmith backpacks features a male rock climber ascending the sheer face of a cliff. He is not wearing his pack like a pack animal, but has instead hooked up a clever system of pulleys and ropes with his mountaineering equipment. He is roped firmly to the sheer face, with his feet planted widely and securely against the rock. The text leaps out in enormous capital letters:

"MASTERS OF THE CRAFT." There is no uncertainty or dismissal. Comparing these two images, males who backpack are masters, secure in their skills, while women who backpack are novices in great danger of toppling over. Linking this image to women's rise "to the top" in the business world, this message implies that men know what they are doing at the top while women are still wobbly and unskilled.

Double Take 2: Built for Paths That Already Have Been Carved

Cued for hidden messages of precariousness and weakness by the Dana Designs image, we look again at this black-and-white image of a female hiker in her Merrell boots. She, too, is not near the highest peak; another ridge looms behind her. She, too, is bending over, apparently speaking to her tail-wagging dog, which strikes the viewer as a frivolous and sentimental act. She smiles, yet her hand is clenched in a fist as if she is nervous and on the defensive. Her bare legs are revealed beneath her hiking shorts, yet she wears a turtleneck sweater and a lightweight insulated vest, conveying the message that no matter how cold it might be at high altitudes, women are expected to show some skin. The text states "Built for any path you take," which upon closer analysis reveals that her path is already carved. She has to follow where others before her have led.

In contrast, the Merrell boots ad featuring males conveys a different message. Here a man's leg and hiking boot splash in vivid color through a raging stream. Not only is he in a more expensive ad (4-color printing is far more expensive than black and white), but his image is engaged in full action, crossing a stream and forging a new path rather than following a path already carved. The smaller inset photos show men ascending the top of peaks and then boot-skiing down the face of a glacier, both are exceedingly difficult and often dangerous. The text downplays any struggle that men might experience in this ascent when it states matter-of-factly, "You climb up. You climb down. Your feet stay dry and comfortable. This is not rocket science." The message is that men's attainment and success is not difficult and precarious as it is for women, but instead men's success is portrayed as effortless and natural.

Double Take 3: Body Building with Dumbbells

Returning to our athletic female model in the Secret antiperspirant ad, we notice that although this model has wide shoulders, they are not necessarily muscular. Her arms are at rest rather than in action, conveying a stereotypical image of feminine passivity. Furthermore, her hands loosely hold two weights also known as "dumbbells." Women's intelligence has often been downplayed, and "dumbbell" is a word often used on elementary school playgrounds to indicate what boys think of girls. Her body is turned at an angle with her weight on one hip, neither a serious weightlifting stance nor a position of balance and strength despite the text's claim that Secret is "pH balanced for a woman." She looks down, demurely, in her state of repose as if she is tired or possibly defeated.

In contrast, the Secret ad for men shows an extremely muscular man with his biceps curled and his lateral muscles strained in action. His elbows burst out of the frame, and his head is held high. His feet are planted firmly apart and even the muscles in his thighs and posterior are flexed. Strength and power are conveyed, and the text reinforces this image: "Strong enough for a man." Once again, by viewing these advertisements in contrast to one another, we see that women are more likely to be portrayed as off-balance, inactive, and uncertain while men are portrayed as secure, active, and certain.

Double Take 4: Computers as Toys: Computers as Tools

Revisiting our ambitious young Asian American girl with her personal computer, we notice that the text poses a question rather than asserts a claim: "WILL a PC give your kids an edge?" Questions are more prevalent in ads featuring girls and women, conveying a sense of uncertainty and playing on stereotypes of women as indecisive. The cartoon drawings around her are also symbolic of stereotypical femininity. The fuzzy kitten is a common character in girls' bedrooms and bedtime stories. Even more troubling is the synonym for kitten, a word that is often used to describe women's sexual parts. This further sexualizes and belittles the female model, and suggests dangerous possibilities in this age of rampant sexual abuse against children. On the screen, a cartoon image of an Egyptian Sphinx radiates in shades of magenta and pink. Whether the student is doing a report about Egypt or playing a cartoon game that takes place in Egypt is difficult to discern, raising questions regarding the seriousness with which girls and women might use computers. Furthermore, it should be remembered that the Sphinx is a symbol of mythological cruelty, tricking travelers with unanswerable riddles and condemning them to death. The evil side of women has often been caricatured in this way, equating women's mysterious nature not with strength but with deception and treachery. This ad, upon second glance, appears to be filled with disturbing and stereotypical symbolism.

An ad aimed at boys, featuring the same Macintosh Proforma computer, clearly conveys a contrasting message. In this image, the boy is not studying. Instead he is playing with his father, standing wide-legged in front of him as his father leans over laughing. The image conveys a scene of male bonding. Instead of a cartoon "kitty" there is a cartoon "screwdriver." The sexual innuendo is not difficult to detect. Rather than a Sphinx or an image of riddles and tricks, there are tools. A telephone waits ready to be hooked up to a modem; a mouse snakes across the page ready to be used. There is no glaring headline asking whether or not this child WILL be able to use the product. Instead, at the end of a page of fine print woven around the boy and his father, there is a simple declarative statement: "The power to be your best." Once again, in subtle and subliminal ways, we receive two different messages regarding women's inabilities and men's abilities.

Double Take 5: To Monitor or to Be Monitored?

As many viewers might have noticed when we first looked at this image by Nokia, the woman in this advertisement gazes into her Nokia monitor while wearing a nearly backless black dress. She is dressed for an evening out, and appears to be gazing at the monitor to pass the time before going off to her party. Significantly missing is a keyboard; she cannot input information into this computer. She can only receive. The text, "European art comes to the screen, without those annoying subtitles," conveys that she is either incapable of reading subtitles or sufficiently discouraged to find them "annoying." Once again, the advertisement portrays a woman passively receiving, not actively working; using a computer for fun rather than as a tool; and the text questions her intelligence.

In contrast, the ad for Samsung monitors features a man in a shirt and tie, with glasses, ready to work rather than to dash off to an elegant party. He looks directly toward the camera, holding a newspaper in his hand, conveying an image of purposeful activity and educated awareness. On his screen is not superfluous European art, but instead important financial reports. His computer has a keyboard, prominently displayed and ready to be used. The text reads "Samsung monitors. Designed from your point of view." This product is to be used for work and investments, not as a toy or for hobbies, implying that men know how to distinguish between important work and frivolous pastimes.

Double Take 6: Women Doubt: Men Decide

Returning to the black-and-white porch where our pondering woman sits, we notice that her ad is colorless, her clothes are drab, and her questioner ends with a doubtful phrase: "Are you prepared to carry on the tradition?" She is not engaged in an activity, other than passively worrying. She is not portrayed amidst her important job through which she must be accruing these retirement benefits, but rather she is shown in women's "proper place," at home. Although this ad is progressive in addressing women's retirement and investment concerns, it concurrently portrays women as unable to handle this daunting responsibility.

In a similar ad about investment services through Chase Manhattan Bank, a male executive is shown in full color, on the phone, working, thinking, and planning ahead. He appears to have no misgivings and no doubts. The text reads "We pay him to timeshift in this fashion. Because he's thinking. About trust creation. And how your grandchildren can inherit more than your winsome smile." This ad seems to be a direct reply to the female ad, providing a solution to her worries about being "prepared to handle" such decisions. According to the Chase Manhattan ad, all she needs to do is worry about her winsome smile while the confident, full-color, high speed men on Wall Street handle the rest.

Double Take 7: Black Feelings or Black Power?

Advertisers have responded to consumer demands by portraying ethnic models selling various products from fine liquors to hair care products. While gender differences appear between black male models and black female models, these differences are less pronounced than in ads with white models. In some ads, a striking egalitarianism occurs. Comparing the proud and straightforward woman in the African Pride ad with her male counterpart, we find that both ads begin with identical text: "Confidence. Pride. Power." Both ads portray the models in similar poses, looking straight into the camera, bodies relaxed yet serious, in elegant dress clothes. One subtle difference is that the man raises his hands into a relaxed fist, conveying power, while the woman crosses her arms over her body in a gesture of possible protectiveness.

Upon further reading of the text, we discover that the woman's ad goes on to say, "Nothing can help you get that feeling like African Pride Relaxer." The emphasis is on feelings, a somewhat stereotypical way of appealing to women. In contrast, the man's ad goes on to say, "You've got the power to make things happen." Again, power and activity are emphasized. While these subtle gender differences exist, there was not one ad among all of the white models where the models and text were as similar as they are in this set of ads aimed at African Americans. Furthermore, both ads conclude with similarity that emphasizes the common situation of African Americans, male or female. A bold caption signifying courage and pride for men and women is emblazoned across the bottom of each ad: "Keep your head up."

Double Take 8: Fearing Black Men

African American models, male and female, have been almost entirely absent from mainstream advertisements for everyday products such as cars, homes, tools, detergents, or even milk. When African American models are shown in mainstream magazines, they are usually athletes endorsing some brand of equipment. Some theorists suggest that there is an underlying fear of black men in white culture, and mainstream magazines have thus kept African American men stereotyped as brawny but not brainy athletes, or have excluded them altogether. In the following milk ads, we find another trend: to remove the fear of black men by portraying them as nonmasculine.

Returning to Jackie Joyner-Kersee's milk ad, we notice several elements that reduce her impression of physical power. Her body is posed and still; she is not actually in the midst of her record-breaking sprints. Instead, she is standing in front of a photographer's fan that lifts her long hair into a pseudoimage of action. In the text she asserts how "fast" she is, having outrun a jackrabbit, yet the word "fast" has often been used to connote sexual looseness. This stereotype has been applied to African American women since the days of slavery and was often used as justification for their rape by white slave owners.

The male ad for milk shows Spike Lee, the famous director of important films such as "Jungle Fever" and "Get On The Bus." He is looking rather diminutive in his oversized suit with his round-framed glasses that seem to be slipping down his nose. Rather than looking like a powerful director who has shaped images and ideas about race relations through his popular films, he appears to be a tiny and inconsequential little man who poses no threat—either physically or intellectually—to the primarily white audience.

For all of the advances that African Americans have made in achievement and in advertising, these images bring up complex questions. Could it be that black men and women are portrayed as more "equal" because that reduces the perceived masculine threat that black men pose to white culture? Are black men and women portrayed as more equal to one another because that reflects their more egalitarian relationships? For example, studies of housework and decision making in dual-earner black families reveal much higher levels of equality between spouses than in white, Hispanic, or Asian American families. Theorists such as Bell Hooks (1989) have proposed that groups that have been historically marginalized are the groups that bring forth new visions, new arrangements, and new ways of being to the culture.

Conclusion

Are these new ads of powerful women really challenging stereotypes? At first glance, it seems that there are more women appearing in stronger and more powerful portrayals. But in taking the time to view these ads in detail, we find that these new ads are not challenging gender stereotypes to the degree we might have hoped. In many cases, they are simply reinforcing traditional images of women's insecurity and frivolity, using far more subtle means. Furthermore, by comparing women to men in ads, we find that women are still represented as comparatively more vulnerable, less confident, less active, and less independent than men. Women show more skin. Women have more doubts. Women face greater struggles. These themes are less prevalent in ads using African American models, although subtle forms of racism creep in to complicate the sexism. Although women certainly have "come a long way, baby" in terms of gaining political rights and economic access over the years, we have a long way to go in the gendered world of advertising imagery.

References/ Further Reading

Barthel, Diane. 1988. *Putting on Appearances: Gender and Advertising.* Philadelphia: Temple University Press.

Belknap, M., and Leonard, W. M. 1991. "A Conceptual Replication and Extension of Erving Goffman's Study of Gender Advertisements." *Sex Roles* 25: 103–119.

Chafetz, Janet S. et al. 1993. "Gender Depictions of the Professionally Employed: A Content Analysis of Trade Publications, 1960–1990." *Sociological Perspectives* 36(1): 63–82.

Dires, Gail, and Humez, Jean, M. 1995. *Gender, Race and Class In Media: A Text Reader.* Thousand Oaks: Sage Publications.

Dortch, Shannon. 1994. "What's Good For the Goose May Gag the Gander." *American Demographics* 16(5): 15–16.

Ford, J. B., LaTour, M. S., and Lundstrom, W. J. 1991. "Contemporary Women's Evaluation of Female Role Portrayals in Advertising." *Journal of Consumer Marketing* 8(1): 15–28.

Gilligan, C. 1982. *In a Different Voice: Psychological Theory and Women's Developement.* Cambridge, MA: Harvard University Press.

Goffman, Erving. 1976. *Gender Advertisements.* Reprinted in 1979. Cambridge: Harvard University Press.

Griffin, Michael, Viswanath, K., and Schwartz, Dona. 1994. "Gender Advertisements in the U.S. and India: Exporting Cultural Stereotypes." *Media, Culture and Society* 16: 487–507.

Hooks, Bell. 1989. *Talking Back.* Boston: South End Press.

Jensen, Robert. 1996. "Advertising, Sexuality, and Sexism: A Slide Show Spotlights Gender Issues." *SIECUS Report* 24(5): 10–12.

Kilbourne, Jean. 1987. *Still Killing Us Softly.* Cambridge: Cambridge Documentary Films.

Leo, John. 1993. "Madison Avenues Gender Wars." *U.S. News and World Report* 115(16): 25.

Leppard, Wanda, Ogletree, S. M., and Wallen, Emily. 1993. "Gender Stereotypes in Medical Advertising: Much Ado About Something?" *Sex Roles* 29(11/12): 829–838.

Manca, Luigia, and Manc, Alessandra, eds. 1994. Gender and Utopia in Advertising: A Critical Reader. Syracuse: Syracuse University Press and Procopian Press.

Signorielli, Nancy, McLeod, Douglas, and Healy, Elaine. 1994. "Gender Stereotypes in MTV Commercials: The Beat Goes On." *Journal of Broadcasting and Electronic Media* 91–101.

Smith, Lois J. 1994. "A Content Analysis of Gender Differences in Children's Advertising." *Journal of Broadcasting and Electronic Media* 38(3): 323–337.

Tapper, John, Thorson, Esther, and Black, David. 1994. "Variations in Music Videos as a Function of Their Musical Genre." *Journal of Broadcasting and Electronic Media* 38(1): 103–113.

Wilson, C. G., II, and Guitierrez, Felix. 1995. *Race, Multiculturalism and the Media: From Mass to Class Communication.* Thousand Oaks: Sage Publications.

Woodruff, Katie. 1996. "Alcohol Advertising and Violence against Women: A Media Advocacy Case Study." *Health Education Quarterly* 23(3): 330–345.

Article Review Form at end of book.

Stalking is one of the most frightening crimes in our society. However, it is not a new phenomenon. What do you think causes stalking? Is it simply that the people who engage in this activity are psychologically unbalanced or are there sociological explanations for it? How does society prevent stalking? Is there some way we can dissuade individuals from engaging in it? Would additional laws and penalties deter people or must we simply accept stalking as a consequence of living in an industrialized society?

Stalking

N. Jane McCandless

State University of West Georgia

Sue McCarty was changing her clothes in her bedroom the evening it all began. She tried on a yellow sweater, took it off, pulled on a blue one and looked in the mirror. The telephone rang. She was expecting a call from her boyfriend. They had plans for dinner. But she didn't recognize the male voice on the phone. "Put the yellow one back on. I like it better." Someone she didn't know had access to her bedroom. . . . "Oh, don't turn away from me," the voice teased. . . . Better yet, don't wear anything at all—like this morning, before you went to work," said the voice. . . . Still, it wasn't until the next day, when the voice began calling her at work, and then later at a nail salon that McCarty, a twenty-eight-year-old stockbroker, realized she was being stalked, actively followed, and not just the recipient of a few annoying phone calls. (Sherman 1994: 198)

What Is Stalking?

Due to increased media attention, many of us are aware of the crime of stalking and may even have heard of persons who are being, or have been, stalked. In fact,

stalking as a phenomenon has captured the popular imagination. Sensational stories on crazed fans fuel tabloid journalism and are often tucked between tales of stars and strippers on TV's Hard Copy. Stalking references have become the joke du jour for '90s stand-up comics and sitcom wisecrackers, and the subject of films such as The Fan and Misery. (Ali 1996: 29–30)

So what is stalking? The National Criminal Justice Association in making recommendations on the development of antistalking codes stated,

In general terms, stalking involves one person's obsessive behavior toward another person. The stalker's actions may be motivated by an intense affection for or an extreme dislike of the victim. Stalking behavior may be overtly irrational or violent or be centered upon benign acts that in another context might be welcomed or considered flattering by the receiving party. Over time, the stalker's behavior may have life threatening consequences for the victim. (1993: 92)

Analyzing this definition of stalking by the National Criminal Justice Association we must recognize that:

(a) the crime of stalking requires a series of harassing acts, not just one isolated incidence;

(b) the harassing actions must be willful, purposeful, and intentional;

(c) the harassing acts directed at a specific individual must be unwanted and nonreciprocal in nature;

(d) and the harassing acts must cause some physical and/or emotional distress for the victim. (See Perez 1993.)

In the state of California, the first state to implement a stalking law, the stalking statute indicates the crime of stalking is,

repeated behavior (that) includes following or harassing conduct that would cause a reasonable person to suffer substantial emotional distress and actually causes distress, and which seriously alarms, annoys, torments, or terrorizes the victim. (Stalking Laws 1995: 3)

Generally speaking, stalkers are persons who become obsessed with another person, sometimes believing that the person they are stalking is the only one who can fulfill their needs, wants, and desires. As ironic as it may sound, stalkers may also stalk because they believe they have been spurned or rejected by the person they are stalking. For either reason, a stalker will do whatever it

takes to contact, or to come into contact with, their victim for the purpose of expressing their feelings toward the victim. In the beginning the stalker may attempt to gain the attention of his/her victim by sending an assortment of items. Included in the stalker's repertoire of actions are sending letters, photos, videos, gifts, and/or flowers. However, as the stalker's advances are continually spurned by the victim, the stalker may then begin to increase her/his contact to include following the victim; phoning the victim at all hours of the day or night; sending a barrage of letters, photos, or videos; stealing the victim's mail; tapping their phone; driving by the victim's place of residence or employment; watching the victim from obscure and undetected places; contacting persons around the victim to find out detailed information about the victim; and/or making appearances at grocery stores, styling salons, shopping centers, restaurants, or any other place where the stalker believes the victim might be. Sometimes the harassing behaviors and intrusions into the life of the victim escalate to intimidation or threats, as a stalker might vandalize the property of the victim or provide enclosures with his/her communications. In a study of threatening letters sent to Hollywood celebrities, Dietz et al. (1991: 197) noted that such enclosures "ranged from the innocuous (for example, business cards) to the bizarre (for example, semen, blood, or a coyote head)." Unfortunately this persistent pattern of behavior may end in seriously violent acts toward and/or the murder of the victim. The evolution of the stalker's thought pattern (can) progress from, If I can just prove to you how much I love you, to I can make you love me, to if I can't have you, nobody else will (Infolink 1995a: 4).

"The variety of specific strategies employed and behaviors displayed by stalkers are limited only by the creativity and ingenuity of the stalkers themselves" (Infolink 1995a: 1).

Classifying Stalkers

Some researchers have classified stalkers, creating specific types or categories of stalkers. Zona, Sharma, and Lane (1993) identified three distinctive groups of stalkers: (a) the erotomanic group; (b) the love obsessional group; and (c) the simple obsessional group.

The first classification of stalkers is referred to as the erotomanic group, labeled the "delusional stalker" by Wright et al. (1996). Erotomania, also known as de Clerambault's Syndrome for the French psychiatrist who defined the disorder in 1921, is listed as a specific subtype of delusional (paranoid) disorder in the *Diagnostic and Statistical Manual of Mental Disorders* (1987: 199). Once described as a female delusional disorder, the central theme of erotomania is that a person (stalker) has a delusional belief that they are passionately loved by someone else (victim). That is, an erotomanic will project her/his own feelings of love onto the victim, becoming convinced that the victim loves them in return. Usually the person of the erotomanic's delusion is a person of higher status.

While erotomanics stalk persons within their immediate environment, quite often an erotomanic stalks media personalities. Mark David Chapman, the man who shot and killed John Lennon; Robert Dewey Oskins, who appeared at Madonna's home on several occasions, once threatening to "slit her throat from ear to ear"; and Margaret Ray, who broke into David Letterman's home on several occasions, have shared the national spotlight as erotomanic stalkers (Ali 1996: 29). Whitney Houston, Janet Jackson, and Michael J. Fox, among others, have also been stalked by erotomanics. David Beatty, director of Public Affairs for the National Victim Center in Arlington, Virginia, stated that "because of their high profile, erotomanics get 90 percent of the publicity while accounting for only 20 percent of all stalking cases" (Blanchard 1994: 148).

What is interesting about erotomania is that the delusional belief or psychological fixation on the victim is based on an "idealized romantic love and spiritual union rather than a sexual attraction" (*Diagnostic Statistical Manual III* 1990). From absolutely no personal interaction or only the briefest of contact, such as in the case of a response to fan mail, an erotomanic is convinced that the victim loves him/her and will create an entire, though fictional, life with the victim in his/her mind. Unfortunately, this preoccupation with the victim becomes consuming and is most often long term, primarily because (a) the erotomanic rejects any evidence indicating that the victim feels otherwise, and (b) "delusions are among the most difficult symptoms to treat" (Orion 1997: 11). Often the erotomanic, particularly male erotomanics, act out their fantasy in a violent fashion.

Consider the case of Theresa Saldana, star in the drama series *The Commish.*

On the morning of March 15, 1982, Jackson, 47, was waiting near Theresa Saldana's West Hollywood apartment house. As Saldana, 27, rushed out to a music class at Los Angeles City College, Jackson approached. When

Saldana paused to unlock her car, Jackson asked, "Excuse me, are you Theresa Saldana?" When she answered in the affirmative and her identity confirmed, Jackson began stabbing Saldana with a hunting knife. He stabbed and slashed her so hard and so often that the knife bent. Hearing Saldana's screams, a delivery man rushed to her aid and wrested the weapon away from Jackson. The intervention of the delivery man, heart-lung surgery, and 26 pints of blood saved Saldana's life. Jackson, convicted of attempted murder and inflicting great bodily injury, was given the maximum sentence of 12 years in prison. (Wright et al. 1996: 498–499)

A second group of stalkers is referred to as the "love obsessional group" (Zona et al. 1993), similar to Meloy's (1989) borderline erotomanic and Wright et al's. (1996) nondomestic-organized stalker. The love obsessional stalker, like the erotomanic, will stalk persons within their immediate environment or a media personality or public official. John Hinckley, Jr. is among those best known as love obsessional stalkers. Hinckley's attempt on the life of President Reagan was designed to capture Jodie Foster's attention. In a letter to Ms. Foster, dated March 30, 1981, Mr. Hinckley stated: "I will admit to you that the reason I'm going ahead with this attempt now is because I just cannot wait any longer to impress you. I've got to do something now to make you understand, in no uncertain terms, that I am doing all of this for your sake" (Caplan 1984: 11).

The difference between the erotomanic and the love obsessional stalker is that the love obsessional stalker is not delusional and does not always believe that the victim loves her/him in return. The love obsessive person may look across a room and fall in love, or, according to Meloy (1989), develop their obsession with the victim from a friendly glance or smile. "Experts have some difficulty in determining whether people who are love obsessive are dangerous, because almost everyone has been affected with the syndrome to a varying degree at one time or another" (Perez 1993: 274).

Nonetheless, the love obsessional stalker begins a campaign to make his/her existence known to the victim, perhaps even hoping that the victim might love him/her in return (Zona et al. 1993). The love obsessional stalker comes to believe that if she/he pursues the victim hard enough and long enough, the victim will certainly reciprocate the affections. As Wright et al. (1996: 496) described, this type of stalking is a "long-term crime without a traditional crime scene." Consider the following case:

Jane McAllister, a human-resources expert in Richmond, Virginia, somberly recalls the day she spoke before a self-help group, unaware that an unknown man in the audience was about to change her life forever. "I had never met him," says Jane, forty-seven. "He literally picked me out of a crowd."

Paul (not his real name) proceeded to follow and harass Jane off and on for more than a decade after that 1981 speech, continually writing, calling and showing up in places she often visited. Yet the police were unable to intervene because at the time, these actions were not considered illegal. Jane tried to convince herself it wasn't a serious matter—until one Sunday night when, expecting a call, she picked up the phone as it rang. With mounting fear, she listened as Paul talked for forty-five minutes, saying he couldn't stop thinking about her. "He said he had a place already set up for us to live together," she says. "He described it to me down to the rugs." (Anonymous 1994: 153)

A third group of stalkers is referred to as the "simple obsessional stalker" (Zona et al. 1993), or the domestic stalker (Wright et al. 1996). Simple obsessional stalkers account for the majority of stalking cases, as these stalkers know their victims and may have had a prior relationship with them. While the type of relationship between the stalker and the victim may vary from a simple acquaintance to a professional encounter, the victim did not return the stalker's attentions and the stalker felt mistreated or rejected by the victim.

Frequently found among simple obsessional stalkers are persons who have been in intimate relationships with their victims, but the relationship was terminated by the victim. The simple obsessional stalker is often motivated by a desire to reestablish the relationship, to win back the former lover or spouse. In these cases, it is not unusual that the previous relationship between the stalker and the victim had a history of jealousy, possessiveness, physical and/or emotional abuse. The simple obsessional stalker "begins a campaign either to rectify the schism, or to seek some type of retribution" (Zona et al. 1993: 896). Often such actions end with a violent attack upon the victim. Consider the following case:

Tiffiney Graham didn't know the ugly side of Thaddeus Davis. Her older sister wondered if a relationship with a man whose father had killed his mother could turn out any way but bad. But Tiffiney loved Thaddeus until the possessive, jealous part of him surfaced after she ended their affair.

Thaddeus's angry threats and countless phone calls frightened Tiffiney. She begged her family not to tell him when she was home, and her coworkers knew never to say she was at work. She even carried a can of mace to spray in his face if their paths crossed. But in the end, nothing mattered. One February day, as she ran from him onto a subway car, Thaddeus put a single bullet through her head and then shot a conductor who tried to help her. (Serant 1993: 72)

Profiling Stalkers

Though the legal definition of stalking is not sex specific, if we were to rely on the popular press or Hollywood's presentation of the stalker, we might conclude that the crime of stalking is exclusively a male activity. Indeed, the largest percentage of stalkers are male, and an astounding number of women are stalked.

However, women also engage in the crime of stalking. Some authors have suggested that as many as 25 percent of stalkers are female (Infolink 1995a). Using the Federal Bureau of Investigation Crime Reports (1993), 76 percent of women arrested are arrested for the crime of larceny theft. However, women account for only 18 percent of the total arrests made for the crime of larceny theft, as men account for 82 percent of all larceny theft arrests. If women do constitute 25 percent of stalkers, and men account for the remaining 75 percent, then the largest percentage of females committing crimes are committing the crime of stalking.

As we cannot assume that all stalkers are male, it is also difficult to create a single profile of a stalker or predict who might become a stalker. Meloy and Gothard (1995) conducted what they believed to be the first comparative clinical study of a group of obsessional followers. In the study they found obsessional followers were typically older, smarter, and better educated. Based on these findings Meloy and Gothard stated "the obsessional follower, on average, will have the capability of being quite resourceful and manipulative in his or her pursuits" (1995: 261). In this author's review of the stalking literature, however, stalkers were defined or described as

above average intellectually, codependent, desiring attention, desiring recognition, a substance abuser, unsuccessful in establishing an identity, unable to develop meaningful relationships, maladjusted, interested in the media, cruel, domineering, emotionally immature, insecure, jealous, one with low self-esteem, mentally ill, a product of a home where women were battered, paranoid, having a personality disorder, physically or emotionally abusive, physically unattractive, possessing poor social skills, possessive, powerless, preoccupied with violent ideas and fantasies, quick to anger, unable to form friendships or relationships, vindictive, and/or violent.

We must then conclude, to date, there is not a single profile of a stalker and anyone can engage in the crime of stalking, regardless of sex, race, sexual orientation, social class, or geographical location. The interesting twist is that those who stalk are apparently normal in their behavior when their stalking behaviors are not being discussed or acted upon.

Why Do Stalkers Stalk?

There are several possible explanations for why stalkers stalk. In some cases, particularly in the case of female stalkers, stalkers stalk because of a psychological disorder, that is erotomania. It is beyond the scope of this chapter to discuss the reasons for which a person with a psychological disorder might engage in the crime of stalking. However, if we consider the most common case, that of the simple obsessional stalker, we can offer some explanation.

Wright et al. (1996) in their study of stalking cases classified the stalker's motive into the following categories: infatuation, possession, anger/retaliation, or other. In their study of thirty stalkers, the authors found that in the majority of cases the motivation for stalking was classified as angry/retaliating.

According to Dr. James Wulach, a forensic-psychology professor at John Jay College of Criminal Justice, when some men suffer a blow to their self-esteem, such as unrequited love or a terminated relationship, they use aggression in an attempt to restore their sense of self and individual power (Serant 1993). Stalking, a form of aggression, can indeed bolster a man's self-esteem and allow him to regain some sense of power (Infolink 1995a). The question then becomes why do some men use the violent act of stalking against women as a means to enhance their self-esteem or restore their sense of power?

Experts who study what leads some men to commit crimes against women cite a number of biological, psychological, and sociological theories. While we cannot suggest that a single cause exists to explain violence against women, we can suggest that part of the answer is found in traditional sex role stereotypes and the sexism that exists within our society.

Our socialization process continues to include the message that to be masculine is to be aggressive, dominant, powerful, and in control, whereas to be feminine is to be passive, submissive, powerless, and to be controlled. Coupling these stereotypes, transmitted by our agents of socialization, with the sex-differentiated society in which we live, men and women not only learn about such roles but come to incorporate these roles into their lives.

Parents, peers, and educators actively reinforce traditional sex role stereotypes. "Both directly and indirectly—through modeling and reinforcement—and as a function of their level of cognitive development, children are steered toward different modes of behavior through a developing gender schema" (Basow 1986: 128). As a result, children become fully aware of sex-appropriate attitudes, values, and behaviors early in life and act and react accordingly. In addition, television and the print media, films, and popular music convey traditional sex role stereotypes, sometimes in the most exaggerated ways. Basow states, "The male image is far from realistic. Boys generally do not fight grizzly bears, cannot solve all problems with a show of physical force, and certainly experience emotions other than anger" (1986: 146). Furthermore, the society in which we live devalues the roles of women in our major social institutions. One needs to look no farther than to the salaries that men and women receive for the work that they do to conclude that there is sexism within the occupational arena. As a result, persons who are unaggressive, submissive, passive, and weak, and who are devalued for their contributions to society, are often victims to those who are aggressive, dominant, active, and strong.

If some men use aggression as a way to enhance their self-esteem and restore their sense of power after experiencing a terminated relationship, do some women respond the same way under the same circumstances?

The answer to this question is that, like men, women may indeed become angry and retaliate in the case of unrequited love or a terminated relationship. However, based on traditional sex role stereotypes, women may not become as aggressive as men in their retaliatory acts, nor retaliate in an effort to regain a sense of power. Again, part of the explanation for this reaction is found in the socialization process.

Traditional sex role stereotypes include the message that the most important roles for women are those of wife and mother. From birth, females are socialized to eventually assume the role of wife and mother. For example, parents will assign household tasks and provide toys that appropriately enhance the development of nurturing and caretaking skills in their female children. A female's peers continue to reinforce the same messages learned within the home. Particularly important during adolescence is a female's popularity with boys. This emphasis upon the importance of the roles of wife and mother for women is further reinforced by the educational, political, economic, and religious institutions within our society The religious institution maintains a powerful hold over the roles considered to be appropriate for men versus those roles considered to be appropriate for women.

As a result, some women who confront an unrequited lover or a terminated relationship may try to restore the relationship through whatever means possible —not because these women want to enhance their sense of power, but rather because they want to regain that which could lead to the roles of wife and mother. Consider the following case:

> The (female) stalker had flowers delivered, sent cards, placed the victim's name on numerous mailing lists, mailed love notes, moved into the victim's apartment complex, began showing up at the victim's residence and following the victim in public places. (Civil Action 94–V–107 1994: 2-3)

How Many Are Stalked?

While we do not have statistics to indicate the actual number of stalking cases, it is estimated that 200,000 persons are currently being stalked (Infolink 1995a). As with other crimes, we might suspect that there is an underreporting of the number of persons actually stalked.

First, if a crime is not labeled a crime, it cannot be treated as such. This is particularly important in the case of stalking. Stalkers often engage in subtle and elusive behaviors that are difficult to detect. Sometimes the benign acts that stalkers engage in may, at first, be considered flattering. For example, not everyone would immediately define cards from a "distant admirer," or flowers from "someone watching you from afar" as unwelcome and obtrusive. It is also possible that the stalker is a stranger, which makes it difficult to identify him/her once the victim becomes aware of the unwanted attention. As we will discuss later in this chapter, before a victim can begin to document the crime of stalking, she/he must first recognize the behavior, label the obsessive behavior as criminal, and identify the person committing the crime.

Second, the crime of stalking may go unreported when the stalker is a woman and the victim is a man. In this case, it would be easy to respond to the stalking behavior of women by ignoring it or concluding that it is difficult, if not impossible, for a woman to cause a man emotional distress and/or place him in reasonable fear of bodily injury. After all, traditional sex role stereotypes continue to define women as unaggressive, emotional, and passive. Believing that men are able to defend themselves against women, a man may not only refuse to report the behaviors or actions of the female stalker, but such a report might be treated with bemusement by law enforcement agents.

Finally, according to Infolink (1995a), while stalking is as old as the history of human relationships, stalking is a relatively new crime. "Law enforcement officials do not track the incidence of stalking offenses as part of their normal crime reporting process" (Infolink 1995a: 1). Even in states that have established stalking as a crime, we cannot be sure that law enforcement personnel are aware of these laws. If either of these situations are the case, the crime of stalking may be recorded as a crime of harassment, criminal trespassing, aggravated assault, or "other."

Vulnerability to Stalking

While no one can predict who will be a victim of stalking, some persons are more vulnerable than others. Among the most vulnerable are women. According to Infolink (1995a) it is estimated that one in twenty women will experience an unwanted pursuit in their lifetime. This statistic reveals that stalking against women is a serious problem.

Survivors of abusive relationships also face the possibility of being stalked, particularly after the abusive relationship has been terminated. Of all the women killed in the United States, almost one-third were murdered by their husbands or boyfriends, and it is suggested that 90 percent of these women were first stalked by their killers (Furio 1993). Ex-husbands and ex-boyfriends have shown persistence in pursuing women who try to leave abusive relationships.

Responding to the Victimization

Anyone victimized by a stalker can manifest a variety of physical and emotional problems during and after their victimization. Wright et al. notes that "targets of stalkers often feel trapped in an environment filled with anxiety, stress, and fear that often results in their having to make drastic adjustments in how they live their lives" (1996: 495).

All of us are, to some extent, aware of the literature detailing the effect that stress has upon our lives. Stress plays a major role in the development of many physical illnesses. In the beginning, victims of stalking may attempt to deal with the stress their victimization has upon their lives. However, over time, prolonged stress exhausts the body's ability to effectively ward off the stress and leaves one vulnerable and susceptible to illnesses. Stress has been associated with a variety of physical symptoms, including, but not limited to, anxiety, digestive problems, headaches, inability to concentrate, and sleep disturbances. Stress can also lead to an increase in alcohol use, drug use, smoking, and eating, which then further complicates an already complicated situation.

Fear is also draining on one's physical and emotional well-being. When one is living in fear, the fear drains an individual physically and, again, makes him/her more vulnerable to disease. Fear can also interfere with an individual's daily functioning. Constant intrusions by the stalker, and the inability to predict when the stalker's next contact will be, steals an individual's sense of security. One victim of stalking described how the fear associated with being stalked prevented her from answering her phone, going to her mailbox, sleeping after dark, and even going to her place of employment (Civil Action 94–V–107 1994). Kathleen Krueger, whose family has been stalked for over eight years by the man who piloted a plane her family used during her husband's campaign for the Senate, stated, "I am afraid to be alone, alone in my home, whether it be day or night, alone with our children, whether it be in our backyard or walking to New Barunfels Square" (Hearing 1993: 26).

In the case of stalking it is often recommended that the victim change something in her/his life. Consider the ten recommendations from the *Helpful Guide for Stalking Victims* (Infolink 1995b: 4):

- Install solid core doors with dead bolts. If victim cannot account for all keys, change locks and secure spare keys.
- If possible, install adequate outside lighting. Trim bushes and vegetation around residence.
- Maintain an unlisted phone number. If harassing calls persist, notify local law enforcement, but also keep a written log of harassing calls and any answering machine tapes of calls with the stalker's voice and messages.

- Treat any threats as legitimate and inform law enforcement immediately.
- Vary travel routes, stores, and restaurants, etc., which are regularly used. Limit time walking, jogging, etc.
- Inform a trusted neighbor and/or colleagues about the situation. Provide them with a photo or description of the suspect and any possible vehicles he/she may drive.
- If residing in an apartment with an onsite property manager, provide the manager with a picture of the suspect.
- Have co-workers screen all calls and visitors.
- When out of the house or work environment, try not to travel alone if at all possible, and try to stay in public areas. If you ever need assistance, yell "FIRE" to get immediate attention, as people more readily respond to this cry for assistance than any other.
- If financial means exist, use a "dummy" answering machine connected to a published phone line. The number to the private unlisted line can be reserved for close friends and family, then the stalker may not realize you have another line.
- Installing doors, locks, additional lighting, and maintaining an unlisted phone number are all financial impositions upon a victim who simply wishes to be left alone. Often victims have no other choice but to move, sometimes to other cities and states. In addition to the direct costs associated with a move, a victim can also lose opportunity costs, such as professional and personal contacts. Informing neighbors and colleagues is emotionally costly as having to do so can cause embarrassment and shame.

If we think about it, being victimized by a stalker imposes regulations and limitations to freely moving about on a daily basis. Consider the response of one stalking victim:

> We equipped our home-in-progress with dead bolts on all outside doors, dowels in all sliding glass windows, special motion-detector lighting, and an expensive security alarm system, wired directly into a surveillance company. We minimized any shrubbery near the house to discourage Fran's lying in wait, installed a wide-angle viewer in all primary doors, an electric garage door, and a loud exterior alarm that could be manually activated from various locations.
>
> I used a private mailbox service for all our personal mail. . . . I varied my route when I returned home from work and frequently looked in my rearview mirror to see if anyone was following me. (Orion 1997: 153)

It is also not unusual to find the victim experiencing anger, hate, lowered self-esteem, mistrust, panic, self-blame, withdrawal from family and friends, and thoughts of suicide. Sometimes the victim will even change something about her/himself to prevent the unwanted attentions. Intellectually victims may know that changing something about their lives reflects the unjustified accusation that they may be, in some way, responsible for the stalking situation. Still, victims will try almost anything to stop the behavior of a stalker. Doreen Orion, a psychiatrist who has been stalked by a former patient for over eight years said:

> I would often wonder what I had done wrong, because surely this whole mess could have been avoided somehow. Every time Fran wrote me or phoned, I would spend several sleepless nights ruminating about my own unwilling role in this psychotic melodrama. . . . If we believe we have in some way caused what is happening, perhaps we can also make it stop. (1997: 58)

An additional emotional and financial toll is placed upon the victim when the stalker is finally confronted by law enforcement agencies or personal attorneys. For example, it is not unusual for the victim to provide an account of events quite different from the events described by the stalker. The Schaefer/Brennan case is a good example:

> In April 1991, 41-year-old medical writer Diane Schaefer "almost breathlessly" told a Manhattan jury about her lengthy passionate affair with renowned surgeon Dr. Murray Brennan. She reminisced about conversations long since past, romantic dinners at specific restaurants, trips made together and people encountered on those trips. While testifying, Ms. Schaefer "acted like a woman very much in *love*."
>
> Dr. Brennan's recollections differ. From 1982 until 1990, Ms. Schaefer relentlessly badgered Dr. Brennan. She followed him to medical conferences around the world, inexplicably appeared in airplane seats next to him, tried to jump into taxis with him, left profane messages on his hospital answering machine, sent him dozens of letters and called his friends. On one occasion, she greeted him in his apartment, wearing nothing but a "see-through negligee." In another encounter, she threatened to kill him. "I can't live while you are alive on this earth. I am going to kill you. Kill you or kill myself—I am degraded by your being alive. (Anderson 1993: 171)

As it is not unusual for the perpetrator of a crime and the victim to provide differing accounts, it is also not unusual for the perpetrator of the crime to assume the role of a victim. Meloy and Gothard (1995) indicated that there was a clear tendency for the obsessional follower to use projection, whereupon the stalker attributed aggression, obsessional following, even threatening behavior to the victim. To make sense of such an occurrence, we might want to remember that when one is being stalked, the stalker is in control and has power over the victim. When the victim responds to the stalking situation through appropriate power structures, such as the criminal justice system or the legal system, there is a power shift, a shift that allows the victim to have power over his/her victimizer. To prevent this power shift, the stalker will appropriate the role of the victim. In one case of stalking, the stalker actually sued the victim for emotional distress, pain, and suffering based on the argument that the stalker experienced trauma when the victim brought legal action against her. The stalker argued that she was so traumatized by the legal action, that she experienced bouts of depression that ultimately affected her parenting skills. For that the stalker wanted financial restitution from the victim (Civil Action 94–V–107 1994).

Violating someone's right to be left alone is, as described by Hendricks and Spillane (1993: 68), a crime that is "more personally invasive and threatening than any other."

Response of the Criminal Justice System

As many stalkings have been reported since 1968 as in the previous 175 years (Perez 1993). Part of the explanation for such a large increase in reported stalking cases may be due to the increased media attention and the antistalking laws that have been developed and enacted.

The shooting death of TV star Rebecca Schaeffer, star of the sitcom *My Sister Sam,* sparked the country's first stalking law in the state of California in 1990.

> On the morning of the last free day of his life in 1989, 19-year-old Robert Bardo ordered onion rings and cheesecake at a Los Angeles diner. He nodded over his food, then went into the restroom. Inside, he pulled a .357 Magnum pistol out of a red and white plastic grocery bag and put one more hollow-point cartridge into its six-round cylinder, fully loading the gun. Carrying the sack, he walked a few blocks in brilliant sunshine to the doorstep of TV actress Rebecca Schaeffer. Bardo had been there an hour before, when he had a one-minute conversation with the young star and handed her a note. "Take care, take care," she had said as she quickly closed the glass security door and backed down the hallway. On his second visit, as Schaeffer opened the door, Bardo killed her with one shot in the chest and ran away. In December 1991, after a Los Angeles Superior Court trial, Bardo was sentenced to life in prison without parole. (Tharp 1992: 28)

Prior to stalking laws, there was little law enforcement could do for a victim of stalking unless the stalker acted upon the threats made. The only recourse many victims had was to obtain a civil protective order. However, civil protective orders have been problematic and not enough to protect victims of stalking (Thomas 1993). For example, violation of a civil protective order is considered a misdemeanor and most often results in a written citation. State provisions sometimes limit who may apply for a protective order. Some states require that the person seeking a protective order is married to the harasser or at least lived with the harasser at the same residence. Furthermore certain stalking behaviors did not always constitute criminal activity or violate criminal statutes. While unsolicited gifts, such as a dozen roses, may be irritating and unwanted, it is not against the law to send such gifts.

The antistalking laws now provide victims greater protection than the protective orders. Since the early 1990s, antistalking laws have been developed and passed in all fifty states in an effort to protect victims and to give law enforcement the opportunity to intervene before the victim is physically injured or even killed.

However, the stalking laws were initially not as successful as many might have hoped. Prosecutors argued that some stalking laws were so narrow that they excluded many of the common behaviors stalkers engaged in, such as repeated phone calls. Some of these early laws also came under attack due to the broad language used. "Some lower courts actually struck down these laws in a handful of states causing lawmakers in those states to redraft their stalking statutes in order to cure such constitutional defects" (Infolink 1995a: 5). In an effort to help, the National Criminal Justice Administration, in conjunction with other organizations, conducted a one-year study of the various laws enacted by states to produce a model stalking statute.

Since their inception, and the publication of the report by the National Criminal Justice Administration, many states have been amending their laws in some fashion. General trends of amendments include attaching a stronger penalty to stalking, requiring a psychological evaluation of the stalker, and/or allowing for a protective order for up to ten years (Stalking Laws 1995).

Probably the biggest challenge is to move the content of these laws from what is defined as a "credible threat" along the continuum toward "threats implied by conduct." Many stalking laws rely heavily upon the stalker making a credible threat, a written, verbal, or implied threat of violence, as in the phrase "I am going to kill you." This threat, whether made directly by the stalker or through another person, could then place the victim in fear of death, bodily injury, or assault. On the other hand, if the laws were to change the element of "credible threat" to "threats implied by conduct," this would allow the victim to prosecute a stalker, if the victim experienced reasonable fear for her/his safety based on the behavior or conduct of the stalker. That is, the victim would not have to wait for the stalker to make a "credible threat," which, in many cases, does not happen. If these laws were only to require "threats implied by conduct," the key to the successful prosecution would be to argue that the stalker's obsessive behavior was enough to cause the victim fear. Knowing that jurors consider themselves to be reasonable persons, jurors would then decide the case on whether they would have suffered fear under the same circumstances. Still, even this can become problematic when, for example, we consider that men define fear differently than do women. Consider the unidentifiable caller on the phone in the middle of the night. Would these kind of calls produce reasonable fear in men? In women? In college students? Among the elderly? Among the single? Among the married?

Some critics continue to argue that with the addition of "threats implied by conduct," such laws would become so broad that the stalking laws could apply to more cases than those that are stalking in nature. Broad stalking laws might even violate our right to go where we please, to freely associate with those we choose, and, of course, impend our rights to free speech. We might for example argue that a reporter following a politician was in violation of the stalking laws. Too, we must remember that while phone calls may be disturbing, they are not illegal. In effect, these critics argue that stalking laws are unnecessary and insist that existing harassment and assault statutes should be enforced.

Similarly we must consider whether such laws will be effective in dealing with all stalkers. Is it reasonable to assume that a person with a serious psychological disorder, as in the case of the erotomanic, will be dissuaded by antistalking laws? In this regard, mental health treatment may be more effective in stopping an erotomanic than would a jail sentence.

Prosecuting Stalkers

Unfortunately, the criminal prosecution of the stalker is often time-consuming, expensive, and laden with burdens for the victim. Much like other crimes, stalking is not an easy crime to prosecute.

We must remember that stalking begins without the victim's awareness. Rarely does one anticipate that they will be stalked, especially if the stalker is unknown to the victim. As discussed previously, it may take the victim time to notice the subtle and elusive behaviors of a stalker. Before one can even begin to document this criminal activity it requires that the victim first recognize the behavior as criminal. During the initial recognition of the crime of stalking, a victim might try to ignore, avoid, or have no contact with the stalker. As discussed earlier, sometimes victims believe that they are responsible for such behavior and will change something about themselves to stop the stalker. Not one of these strategies guarantees that the stalking will end.

While we might assume we know what we would do if we were confronted with a stalker, often a victim will react with irritation or even amusement, particularly if the stalker is unknown to the victim. Sometimes victims try to take matters into their own hands, by confronting stalkers with the hope that the stalker will cease and desist. Confrontation rarely works when one is dealing with a stalker. Stalkers can easily interpret confrontation as the victim really cares, that the victim is playing hard to get, or that the victim is responding negatively for the benefit of others (Ramsey 1994; Taibbi 1995).

When a victim has concluded that the behavior is stalking, it means having to build a case. It is imperative that the victim document every stalking incident, and keep all notes, cards, letters, gifts, and phone machine messages. The victim must also prove the origins of the gifts, and produce a record of the dates and times of visits or appearances made by the stalker. Without such evidence, it is extremely difficult to prosecute a stalking case (Infolink 1995b).

The successful prosecution of the stalker is also dependent on the law of the state in which the case is being prosecuted. In the state of North Carolina, the stalking law does not require a credible threat, but rather that the actions of the stalker place the victim in reasonable fear of death or bodily injury (Stalking Laws 1995). The North Carolina stalking law also indicates that the stalking behavior must happen on more than one occasion, and that the stalker follows or is in the presence of the victim without a legal purpose. Other states, such as Alabama, Florida, and Illinois, require a credible threat. Again, an individual must threaten to physically harm a person.

In most states the first conviction for stalking is a misdemeanor, punishable by up to a year in jail and a $1,000 fine (Furio 1993). Repeat offensives are felonies and punished more severely. That is, a second offense for the crime of stalking is considered to be a felony in many states and is punishable by incarceration for several years. Some states have increased the punishment for the crime of stalking, if the stalker is in violation of a restraining order or the stalker causes the victim physical harm. There are always civil remedies, including filing civil suits of invasion of privacy, trespassing, and intentional infliction of emotional distress against the stalker. Civil remedies do not provide the victim with any protection from the stalker and may not serve as a deterrent to the stalking behavior. Given the short time these statutes have been in effect, it is still too early to discuss average penalties or the impact these penalties have upon rates of recidivism.

Conclusion

As stalkers begin to brave the new world of electronic communications to find new angles to torment their victims, women and men from all walks of life continue to struggle with having their privacy invaded by an unwanted other. Relentless in their efforts and determined to do all that they can to fulfill their desire to come into contact with the victim of their obsession, stalkers have indeed proven themselves to be manipulative and clever. Justice Brandeis said it best when he said that stalking violates our right to be left alone.

Studying those persons who engage in the crime of stalking is a relatively new area of research for academics and specialists. To date, there exists only a limited number of empirical studies that give a reader insight into the classification and profile of the stalker. With the exception of erotomania, the literature explaining this criminal activity is even more scarce. We are able to conclude that understanding those issues surrounding the criminal activity of stalking is going to require a variety of academic disciplines and professionals. Like so many other contemporary issues, stalking will require an interdisciplinary approach to its analysis.

Approximately 200,000 adults are currently victim to a stalker, and some persons, particularly women, are more vulnerable than others. Personal accounts by many of these victims indicate that a victim to stalking can suffer an undue physical, emotional, and financial toll. As Senator Biden said during a hearing before the United States Senate, "[victims of stalking] are required to, in effect, change their identity, in some cases, change their entire lives, after everything that has been up to that point normal in their lives to accommodate [another who stalks]" (Hearing Before the Committee on the Judiciary 1993: 1).

Since the early 1990s, antistalking laws have been developed in all fifty states in an attempt to provide greater protection to victims of stalkers. With the passage of the 1994 Crime Bill by the U.S. Congress, which mandates the tracking and compilation of stalking crime statistics, experts will be better able to examine the multiple aspects of this crime for the first time (Infolink 1995a: 2). Until then we can only speculate about such issues as the effectiveness of the stalking laws, as well as the effectiveness of the prosecution of the stalker.

There are a multiple of publications available for those who are being, or have been, victimized by a stalker. This new literature provides a number of recommendations on what to do and not to do in the case of stalking. Several organizations also deal with the issue of stalking. The National Victim Center in Arlington, Virginia, and the National Criminal Justice Reference Service provide victims with information and referral services. There are also organizations on the local front, such as the Atlanta Stalking Victim Assistance program, which will not only provide information to victims, but also provides information on how to start an educational or support group.

However, one final question remains to be answered, Does the crime of stalking rise to the level of a social problem?

According to Sullivan (1997: 5) a social problem exists when (a) an influential group defines a social condition as threatening its values, (b) when the condition affects a large number of people, and (c) when the condition can be remedied by collective action.

Reviewing the information presented in this chapter, there is overwhelming evidence to suggest together, victims of stalkers, professionals who have dealt with stalkers, and even the media have become an influential group and have led the way in defining the crime of stalking as a threat to our "right to be left alone." Consider again the development of anti-stalking laws. No doubt the collective of persons mentioned played an important role in bringing the issue of stalking to the attention of policymakers. While women and men have been victims of stalking for decades, policymakers did little to improve laws dealing with stalkers until the early 1990s.

Second, despite the problems associated with accurately predicting the number of persons who are, or will be, victimized by a stalker, stalking affects an astounding number of men and women. Again, with the help of many we have come to recognize that far too many individuals are being stalked, and as a result, are suffering undue personal and social consequences.

Finally, stalking is being vigorously attacked by victims, professionals, and law makers in an effort to remedy the problem. New laws, the formation of expert organizations on the national and local levels, and individual action and concern have laid the groundwork for remedying the crime of stalking. While we may never be able to extinguish this crime, we are better prepared to deal with another social problem.

References

Ali, L. (1996) "Stalkers: Is the Threat of Rock Stars Growing?" *Rolling Stone* 747 (November 14), 29–30.

Anderson, S. C. (1993) "Anti-stalking Laws: Will They Curb the Erotomanic's Obsessive Pursuit?" *Law and Psychology Review* Vol. 17 (Spring), 171–191.

Anonymous. (1994) "Someone is Watching Me." *Ladies Home Journal.* (April), 152–153, 218–221.

Basow, S. (1986) *Gender Stereotypes: Traditions and Altematives.* CA: Brooks/Cole Publishing.

Blanchard, K. (1994) "When a Lover Turns Evil." *Mademoiselle* Vol. 100 (11), 146–149.

Caplan, L. (1984) *The Insanity Defense and the Trial of John W Hinckley, Jr.* MA: David R. Godine.

Civil Action No. 94–V–107 (1994) State Court, Georgia.

Diagnostic and Statistical Manual of Mental Disorders (Third Edition-Revised). (1987) Washington, D.C.: American Psychiatric Association.

Dietz, R. E., D. B. Matthews, C. Ban Duyne, D. A. Marlell, C. D. H. Parry, T. Stewart, J. Warren, and J. D. Crowder. (1991) "Threatening and Otherwise Inappropriate Letters to Hollywood Celebrities." *Journal of Forensic Sciences* Vol. 36 (1), 185–209.

Federal Bureau of Investigation. (1993) *Crime in the United States,* Washington, D.C.: U.S. Department of Justice.

Furio, J. (1993) "Can New State Laws Stop the Stalker?" *Ms* 3 (4), 90–91.

Hearing Before the Committee on the Judiciary, United States Senate. 103rd Congress, First Session on Combating Stalking and Family Violence (March 17, 1993) Serial No. J–1 03–5. Washington, D.C.: U.S. Government Printing Office.

Hendricks, J. E., and L. Spillane. (1993) "Stalking: What Can We Do to Forestall Tragedy?" *The Police Chief* 60, 68–70.

Infolink. (1995a) *At a Glance—Stalking—Questions and Answers.* (No. 43) Arlington, VA: Publication by the National Victim Center.

———. (1995b) *Helpful Guide for Stalking Victims.* (No. 44) Arlington, VA: Publication by the National Victim Center.

Meloy, J. R. (1989) "Unrequited Love and the Wish to Kill." *Bulletin of the Menninger Clinic* (53), 477–492.

Meloy, J. R., and S. Gothard. (1995) "Demographic and Clinical Comparison of Obsessional Followers and Offenders with Mental Disorders." *American Journal of Psychiatry* 152 (2), 258–263.

National Criminal Justice Association. (1993) *Project to Develop a Model Anti-Stalking Code for States.* Washington, D.C.: National Institute of Justice.

Orion, D. (1997) *Know You Really Love Me.* New York: MacMillan.

Perez, C. (1993) "Stalking—When Does Obsession Become a Crime?" *American Journal of Criminal Law* Vol. 20 (2), 263–280.

Ramsey, B. (1994) *Stop the Stalker.* GA: Securus House.

Serant, C. (1993) "Stalked." *Essence* (October), 72–76.

Stalking Laws. (1995) Arlington, VA: Publication by the National Victim Center.

Sullivan, T. (1997) *Introduction to Social Problems.* Boston: Allyn and Bacon.

Taibbi, R. (1995) "Stalking, An Unwelcome Presence." *Current Health* 21 (6), 18–19.

Tharp, M. (1992) "In the Mind of a Stalker." *US News and World Report* 11 2(6), 28–30.

Thomas, K. R. (1993) "How to Stop the Stalker: State Antistalking Laws." *Criminal Law Bulletin* 29 (2), 124–136.

Wright, J. A., A. G. Burgess, A. W. Burgess, A. T. Laszlo, G. O. McCrary, and J. E. Douglas. (1996) "A Typology of Interpersonal Stalking." *Journal of Interpersonal Violence* 11 (4), 487–502.

Zona, M. A., K. K. Sharma, and J. Lane. (1993) "A Comparative Study of Erotomanic and Obsessional Subjects in a Forensic Sample." *Journal of Forensic Sciences* Vol. 38 (4), 894–903.

Article Review Form at end of book.

Do you think that gender equality should entail equality among the sexes, or equal respect and opportunities between the sexes? Do you agree with Smith's assessment that women are still trying to escape their exclusion from the male creation of American culture? How do women's struggles in the military reflect this assessment?

Gender in the Military

Gina Carreño
Florida State University

Today women enjoy rights that their predecessors could only dream of—women can vote, attend college, pursue careers, and raise children as single parents. Despite advances such as these, however, women still suffer from sexist attitudes and practices. Specifically, the United States military represents one of the most challenging arenas for advocates of women's rights. While efforts are being made to integrate women into this previously all-male institution, military women continue to be victimized through sexist practices including sex discrimination, sexual abuse, and domestic violence.

The purpose of this article is to address some of the major issues facing women in the United States' Armed Forces. After briefly highlighting the aforementioned problems of discrimination, abuse, and domestic violence, we will attempt to view these issues in light of sociological theories of gender. Specifically, different types of feminism will be outlined, as well as Harding's and Smith's feminist standpoint theory and Connell's discussion of masculinity.

Problems Facing Women in the Military

Sex Discrimination

One of the most blatant examples of sex discrimination lies in Shannon Faulkner's battle with The Citadel, a public military academy in Charleston, South Carolina. Until Faulkner was accepted after omitting her sex from her application, The Citadel's all-male policy had remained unchallenged for 150 years. After discovering that Faulkner was a woman, the school revoked her acceptance. Faulkner responded by taking her case to court. Ultimately, the courts ruled in her favor: she was allowed to enroll in classes as well as join the Corps of Cadets. Although Faulkner won the legal battle, she had just begun the fight for equal treatment from her fellow—but male—cadets (Faludi 1994).

Sexual Abuse

Once enlisted in the military, many women are victimized by sexual abuse. In September 1990, for example, the Pentagon conducted a study of sexual harassment in the military by surveying over 20,000 active-duty personnel. They found that over one-third of the women surveyed had suffered some type of harassment, ranging from touching and pressures for sexual intercourse to rape. One victim, who stated she was raped by three fellow Army officers, said that women do not seek help at V.A. hospitals because "it is the same male-dominated, abusive system and environment which hurt us before" ("Military women report . . ." 1992: 37).

Sexual abuse of military women is not a fragment of the past. In August 1997 Army Sergeant Major Gene C. McKinney was suspended on charges of sexually harassing retired Sergeant Major Brenda Hoster. Hoster, who served on McKinney's staff, alleged that on an April 1996 trip to Hawaii McKinney went to her hotel room, grabbed and kissed her, and asked her to have sex. When she refused, he left the room. After Hoster's accusations, at least five more women accused McKinney of sexual harassment (Rothberg 1997a).

In addition to the accusations leveled against McKinney, the U.S. Army has been the site of another sex scandal, this time in Aberdeen, Maryland. Captain Derrick Robertson was dismissed from the military after pleading guilty to consensual sodomy, adultery, and other charges. Robertson was cleared of charges of rape, assault, and obstruction of justice. Although sentenced to one year, Robertson will only serve four months in prison ("Army officer in Aberdeen . . ." 1997).

Domestic Violence

In addition to sex discrimination and sexual abuse, military women often suffer from domestic violence. The Defense Advisory Committee on Women in the Services (DACOWITS) is investigating whether military women are hesitant in reporting abuse for fear of damaging their careers. One female military member said that some military women had been abused by their civilian husbands, who had not been punished. Sometimes the military "discouraged a separation from the abusive husband because the servicewoman would be left with more responsibility to care for the children" (Jowers 1995: 26).

The integration of women into the previously all-male U.S. military has not been a smooth, evolutionary process. On the contrary, female and male supporters of women entering the Armed Forces have had to fight for integration. Women are still facing unfair treatment because sexist attitudes and practices pervade our society. Now let us view these problems in terms of sociological theories of gender. First we will consider feminism and attitudes toward the role of women in the military. Then we will consider feminist standpoint theory and theories of masculinity.

Feminism and the Role of Women in the Military

Gender is a salient issue because we are socialized to view the world in terms of "male" and "female." Bem's Enculturated Lens Theory (1993) argues that the culture of any society is composed of a set of hidden assumptions about how members of that society should look, think, feel, and act. These assumptions are embedded in social institutions and individual psyches so that over time specific patterns of thought are invisibly but systematically reproduced. Bem calls these assumptions "lenses." In the United States and most Western cultures, gender lenses influence how we see the world. As a result, gender perceptions play an important role in our daily interactions. Bem argues that these perceptions are so embedded in our society that we are often unaware of their existence, rendering us like " . . . the proverbial fish who is unaware that its environment is wet. After all, what else could it be?" (1993: 140).

According to retired Air Force Colonel Ralph P. Witherspoon, " . . . three major forces—the declining population, the ending of compulsory military service, and the general liberation of women in our society—combined into a single force of profound impact on the way the female soldier is regarded in our society and in our armed forces" (1988: 8). Subsequently the debate continues over women's role in the military.

Historically, feminists have been divided on the issue of women in the military. On one hand, many feminists support the peace movement. These activists, who tend to be liberal, younger, and female, may discourage women from participating in the armed forces because they disapprove of the military's existence as an institution. On the other hand, other feminists support military women on the grounds of equality between the sexes. These feminists strive for equality in all areas, even in those not meeting their approval. In other words, many feminists place a higher value on gender equality than on the pacifist movement (Herbert 1994).

The gender literature differentiates among four types of feminism: liberal, Marxist, socialist, and radical. Each type of feminism, because of their diverse ideologies, will hold a different view of women and the military. Liberal feminists strive for women's equality within the framework of the existing social structure. According to Ramazanoglu (1989), liberal feminism " . . . campaigns for improved rights and opportunities for women without seriously questioning the existing organization of society" (pp. 10–11). Subsequently liberal feminists are likely to support women's participation in the military (Herbert 1994).

Unlike liberal feminists, Marxist feminists seek to undermine the present social structure. They argue that women are oppressed by men because of the existence of capitalism. They maintain that if capitalist relations were eradicated, so would be gender-based domination and subordination. The U.S. military protects capitalism; therefore Marxist feminists are likely to discourage female participation (Herbert 1994).

Socialist feminism goes a step farther by expanding the Marxist view of capitalist relations. Specifically, socialist feminists claim that patterns of domination and subordination extend beyond the capitalist workplace and include the personal sphere of sexuality and reproduction. Like their Marxist counterparts, socialist feminists strive to change the current social structure and are therefore likely to discourage anyone's—female or male—participation in the military (Herbert 1994).

Finally, radical feminism is at the opposite end of the spectrum from liberal feminism. Radical feminists maintain that the subordination and exploitation of women are necessary for the existence of the present social structure. As a result of this view, radical feminists are likely to discourage any participation in the military (Herbert 1994).

Previous research shows that feminism in the general population tends to be liberal. As a result, feminist support for women's integration into the military stems from an endorsement of gender equality. An analysis of the 1982 National Opinion Research Center's General Social Survey shows that "support for women in the military is greater among (1) the better educated, (2) younger adults, (3) Northerners, and (4) the less devout" (Davis, Lauby, and Sheatsley 1983: 38). Further, female and male feminists, whether or not antimilitary, may be more supportive of female participation than conservative, promilitary individuals (Herbert 1994).

Much of the literature on female participation in the military is grounded in the theoretical approach of examining women's effects on the male identity of the military. Brian Mitchell (1989), writing against female participation, states, "Men simply do not aspire to be women or to emulate women, and whatever women are, men will seek to be anything other" (pp. 217–218). Sharon MacDonald (1987) writes, "Where war is defined as a male activity, and where highly-valued masculine characteristics are often associated with war, a female warrior must be seen as inherently unsettling to the social order" (p. 6). Segal and Hansen's 1992 analysis frames the question of female military participation in terms of two opposing value systems: the militarists' goal of military effectiveness versus the feminists' fight for equal opportunity. Their findings suggest that militarists are more likely to discourage female participation, while feminists are more likely to encourage it.

Herbert (1994) also analyzes the 1982 General Social Survey conducted by the National Opinion Research Center. She finds that those individuals holding feminist value systems are likely to support female participation in the military, while those subscribing to militarist values show a small tendency toward discouraging female participation. Subsequently, gender integration in the military appears to be more an issue of gender equality than military policy. As a result of her findings, Herbert contends that the debate should therefore shift from a military focus to a women's issue.

Feminist Standpoint Theory

Feminist standpoint theory, as discussed by Harding (1991) and Smith (1987) provides a useful theoretical framework for addressing the current problems facing women in the U.S. military. In her book *Whose Science? Whose Knowledge? Thinking from Women's Lives,* Sandra Harding puts forth feminist standpoint theory. This book argues that knowledge is socially situated: "The feminist standpoint theories focus on gender differences, on differences between women's and men's situations which give a scientific advantage to those who can make use of the differences" (p. 120). Harding outlines various differences between women's and men's situations, including the devaluing of women's life experiences as well as the viewing of women as the "Other." In other words, women are "outsiders within" (1991: 131).

In her book *The Everyday World as Problematic: A Feminist Sociology,* Dorothy E. Smith (1987) maintains that women have been continuously excluded from men's culture. She points out that culture does not come into being spontaneously. Instead, culture is "manufactured" (p. 19). In other words, culture is socially created. Smith's next primary point flows logically from that contention. If culture is indeed created rather than spontaneously arising, then the next logical question is to ask, *who* creates culture? Smith maintains that "the concerns, interest, and experiences forming 'our' culture are those of men in positions of dominance whose perspectives are built on the silence of women (and of others)" (pp. 19–20).

Smith's discussion of the creation of culture and women's exclusion from that process necessitates the clarification of two concepts: relations of ruling and bifurcated consciousness. Smith defines relations of ruling as a "complex of organized practices, including government, law, business and financial management, professional organizations, and educational institutions as well as the discourses in texts that interpenetrate the multiple sites of power" (p. 3). Smith claims that "we are ruled by forms of organization vested in and mediated by texts and documents, and constituted externally to particular individuals and their personal and familial relationships" (p. 3). As a result, different forms of consciousness are constructed that stem from organizations rather than individuals.

Smith's relations of ruling leads logically into her concept of bifurcated consciousness. Here she maintains that "movement between a consciousness organized within the relations of ruling and a consciousness implicated in the local particularities of home and family transgressed a gender boundary" (1987: 7). Smith goes on to say that women's experiences of life do not fit into the male relations of ruling.

These concepts of relations of ruling and bifurcated consciousness go hand-in-hand. To put it succinctly, relations of ruling means that those men with power are the ones in charge. While women are urged to remain at home in the private sphere, men are the ones running the public sphere of the state and other institutions. Instantly, this dichotomy between public and private creates a boundary between forms of consciousness. This boundary results in Smith's concept of bifurcated consciousness. In other words, women's experiences have been neglected in the creation of the culture and ideologies in which we live. Women, because of this exclusion, cannot call this culture "theirs" because women are indeed the "Other."

The central argument of feminist standpoint theory then is that in our male-dominated society, women are viewed as the "Other" and subsequently lack a voice, lack power. This theory then can shed light on problems facing women in the U.S. military, because in this particular setting women are very much the "Other." Let us consider Shannon Faulkner's battle against The Citadel's 150-year-old practice of sex discrimination. In The Citadel's environment, women are automatically designated the "Other": women are not allowed in communal bathrooms or in barracks, nor are cadets allowed to marry. Female faculty members frequently report crude treatment from the cadets, with male faculty members offering little or no support. Further, Citadel President Claudius Elmer (Bud) Watts III, a retired Air Force lieutenant general and Citadel alumnus, said, "You cannot put a male and a female on that same playing field"—but he could not explain why (Faludi 1994: 65).

Feminist standpoint theory highlights that in our currently male-dominated society, women lack the power to have a voice. This powerlessness can be seen in the problem of domestic violence. Active-duty women abused by their military or even civilian husbands lack the power to voice their victimization and bring their husbands to justice. In one incident, "a servicewoman who was physically abused by her military husband said her commander tried to have her committed to a mental institution, and the incident was noted in *her* records" (Jowers 1995: 26, italics mine). Feminist standpoint theory emphasizes the subordination of women, and this bifurcated consciousness leads to the viewing of women as the "Other." This lack of power clearly occurs in the male-dominated U.S. Armed Forces.

Connell's Theory of Masculinities

In addition to feminist standpoint theory put forth by Harding (1991) and Smith (1987), R.W. Connell's (1996) discussion of masculinities also serves as a useful framework for examining problems women face in the military. According to Connell, gender is constructed and perpetuated in everyday interactions. Social science research on the production and reproduction of masculinity has revealed important findings. First, there are many different masculinities. In other words, there is no single masculinity that exists everywhere. As a result, societies like the United States that are home to a plethora of cultures also exhibit numerous definitions of masculinity. For example, research shows that ideas of what it is to "be a man" varies by ethnicity as well as social class (Connell 1996).

Second, some masculinities are more respected than others. Moreover, some masculinities are dishonored and even marginalized. The form of masculinity that is dominant in a particular culture is known as the hegemonic masculinity. In the United States, for example, the present hegemonic masculinity is often associated with such characteristics as heterosexuality, Whiteness, athleticism, and careerism. Conversely, homosexual and Black masculinities are often looked down upon and marginalized from the rest of society. While revealing how some men are dominant over others, hegemonic masculinity is also dominant in the gender structure as a whole. In other words, hegemonic masculinity reflects the power men collectively hold over women (Connell 1996; 1995).

Third, masculinities do not exist outside of social interaction: they are produced as individuals act. People "do" gender every day, through such behaviors as ways of speaking and styles of dressing. Connell (1995) writes, "Masculinities, it appears, are far from settled. From bodybuilders in the gym, to managers in the boardroom, to boys in the elementary school playground, a whole lot of people are working very hard to produce what they believe to be appropriate masculinities" (p. 209).

Finally, because different masculinities exist in various cultures and time periods, masculinities can change. The "dynamics" of masculinity suggest that different masculinities emerge as well as decay, and that the politics of "doing" gender permeate our lives (Connell 1996).

Connell's discussion of masculinities provides yet another rich theoretical framework for examining the problems women frequently face when joining the military. Specifically, Connell's concept of hegemonic masculinity can help explain why military women encounter so much resistance from men to their integration and equality. As stated previously, U.S. hegemonic masculinity associates "being a man" with such characteristics as Whiteness, heterosexuality, and participating in the labor force. The present hegemonic masculinity, because of this view, rejects such characteristics as Blackness, homosexuality, and not working outside the home. Given these ideas of what it is to "be a man," then, hegemonic masculinity targets women, Blacks, and homosexuals as objects to be subordinated and exploited. Now let us consider the problems of sex discrimination, sexual abuse, and domestic violence in light of the present American hegemonic masculinity.

Sex Discrimination

Recall our discussion of Shannon Faulkner's battle against The Citadel's practice of sex discrimination. Faukner's application was selected for acceptance and was turned down only when her sex was discovered. When the courts ruled that Faulkner must be permitted to enroll, she earned an A in calculus. In previous years, the Math Department had held an annual party to honor its A students. Instead of keeping with this tradition and inviting Faulkner, however, the department chose to limit the party to math majors. The present hegemonic masculinity's shunning of women can be seen at work here. Math professor David Trautman e-mailed fellow faculty members his explanation of the department's decision to exclude Faulkner: "Her presence would put a damper on the evening" (Faludi 1994: 75).

Hegemonic masculinity's subordination and exploitation of the female sex is also evident in the male cadets' crude treatment of women. Some female professors have been called lewd names such as "pussies." One female professor, who photocopied an editorial supporting women's integration into the Corps of Cadets, found the following messages scribbled on her office door: "Dr. Bishop, you are a prime example of why women should not be allowed here" and "Women will destroy the world" (Faludi 1994: 71). In addition to misogynistic acts such as these, many cadets call the all-female (and all-Black) mess hall staff "bitches" and "whores," and a number of cadets are admired for beating their girlfriends at Citadel parties (1994).

At The Citadel, if female victims are not available for subordination and exploitation, hegemonic masculinity still finds a way. Upperclassmen jeer first-year cadets as their heads are shaved: "Oh, you going to get your little girlie locks cut off?" (Faludi 1994: 70). If a young cadet shows any signs of being afraid, his peers may comment, "You look like you're having an abortion," or "Are you menstruating?" (1994: 70). The previous absence of female cadets apparently did not stop Citadel students from acting out hegemonic masculinity:

> When Michael Lake looked back on the abuse he suffered . . . [w]hat he saw was a submerged gender battle, a bitter but definitely fixed contest between the sexes, concealed from view by the fact that men played both parts. The beaten knobs [first-year cadets] were the women, 'stripped' and humiliated, and the predatory upperclassmen were the men, who bullied and pillaged. If they couldn't recreate a male-dominant society in the real world, they could restage the drama by casting male knobs in all the subservient feminine roles. (Faludi 1994: 70)

In addition to subordinating and exploiting women, hegemonic masculinity also targets Blacks. This is precisely why when one talks about gender, one must also talk about race. During Faulkner's first day at The Citadel, African American Cadet Von Mickle shook her hand and paralleled the discrimination against women to that of Blacks. For this action Von Mickle was berated by his peers in The Citadel newspaper *Pimpernel:*

> 'The PIMP doth long to tame the PLASTIC COW on this most

> wondrous of nights. . . . But it seems that we will have a live specimen, a home grown DAIRY QUEEN from the stables of Powdersville. Perhaps NON DICKLE will be the first to saddle up. He is DIVINE BOVINE'S bestfriend after all.' (Faludi 1994: 75)

This quotation reveals not only hegemonic masculinity's misogyny and racism, but also its disdain for homosexuality. Von Mickle publicly supported a woman, so his masculinity was jeered at through such references as "DAIRY QUEEN" and "NON DICKLE."

Cadets at The Citadel clearly practice hegemonic masculinity. One cadet, accused of having a sexual relationship with a male janitor, was rejected by his classmates: homosexual activity is not tolerated. Ironically, though, the cadets at The Citadel frequently display signs of intimacy. Students frequently kiss and hug each other. The "Nude Platoon" is notorious for stripping and then wrestling naked on the ground. Acts of intimacy even extend to cadets dressing one another:

> The [shirt] tuck requires that a cadet unzip his pants halfway and fold down his waistband, then stand still while his helper approaches him from the back, puts his arms around the cadet's waist, pulls the loose shirt material firmly to the back, jams it as far down as he can and then pulls the cadet's pants up. (Faludi 1994: 79)

It appears that this previously all-male environment had served as a means of escaping our society's standards of what it is to "be a man": here cadets could act affectionate and even vulnerable without fearing reprimand: "Behind the martial backdrop . . . you don't have to be a leader. You can play back seat. It's a great relief. You can act like a human being and not have to act like a man" (Faludi 1994: 81).

In addition to some Citadel cadets' racist attitudes that fall in line with hegemonic masculinity, the U.S. military in general also reveals the intersection between gender and race. Cheatham and Seem (1990) examined occupation equity in the American Armed Forces, focusing especially upon African American women. They found that women, especially African American women, were underrepresented in the core technical occupations and overrepresented in the nontechnical support occupations. The converse is true for White males. In other words, in the military it is advantageous to be White and male. This study strongly suggests that African American women are victims of "'double jeopardy,' that is, from the interactive effects of race and gender" (1990: 77). Cheatham and Seem write:

> . . . the U.S. military has not accomplished its goal of providing occupation equity, and particularly so for African-American women. This inequity further affects these women's opportunities to obtain placement in traditionally male-dominated occupations which command higher salaries and status than do traditionally female-dominated occupations upon completion of enlisted service. (1990: 77)

Sexual Abuse

Recall our discussion of Brenda Hoster's accusation that Gene C. McKinney sexually harassed her on an Army trip to Hawaii. Again hegemonic masculinity comes into play. Sexual harassment of women allows men to subordinate and exploit the female sex. In this particular case, a man allegedly used his higher rank to pressure a woman for sexual favors. The McKinney scandal also brings a race issue to bear. A number of newspaper articles pointed out that McKinney was the first Black to hold the post of Army Sergeant Major. McKinney has claimed that Hoster has accused him of sexual harassment because she is White.

In addition to the issues of gender and race, the McKinney scandal also revealed hegemonic masculinity's derision of homosexuality. In one cross-examination, McKinney's defense lawyer asked Hoster if she had ever been seen in public holding hands with Command Sergeant Major Zulma Santiago. Hoster had testified that she had once lived in the same house as Santiago, who she described as her landlord and friend. Clearly McKinney's defense lawyer was attempting to depict Hoster as a lesbian. Although Hoster maintains she is not a lesbian, her sex life is irrelevant to the charges she made against McKinney (Rothberg 1997b).

Domestic Violence

Recall that a number of women serving in the U.S. military have been verbally and physically abused by their husbands. As discussed previously, sometimes the military command discourages the woman from divorcing her abusive husband, claiming that the woman may be left to care for the children (Jowers 1995). As Connell notes, hegemonic masculinity privileges all men over women. Many women are pressured to sacrifice their career aspirations and instead take on the responsibilities of child rearing because of women's lack of power in our society's current gender structure and social order. The military's discouragement of divorce not only acknowledges but also reinforces and legitimates our society's expectations of so-called "proper" gender roles.

Conclusion

The problems facing women in the military appear to be far from over. The U.S. military is not a vacuum, a bubble isolated from the rest of society. Like other institutions, the military is the product of our culture's beliefs and value systems. In our culture, the present social structure identifies individuals in terms of gender. Ursula Le Guin (1969) points this out: "What is the first question we ask about a newborn baby?" (p. 94). As long as we view the world in terms of gender, and as long as we favor maleness over femaleness, men will dominate women. This subordination and exploitation will continue through such practices as sex discrimination, sexual abuse, and domestic violence. Only through making people aware of these issues can we make changes. Only by acknowledging that women are presently viewed as the "Other" can we decrease sexism. Only by redefining hegemonic masculinity, changing our idea of what it is to "be a man" can we collectively move toward a more egalitarian society.

References

"Army Officer in Aberdeen in Sex Scandal Gets Jail Time." 1997. *Jet* 91(20): 54.

Bem, Sandra L. 1993. *The Lenses of Gender: Transforming the Debate on Sexual Inequality.* New Haven: Yale University Press.

Cheatham, Harold, and Susan Seem. 1990. "Occupation Equality: A Black and White Portrait of Women in the United States Military." *Review of Black Political Economy* 19(1): 65–78.

Connell, R.W. 1995. *Masculinities.* Berkeley: University of California Press.

———. 1996. "Teaching the Boys: New Research on Masculinity, and Gender Strategies for Schools." *Teachers College Record* 98(2): 206–235.

Davis, James A., Jennifer Lauby, and Paul B. Sheatsley. 1983. "Americans View the Military." *NORC Report* No. 131. National Opinion Research Center.

Faludi, Susan. 1994. "The Naked Citadel." *The New Yorker* Sept. 5: 62–81.

Harding, Sandra. 1991. *Whose Science? Whose Knowledge? Thinking from Women's Lives.* New York: Cornell University Press.

Herbert, Melissa. 1994. "Feminism, Militarism, and Attitudes toward the Role of Women in the Military." *Feminist Issues* 14: 25–49.

Jowers, Karen. 1995. "Abuse Feared Hidden for Military Women." *Army Times* 56(16): 26–28.

MacDonald, Sharon. 1987. "Drawing the Lines—Gender, Peace and War: An Introduction." *Images of Women in Peace and War: Cross-Cultural and Historical Perspectives* ed. Sharon MacDonald, Pat Holden, and Shirley Ardener. Madison: University of Wisconsin Press.

"Military Women Report Pervasive Sexual Abuse by Servicemen." 1992. *Women's International Network News* 18(3): 37–39.

Mitchell, Brian. 1989. *Weak Link: The Feminization of the American Military.* Washington, D.C.: Regnery Gateway.

Ramazanoglu, Caroline. 1989. *Feminism and the Contradictions of Oppression.* New York: Routledge.

Rothberg, Donald M. 1997a. "'I'm the Victim, Angry Witness Tells Defense Lawyer." *Tallahassee Democrat* July 27: 3A.

———. 1997. "McKinney Accuser Finds Support." *Tallahassee Democrat* July 30: 3A.

Segal, M. W., and A. F. Hansen. 1992. "Value Rationalities in Policy Debates on Women in the Military: A Content Analysis of Congressional Testimony, 1941–1985." *Social Science Quarterly* 73: 296–309.

Smith, Dorothy E. 1987. *The Everyday World as Problematic: A Feminist Sociology.* Boston: Northeastern University Press.

———. 1997. "Comment on Hekman's 'Truth and Method: Feminist Standpoint Theory Revisited.'" *Signs* 22(2): 392–398.

Witherspoon, Ralph P. 1988. "Female Soldiers in Combat—A Policy Adrift." *Minerva: Quarterly Report on Women and the Military VI*: 1–28.

Article Review Form at end of book.

WiseGuide Wrap-Up

In many ways, we have come farther in our understanding of and sympathy for racial issues than we have with regard to gender issues. For example, while no one would question the appropriateness of an African American attending an all-white school, some people balk at the idea of a female entering an all-male institution. As the readings in this section have demonstrated, on many issues, women are overlooked, marginalized, or ignored. Moreover, a general lack of understanding of women in society has been underscored by stereotypical images of their attitudes, values, and beliefs. Recently, the crime of stalking has been created to identify cases in which the marginalization of women has become problematic. Thus, in terms of a theme, the readings in this section pointed out both the significance of the problem as well as how easily it is overlooked.

R.E.A.L. Sites

This list provides a print preview of typical **coursewise** R.E.A.L. sites. (There are over 100 such sites at the **courselinks**™ site.) The danger in printing URLs is that web sites can change overnight. As we went to press, these sites were functional using the URLs provided. If you come across one that isn't, please let us know via email to: webmaster@coursewise.com. Use your Passport to access the most current list of R.E.A.L. sites at the **courselinks**™ site.

Site name: The Stalking Victims' Sanctuary

URL: http://www.stalkingvictims.com

Why is it R.E.A.L.? This site provides a comprehensive assessment of stalking. The topics range from information about stalking and stalkers to support group information, games that help victims cope with the stress involved in being stalked, and other resources that assist victims and researchers.

Key topics: profiling a stalker, how to cope with being stalked, support groups and stalking

Site name: Victim Advocacy Center

URL: http://www.fiu.edu/-victimad/index.htm

Why is it R.E.A.L.? This site is the Victim Advocacy Center at Florida International University in Miami, and was established with the mission to provide support services to victims and survivors of crime and abuse, and to increase awareness of violence and victimization in the South Florida community.

Key topics: domestic violence, legal aid, victims of crime

Index

References in boldface type are authors of Readings.
References to endnotes are indicated by *n* followed by note number.

Putting it in *Perspectives*
-Review Form-

Your name:______________________________ Date: ______________

Reading title: ____

Summarize: Provide a one-sentence summary of this reading. ____

____

____

____

Follow the Thinking: How does the author back the main premise of the reading? Are the facts/opinions appropriately supported by research or available data? Is the author's thinking logical?

____

____

____

____

____

____

Develop a Context (answer one or both questions): How does this reading contrast or compliment your professor's lecture treatment of the subject matter? How does this reading compare to your textbook's coverage?

____

____

____

____

____

____

____

Question Authority: Explain why you agree/disagree with the author's main premise.

____

____

____

____

____

____

____

COPY ME! Copy this form as needed. This form is also available at http://www.coursewise.com
Click on: *Perspectives*.